Concert of

# VOICES

"To redeem the word from the superstition of the word is to humanize it, to make it participate once more in a living concert of voices . . ."

Geoffrey Hartman, *Beyond Formalism*

Concert of

# VOICES

## An Anthology
of World Writing
in English

edited by
Victor J. Ramraj

broadview

**Canadian Cataloguing in Publication Data**

Main entry under title:

Concert of voices: an anthology of world writing in English

Includes bibliographical references and index.
ISBN 1-55111-025-3

1. English literature - 20th century. I. Ramraj, Victor Jammona, 1941-

PM6014.775 1994    808'.0427    C94-932141-9

Broadview Press:
71 Princess St., Post Office Box 1243, Peterborough ON  Canada

in the United States of America:
3576 California Rd., Orchard Park, NY  14127

in the United Kingdom
c/o Drake Marketing, Saint Fagan's Rd., Fairwater, Cardiff, CF53AE

Broadview Press gratefully acknowledges the support of the Canada Council, the Onrtario Arts Council, the Ontario Publishing Centre, and the Ministry of Canadian Heritage

PRINTED IN CANADA

# Table of Contents

# *Table of Contents: Genres*

## *Fiction*

## *Poetry*

# *Table of Contents: Regions*

## *Africa*

## *Canada*

## The Indian Subcontinent

# Acknowledgements

Chinua Achebe, "Girls At War" from *Girls At War and Other Stories.* London: Heinemann, 1972. Reprinted by permission of the author.

Ama Ata Aidoo, "No Sweetness Here" from *No Sweetness Here.* London: Longman, 1970. Reprinted by permission of the author.

Agha Shahid Ali, "Snowmen" from *The Half-Inch Himalayas.* Wesleyan University Press. Reprinted with permission.

Mulk Raj Anand, "Duty" from *The Barber's Trade Union and Other Stories.* London: Cape, 1944. Reprinted by permission of the author.

Jean Arasanayagam, "I Have No Country" from *Reddened Water Flows Clear.* London: Forest Books. Reprinted by permission of the author.

Ven Begamudré, "Honestly, as in the Day" from *A Planet of Eccentrics.* Lantzville, BC: Oolichan Books, 1990. Reprinted by permission of the author and publisher.

Louise Bennett, "Anancy an Ticks" from *Anancy and Miss Lou.* Kingston: Sangster's Book Stores Ltd., 1979. Reprinted by permission of Sangster's Book Stores Ltd.

Neil Bissoondath, "Man as Plaything, Life as Mockery" from *Digging Up the Mountains.* Toronto: Macmillan, 1985. Reprinted by permission of the publisher.

Gerry Bostock, "Here Comes the Nigger" from *Paperbark*, ed. Jack Davis. St. Lucia: University of Queensland Press, 1990. Reprinted by permission of the author.

Dionne Brand, "Return I" from *No Language is Neutral.* Copyright © Dionne Brand 1990. Reprinted by permission of Coach House Press. ". . . Seen" from *Sans Souci and Other Stories.* Stratford: Williams-Wallace, 1988. Reprinted by permission of Women's Press.

Edward Kamau Brathwaite, "Red Rising" from *Sun Poem* © Edward Kamau Braithwaite, 1982. Reprinted by permission of Oxford University Press.

Dennis Brutus, "I am Alien in Africa and Everywhere" from *Thoughts Abroad.* Blackwood: Troubador Press. "I Am Out of Love With You For Now" from *A Simple Lust.* London: Heinemann. Reprinted by permission of the author.

Buhkwujjenene, "Nanaboozhoo Creates the World" from *First People, First Voices.* Toronto: University of Toronto Press, 1983. Reprinted by permission of University of Toronto Press.

Willi Chen, "Assam's Iron Chest" from *King of the Carnival and Other Stories.* London: Hansib, 1988. Reprinted by permission of the publisher.

Austin Clarke, "The Man" from *When Women Rule.* Toronto: McClelland & Stewart, 1985. Reprinted by permission.

Saros Cowasjee, "His Father's Medals" from *More Stories From the Raj and After.* London: Grafton Books, 1986. Reprinted by permission of the author.

Rienzi Crusz, "Roots" from *A Time for Loving.* Toronto: TSAR, 1986. Reprinted by permission of the publisher.

Fred D'Aguiar, "Home," first published *ARIEL* 24 (January 1993). Reprinted by permission of the publisher.

Cyril Dabydeen, "Señorita" and "Elephants Make Good Stepladders" from *Coastland: New and Selected Poems 1973-1987.* Oakville: Mosaic, 1989. Reprinted by permission of the author.

David Dabydeen, "Catching Crabs" and "The New Poetry" from *Coolie Odyssey.* London: Hansib, 1988. Reprinted by permission of the publisher.

Jayanta Mahapatra, "The Abandoned British Cemetery at Balasore" from *The False Start*, 1980. First published in *Sewanee Review*. Reprinted by permission.

Lee Maracle, "Charlie" from *Soujourner's Truth and Other Storis*. Vancouver: Press Gang, 1980. Reprinted by permission.

Dambudzo Marechera, "Black Skin What Mask" from *The House of Hunger*. London: Heinemann, 1978. Reprinted by permission.

Pauline Melville, "The Truth is in the Clothes" from *Shape-Shifter* by Pauline Melville, first published by The Women's Press Ltd, 1990, 34 Great Sutton Street, London EC1V 0DX. c Pauline Melville 1990. Reprinted by permission of the author.

Sudesh Mishra, "Mt. Abu: St. Xavier's Church" and "The Black Pagoda: Konarak" from *Memoirs of a Reluctant Traveller*. Adelaide: CRNLE, Flinders University, 1994. Reprinted by permission of the author.

Rohinton Mistry, "Swimming Lessons" from *Tales from Firozsha Baag* by Rohinton Mistry. Reprinted by permission of The Canadian Publishers, McClelland & Stewart, Toronto. "Swimming Lessons" from *Swimming Lessons*. Copyright © 1987 by Rohinton Mistry. Reprinted by permission of Houghton Mifflin Co. All rights reserved.

Tololwa Marti Mollel, "A Night Out" from *Contemporary African Short Stories*. Oxford: Heinemann, 1992. Reprinted by permission of the author.

Timothy Mo, "One of Billy's Boys," first published in *Eastern Express (Weekend)*, 5 February 1994. Reprinted by permission.

Toshio Mori, "Slant-Eyed Americans" from *Yokohama, California*. Caldwell, ID: Caxton Printers. Reprinted by permission of the author.

Mervyn Morris, "To An Expatriate Friend" and "Family Pictures" from *The Pond*. London: New Beacon, 1973. Reprinted by permission.

Es'kia Mphahlele, "The Coffee-Cart Girl" from *In Corner B: Short Stories*. Dar es Salam: East Africa Publishing House, 1967. Reprinted by permission of the author.

Bharati Mukherjee, "Hindus" from *Darkness* (1985) by Bharati Mukherjee. Copyright © Bharati Mukherjee. Reprinted by permission of Penguin Books Canada Limited.

V. S. Naipaul, "B. Wordsworth" from *Miguel Street*. London: Deutsch, 1959. "Jasmine" from *The Overcrowded Barracoon*. London: Deutsch, 1972. Reprinted by permission of the author.

Satendra Nandan, "Fiji: A Return to a Certain Darkness," first published in *Meanjin* Summer 1993. Reprinted by permission of the author.

R. K. Narayan, "Mother and Son" from *Malgudi Days*. Copyright © 1972, 1975, 1978, 1980, 1981, 1982 by R.K. Narayan. Reprinted by permission of the Viking Penguin, a division of Penguin Books, USA Inc.

Mudrooroo Narogin, "A Missionary Would I Have Been" from *Westerly*, March 1975. Reprinted by permission of the author.

Njabulo S. Ndebele, "Guilt and Atonement: Unmasking History for the Future" from *South African Literature and Culture*. Manchester: University of Manchester Press, 1994. Reprinted by permission of the author.

Ngitji Ngitji, "The Possum Woman" from *Paperbark*, ed. Jack Davis. St. Lucia: University of Queensland Press, 1990. Reprinted by permission of the author.

Ngugi wa Thiong'o, "Goodbye Africa" from *Secret Lives and Other Stories*. London: Heinemann, 1975. Reprinted by permission.

Oodgeroo Noonuccal (formerly Kath Walker), "Gooboora, the Silent Pool" and "The Past" from *My People*. Queensland: Jacaranda Press, 1990. Reprinted by permission of the publisher.

Gabriel Okara, "The Snowflakes Sail Gently Down" from *The Fisherman's Invocation*. London: Heinemann. Reprinted by permission of the author.

Michael Ondaatje, "Light" from *There's a Trick with a Knife I'm Learning to Do*. Toronto: McClelland & Stewart, 1979. Reprinted by permission of the author.

Sasenarine Persaud, "Tiger Swami" from *Between the Dash and the Comma*. 1989. Reprinted by permission of the author.

M. Nourbese Philip, "She Tries Her Tongue; Her Silence Softly Breaks" and "Transfiguration" from *She Tries Her Tongue, Her Silence Softly Breaks*. Charlottetown: Ragweed Press, 1989. Reprinted by permission of the author.

Jean Rhys, "I Used to Live Here Once" from *Sleep It Off, Lady*. Penguin Books, 1979. First published by Andre Deutsch, 1976. © Jean Rhys, 1976. Reprinted by permission of Penguin Books.

Salman Rushdie, "'Commonwealth Literature' Does Not Exist" from *Imaginary Homelands*. London: Granta Books, 1981. Reprinted by permission.

Sam Selvon, "Brackley and the Bed" from *Ways of Sunlight* (1957). "Turning Christian" from *Foreday Morning* (1989). Reprinted by permission of the estate of Sam Selvon.

Olive Senior, "The Boy Who Loved Ice Cream" from *Summer Lightning and Other Stories*. Essex: Longman, 1986. Reprinted by permission of the author and the publisher.

Vikram Seth, 12.1-12.8 from *The Golden Gate*. New York: Random House, 1986. Reprinted by permission of the author.

Philip Sherlock, "The Warau People Discover the Earth" from *West Indian Folk-Tales* by Philip Sherlock. © Philip Sherlock 1966. Reprinted by permission of Oxford University Press.

Leslie Marmon Silko, "Yellow Woman" from *The Man to Send Rain Clouds*. New York: Viking-Penguin, 1974. Reprinted by permission.

Wole Soyinka, "The Trials of Brother Jero" from *Collected Plays 2* 1974. © Wole Soyinka 1964. Reprinted by permission of Oxford University Press.

Subramani, "Sautu" from *The Fantasy Eaters* (1988). Washington: Three Continents Press. Reprinted by permission of author.

Mary TallMountain, "There Is No Word for Goodbye" from *There Is No Word for Goodbye*, 1981. Reprinted by permission of the literary executor of the TallMountain estate.

Edwin Thumboo, "Ulysses by the Merlion" from *Ulysses by the Merlion*. Oxford: Heinemann, 1979. Reprinted by permission of the author.

M. G. Vassanji, "The London-Returned" from *Uhuru Street*. Oxford: Heinemann, 1991. Reprinted by permission of Heinemann and of McClelland & Stewart, Toronto.

Alafina Vuki, "Four-Year Wisdom" from *Creative Writing*, ed. Satendra Nandan. Suva: Fiji Writers' Association, 1985. Reprinted of permission of the editor.

Fred Wah, "Breathin' My Name with a Sigh" from *Breathin' My Name with a Sigh*. Vancouver: Talon Books, 1981. Reprinted by permission of the author.

Derek Walcott, "Midsummer LII" from *Midsummer*. London: Faber & Faber, 1981. "A Letter From Brooklyn" and "Ruins of a Great House" from *Collected Poems 1948-1984*. Farrar, Straus & Giroux, Inc. Reprinted by permission of the publisher.

Albert Wendt, "Crocodile" from *The Birth and Death of the Miracle Man*. London: Penguin, 1986. Reprinted by permission.

May Wong, "The Shroud" from *Critical Engagements*, ed. Kirpal Singh. Singapore: Heinemann (Asia), 1986. Reprinted by permission of the author and publisher.

Arthur Yap, "2 Mothers in a HDB Playground" from *Critical Engagements*, ed. Kirpal Singh. Singapore: Heinemann (Asia), 1986. Reprinted by permission of the author and publisher.

The publisher has made every effort to locate all copyright holders of the texts published in this anthology and would be pleased to hear from any party not duly acknowledged.

# Introduction

The literary community from which *Concert of Voices: An Anthology of World Writing in English* draws its material is one linked by a common language imposed by centuries of British imperial expansion. In many instances, the language has acquired local linguistic features but the various versions retain strong affinities with each other and with British English. This vast literary community extends into every continent and encompasses many different cultures and traditions and hundreds of poets, essayists, novelists, and dramatists, whose works have appeared in a range of local and international publications. To select for this anthology a representative set of short essays, fiction, plays, and poems from this multifarious literary community was a formidable task, one that eventually required reining in ambitiousness with practicality and tempering selectivity with arbitrariness. Although a number of anthologies of national or regional writings are readily available, it is difficult to find one that spans these contiguous literatures and addresses the requirements of survey courses or the needs of readers who want an introductory overview. *Concert of Voices* is an attempt to provide such a text.

The parameter this collection adopts to cope with the formidable quantity of material is to regard itself as an anthology of work by writers who have had to define themselves in relation to current or residual imperial presences, or to dominant cultures within their societies (whether it is the Japanese-Canadian Joy Kogawa in Canada, the Aboriginal Gerry Bostock in Australia, or the Welsh-Dominican Jean Rhys in the Caribbean), or to both. As such, the anthology is both cross-cultural and multicultural in scope. The intention in the first instance is to provide an *alternative* text to anthologies of traditional and established writings (in which the new writings in English invariably are displaced and marginalized) and at the same time to *complement* these anthologies. In this regard, the word "other" — which points up apartness and division — was found wanting and dropped from the main title. Its omission draws attention to a concept (and conviction) operative in the construction of the anthology: despite historical and cultural specificities (the focus of cross-cultural and multicultural studies), commonalities and affinities exist among these writings and between writings on both sides of the hegemonic divide. The anthology, then, is not intended simply as an offering of sociological or anthropological insights into these "different" peoples. The selections can be used to show that literature alerts us to the common and shared in human experience, whatever our own particular cultural, ethnic, historical, national, or political attachments. As Timothy Mo's protagonist puts it in *An Insular Possession,* under "the different veneers of varying laws, institutions, and civilizations . . . the Old Adam is the same. His nature contains the same admixture of bad and good . . . whether . . . subsumed under an integument which is yellow, black, red, white, coffee, or any combination of fleshly tints" (257). The pieces in *Concert of Voices* demonstrate that imaginative writings can evolve from the cocoon of particularities into what can be called — modifying a catch-phase of certain other disciplines — Literature Without Borders. To put it another way, they illustrate what Northrop Frye identified as *primary* and *secondary* concerns in literature: *primary* concerns, according to Frye, are akin to Wordsworth's notion of the "primary laws of our nature," which are shared by all peoples of all times and include the "essential passions of the heart", and the desire to live comfortably with food, shelter, and companionship. *Secondary* concerns include "loyalty to one's place in the class structure, and in short to everything that comes under the heading of ideology" (21).

These *secondary* concerns are much in evidence in many of the selections in this text, particularly in the writers' responses to centuries of domination by imperial cultures. Many of these writers whose languages and cultures were (and are) relegated to the margins in their own communities and dismissed as inferior by the imperial centre or the dominant culture now reclaim and celebrate their distinct identities and traditions. Others possessed of a bicultural or multicultural imagination that encompasses both the local and the metropolitan, the marginal and the dominant, exhibit ambivalences and divided psyches, which — if and when they are resolved — may result in denial of one side of their bipolarity or in a philosophical recognition of the complementarity of their binary opposites.

Similar responses are to be seen in the writers' relationship with the English language. Those who perceive language to be inseparable from cultural identity and interpret continued use of imposed imperial languages as a prolonging of colonialism reject English in favour of indigenous languages. (They are likely to contend that an anthology of this kind, which takes its selection from former English-speaking colonies, is complicitly engaged in perpetuating colonialism.) Others who have lost touch with the languages of their ancestors and for whom

English is their first and often only language continue to use it self-consciously, and are aware of the irony of their situation, particularly when they employ it to write back to the centre. For others yet English is a lingua franca—in which as much as three-quarters of its words are foreign-born; it belongs to them; it is theirs to master and, if they so wish, to modify and transform into nation languages to serve local needs.

The colonial-imperial, marginal-central binary informs much of the writings of this linguistic community but it is not the exclusive or overriding precoccupation of the writers. They do not confine themselves to political and ideological issues or subsume beneath them other geneses and dimensions of experiences of love, ambition, resentment, envy, generosity, anger, and the range of responses that make humans human. To do so would be to simplify and falsify their complex lives. Moreover, to trace all experiences to hegemonic politics is to deny individuals and communities agency and responsibility for their own fates, and to ignore that in some locations home-grown tyrants have supplanted foreign imperialists, and that individuals can have feelings and thoughts only tangentially related to the political and ideological, if at all.

The subtitle claims that this is an anthology of "World Writing in English." What might this mean? A decade or two ago, perhaps the term "Commonwealth Literature" would have been used to cover a great deal of this material, but that would have meant dispensing with such writings in English as those by Natives in the U.S.A. and by South Africans. Moreover, nowadays for many this is an outmoded term for works forged in and by an age of decolonization and dissolution of imperial ties. The currently fashionable term "Postcolonial Literature," on the other hand, is not confined to writings in English; and it is considered by some as yet another political concept that now imposes coloniality on all current issues, forces homogeneity on countries and regions with different histories of colonization, and ignores that colonialism in various guises is still around. "New Literatures in English" may appear to be politically neutral, but for some it relegates to a junior status literatures some of which have been around for more than two centuries. This anthology therefore settled on "World Writing in English" as the most convenient term, even though it excludes—like its affiliates "World Literature Written in English" or "International English Literature"—traditional and established texts from the U.S.A. and the U.K. (Once again, the book is quite consciously an *alternative* to traditional mainstream anthologies.)

*Concert of Voices* attempts to include many of the established writers with solid reputations at home and abroad and to balance these with new and not-so-well-known voices, yet — as is to be expected of a short anthology — a number of significant writers and writings had to be omitted even within the set parameters. To do justice to this body of writing and to do anything more than provide a limited sampling of the writings and the ideological, artistic, and cultural underpinnings of these literatures would require a multi-volume anthology. Perhaps survey courses of these literatures could compensate for these omissions by supplementing the works included here with a selection of novels and extended plays from the different regions and communities.

The selections are organized alphabetically under the authors' names, and (to serve the needs of those who would like regional or genre entree to the authors and works, two additional tables of contents are provided. The regional table of contents groups the selections under Africa, Canada, the Caribbean, the Indian Subcontinent, South-East Asia, the South Pacific, and the U.K. and U.S.A. Authors with dual national or regional affiliations are listed in both regions. In the genre table of contents, selections are grouped under fiction, poetry, drama, and essays. An index of titles and brief biographical notes on each author are included. I would like to thank my colleagues and friends in the field of International English literature (or whatever term they deem appropriate) for their very helpful comments on my selections: Karin Beeler, Frank Birbalsingh, Anthony Boxill, Cherry Clayton, Saros Cowasjee, Kwame Dawes, Susan Gingell, Robert Hamner, Kelly Hewson, Shamsul Islam, Chelva Kanaganayakam, Carol Morrell, Kenneth Ramchand, Sumana Sen-Bagchee, Pat Srebrnik, John Thieme, H. Nigel Thomas, Michael Thorpe, and Tracy Ware. Yaw Asante, George Fitzpatrick, Jennifer Kelly, Don LePan, and Guangtian Li had a hand in the production of this anthology and I acknowledge with thanks their assistance. I am indebted to Myrna Sentes and Sharoj Tiwari, who generously let me avail myself of their faxing and word-processing skills. And I am particularly grateful to Ruby Ramraj, without whose support and assistance this anthology would not have seen publication.

WORKS CITED

Frye, Northrop. "Literary and Linguistic Scholarship in a Postliterate World." *Myth and Metaphor: Collected Essays 1974-1988*. Ed. Robert Denham. Charlotteville: U of Virginia P, 1990.

Mo, Timothy. *An Insular Possession*. London: Chatto & Windus, 1986.

# Chinua Achebe

## *Girls at War*

The first time their paths crossed nothing happened. That was in the first heady days of warlike preparation when thousands of young men (and sometimes women too) were daily turned away from enlistment centres because far too many of them were coming forward burning with readiness to bear arms in defence of the exciting new nation.

The second time they met was at a check-point at Awka. Then the war had started and was slowly moving southwards from the distant northern sector. He was driving from Onitsha to Enugu and was in a hurry. Although intellectually he approved of thorough searches at road-blocks, emotionally he was always offended whenever he had to submit to them. He would probably not admit it but the feeling people got was that if you were put through a search then you could not really be one of the big people. Generally he got away without a search by pronouncing in his deep, authoritative voice: "Reginald Nwankwo, Ministry of Justice." That almost always did it. But sometimes either through ignorance or sheer cussedness the crowd at the odd check-point would refuse to be impressed. As happened now at Awka. Two constables carrying heavy Mark 4 rifles were watching distantly from the roadside leaving the actual searching to local vigilantes.

"I am in a hurry," he said to the girl who now came up to his car. "My name is Reginald Nwankwo, Ministry of Justice."

"Good afternoon, sir. I want to see your boot."

"Oh Christ! What do you think is in the boot?"

"I don't know, sir."

He got out of the car in suppressed rage, stalked to the back, opened the boot and holding the lid up with his left hand he motioned with the right as if to say: After you!

"Are you satisfied?" he demanded.

"Yes, sir. Can I see your pigeon-hole?"

"Christ Almighty!"

"Sorry to delay you, sir. But you people gave us this job to do."

"Never mind. You are damn right. It's just that I happen to be in a hurry. But never mind. That's the glove-box. Nothing there as you can see."

"All right sir, close it." Then she opened the rear door and bent down to inspect under the seats. It was then he took the first real look at her, starting from behind. She was a beautiful girl in a breasty blue jersey, khaki jeans and canvas shoes with the new-style hair-plait which gave a girl a defiant look and which they called—for reasons of their own—"air force base"; and she looked vaguely familiar.

"I am all right, sir," she said at last meaning she was through with her task. "You don't recognize me?"

"No. Should I?"

"You gave me a lift to Enugu that time I left my school to go and join the militia."

"Ah, yes, you were the girl. I told you, didn't I, to go back to school because girls were not required in the militia. What happened?"

"They told me to go back to my school or join the Red Cross."

"You see I was right. So, what are you doing now?"

"Just patching up with Civil Defence."

"Well, good luck to you. Believe me you are a great girl."

That was the day he finally believed there might be something in this talk about revolution. He had seen plenty of girls and women marching and demonstrating before now. But somehow he had never been able to give it much thought. He didn't doubt that the girls and the women took themselves seriously, they obviously did. But so did the little kids who marched up and down the streets at the time drilling with sticks and wearing their mothers' soup bowls for steel helmets. The prime joke of the time among his friends was the contingent of girls from a local secondary school marching behind a banner: WE ARE IMPREGNABLE!

But after that encounter at the Awka check-point he simply could not sneer at the girls again, nor at the talk of revolution, for he had seen it in action in that young woman whose devotion had simply and without self-righteousness convicted him of gross levity. What were her words? We are doing the work you asked us to do. She wasn't going to make an exception even for one who once did her a favour. He was sure she would have searched her own father just as rigorously.

When their paths crossed a third time, at least eighteen months later, things had got very bad. Death and starvation having long chased out the headiness of the early days, now left in some places blank resignation, in others a rock-like, even suicidal, defiance. But surprisingly enough there were many at this time who had no other desire than to corner whatever good things were still going and to enjoy themselves to the limit. For such people a strange normalcy had returned to the world. All those nervous check-points disappeared. Girls became girls once more and boys boys. It was a tight, blockaded and desperate world but none the less a world—with some goodness and some badness and plenty of heroism which, however, happened most times far, far below the eye-level of the people in this story—in out-of-the-way refugee camps, in the damp tatters, in the hungry and bare-handed courage of the first line of fire.

Reginald Nwankwo lived in Owerri then. But that day he had gone to Nkwerri in search of relief. He had got from Caritas in Owerri a few heads of stock-fish, some tinned meat, and the dreadful American stuff called Formula Two which he felt certain was some kind of animal feed. But he always had a vague suspicion that not being a Catholic put one at a disadvantage with Caritas. So he went now to see an old friend who ran the WCC depot at Nkwerri to get other items like rice, beans and that excellent cereal commonly called Gabon gari.

He left Owerri at six in the morning so as to catch his friend at the depot where he was known never to linger beyond 8.30 for fear of air-raids. Nwankwo was very fortunate that day. The depot had received on the previous day large supplies of new stock as a result of an unusual number of plane landings a few nights earlier. As his driver loaded tins and bags and cartons into his car the starved crowds that perpetually hung around relief centres made crude, ungracious remarks like "War Can Continue!" meaning the WCC! Somebody else shouted "Irevolu!" and his friends replied "shum!" "Irevolu!" "shum!" "Isofeli?" "shum!" "Isofeli?" "Mba!"

Nwankwo was deeply embarrassed not by the jeers of this scarecrow crowd of rags and floating ribs but by the independent accusation of their wasted bodies and sunken eyes. Indeed he would probably have felt much worse had they said nothing, simply looked on in silence, as his boot was loaded with milk, and powdered egg and oats and tinned meat and stock-fish. By nature such singular good fortune in the midst of a general desolation was certain to embarrass him. But what could a man do? He had a wife and four children living in the remote village of Ogbu and completely dependent on what relief he could find and send them. He couldn't abandon them to kwashiokor. The best he could do—and did do as a matter of fact—was to make sure that whenever he got sizeable supplies like now he made over some of it to his driver, Johnson, with a wife and six, or was it seven?, children and a salary of ten pounds a month when gari in the market was climbing to one pound per cigarette cup. In such a situation one could do nothing at all for crowds; at best one could try to be of some use to one's immediate neighbours. That was all.

On his way back to Owerri a very attractive girl by the roadside waved for a lift. He ordered the driver to stop. Scores of pedestrians, dusty and exhausted, some military, some civil, swooped down on the car from all directions.

"No, no, no," said Nwankwo firmly. "It's the young woman I stopped for. I have a bad tyre and can only take one person. Sorry."

"My son, please," cried one old woman in despair, gripping the door-handle.

"Old woman, you want to be killed?" shouted the driver as he pulled away, shaking her off. Nwankwo had already opened a book and sunk his eyes there. For at least a mile after that he did not even look at the girl until she finding, perhaps, the silence too heavy said:

"You've saved me today. Thank you."

"Not at all. Where are you going?"

"To Owerri. You don't recognize me?"

"Oh yes, of course. What a fool I am . . . You are . . . "

"Gladys."

"That's right, the militia girl. You've changed, Gladys. You were always beautiful of course, but now you are a beauty queen. What do you do these days?"

"I am in the Fuel Directorate."

"That's wonderful."

It was wonderful, he thought, but even more it was tragic. She wore a high-tinted wig and a very expensive skirt and low-cut blouse. Her shoes, obviously from Gabon, must have cost a fortune. In short, thought Nwankwo, she had to be in the keep of some well-placed gentleman, one of those piling up money out of the war.

"I broke my rule today to give you a lift. I never give lifts these days."

"Why?"

"How many people can you carry? It is better not to try at all. Look at that old woman."

"I thought you would carry her."

He said nothing to that and after another spell of silence Gladys thought maybe he was offended and so added: "Thank you for breaking your rule for me." She was scanning his face, turned slightly away. He smiled, turned, and tapped her on the lap.

"What are you going to Owerri to do?"

"I am going to visit my girl friend."

"Girl friend? You sure?"

"Why not? . . . If you drop me at her house you can see her. Only I pray God she hasn't gone on weekend today; it will be serious."

"Why?"

"Because if she is not at home I will sleep on the road today."

"I pray to God that she is not at home."

"Why?"

"Because if she is not at home I will offer you bed and breakfast . . . What is that?" he asked the driver who had brought the car to an abrupt stop. There was no need for an answer. The small crowd ahead was looking upwards. The three scrambled out of the car and stumbled for the bush, necks twisted in a backward search of the sky. But the alarm was false. The sky was silent and clear except for two high-flying vultures. A humorist in the crowd called them Fighter and Bomber and everyone laughed in relief. The three climbed into their car again and continued their journey.

"It is much too early for raids," he said to Gladys, who had both her palms on her breast as though to still a thumping heart. "They rarely come before ten o'clock."

But she remained tongue-tied from her recent fright. Nwankwo saw an opportunity there and took it at once.

"Where does your friend live?"

"250 Douglas Road."

"Ah! that's the very centre of town—a terrible place. No bunkers, nothing. I won't advise you to go there before 6 p.m.; it's not safe. If you don't mind I will take you to my place where there is a good bunker and then as soon as it is safe, around six, I shall drive you to your friend. How's that?"

"It's all right," she said lifelessly. "I am so frightened of this thing. That's why I refused to work in Owerri. I don't even know who asked me to come out today."

"You'll be all right. We are used to it."

"But your family is not there with you?"

"No," he said. "Nobody has his family there. We like to say it is because of air-raids but I can assure you there is more to it. Owerri is a real swinging town and we live the life of gay bachelors."

"That is what I have heard."

"You will not just hear it; you will see it today. I shall take you to a real swinging party. A friend of mine, a Lieutenant-Colonel, is having a birthday party. He's hired the Sound Smashers to play. I'm sure you'll enjoy it."

He was immediately and thoroughly ashamed of himself. He hated the parties and frivolities to which his friends clung like drowning men. And to talk so approvingly of them because he wanted to take a girl home! And this particular girl too, who had once had such beautiful faith in the struggle and was betrayed (no doubt about it) by some man like him out for a good time. He shook his head sadly.

"What is it?" asked Gladys.

"Nothing. Just my thoughts."

They made the rest of the journey to Owerri practically in silence.

She made herself at home very quickly as if she was a regular girl friend of his. She changed into a house dress and put away her auburn wig.

"That is a lovely hair-do. Why do you hide it with a wig?"

"Thank you," she said leaving his question unanswered for a while. Then she said: "Men are funny."

"Why do you say that?"

"You are now a beauty queen," she mimicked.

"Oh, that! I mean every word of it." He pulled her to him and kissed her. She neither refused nor yielded fully, which he liked for a start. Too many girls were simply too easy those days. War sickness, some called it.

He drove off a little later to look in at the office and she busied herself in the kitchen helping his boy with lunch. It must have been literally a look-in, for he was back within half an hour, rubbing his hands and saying he could not stay away too long from his beauty queen.

As they sat down to lunch she said: "You have nothing in your fridge."

"Like what?" he asked, half-offended.

"Like meat," she replied undaunted.

"Do you still eat meat?" he challenged.

"Who am I? But other big men like you eat."

"I don't know which big men you have in mind. But they are not like me. I don't make money trading with the enemy or selling relief or . . ."

"Augusta's boy friend doesn't do that. He just gets foreign exchange."

"How does he get it? He swindles the government — that's how he gets foreign exchange, whoever he is. Who is Augusta, by the way?"

"My girl friend."

"I see."

"She gave me three dollars last time which I changed to forty-five pounds. The man gave her fifty dollars."

"Well, my dear girl, I don't traffic in foreign exchange and I don't have meat in my fridge. We are fighting a war and I happen to know that some young boys at the front drink gari and water once in three days."

"It is true," she said simply. "Monkey de work, baboon de chop."

"It is not even that; it is worse," he said, his voice beginning to shake. "People are dying every day. As we talk now somebody is dying."

"It is true," she said again.

"Plane!" screamed his boy from the kitchen.

"My mother!" screamed Gladys. As they scuttled towards the bunker of palm stems and red earth, covering their heads with their hands and stooping slightly in their flight, the entire sky was exploding with the clamour of jets and the huge noise of home-made anti-aircraft rockets.

Inside the bunker she clung to him even after the plane had gone and the guns, late to start and also to end, had all died down again.

"It was only passing," he told her, his voice a little shaky. "It didn't drop anything. From its direction I should say it was going to the war front. Perhaps our people are pressing them. That's what they always do. Whenever our boys press them, they send an SOS to the Russians and Egyptians to bring the planes." He drew a long breath.

She said nothing, just clung to him. They could hear his boy telling the servant from the next house that there were two of them and one dived like this and the other dived like that.

"I see dem well well," said the other with equal excitement. "If no to say de ting de kill porson e for sweet for eye. To God."

"Imagine!" said Gladys, finding her voice at last. She had a way, he thought, of conveying with a few words or even a single word whole layers of meaning. Now it was at once her astonishment as well as reproof, tinged perhaps with grudging admiration for people who could be so light-hearted about these bringers of death.

"Don't be so scared," he said. She moved closer and he began to kiss her and squeeze her breasts. She yielded more and more and then fully. The bunker was dark and unswept and might harbour crawling things. He thought of bringing a mat from the main house but reluctantly decided against it. Another plane might pass and send a neighbour or simply a chance passer-by crashing into them. That would be only slightly better than a certain gentleman in another air-raid who was seen in broad daylight fleeing his bedroom for his bunker stark-naked pursued by a woman in a similar state!

Just as Gladys had feared, her friend was not in town. It would seem her powerful boy friend had wangled for her a flight to Libreville to shop. So her neighbours thought anyway.

"Great!" said Nwankwo as they drove away. "She will come back on an arms plane loaded with shoes, wigs, pants, bras, cosmetics and what have you, which she will then sell and make thousands of pounds. You girls are really at war, aren't you?"

She said nothing and he thought he had got through at last to her. Then suddenly she said, "That is what you men want us to do."

"Well," he said, "here is one man who doesn't want you to do that. Do you remember that girl in khaki jeans who searched me without mercy at the check-point?"

She began to laugh.

"That is the girl I want you to become again. Do you remember her? No wig. I don't even think she had any earrings . . ."

"Ah, na lie-o. I had earrings."

"All right. But you know what I mean."

"That time done pass. Now everybody want survival. They call it number six. You put your number six; I put my number six. Everything all right."

The Lieutenant-Colonel's party turned into something quite unexpected. But before it did things had been going well enough. There was goat-meat, some chicken and rice and plenty of home-made spirits. There was one fiery brand nicknamed "tracer" which indeed sent a flame down your gullet. The funny thing was looking at it in the bottle it had the innocent appearance of an orange drink. But the thing that caused the greatest stir was the bread—one little roll for each person! It was the size of a golf-ball and about the same consistency too! But it was real bread. The band was good too and there were many girls. And to improve matters even further two white Red Cross people soon arrived with a bottle of Courvoisier and a bottle of Scotch! The party gave them a standing ovation and then scrambled to get a drop. It soon turned out from his general behaviour, however, that one of the white men had probably drunk too much already. And the reason it would seem was that a pilot he knew well had been killed in a crash at the airport last night, flying in relief in awful weather.

Few people at the party had heard of the crash by then. So there was an immediate damping of the air. Some dancing couples went back to their seats and the band stopped. Then for some strange reason the drunken Red Cross man just exploded.

"Why should a man, a decent man, throw away his life. For nothing!

Charley didn't need to die. Not for this stinking place. Yes, everything stinks here. Even these girls who come here all dolled up and smiling, what are they worth? Don't I know? A head of stock-fish, that's all, or one American dollar and they are ready to tumble into bed."

In the threatening silence following the explosion one of the young officers walked up to him and gave him three thundering slaps — right! left! right! — pulled him up from his seat and (there were things like tears in his eyes) shoved him outside. His friend, who had tried in vain to shut him up, followed him out and the silenced party heard them drive off. The officer who did the job returned dusting his palms.

"Fucking beast!" said he with an impressive coolness. And all the girls showed with their eyes that they rated him a man and a hero.

"Do you know him?" Gladys asked Nwankwo.

He didn't answer her. Instead he spoke generally to the party:

"The fellow was clearly drunk," he said.

"I don't care," said the officer. "It is when a man is drunk that he speaks what is on his mind."

"So you beat him for what was on his mind," said the host, "that is the spirit, Joe."

"Thank you, sir," said Joe, saluting.

"His name is Joe," Gladys and the girl on her left said in unison, turning to each other.

At the same time Nwankwo and a friend on the other side of him were saying quietly, very quietly, that although the man had been rude and offensive what he had said about the girls was unfortunately the bitter truth, only he was the wrong man to say it.

When the dancing resumed Captain Joe came to Gladys for a dance. She sprang to her feet even before the word was out of his mouth. Then she remembered immediately and turned round to take permission from Nwankwo. At the same time the Captain also turned to him and said, "Excuse me."

"Go ahead," said Nwankwo, looking somewhere between the two.

It was a long dance and he followed them with his eyes without appearing to do so. Occasionally a relief plane passed overhead and somebody immediately switched off the lights saying it might be the Intruder. But it was only an excuse to dance in the dark and make the girls giggle, for the sound of the Intruder was well known.

Gladys came back feeling very self-conscious and asked Nwankwo to dance with her. But he wouldn't. "Don't bother about me," he said, "I am enjoying myself perfectly sitting here and watching those of you who dance."

"Then let's go," she said, "if you won't dance."

"But I never dance, believe me. So please enjoy yourself."

She danced next with the Lieutenant-Colonel and again with Captain Joe, and then Nwankwo agreed to take her home.

"I am sorry I didn't dance," he said as they drove away. "But I swore never to dance as long as this war lasts."

She said nothing.

"When I think of somebody like that pilot who got killed last night. And he had no hand whatever in the quarrel. All his concern was to bring us food . . ."

"I hope that his friend is not like him," said Gladys.

"The man was just upset by his friend's death. But what I am saying is that with people like that getting killed and our own boys suffering and dying at the war fronts I don't see why we should sit around throwing parties and dancing."

"You took me there," said she in final revolt. "They are your friends. I don't know them before."

"Look, my dear, I am not blaming you. I am merely telling you why I personally refuse to dance. Anyway, let's change the subject . . . Do you still say you want to go back tomorrow? My driver can take you early enough on Monday morning for you to go to work. No? All right, just as you wish. You are the boss."

She gave him a shock by the readiness with which she followed him to bed and by her language.

"You want to shell?" she asked. And without waiting for an answer said, "Go ahead but don't pour in troops!"

He didn't want to pour in troops either and so it was all right. But she wanted visual assurance and so he showed her.

One of the ingenious economics taught by the war was that a rubber condom could be used over and over again. All you had to do was wash it out, dry it and shake a lot of talcum powder over it to prevent its sticking; and it was as good as new. It had to be the real British thing, though, not some of the cheap stuff they brought in from Lisbon which was about as strong as a dry cocoyam leaf in the harmattan.

He had his pleasure but wrote the girl off. He might just as well have slept with a prostitute, he thought. It was clear as daylight to him now that she was kept by some army officer. What a terrible transformation in the short period of less than two years! Wasn't it a miracle that she still had memories of the other life, that she even remembered her name? If the affair of the drunken Red Cross man should happen again now, he said to himself, he would stand up beside the fellow and tell the party that here was a man of truth. What a terrible fate to befall a whole generation! The mothers of tomorrow!

By morning he was feeling a little better and more generous in his judgements. Gladys, he thought, was just a mirror reflecting a society that had gone completely rotten and maggotty at the centre. The mirror itself was intact; a lot of smudge but no more. All that was needed was a clean duster. "I have a duty to her," he told himself, "the little girl that once revealed to me our situation. Now she is in danger, under some terrible influence."

He wanted to get to the bottom of this deadly influence. It was clearly not just her good-time girl friend, Augusta, or whatever her name was. There must be some man at the centre of it, perhaps one of these heartless attack-traders who traffic in foreign currencies and make their hundreds of thousands by sending young men to hazard their lives bartering looted goods for cigarettes behind enemy lines, or one of those contractors who receive piles of money daily for food they never deliver to the army. Or perhaps some vulgar and cowardly army officer full of filthy barrack talk and fictitious stories of heroism. He decided he had to find out. Last night he had thought of sending his driver alone to take her home. But no, he must go and see for himself where she lived. Something was bound to reveal itself there. Something on which he could anchor his saving operation. As he prepared for the trip his feeling towards her softened with every passing minute. He assembled for her half of the food he had received at the relief centre the day before. Difficult as things were, he thought, a girl who had something to eat would be spared, not all, but some of the temptation. He would arrange with his friend at the WCC to deliver something to her every fortnight.

Tears came to Gladys's eyes when she saw the gifts. Nwankwo didn't have too much cash on him but he got together twenty pounds and handed it over to her.

"I don't have foreign exchange, and I know this won't go far at all, but . . ."

She just came and threw herself at him, sobbing. He kissed her lips and eyes and mumbled something about victims of circumstance, which went over her head. In deference to him, he thought with exultation, she had put away her high-tinted wig in her bag.

"I want you to promise me something," he said.

"What?"

"Never use that expression about shelling again."

She smiled with tears in her eyes. "You don't like it? That's what all the girls call it."

"Well, you are different from all the girls. Will you promise?"

"OK."

Naturally their departure had become a little delayed. And when they got into the car it refused to start. After poking around the engine the driver decided that the battery was flat. Nwankwo was aghast. He had that very week paid thirty-four pounds to change two of the cells and the mechanic who performed it had promised him six months' service. A new battery, which was then running at two hundred and fifty pounds was simply out of the question. The driver must have been careless with something, he thought.

"It must be because of last night," said the driver.

"What happened last night?" asked Nwankwo sharply, wondering what insolence was on the way. But none was intended.

"Because we use the head light."

"Am I supposed not to use my light then? Go and get some people and try pushing it." He got out again with Gladys and returned to the house while the driver went over to neighbouring houses to seek the help of other servants.

After at least half an hour of pushing it up and down the street, and a lot of noisy advice from the pushers, the car finally spluttered to life shooting out enormous clouds of black smoke from the exhaust.

It was eight-thirty by his watch when they set out. A few miles away a disabled soldier waved for a lift.

"Stop!" screamed Nwankwo. The driver jammed his foot on the brakes and then turned his head towards his master in bewilderment.

"Don't you see the soldier waving? Reverse and pick him up!"

"Sorry, sir," said the driver. "I don't know Master wan to pick him."

"If you don't know you should ask. Reverse back."

The soldier, a mere boy, in filthy khaki drenched in sweat lacked his right leg from the knee down. He seemed not only grateful that a car should stop for him but greatly surprised. He first handed in his crude wooden crutches which the driver arranged between the two front seats, then painfully he levered himself in.

"Thank sir," he said turning his neck to look at the back and completely out of breath.

"I am very grateful. Madame, thank you."

"The pleasure is ours," said Nwankwo. "Where did you get your wound?"

"At Azumini, sir. On tenth of January."

"Never mind. Everything will be all right. We are proud of you boys and will make sure you receive your due reward when it is all over."

"I pray God, sir."

They drove on in silence for the next half-hour or so. Then as the car sped down a slope towards a bridge somebody screamed — perhaps the driver, perhaps the soldier — "They have come!" The screech of the brakes merged into the scream and the shattering of the sky overhead. The doors flew open even before the car had come to a stop and they were fleeing blindly to the bush. Gladys was a little ahead of Nwankwo when they heard through the drowning tumult the soldier's voice crying: "Please come and open for me!" Vaguely he saw Gladys stop; he pushed past her shouting to her at the same time to come on. Then a high whistle descended like a spear through the chaos and exploded in a vast noise and motion that smashed up everything. A tree he had embraced flung him away through the bush. Then another terrible whistle starting high up and ending again in a monumental crash of the world; and then another, and Nwankwo heard no more.

He woke up to human voices and weeping and the smell and smoke of a charred world. He dragged himself up and staggered towards the source of the sounds.

From afar he saw his driver running towards him in tears and blood. He saw the remains of his car smoking and the entangled remains of the girl and the soldier. And he let out a piercing cry and fell down again.

# Ama Ata Aidoo

## *No Sweetness Here*

He was beautiful, but that was not important. Beauty does not play such a vital role in a man's life as it does in a woman's, or so people think. If a man's beauty is so ill-mannered as to be noticeable, people discreetly ignore its existence. Only an immodest girl like me would dare comment on a boy's beauty. "Kwesi is so handsome," I was always telling his mother. "If ever I am transferred from this place, I will kidnap him." I enjoyed teasing the dear woman and she enjoyed being teased about him. She would look scandalised, pleased and alarmed all in one fleeting moment.

"Ei, Chicha. You should not say such things. The boy is not very handsome really." But she knew she was lying. "Besides, Chicha, who cares whether a boy is handsome or not?" Again she knew that at least she cared, for, after all, didn't the boy's wonderful personality throw a warm light on the mother's lively though already waning beauty? Then gingerly, but in a remarkably matter-of-fact tone, she would voice out her gnawing fear. "Please Chicha, I always know you are just making fun of me, but please, promise me you won't take Kwesi away with you." Almost at once her tiny mouth would quiver and she would hide her eyes in her cloth as if ashamed of her great love and her fears. But I understood. "O, Maami, don't cry, you know I don't mean it."

"Chicha I am sorry, and I trust you. Only I can't help fearing, can I? What will I do, Chicha, what would I do, should something happen to my child?" She would raise her pretty eyes, glistening with unshed tears.

"Nothing will happen to him," I would assure her. "He is a good boy. He does not fight and therefore there is no chance of anyone beating him. He is not dull, at least not too dull, which means he does not get more cane-lashes than the rest of his mates. . . ."

"Chicha, I shall willingly submit to your canes if he gets his sums wrong," she would hastily intervene.

"Don't be funny. A little warming-up on a cold morning wouldn't do him any harm. But if you say so, I won't object to hitting that soft flesh of yours." At this, the tension would break and both of us begin laughing. Yet I always went away with the image of her quivering mouth and unshed tears in my mind.

Maami Ama loved her son; and this is a silly statement, as silly as saying Maami Ama is a woman. Which mother would not? At the time of this story, he had just turned ten years old. He was in Primary Class Four and quite tall for his age. His skin was as smooth as shea-butter and as dark as charcoal. His black hair was as soft as his mother's. His eyes were of the kind that always remind one of a long dream on a hot afternoon. It is indecent to dwell on a boy's physical appearance, but then Kwesi's beauty was indecent.

The evening was not yet come. My watch read 4.15 p.m., that ambiguous time of the day which these people, despite their great ancient astronomic knowledge, have always failed to identify. For the very young and very old, it is certainly evening, for they've stayed at home all day and they begin to persuade themselves that the day is ending. Bored with their own company, they sprawl in the market-place or by their own walls. The children begin to whimper for their mothers, for they are tired with playing "house." Fancying themselves starving, they go back to what was left of their lunch, but really they only pray that mother will come home from the farm soon. The very old certainly do not go back on lunch remains but they do bite back at old conversational topics which were fresh at ten o'clock.

"I say, Kwame, as I was saying this morning, my first wife was a most beautiful woman," old Kofi would say.

"Oh! yes, yes, she was an unusually beautiful girl. I remember her." Old Kwame would nod his head but the truth was he was tired of the story and he was sleepy. "It's high time the young people came back from the farm."

But I was a teacher, and I went the white man's way. School was over. Maami Ama's hut was at one end of the village and the school was at the other. Nevertheless it was not a long walk from the school to her place because Bamso is not really a big village. I had left my books to little Grace Ason to take home for me; so I had only my little clock in my hand and I was walking in a leisurely way. As I passed the old people, they shouted their greetings. It was always the Fanticised form of the English.

"Kudiimin-o, Chicha." Then I would answer, "Kudiimin, Nana." When I greeted first, the response was "Tanchiw."

"Chicha, how are you?"

"Nana, I am well."

"And how are the children?"

"Nana, they are well."

"*Yoo*, that is good." When an old man felt inclined to be talkative, especially if he had more than me for audience, he would compliment me on the work I was doing. Then he would go on to the assets of education, especially female education, ending up with quoting Dr. Aggrey.

So this evening too, I was delayed: but it was as well, for when I arrived at the hut, Maami Ama had just arrived from the farm. The door opened, facing the village, and so I could see her. Oh, that picture is still vivid in my mind. She was sitting on a low stool with her load before her. Like all the loads the other women would bring from the farms into their homes, it was colourful with miscellaneous articles. At the very bottom of the wide wooden tray were the cassava and yam tubers, rich muddy brown, the colour of the earth. Next were the plantain, of the green colour of the woods from which they came. Then there were the gay vegetables, the scarlet pepper, garden eggs, golden pawpaw and crimson tomatoes. Over this riot of colours the little woman's eyes were fixed, absorbed, while the tiny hands delicately picked the pepper. I made a scratchy noise at the door. She looked up and smiled. Her smile was a wonderful flashing whiteness.

"Oh Chicha, I have just arrived."

"So I see. *Ayekoo*."

"*Yaa*, my own. And how are you, my child?"

"Very well, Mother. And you?"

"Tanchiw. Do sit down, there's a stool in that corner. Sit down. Mmmm. . . . Life is a battle. What can we do? We are just trying, my daughter."

"Why were you longer at the farm today?"

"After weeding that plot I told you about last week, I thought I would go for one or two yams."

"Ah!" I cried.

"You know tomorrow is Ahobaa. Even if one does not feel happy, one must have some yam for old Ahor."

"Yes. So I understand. The old saviour deserves it. After all it is not often that a man offers himself as a sacrifice to the gods to save his people from a pestilence."

"No, Chicha, we were so lucky."

"But Maami Ama, why do you look so sad? After all, the yams are quite big." She gave me a small grin, looking at the yams she had now packed at the corner.

"Do you think so? Well, they are the best of the lot. My daughter, when life fails you, it fails you totally. One's yams reflect the total sum of one's life. And mine look wretched enough."

"O, Maami, why are you always speaking in this way? Look at Kwesi, how many mothers can boast of such a son? Even though he is only one, consider those who have none at all. Perhaps some woman is sitting at some corner envying you."

She chuckled. "What an unhappy woman she must be who would envy Ama! But thank you, I should be grateful for Kwesi."

After that we were quiet for a while. I always loved to see her moving quietly about her work. Having finished unpacking, she knocked the dirt out of the tray and started making fire to prepare the evening meal. She started humming a religious lyric. She was a Methodist.

*We are fighting*
*We are fighting*
*We are fighting for Canaan, the Heavenly Kingdom above.*

I watched her and my eyes became misty, she looked so much like my own mother. Presently, the fire began to smoke. She turned round. "Chicha."

"Maami Ama."

"Do you know that tomorrow I am going to have a formal divorce?"

"Oh!" And I could not help the dismay in my voice.

I had heard, soon after my arrival in the village, that the parents of that most beautiful boy were as good as divorced. I had hoped they would come to a respectful understanding for the boy's sake. Later on when I got to know his mother, I had wished for this, for her own sweet self's sake too. But as time went on I had realised this could not be or was not even desirable. Kodjo Fi was a selfish and bullying man, whom no decent woman ought to have married. He got on marvellously with his two other wives but they were three of a feather. Yet I was sorry to hear Maami was going to have a final breach with him.

"Yes, I am," she went on. "I should. What am I going on like this for? What is man struggling after? Seven years is a long time to bear ill-usage from a man coupled with contempt and insults from his wives. What have I done to deserve the abuse of his sisters? And his mother!"

"Does she insult you too?" I exclaimed.

"Why not? Don't you think she would? Considering that I don't buy her the most expensive cloths on the market and I don't give her the best fish from my soup, like her daughters-in-law do."

I laughed. "The mean old witch!"

"Chicha, don't laugh. I am quite sure she wanted to eat Kwesi but I baptised him and she couldn't."

"Oh, don't say that, Maami. I am quite sure they all like you, only you don't know."

"My child, they don't. They hate me."

"But what happened?" I asked the question I had wanted to ask for so long.

"You would ask, Chicha! I don't know. They suddenly began hating me when Kwesi was barely two. Kodjo Fi reduced my housekeeping money and sometimes he refused to give me anything at all. He wouldn't eat my food. At first, I used to ask him why. He always replied, "It is nothing." If I had not been such an unlucky woman, his mother and sisters might have taken my side, but for me there was no one. That planting time, although I was his first wife, he allotted to me the smallest, thorniest plot."

"Ei, what did you say about it?"

"What could I say? At that time my mother was alive, though my father was already dead. When I complained to her about the treatment I was getting from my husband, she told me that in marriage, a woman must sometimes be a fool. But I have been a fool for far too long a time."

"Oh!" I frowned.

"Mother has died and left me and I was an only child too. My aunts are very busy looking after the affairs of their own daughters. I've told my uncles several times but they never take me seriously. They feel I am only a discontented woman."

"You?" I asked in surprise.

"Perhaps you would not think so. But there are several who do feel like that in this village."

She paused for a while, while she stared at the floor.

"You don't know, but I've been the topic of gossip for many years. Now, I only want to live on my own looking after my child. I don't think I will ever get any more children. Chicha, our people say a bad marriage kills the soul. Mine is fit for burial."

"Maami, don't grieve."

"My daughter, my mother and father who brought me to this world have left me alone and I've stopped grieving for them. When death summoned them, they were glad to lay down their tools and go to their parents. Yes, they loved me all right but even they had to leave me.

Why should I make myself unhappy about a man for whom I ceased to exist a long time ago?"

She went to the big basket, took out some cassava and plantain, and sitting down began peeling them. Remembering she had forgotten the wooden bowl into which she would put the food, she got up to go for it.

"In this case," I continued the conversation, "what will happen to Kwesi?"

"What will happen to him?" she asked in surprise. "This is no problem. They may tell me to give him to his father."

"And would you?"

"No, I wouldn't."

"And would you succeed in keeping him if his father insisted?"

"Well, I would struggle, for my son is his father's child but he belongs to my family."

I sat there listening to these references to the age-old customs of which I had been ignorant. I was surprised. She washed the food, now cut into lumps, and arranged it in the cooking-pot. She added water and put it on the fire. She blew at it and it burst into flames.

"Maami Ama, has not your husband got a right to take Kwesi from you?" I asked her.

"He has, I suppose, but not entirely. Anyway, if the elders who would make the divorce settlement ask me to let him go and stay with his father, I wouldn't refuse."

"You are a brave woman."

"Life has taught me to be brave," she said, looking at me and smiling, "By the way, what is the time?"

I told her, "It is six minutes to six o'clock."

"And Kwesi has not yet come home?" she exclaimed.

"Mama, here I am," a piping voice announced.

"My husband, my brother, my father, my all-in-all, where are you?" And there he was. All at once, for the care-worn village woman, the sun might well have been rising from the east instead of setting behind the coconut palms. Her eyes shone. Kwesi saluted me and then his mother. He was a little shy of me and he ran away to the inner chamber. There was a thud which meant he had thrown his books down.

"Kwesi," his mother called out to him. "I have always told you to put your books down gently. I did not buy them with sand, and you ought to be careful with them."

He returned to where we were. I looked at him. He was very dirty. There was sand in his hair, ears and eyes. His uniform was smeared with mud, crayon and berry-juice. His braces were hanging down on one side. His mother gave an affectionate frown. "Kwesi, you are very dirty, just look at yourself. You are a disgrace to me. Anyone would think your mother does not look after you well." I was very much amused, for I knew she meant this for my ears. Kwesi just stood there, without a care in the world.

"Can't you play without putting sand in your hair?" his mother persisted.

"I am hungry," he announced. I laughed.

"Shame, shame, and your chicha is here. Chicha, you see? He does not fetch me water. He does not fetch me firewood. He does not weed my farm on Saturdays as other schoolboys do for their mothers. He only eats and eats." I looked at him; he fled again into the inner chamber for shame. We both started laughing at him. After a time I got up to go.

"Chicha, I would have liked you to eat before you went away; that's why I am hurrying up with the food." Maami tried to detain me.

"Oh, it does not matter. You know I eat here when I come, but today I must go away. I have the children's books to mark."

"Then I must not keep you away from your work."

"Tomorrow I will come to see you," I promised.

"*Yoo*, thank you."

"Sleep well, Maami."

"Sleep well, my daughter." I stepped into the open air. The sun was far receding. I walked slowly away. Just before I was out of earshot, Maami shouted after me, "And remember, if Kwesi gets his sums wrong, I will come to school to receive his lashes, if only you would tell me."

"*Yoo*," I shouted back. Then I went away.

The next day was Ahobaada. It was a day of rejoicing for everyone. In the morning, old family quarrels were being patched up. In Maami Ama's family all became peaceful. Her aunts had—or thought they had—reconciled themselves to the fact that, when Maami Ama's mother was dying, she had instructed her sisters, much to their chagrin, to give all her jewels to her only child. This had been one of the reasons why the aunts and cousins had left Ama so much to her own devices. "After all, she has her mother's goods, what else does she need?" they were often saying. However, today, aunts, cousins and nieces have come to a better understanding. Ahobaa is a season of goodwill! Nevertheless, Ama is going to have a formal divorce today. . . .

It had not been laid down anywhere in the Education Ordinance that schoolchildren were to be given holidays during local festivals. And so no matter how much I sympathised with the kids, I could not give them a holiday, although Ahobaa was such an important occasion for them; they naturally felt it a grievance to be forced to go to school while their friends at home were eating so much yam and meat. But they had their revenge on me. They fidgeted the whole day. What was worse, the schoolroom was actually just one big shed. When I left the Class One chicks to look at the older ones, they chattered; when I turned to them, Class Two and Class Three began shouting. Oh, it was a fine situation. In the afternoon, after having gone home to taste some of the festival dishes, they nearly drove me mad. So I was relieved when it was three o'clock. Feeling no sense of guilt, I turned them all out to play. They rushed out to the field. I packed my books on the table for little Grace to take home. My intention was to go and see the divorce proceedings which had begun at one o'clock and then come back at four to dismiss them. These divorce cases took hours to settle, and I hoped I would hear some of it.

As I walked down between the rows of desks, I hit my leg against one. The books on it tumbled down. As I picked them up I saw they belonged to Kwesi. It was the desk he shared with a little girl. I began thinking about him and the unhappy connection he had with what was going on at that moment down in the village. I remembered every word of the conversation I had had with his mother the previous evening. I became sad at the prospect of a possible separation from the mother who loved him so much and whom he loved. From his infancy they had known only each other, a lonely mother and a lonely son. Through the hot sun, she had carried him on her back as she weeded her cornfield. How could she dare to put him down under a tree in the shade when there was no one to look after him? Other women had their own younger sisters or those of their husbands to help with the baby; but she had had no one. The only face the little one had known was his mother's. And now . . .

"But," I told myself, "I am sure it will be all right with him."

"Will it?" I asked myself.

"Why not? He is a happy child."

"Does that solve the problem?"

"Not altogether, but . . . "

"No buts; one should think of the house into which he would be taken now. He may not be a favourite there."

But my other voice told me that a child need not be a favourite to be happy.

I had to bring the one-man argument to an end. I had to hurry.

Passing by the field, I saw some of the boys playing football. At the goal at the further end was a headful of hair shining in the afternoon sun. I knew the body to which it belonged. A goalkeeper is a dubious character in infant soccer. He is either a good goalkeeper and that is why he is at the goal, which is usually difficult to know in a child, or he is a bad player. If he is a bad player, he might as well be in the goal as anywhere else. Kwesi loved football, that was certain, and he was always the goalkeeper. Whether he was good or not I had never been able to see. Just as I passed, he caught a ball and his team clapped. I heard him give the little squeaky noise that passed for his laugh. No doubt he was a happy child.

Now I really ran into the village. I immediately made my way to Nana Kum's house, for the case was going on there. There was a great crowd in front of the house. Why were there so many people about? Then I remembered that it being a holiday, everyone was at home. And of course, after the eating and the drinking of palm-wine in the morning and midday, divorce proceedings certainly provide an agreeable diversion, especially when other people are involved and not ourselves.

The courtyard was a long one and as I jostled to where Maami Ama was sitting, pieces of comments floated into my ears. "The elders certainly have settled the case fairly," someone was saying. "But it seemed as if Kodjo Fi had no strong proofs for his arguments," another was saying. "Well, they both have been sensible. If one feels one can't live with a woman, one might as well divorce her. And I hate a woman who cringes to a man," a third said. Finally I reached her side. Around her were her family, her two aunts, Esi and Ama, her two cousins and the two uncles. To the right were the elders who were judging the case; opposite were Kodjo Fi and his family.

"I have come, Maami Ama," I announced myself.

She looked at me. "You ought to have been here earlier, the case has been settled already."

"And how are things?" I inquired.

"I am a divorced woman."

"What were his grounds for wanting to divorce you?"

"He said I had done nothing, he only wanted to . . . "

"Eh! Only the two of you know what went wrong," the younger aunt cried out, reproachfully. "If after his saying that, you had refused to be divorced, he would have had to pay the Ejecting Fee, but now he has got the better of you."

"But aunt," Maami protested, "how could I refuse to be divorced?"

"It's up to you. I know it's your own affair, only I wouldn't like your mother's ghost to think that we haven't looked after you well."

"I agree with you," the elder aunt said.

"Maami Ama, what was your debt?" I asked her.

"It is quite a big sum."

"I hope you too had something to reckon against him?"

"I did. He reckoned the dowry, the ten cloths he gave me, the Knocking Fee . . . ."

All this had been heard by Kodjo Fi and his family and soon they made us aware of it.

"Kodjo," his youngest sister burst out, "you forgot to reckon the Knife Fee."

"No. *Yaa*, I did not forget," Kodjo Fi told her. "She had no brothers to whom I would give the fee."

"It's all right then," his second sister added.

But the rest of his womenfolk took this to be a signal for more free comments.

"She is a bad woman and I think you are well rid of her," one aunt screamed.

"I think she is a witch," the youngest sister said.

"Oh, that she is. Anyway, only witches have no brothers or sisters. They eat them in the mother's womb long before they are born."

Ama's aunts and cousins had said nothing so far. They were inclined to believe Ama was a witch too. But Maami sat still. When the comments had gone down a bit, she resumed the conversation with me.

"As I was saying, Chicha, he also reckoned the price of the trunk he had given me and all the cost of the medicine he gave me to make me have more children. There was only the Cooking Cost for me to reckon against his."

"Have you got money to pay the debt?" I asked her.

"No, but I am not going to pay it. My uncles will pay it out of the family fund and put the debt down against my name."

"Oh!"

"But you are a fool," Maami Ama's eldest aunt shouted at her.

"I say you are a fool," she insisted.

"But aunt . . ." Maami Ama began to protest.

"Yes! And I hope you are not going to answer back. I was born before your mother and now that she is dead, I'm your mother! Besides, when she was alive I could scold her when she went wrong, and now I say you are a fool. For seven years you have struggled to look after a child. Whether he ate or not was your affair alone. Whether he had any cloth or not did not concern any other person. When Kwesi was a child he had no father. When he nearly died of measles, no grandmother looked in. As for aunts, he began getting them when he started going to school. And now you are allowing them to take him away from you. Now that he is grown enough to be counted among the living, a father knows he has got a son."

"So, so!" Kodjo Fi's mother sneered at her. "What did you think? That Kodjo would give his son as a present to you, eh? The boy belongs to his family, but he must be of some service to his father too."

"Have I called your name?" Ama's aunt asked the old woman.

"You have not called her name but you were speaking against her son." This again was from Kodjo Fi's youngest sister.

"And who are you to answer my mother back?" Ama's two cousins demanded of her.

"Go away. But who are you people?"

"Go away, too, you greedy lot."

"It is you who are greedy, witches."

"You are always calling other people witches. Only a witch can know a witch."

Soon everyone was shouting at everyone else. The people who had come started going home, and only the most curious ones stood by to listen. Maami Ama was murmuring something under her breath which I could not hear. I persuaded her to come with me. All that time no word had passed between her and her ex-husband. As we turned to go, Kodjo Fi's mother shouted at her, "You are hurt. But that is what you deserve. We will get the child. We will! What did you want to do with him?"

Maami Ama turned round to look at her. "What are you putting yourself to so much trouble for? When Nana Kum said the boy ought to go and stay with his father, did I make any objection? He is at the school. Go and fetch him. Tomorrow, you can send your carriers to come and fetch his belongings from my hut." These words were said quietly.

Then I remembered suddenly that I had to hurry to school to dismiss the children. I told Maami Ama to go home but that I would try to see her before night.

This time I did not go by the main street. I took the back door through back streets and lanes. It was past four already. As I hurried along, I heard a loud roaring sound which I took to be echoes of the quarrel, so I went my way. When I reached the school, I did not like what I saw. There was not a single childish soul anywhere. But everyone's books were there. The shed was as untidy as ever. Little

Grace had left my books too.

Of course I was more than puzzled. "How naughty these children are. How did they dare to disobey me when I had told them to wait here until I came to dismiss them?" It was no use looking around the place. They were not there. "They need discipline," I threatened to the empty shed. I picked up my books and clock. Then I noticed that Kwesi's desk was clean of all his books. Nothing need be queer about this; he had probably taken his home. As I was descending the hill the second time that afternoon, I saw that the whole school was at the other end of the main street. What were the children doing so near Maami Ama's place? I ran towards them.

I was not prepared for what I saw. As if intentionally, the children had formed a circle. When some of them saw me, they all began to tell me what had happened. But I did not hear a word. In the middle of the circle, Kwesi was lying flat on his back. His shirt was off. His right arm was swollen to the size of his head. I simply stood there with my mouth open. From the back yard, Maami Ama screamed, "I am drowning people of Bamso, come and save me!" Soon the whole village was there.

What is the matter? What has happened? Kwesi has been bitten by a snake. Where? Where? At school. He was playing football. Where? What has happened? Bitten by a snake, a snake, a snake.

Questions and answers were tossed from mouth to mouth in the shocked evening air. Meanwhile, those who knew about snake-bites were giving the names of different cures. Kwesi's father was looking anxiously at his son. That strong powerful man was almost stupid with shock and alarm. Dose upon dose was forced down the reluctant throat but nothing seemed to have any effect. Women paced up and down around the hut, totally oblivious of the fact that they had left their festival meals half prepared. Each one was trying to imagine how she would have felt if Kwesi had been her child, and in imagination they suffered more than the suffering mother. "The gods and spirits of our fathers protect us from calamity!"

After what seemed an unbearably long time, the messenger who had been earlier sent to Surdo, the village next to Bamso, to summon the chief medicine man arrived, followed by the eminent doctor himself. He was renowned for his cure of snake-bites. When he appeared, everyone gave a sigh of relief. They all remembered someone, perhaps a father, brother or husband, he had snatched from the jaws of death. When he gave his potion to the boy, he would be violently sick, and then of course, he would be out of danger. The potion was given. Thirty minutes; an hour; two hours; three, four hours. He had not retched. Before midnight, he was dead. No grown-up in Bamso village slept that night. Kwesi was the first boy to have died since the school was inaugurated some six years previously. "And he was his mother's only child. She has no one now. We do not understand it. Life is not sweet!" Thus ran the verdict.

The morning was very beautiful. It seemed as if every natural object in and around the village had kept vigil too. So they too were tired. I was tired too. I had gone to bed at about five o'clock in the morning and since it was a Saturday I could have a long sleep. At ten o'clock, I was suddenly roused from sleep by shouting. I opened my window but I could not see the speakers. Presently Kweku Sam, one of the young men in the village, came past my window. "Good morning, Chicha." He shouted his greeting to me.

"Good morning, Kweku," I responded. "What is the shouting about?"

"They are quarrelling."

"And what are they quarrelling about now?"

"Each is accusing the other of having been responsible for the boy's death."

"How?"

"Chicha, I don't know. Only women make too much trouble for themselves. It seems as if they are never content to sit quiet but they must always hurl abuse at each other. What has happened is too serious to be a subject for quarrels. Perhaps the village has displeased the gods in some unknown way and that is why they have taken away this boy." He sighed. I could not say anything to that. I could not explain it myself, and if the villagers believed there was something more in Kwesi's death than the ordinary human mind could explain, who was I to argue?

"Is Maami Ama herself there?"

"No, I have not seen her there."

He was quiet and I was quiet.

"Chicha, I think I should go away now. I have just heard that my sister has given birth to a girl."

"So," I smiled to myself. "Give her my congratulations and tell her I will come to see her tomorrow."

"*Yoo.*"

He walked away to greet his new niece. I stood for a long time at the window staring at nothing, while I heard snatches of words and phrases from the quarrel. And these were mingled with weeping. Then I turned from the window. Looking into the little mirror on the wall, I was not surprised to see my whole face bathed in unconscious tears. I did not feel like going to bed. I did not feel like doing anything at all. I toyed with the idea of going to see Maami Ama and then finally decided against it. I could not bear to face her; at least, not yet. So I sat down thinking about him. I went over the most presumptuous daydreams I had indulged in on his account. "I would have taken him away with me in spite of his mother's protests." She was just being absurd. "The child is a boy, and sooner or later, she must learn to live without him. The highest class here is Primary Six and when I am going away, I will take him. I will give him a grammar education. Perhaps, who knows, one day he may win a scholarship to the university." In my daydreams, I had never determined what career he would have followed, but he would be famous, that was certain. Devastatingly handsome, he would be the idol of women and the envy of every man. He would visit Britain, America and all those countries we have heard so much about. He would see all the seven wonders of the world. "Maami shall be happy in the end," I had told myself. "People will flock to see the mother of such an illustrious man. Although she has not had many children, she will be surrounded by her grandchildren. Of course, away from the village." In all these reveries his father never had a place, but there was I, and there was Maami Ama, and there was his father, and he, that bone of contention, was lost to all three. I saw the highest castles I had built for him come tumbling down, noiselessly and swiftly.

He was buried at four o'clock. I had taken the schoolchildren to where he lay in state. When his different relatives saw the little uniformed figure they all forgot their differences and burst into loud lamentations. "Chicha, O Chicha, what shall I do now that Kwesi is dead?" His grandmother addressed me. "Kwesi, my Beauty, Kwesi my Master, Kwesi-my-own-Kwesi," one aunt was chanting, "Father Death has done me an ill turn."

"Chicha," the grandmother continued, "my washing days are over, for who will give me water? My eating days are over, for who will give me food?" I stood there, saying nothing. I had let the children sing "Saviour Blessed Saviour." And we had gone to the cemetery with him.

After the funeral, I went to the House of Mourning as one should do after a burial. No one was supposed to weep again for the rest of the day. I sat there listening to visitors who had come from the neighbouring villages.

"This is certainly sad, and it is most strange. School has become like business; those who found it earlier for their children are eating more than the children themselves. To have a schoolboy snatched away like this is unbearable indeed," one woman said.

"Ah, do not speak," his father's youngest sister broke in. "We have lost a treasure."

"My daughter," said the grandmother again, "Kwesi is gone, gone for ever to our forefathers. And what can we do?"

"What can we do indeed? When flour is scattered in the sand, who can sift it? But this is the saddest I've heard, that he was his mother's only one."

"Is that so?" another visitor cried. "I always thought she had other children. What does one do, when one's only water-pot breaks?" she whispered. The question was left hanging in the air. No one dared say anything more.

I went out. I never knew how I got there, but I saw myself approaching Maami Ama's hut. As usual, the door was open. I entered the outer room. She was not there. Only sheep and goats from the village were busy munching at the cassava and the yams. I looked into the inner chamber. She was there. Still clad in the cloth she had worn to the divorce proceedings, she was not sitting, standing or lying down. She was kneeling, and like one drowning who catches at a straw, she was clutching Kwesi's books and school uniform to her breast. "Maami Ama, Maami Ama," I called out to her. She did not move. I left her alone. Having driven the sheep and goats away, I went out, shutting the door behind me. "I must go home now," I spoke to myself once more. The sun was sinking behind the coconut palm. I looked at my watch. It was six o'clock; but this time, I did not run.

# Agha Shahid Ali

## *Snowmen*

My ancestor, a man
of Himalayan snow,
came to Kashmir from Samarkand,
carrying a bag
of whale bones:
heirlooms from sea funerals.
His skeleton
carved from glaciers, his breath
arctic,
he froze women in his embrace.
His wife thawed into stony water,
her old age a clear
evaporation.

This heirloom,
his skeleton under my skin, passed
from son to grandson,
generations of snowmen on my back.
They tap every year on my window,
their voices hushed to ice.

No, they won't let me out of winter,
and I've promised myself,
even if I'm the last snowman,
that I'll ride into spring
on their melting shoulders.

# Mulk Raj Anand

## Duty

The midday sun blasts everything in the Indian summer: it scorches the earth till its upper layers crack into a million fissures; it sets fire to the water till the lakes and pools and swamps bubble, evaporate and dry up; it shrivels up the lives of birds, beasts and flowers; it burns into one like red pepper and leaves one gasping for breath with a bulging tongue till one spends one's time looking for some shady spot for even the most precarious shelter.

Mangal Singh, the policeman who had been posted on duty at the point where the branch road from the village of Vadala enters the Mall Road of Chetpur, had taken shelter under the sparse foliage of a kikar tree beyond the layers of white dust, after having stood in the sun for five and a half hours since dawn. In a little while sepoy Rahmat-Ullah would come and relieve him, and he felt that he could cool down a little and prepare to go to the barracks.

The sun was penetrating even the leaves of the wayside trees, and there was not much comfort in the humid airless atmosphere, but after the cracking heat of the open, Mangal felt that this comparative shade was a blessing.

He was not, of course, like the delicate Lallas, rich Hindu merchants, who rode out into the gardens early in the morning and withdrew after "eating" the fresh air at sunrise and never appeared till sunset, sitting in the laps of their wives drinking milk-water or lying sprawled about on the front boards of their shops under the cool air of electric fans. . . . No, he didn't say as they would: "I go for a pice worth of salt, bring me a palanquin." Nor could he "quench his thirst by drinking dew." No, he was proud that he came from strong peasant stock and was a hardy policeman who could rough it: indeed, this police service was not active enough for him and he felt it a pity that he had not become a real sepoy; for there was more pay in the paltans and there were better uniforms, also free mufti and free rations. So he had heard after he had put the mark of his thumb down and joined the police force—but once done cannot be undone. And it was the blessing of the Gurus, as there was little chance of earning any extra money in the military; while, apart from the fifteen rupees' pay, there were other small sums so long as confectioners continued to mix milk with water and so long as there was a murder or two in the prostitutes' bazaar, and so long as there were respectable Lallas who would pay rather than have their names mentioned. . . . Why, even here on point-duty in the waste land — "your own is your own and another's is also yours." For if the peasants offered tokens of grain and butter and sugar to the Munshi at the customs house, then why not to the police? That skinny little Babu at the octroi post had not the strong arm of the sepoy to protect them when they were being looted by the thugs in the market. . . . He knew. After wisdom the club. If only he had been able to pay a nazar to the Tehsildar he would never have lost his land to Seth Jhinda Ram. . . . But God's work was well done, man's badly. And, truly, if he had not pressed the limbs of the landlord he would never have got the recommendation to join the police. And you learnt a great deal in the service of the Sarkar. And there was nothing better than service: no worry, and there was so much izzat in it that these very cowardly city folk who laughed at you if you were a peasant joined their hands in obeisance to you if you wielded a truncheon. And the rustics who had no notion of discipline or duty could be made to obey authority with the might of the stave, and if they didn't obey that, the fear of the handcuff — even a daring robber like Barkat Ali could not escape because one could blow the whistle and call the entire police force out. And the Sarkar is truly powerful. Like Alamgir, it leaves no fire in the hearth, nor water in the jar, to bring a man to justice. . . .

He glanced at his dust-covered feet in the regulation shoes of rough cow-hide, even as he congratulated himself on his lucky position as a member of the much-feared police service and wished he had really been in the army, for there the sepoys had boots given them. His puttees too were old and faded and there was something loose about the khaki uniform with the black belt. The uniform of the army was so tight-fitting. Perhaps the whistle-chain and the truncheon improved this and the red-and-blue turban was nice, but — he lifted his hand to caress the folds of his head-dress and to adjust it, as it was heavy and got soaked with the sweat that flowed from his fuming scalp burdened by long hair on the lower edges. . . .

The sun poured down a flood of fire on the earth, and it seemed as if the desolate fields covered with dense brown thickets and stalks of grass and cacti were crackling like cinders and would soon be reduced to ashes. A partridge hummed in its nest somewhere and a dove cooed from the tree overhead, giving that depth to the shade which fills the air with long, endless silences and with the desolate peace of loneliness.

Mangal Singh drifted a few steps from where he was standing and halted on a spot where the shade was thicker than it was anywhere else under the kikar trees. And, blowing a hot breath, he cupped his palms over the knob of his stave and leaned his chin on the knuckles of his joined hands and stood contemplating the scene with half-closed eyes like a dog who rests his muzzle on his front paws and lies in wait for his prey.

Layers of white-sheeted mist floated past his eyes in the sun-soaked fields, the anguish of a thousand heat-singed bushes, while the parched leaves of the hanging boughs of the wayside trees rustled at the touch of a scorching breeze.

One breath, a thousand hopes, they say, and there never comes a day without evening — but it would be very difficult to walk down to the barracks through this terrible heat. And he wished his duty was not up, that someone could fetch his food for him and that he could borrow a charpai from the octroi and go to sleep in the grove of neem trees by the garden of Rais Jagjiwan Das, or sit and talk to the grass-cutter's wife who had breasts like turnips. Only Rahmat-Ullah had an eye on her too, and he was sure to be here, as he preferred the desolate afternoon, thinking that he might get a chance when no one was about.

"I will have to walk back to the lines," he muttered to himself and yawned. He felt heavy and tired at the prospect and his legs seemed to weaken from the knowledge of the unending trudge of three miles. He shook his head and tried to be alert, but the invisible presence of some overwhelming force seemed to be descending on him and his heavy-lidded eyes were closing against his will. He took a deep breath and made another effort to open his eyes wide through the drowsy stupor of the shade that weighed down from the trees. For a moment his body steadied and his eyes half opened. But how hateful was the glare, and how cruel, how meaningless, was life outside. . . . And what peace, what quiet below the trees, beneath the eyes. . . .

If a God should be standing here he could not help closing his eyes for a minute, he felt; and sleep came creeping into his bones with a whiff of breeze that was like a soft beauty retreating coyly before the thousand glares of the torrid sun which burnt so passionately above the silent fields. . . . The heat seemed to be melting the fat in his head and to be blinding his eyes, and he let himself be seduced by the placid stillness into a trance of half-sleep. . . .

Through sleepy eyes he was conscious of the whispering elements as he dozed, and his body still stood more or less erect, though his head was bent on the knuckles of his hand above the stave, and the corners of his mouth dribbled slightly. . . .

"Shoop . . . shoop . . . shoop . . . " a snake seemed to lash his face at the same time as he saw the soothing vision of a dim city through the stealthy corners of whose lanes he was passing suavely into a house was effaced. . . .

"Shoop . . . shoop. . . ."

He came to suddenly and saw Thanedar Abdul Kerim standing before him, his young face red with anger under the affected Afghan turban, his tall lanky form tight-stretched, a cane in his hand, and his bicycle leaning against his legs. . . .

"Wake up! Wake up, you ox of a Sikh! Is it because it is past twelve that your senses have left you?"

Mangal reeled, then steadied himself, his hands climbing automatically to his turban which had been shaken by the Inspector's onslaught.

"Shoop . . . shoop," the cane struck his side again and stung his skin like a hundred scorpions. And a welter of abuse fell upon his ears: "Bahin chod, the D.S.P. might have passed, and you are supposed to be on *duty*. Wake up and come to your senses, Madar chod!"

Quite involuntarily Mangal's right band left the turban and shot up to his forehead in a salute, and his thick, trembling lips phewed some hot stale breath: "Huzoor Mai-bap."

"You eat the bread of illegality," the Thanedar shouted. "I will be reprimanded and my promotion stopped, you swine!"

And he lifted his cane to strike Mangal again, but the sepoy was shaking with fright so that his stave dropped from his hand.

Mangal bent and picked up his lathi.

"Go and be on your point-duty!" ordered the Thanedar sternly and, putting his foot on the pedal, rode shakily away on his bicycle.

Mangal walked out of the shade, his shins and thighs still trembling and his heart thumping in spite of himself, though he was less afraid than conscience-stricken for neglecting his duty.

The heat of the sun made the skin of his face smart with a sharp pain where the perspiration flowed profusely down his neck. He rubbed his hand across it and felt the sweat tingle like a raw wound.

He shook himself and his head twitched, and he looked about in order to see if anyone had seen him being beaten. He wanted to bear the pain like a man. But his eyes, startled by the suddenness with which they had opened, were full of a boiling liquid that melted into fumes as he raised his head.

His throat was parched dry and he coughed with an effort so that his big brown face above the shaggy beard reddened. Then he paused to spit on the road and felt his legs trembling and shaking more than ever. He twisted his face in the endeavour to control his limbs and lunged forward. . . .

"Ohe, may you die, ohe asses, ohe, may you die," came a voice from behind him.

As he turned round he saw a herd of donkeys come stampeding up the road in a wild rush, which became wilder as their driver trotted fast behind them in an attempt to keep them from entering the Mall Road at that pace.

For a moment the cloud of dust the herd had raised on the sides of the deeply rutted Vadala Road obscured Mangal's view of the man, but then suddenly he could hear him shouting: "Ohe, may you die, asses!"

Mangal ran with his stave upraised in a wild scurry towards the driver of the stampeding donkeys, scattering them helter-skelter till some of them cantered the more quickly into the Mall and the others turned back and came to a standstill. He caught the driver up before the man had escaped into a ditch by the banana field. And, grinding a half-expressed curse between his teeth, he struck him with his stave hard, hard, harder, so that the blows fell edgewise on a donkey's neck, on the driver's arms, on a donkey's back, on a donkey's head, on the man's legs. . . .

"Oh, forgive, Sarkar, it is not my fault," the man shouted in an angry, indignant voice while he rubbed his limbs and spread his hands to ward off more blows.

"You, son of a dog," hissed Mangal as he struck again and again, harder and harder as if he had gone mad, till his stave seemed to ring as a bamboo stick does when it is splitting into shreds.

# Jean Arasanayagam

## *I Have No Country*

I have no country now but self
I mark my boundaries extend demesnes
Even beyond the darkness of those regions
Still to be explored, chart my ocean voyages
In blood or stay becalmed watching a gull
Impale its shadow on a thorn of wave.
Waiting for the winds to blow to set once more
In motion the pattern of the sea, a ripple stir
Into a wave that sweeps, tidal, wide horizons,
Rises above a cloud to drench the sky
And pours its deluge on the stars to drown
All lights and in that darkness find again
New brightness from a self created firmament
The cosmic mind imagines, to choose one star
Out of a galaxy or constellation, constant as
The Pole's unmoving light whose spokes glittered
On the waves to guide through an unknown and
Blinding dark, the voyages of ancient mariners
Through oceans to reach those lands as yet unmapped
And undiscovered.

Once more to journey on a chartered course
To reach which country? One that I must know
Before this birth or one that others more intrepid
Had discovered so that for me there's no new
Adventure left and nothing new for exploration
Except the landmarks racing through my blood
Or found in ruined fortresses and artefacts
In archives and in museums.

What subterfuge of islands draw me near
Destruction, here, snares already set, the pit is staked

With poisoned thorns and ragged branches,
My footsteps trapped with guile, I fell headlong
Through the camouflage, the hunt made easy
For both hunter and for poacher. And remain
My gait now fractured, couched on a bed of thorns
Wait for what death will come, through knife or bullet.
This was perhaps my choice. So I stay here
Iconoclastic of all statues, images
Covering the walls of sacred places,
The saints too good, too pure and too unreal
To be my guides although they too follow paths
That can only spell new dangers.
Heretical my thought and that of all unbelievers
Yet out of a loss of faith
For our salvation, we seek once more
A stronger faith; my fear is that escape
From martyrdom makes our complexion and
Our stature, coward. Cowering for safety
In the camps to which we flee for refuge
And remain with other fugitives who have escaped
From fire and slaughter for all time disinherited.

## *We Have Our Genealogies*

We have our genealogies but what do they mean?
Nothing. They tell us, those historians that our beginnings
Were invasions, that we walked through blood trails
Sucking like leeches the rich ruby that spilled
From gempits of flesh; we wore those blood splotches
Like jewels sparkling on our wrists, our breasts.

Flesh still cries for the power of that beauty
Reflected in the flashed blood mirrors,
That show our image bathed in its glitter while, tied
To the stake, conflagrations of heretics blaze away
As the fire faggots ignite crackle before they topple,
Fall like great silver candle sconces

Sometimes wearing nailcrowns hammered into the
Skull before they roll away scattered helter skelter
As in a game of bowls on a well trimmed lawn,
Invasions were nothing compared now to the taste
Death has for these hedonists, lovers of torture
And all its titillations of necrophilic flesh, suddenly
To turn voluptuary as the groin screams and the
Air breaks apart into tremendous glass fissures
As the power enters them to speak in tongues
As on the Day of Pentecost, in a language only the
torturer understands,

Saliva blots the lips that are now still, silenced,
A forgotten script bitten into chiselled stone
And no one cares to pause so much as to kick
Even with a blunt naked toe that has walked
Always barefoot over so much rutty terrain —
The path knotted with chains of corpses.

You find yourself wandering demented through
Feudal gardens where the frozen serfs rolled off
Pedestals flesh turning to marbled ice as the
Snow fall mantled the black firs
It was only the great manor houses that shook
With the lights of a thousand candles as the sky
A heavy branched candelabra swung with stars,
Read me again those pages that tell of Azavedo
Of Westerwold, of D'Oyly, those diaries in archives of
Centuries which dwell like so many silver fish malingering
Among the parchment scrolls like mummified skin,

What's flung in your face are the documents
Written on leaves of flesh as on the ola leaves
Of ancient temples, yellow-brown, brittle, stiff
And the lettering so richly archaic so scholarly
Scripted with the fine tools torture has etched.

# Ven Begamudré

## Honestly, as in the Day

I cannot deny it: I am an old man.

My small house occupies a rear corner of my son's lot. In India, such dwellings are often built behind large houses in order to secure rent. They are called outhouses. My daughter-in-law bridles if I tell people this. I therefore call my dwelling by its proper name here: a granny flat.

My son finds both terms equally humorous. He would rather I lived under his roof, but I prefer staying out of my daughter-in-law's way. If my grandchildren wish to see me, they skip through the garden, mince between the pine trees, and knock at my door.

Every Sunday, I eat lunch with my son's family. My daughter-in-law prepares the meal after they return from church. All other times, I eat alone so I can read. I long ago perfected the art of wielding a book with my left hand while eating with my right. I do use cutlery at my son's table, however, because even he considers eating with one's hand to be quaint.

Some of my habits I can hide, but I am unable to change the few that most irritate my daughter-in-law. For instance, I seldom refer to my relations by name. I do address them by name, but I habitually refer to them as my son, my daughter-in-law, and so on. She does not understand when I say that, for me, my relation to another is more important than his name. She claims I am as detached as my house.

One thing else irritates her: my practice of not spending Christmas with them. Each year, after Thanksgiving Day in October, I leave Regina for Victoria, one queenly city for another. I return on the first day of April. I used to say, when she came to fetch me at the airport, "April Fools, I am still alive!"

I ceased this practice after my son confided that my greeting upset her. He no doubt relayed her words diplomatically. She still smiles, however, when I claim she secretly gives thanks on Thanksgiving Day for my impending departure. She reminds me that if she and my son wish to fulfill their social obligations during my absence, then she must hire a sitter for the children.

She has developed the notion that I have a fortune set aside for my grandchildren to inherit, funds I could better spend on them during my lifetime. The matter has become a serious irritant for her, because the children have begun pleading with my son to take them to Walt Disney World. They do not understand when he explains he is experiencing some difficulty with his practice.

It surprises few people that he is an MD. They expect such things from Indians here. I still find it surprising that the son of a mere college lecturer should have become not only a physician but also a specialist. His practice is not yet so established that he may take his family on exotic holidays, however. The family spends most holidays on the farm owned by the parents of my daughter-in-law.

They are somewhat religious people in the sense that they feel compelled to reaffirm their faith weekly. That is why my daughter-in-law recently mentioned some people in her church were becoming curious about me. They have welcomed my son to their fold, but I appear enigmatic to them. I suppose I should be flattered.

"I was talking to Reverend Miller," she announced. She was clearing the dishes after last Sunday's lunch. "He's dying to meet you. He even said how much he'd love it if you'd come give the lesson next week. He's read some of your stuff."

I had been wondering when such a thing might happen. Most of my works once appeared only in British or Indian periodicals. Now certain college presses have begun distributing collections of my more popular tales in the United States and Canada. I suspect this latter is more by default than by design.

I must admit I hold my work in low regard because, like me, it is from another age. It reminds me too much of moralistic fables with surprising endings: the sort favoured by the Frenchman Guy de Maupassant and the American O. Henry. I trust my admirers will not immortalize my name on a chocolate bar.

After my son nudged my foot under the table, I looked up from stirring my tea. "Is that so?" I inquired.

"Yeah," she said. She never says yes. Neither does my son, although I corrected him often when he was young.

Some habits I have never acquired during the forty years I have lived on this continent. Among them is the practice of comfortably using the vernacular. Even now I speak slowly, not because I am old but because I must first translate everything into my native tongue and then back to English.

"So," she repeated, "Reverend Miller said how much he'd love it if you'd come give the lesson next week. It's not like a sermon or anything. You can even pick your own topic. Today Mrs. Sargent — she's organizing the fowl supper again — gave the lesson about charity."

"Did your Mrs. Sargent speak about the Good Samaritan?" I inquired. Old age has improved my ability to detect subterfuge.

"I didn't know you've read the Bible," my daughter-in-law exclaimed.

"Oh yes," I replied, "three times. But I have read the Koran only twice."

My son grinned. He raised his hand to his mouth and coughed before she noticed he had allowed himself a temporary taking of sides.

"It doesn't have to be from the Bible," she said, "as long as it's a lesson."

"Tell them the one about the Bombay talkie producer, Dad," my son said. He calls me Appa, which means father in my tongue, only when we find ourselves alone. That now seldom occurs. He frowned eagerly at me. "I love that part about Hollywood trying to produce a musical about Gandhi."

"It is too long," I said. "Besides that, it would not do to have your congregation roll in the pews."

"That's aisles, Grandpa," my elder granddaughter said.

When I rose, she quietly pulled my chair back from the table.

She thinks I never notice such things. I continue pretending I do not. She and her sibling might otherwise grow to think I expect such kindness, and so not give it freely.

My daughter-in-law seized the opportunity, as always, to speak the final word. "Don't strain yourself," she said.

I returned to my dwelling and searched among dusty boxes for my journals. Then I made minor corrections to an unpublished tale. It has been some years since I wrote anything new, for I find it taxing to put words on paper. They are no longer as malleable as I once thought them. Either that, or my mind is no longer nimble enough to knead and reshape them before they set on the page.

This morning my son assisted me up the steps of my daughter-in-law's church. I clutched a sheaf of yellow papers. On the lawn stood a signboard proclaiming, in white plastic letters, that today's sermon would be about wrath. I permitted myself a smile.

Reverend Miller mistook it for one of greeting. He pressed my hand between both of his. He had telephoned some days before to inquire about the subject of my lesson, so he could plan his sermon. I realized now I had misled him, for I had answered cryptically, "You will find my subject in the Book of Job, chapter five, verse two." He introduced me to various strangers, whose names I immediately forgot.

I did notice he always introduced me as Mr. So-and-So. If I have one complaint about growing old, it is that no one addresses me by my given name. Most of my contemporaries are dead; I shall soon join them. I should like to have my ashes immersed in the Kabini River, which flows past my birthplace. I suspect my son will merely scatter them on Wascana Lake.

After we took our seats, Reverend Miller greeted his congregation, and the choir sang a hymn. Then he announced that the congregation was in for a surprise. The two people about to be most surprised were my daughter-in-law and the Reverend himself. I could do nothing to help him, however, so I took my place at the lectern, adjusted the microphone, and began to read.

I confess I felt nervous. It has been some fifteen years, after all, since I lectured. That is why I never looked up from my papers. I trust everyone was delighted. The only beaming face I recall was that of Mrs. Reverend Miller. She sat hunched over the keyboard of an organ. I hoped she would not pounce on its keys if I myself struck a discordant note. She fortunately sat with her hands in her lap while I read this tale:

## Her Sister's Shadow

The rivalry between Sharada and Vasanta began in their mother's womb, yet it went unnoticed in our village of Debur until they reached womanhood. As infants, the twins slept in hammocks joined so their mother could rock both of them by pushing only one. As toddlers, they left a single track in the dust outside their hut, since Vasanta followed Sharada more closely than a shadow. Once, when Sharada stopped to pet one of the village curs, Vasanta bumped into her so that Sharada found herself trapped between her sister and the snarling dog. Sharada clambered over her sister to safety. When Vasanta began to shriek, their mother kicked the dog aside and scooped Vasanta up. Villagers who saw what had happened merely shook their heads and smiled behind the mother's back. For some time, she suspected both girls were idiots, for they rarely exchanged a word. Sometimes, though, when she caught them eyeing one another guardedly, she thought each resented the other's existence.

In truth, each girl grew to envy the other. Except for a nose too sharply hooked, Sharada had perfect features with large, almost sultry eyes and a wide, almost sensuous mouth. Sharada means autumn, and though she was the elder by a mere twenty minutes, she developed a mature beauty that overshadowed Vasanta's innocent looks. Vasanta means spring, but her beauty was like the spring of promise, forever on the verge of bloom. Her face had neither perfect proportions nor a charming imperfection to make it lovely; yet one could have understood a blind man's assuming Vasanta was the beautiful sister and Sharada the plain one. While Sharada rarely smiled or sang, the sight of a common parakeet sent Vasanta clapping with delight or humming an improvised tune. No wonder, then, that when their parents searched for Sharada's future husband, they received offers only for Vasanta. Sometimes Vasanta's despair over having to wait until Sharada married upset the entire family; more often, Vasanta gloated. Sharada betrayed no ill will, for in response to Vasanta's extreme moods, Sharada had cultivated her natural calm into aloofness. They became two faces of the Kabini River: Sharada its rock-strewn bed easily forded in the dry season; Vasanta its waters swelled by the monsoon, shallow in spots, unpredictably deep in others.

After two years of unsuccessful inquiries beyond our district, the parents agreed to match Vasanta to the Kempe Gowdas' eldest son provided his brother married Sharada in a joint ceremony. Such an event had rarely occurred in our village. At first, Mrs. Kempe Gowda opposed the agreement since she, too, wanted her children to marry outside the district, but for all their land, the Kempe Gowdas lacked the status to attract city-bred wives for their sons. On an auspicious day in February, soon after everyone had washed the dyes and coloured water of the Holi festival from their clothes, Sharada wed the younger son, and Vasanta wed the elder. Sharada's husband was nicknamed Iruve, or ant, for his nervous energy. Vasanta's husband was nicknamed Nona, or fly, for his protruding eyes. During the month it took Iruve to build a bungalow north of the Debur-Nanjangud Road, Sharada lived with her parents in our village, but Vasanta immediately moved into the Kempe Gowdas' home south of the road. To distinguish the two houses, local wags called Iruve's smaller one the Lokh Sabha after the Commons and the Kempe Gowdas' larger one the Rajya Sabha after the Senate.

Within the year, Mrs. Kempe Gowda died. Her husband soon followed her — according to many, from grief; according to local wags, from boredom, since he no longer had to defend himself from her tongue. The village council voted as one man to split the Kempe Gowdas' land equally between Iruve and Nona with the Debur-Nanjangud Road as the boundary. To compensate Sharada for living in the smaller house, Vasanta begged Nona to give Sharada all his mother's jewellery. Secure in his position as schoolmaster of Debur, he agreed. Before handing the necklaces and ear rings to Sharada, he stared at them as though with regret, but Vasanta knew him well enough to realize he never merely looked at anything; he stared with his fly-like eyes. On the first anniversary of her father-in-law's death, she invited her parents to leave their hut in Debur and move into the Rajya Sabha. Aside from the grand joke of having finally acquired a seat in the Senate, her father cherished her gesture, for he had not only escaped our village but also moved to within a mile of the town.

One day, the district engineer announced plans to build two irrigation canals parallel to the Debur-Nanjangud Road. Each four miles in length, the canals were completed in what for us seemed a record time of five years. By then, Sharada had borne three daughters while Vasanta had borne three sons, but the canals separated the sisters further than the shame Sharada had brought Iruve and the honour Vasanta had brought Nona. The canals reversed the sisters' fortunes.

Nona lacked the funds to install an irrigation pump to tap the waters of the upper canal, which passed south of his land. Mainly dependent on the monsoons, his land continued producing only tomatoes. He hauled water from the well into his fields before leaving for his school, but the hotter the weather grew, the more slowly he moved. Toward the end of the dry season, he refused to stir from his bedroll to tend his land. Instead, he waved his limbs like a helpless fly and gestured for drinking water while cracks snaked through his fields. The lower canal, however, bounded the northern edge of Iruve's land. It took little urging from Sharada to set him digging a channel into his fields. True to his nickname, he worked as industriously as an ant. Since the land sloped down, past the canal toward the river, he hired a youth from our village to scoop water up from the canal into the channel. Iruve then gave in to Sharada's demand that he use his entire salary as buyer for the Ganesha Rice Mill to replace his tomato crops with sugar cane. At Deepavali, the festival of lights, when he closed his account book for the old year and opened one for the new, he found himself surprisingly well off. He beamed when Sharada bought the first silk sari ever owned by a girl from our village. She rewarded Vasanta's earlier generosity by presenting her with an embroidered sari made of Lancashire cotton. True to form, Vasanta gave the sari to her mother, who never wore it for fear of upsetting Sharada.

The years passed, and power lines appeared on the Debur-Nanjangud Road. A diesel train shuttled between the town and

Mysore City. Vasanta gave birth to three more boys; Sharada, cursed by having borne five girls in all, finally presented Iruve with a son. She had grown so broad and heavy-limbed that her bangles settled into furrows on her wrists; yet while the worries of feeding and clothing six sons, a husband, and two aged parents subdued Vasanta's spirits, Sharada's rose with the birth of her son. She became prone to extremes while her sister lapsed into silence. Even more noticeable, Vasanta's face grew pinched and dry while Sharada's remained curiously unchanged. She spent a small fortune on lightening creams ordered through the post all the way from Delhi. She mounted face mirrors in every room of the new house Iruve had built for her in the town. While supervising the servant who swept the house daily, Sharada admired herself full-faced and in profile.

Unknown to everyone except the postmaster of Debur, whose silence she bought with Iruve's threadbare shirts, she also received illustrated magazines. In one, from Bombay, she read about a star who had paid to have his jowls tucked and about a starlet who had paid for injections of silicone in unmentionable areas of her body. Convinced this new technique, called cosmetic surgery, could correct her nearly perfect face, Sharada discreetly secured the name of a reputable surgeon in Bangalore, the largest city in our state. He had learned his craft in America and returned to establish the MGM Clinic. His fee equalled the value of Mrs. Kempe Gowda's jewellery, but since the novelty of showing off her son had paled, Sharada had sought a new goal. She told Iruve she planned to visit Bangalore for a nature cure and paid Vasanta a farewell visit. It was their first meeting since the wedding of Vasanta's eldest son, which had been celebrated the previous year.

Sharada blocked the light by which Vasanta patched her husband's umbrella, yet Vasanta did not notice the shadow cast upon her. She raised her head only after Sharada greeted her cheerfully. Vasanta's hands fumbled when she put her sewing aside. Shading her eyes, she smiled with embarrassment. She turned from the sunlight and sat with her ear tilted toward her shoulder as though more eager to listen to Sharada than to look at her. They spoke of whose cattle would balk at the flames lit during Sankranti, to separate cows that would be bred from those that would not. The sisters spoke of this in inflated tones until Vasanta's youngest sons ran home from Debur School. They collapsed giggling into her lap. Their affection infuriated Sharada, for lately her only son had begun whining if she petted him. She abruptly stood and made her farewell. She suffered her nephews to kiss her cheek and observed it would be some time before they saw her face again. During the walk back to the town, she consoled herself by imagining the well-bred sons she would find for her daughters. The next morning, she took the diesel train to Mysore City, where she changed to the longer steam train for Bangalore.

She returned two months later with a new compact mirror clutched in one hand and a kerchief in the other. If she noticed fellow passengers' questioning frowns each time she gazed triumphantly into the mirror, she betrayed nothing. She inwardly laughed. Almost as often as she checked the mirror, she dabbed at her nostrils with the kerchief. The surgeon had cautioned her against blowing her nose, however carefully, until the pressure in her sinuses had eased. At Mysore Railway Station, her spirits rose so high that she gave one rupee to an astonished beggar limping down the platform. At Nanjangud Railway Station, she agonized over whether to go home and change into her newest sari, acquired at Shantala Silk House in Bangalore, or whether to leave directly for the Rajya Sabha. Impatience overruled both her vanity and frugality, so she hired a horse-drawn cart. She chafed until Nona's flat brown land appeared on her left and Iruve's green sugar cane fields rose on her right.

After the cart finally stopped, she hurried through Vasanta's garden, planted with groundnuts so as not to waste a patch of soil, and entered the house uninvited. The veranda was empty. When she shouted her sister's name, Vasanta's daughter-in-law appeared from the kitchen to explain she sat behind the house in the sun. In the twenty years since they had left our village, Sharada had never known Vasanta to indulge in anything as frivolous as sunning herself. Puzzled, Sharada followed the girl back through the veranda and around the house to the well.

Seated on its stone edge, Vasanta leaned against the beam supporting the pulley. She faced directly south toward the distant upper canal with her face tilted to the sun. The girl announced Sharada's arrival and left the sisters alone. Sharada drew near and pointedly sidestepped her sister's shadow. Gripping the beam for balance, Vasanta carefully turned. Sharada dabbed at her painful nostrils one last time and tucked the soiled kerchief into the waist of her nylon sari. Her opening words, "Yes, it is really me," so often rehearsed during her convalescence, died on her lips.

Vasanta's right eye had turned the colour of diluted milk. Her left eye had turned even whiter than the blinding sun.

I returned to my place while Mrs. Reverend Miller played the organ.

Reverend Miller proved to be as quick of mind as I am slow of foot. After the congregation was apprised of certain upcoming events, after the brass plates for the offering were circulated and after yet another hymn was sung, he began his sermon. "We read in the Book of Job, chapter five, verse two," he said, "'Wrath killeth the foolish man, and envy slayeth the silly one.' Our guest dealt with envy, so I'll deal with wrath."

I wondered how I should deal with my daughter-in-law's wrath. She could not have supposed, after all, that I might presume to teach her the lesson. She remained unusually quiet during our drive home, and I wondered whether my son would suggest I consider an early retreat to my winter home. He would no doubt relay her words diplomatically.

My elder granddaughter helped me from my son's posh automobile. I turned toward the path which skirts my son's house and leads to my own.

"Aren't you coming in?" he called.

I glanced at my daughter-in-law. He doubtless anticipated a confrontation, so he shepherded the children into the house. I found myself abandoned to her judgement.

"I wasn't trying to put you on the spot by saying you'd give the lesson," she insisted.

"Nor was I trying to embarrass you by choosing to speak of envy," I said. I placed my hand upon her arm. "Come," I declared, "Let us walk honestly, as in the day; not in rioting and drunkenness, not in chambering and wantonness, not in strife and envying."

"More Bible?" she inquired.

"Yes," I admitted. "From the Book of Romans, I believe."

"What happened to the two sisters?" she inquired.

"I do not know," I answered. "I suppose they made a peace of sorts." I squinted at the sun, already lower in the sky than the sun of summer. "I have been thinking a change would do me some good," I said. "If I spent my winters in Florida, do you suppose all of you might visit me there?"

"I'm sure we could swing it," she replied. "Some day."

I turned toward my son's house. "I make only one condition," I said. "I shall purchase the children passes to Walt Disney World as their Christmas gift. However, I shall not be taken, as one might say here, for a ride."

I expected her to raise the no doubt transitory nature of our truce, but she said nothing. She merely chuckled. I trust she appreciated, at last, the prerogative of an old man to speak the final word.

# Louise Bennett

## *Anancy an Ticks*

Once upon a time Anancy an Ticks use to live nex door to one anada[1]. Anancy had a goat an Ticks had a cow, but Anancy coulda read an Ticks couldn't read. An eena[2] dem days dem nevah got no Literacy Campaign.

Well, one day Anancy read eena newspaper seh[3] dat a gentleman want a cow an a man fi[4] hire, an de man haffi[5] ride de cow fi do certain kine a job wat de gentleman had. Anancy memba[6] Bredda Ticks cow an him study a brain[7] fi work pon Ticks.

One evenin wen Ticks was a put up him cow fi de night, Anancy chop off him[8] goat head an push it eena de tick[9] bush between him an Ticks yard. Him hole awn pon de head an gwan like him a try fi pulli out.[10]

Hear him: "Mmmmmi woan[11] come out, mmmmi fasten."

Bredda Ticks seh: "Wat happen, Anancy?"

Hear Anancy: "Me goat, Bredda Ticks — him fasten ina de bush yah[12], an all de draw me dah draw me cyaan[13] get him out. Come help me, Bredda Ticks."

Ticks like a big fool go ovah Anancy yard, hole awn[14] pon de goat head an meck[15] one pull wid all him strengt. Plaps! de goat head come out ina him han[16].

Anancy jump up ina tempa[17] an seh: "Eehi[18] now, Bredda Ticks, yuh see weh yuh do? De one deggeh[19] goat me got yuh teck grudgeful kill him! Bredda Ticks, i naw go soh! Bad tings a goh happen between me an yuh!"

Po[20] Ticks so frighten, hear him: "Cho, Anancy — noh gwan so. Is accident."

Hear Anancy: "Me goat jine tird party insurance an is bans a truvel[21] fi yuh, Bredda Ticks. Me an yuh dah go a law, an yuh wi haffi[22] pay fi me goat weh yuh kill!"

Po Ticks start cry an seh: "Bredda Anancy, me noh got noh money, as yuh know — all me got is a cow!"

Anancy seh: "Well yuh wi haffi gi me de cow."

Ticks seh: "Ef me gi yuh di cow is wat me gwine teck meck me[23] livin?"

Hear Anancy: "Bredda Ticks, ah sorry fi yuh, so ah gwine ease yuh up. Ef yuh willin fi work yuh cow an pay me back fi me goat, me know a way how yuh can do it."

Ticks seh: "Yes, Bredda Nancy, me wi tenkful."[24]

Anancy seh: "Me know a gentleman wat want smaddy[25] fi ride a cow an do some work fi him. Meck we go to him now, an yuh work an pay me, back."

So Anancy teck Ticks to de man an hire him out wid de cow, an Anancy collec de pay. An up to now Ticks no done pay Anancy yet. Das why till teday Ticks still live in a cow back. Is Anancy meck it.

Jack Mandora, me noh choose none.[26]

[1] another  [2] in  [3] say  [4] for  [5] has to  [6] remember
[7] trick or plan  [8] his  [9] thick  [10] He held on upon his head and go on as if he is trying to pull it out.  [11] won't  [12] here  [13] can't  [14] on
[15] make  [16] hand  [17] temper  [18] Eh, eh  [19] one and only  [20] poor
[21] lots of trouble  [22] will have to  [23] going to make my  [24] I will be thankful  [25] somebody  [26] Many Anancy stories end with this declaration. (Jack Mandora is "keeper of heaven's door"; "Me noh choose none" means "It is not of my choosing.")

# Neil Bissoondath

## Man as Plaything, Life as Mockery

It had rained earlier that morning. Then a wind had arisen and driven away the clouds that had made a rumpled grey sweater of the morning sky. Aspect changed dramatically: the wind, cold and with a bite, brought in its own cloud, low, white, rapid with the urgency of a miracle sky. There was a play of light and shadow that altered the view more rapidly than the eye could seize it. It was like viewing, in rapid succession, the positive and negative of the same photograph: the vision was tricked, the substantial lost, so that even the angular concrete of the airport carpark across the way was emptied, became unreal.

His stance, feet apart, hands clasped behind his back, was casual. It was an attitude struck, a pose. Only the fingers could give him away: even intertwined, they were in motion, playing with one another, rubbing at one another, dissipating energy in small spurts, like dust. They held a scrap of paper that might have been a large theatre ticket, or a grocery list. But a closer glance revealed more history, its creases and lines filled in with the luminous brown that comes not from dirt but from years of handling.

He unclasped his hands, taking the paper in his right palm. He raised it but didn't look at it immediately. A lengthy darkening of the outside view caused his reflection to be etched in the glass wall in front of him and for a moment he studied his face: square, pudgy, with inexpressive eyes caught in the middle of thick, circular spectacle frames, hair so thinned that in the muted light he looked bald. Then his body: a raincoat of unarresting cut, an impression of bulk compressed onto a small frame, a sturdiness that surprised him.

The sun flashed suddenly and his image was effaced. Outside, a man in white coveralls, carrying a broom and a garbage bag, shuffled by chasing a wayward paper cup. The absurd figure, a tragi-comedy on legs, irritated him. He turned his lips down, deepening the hollows that defined his cheeks, and finally, as if in anger, looked at the paper in his hand.

It was a photograph, the outlines of black, white, and grey blurring through time into a desperate fuzziness, so that there was no distinction, no sharpness to the image, like an ink drawing on cheap paper. But his memory sharpened the lines, defined the contours, and to his practised eye a youthful female face came clear. Her smile was thin, not hesitant but threadbare, a gesture, he could tell, summoned for the camera from a carefully rationed reserve.

The photograph produced no effect in him. It had become too familiar over the years and he searched it now only for the way things might have gone: how the cheeks might have sagged, the eyes bagged, the forehead crinkled. But the effort was beyond him. The image was too static, had replaced the vivid elasticity of memory so that the face was no longer a face but a frozen combination of features.

The woman, his wife, had almost ceased to be real.

He slipped the photograph into his coat pocket, half-turning to glance at the arrival monitor that hung from the far wall behind him. There had been a change: the letters ARR now commented on her flight number.

Something within him jumped.

It was not that he had hoped to avoid memory. That would have required an effort beyond his resources.

And he had recognized that, for him, it could never be myth. The transformation would have depleted him, would have used him up; and that depletion, that sense of a life gone by, would have been bequeathed to their daughter, an unfair inheritance. So that what for him could never be myth had, for their daughter, quickly taken on atmosphere. She was denied perspective, save for that of the novel. He saw this as strength: it was a way of moving forward.

She was now twenty-seven. Then she had been five.

He was now fifty-four. Then he had been thirty-two.

Twenty-two years: it was a lifetime.

Still, he remembered. The rain, the mud turning the night into a glutinous surge: the thunder of heavy guns, seeming always close, gouging then dulling the senses; the banks of black smoke for days on end defining the sun into a circle of red-hot metal; the corpses and pieces of corpses backing up in the ditches by night, rotting in the ditches by day; and the flow of people — in front, beside, behind — men, women, children, faces blank with misery, possessions abandoned, moving without urgency, like people stripped of all but the automatic, offered nothing now but a knowledge of loss and a numbing sense of violation, victims of a mass rape. Even terror, then, had been beyond them.

And yet no memory was as vivid as the warmth that had filled his hand, that had pressed limply against his chest, exuding exhaustion.

He had shielded his daughter from nothing. She saw, as he did, the severed head of a neighbor lying beside the road; had helped him fight off the dogs driven crazy by hunger; had foraged for roots in soil long dredged; had watched, with him in a torpor, as a mother prepared to carve her husband's body so her children, hollow-eyed approximations of themselves, could eat.

He was grateful that none of this had remained with her. She recalled only playing with sand, playing with dogs, faces and movement; memories edited of carnage.

He himself had lost none of it. But he had retained too the memory of her warmth, a warmth that held its own terror, of night, of contemplated infanticide, of horror of his own hands, of utter senselessness. And yet, in an unfathomable way, it was a positive memory.

It had been a grey, violent time, a time in which the rules of human life had been usurped by human madness, an experience of images that formed no whole, that took no shape, an experience without parentheses. It was history in the making, episodic, he and his daughter particles insignificant in the upheaval of event. None of the usual prejudices applied. It was an extraordinary time, requiring extraordinary responses, eliciting extraordinary ends. The centre had been lost, all had become unpredictable.

So they had trudged, father and daughter, across the bridge of black iron that offered an unrelieving safety, separated from the wife, the mother, by hundreds, by thousands of miles of chaos, just another attenuated refugee family among countless other attenuated refugee families, misery blending them into a whole for the news photographers who scurried around, absorbed, flashbulbs popping.

Attenuated: by profession, by civil war. The wounded needed a doctor; his right hand was bulbous with pus from a wound by an infected scalpel. His wife, a surgeon more skilful than he, went off into the night with her bundle of instruments. He knew the horrors that awaited her: amputations without anaesthetic, stomachs that spilled their contents, bodies with more rips than pores, blood less precious than water. The images, red, gleaming, startling in their intensity, had come to him through a feverish haze as he watched her retreating back, her bundle. He knew he had felt pain; he had retained the knowledge of it. Pain, he had learnt, could not be a memory; the mind resisted, and only the absence of well-being could be submitted to review, in a withdrawn, intellectual way.

Hours, days, weeks: he didn't know how much time passed. Night and day switched places, and back again. His wife didn't return. He didn't know where she had gone, which of the many groups she had left with. Heavy artillery blended dusk with dawn as the fight closed in. Still she didn't return. And when the guns caused their town to split in two, spilling its guts like an overripe corpse, he fled with his daughter, following the tide.

No one talked of safety. No one talked of direction. No one talked. They trudged, through a landscape overturned.

He remembered the first evening of safety, a night spent in a churchyard, in a rain that couldn't cleanse. The church had been crowded, the pews, the alter, the corners disappearing under black, heaving bundles of sighs. He had found a spot against an outside wall, had sat, his back to the wall, his raised knees covered by a piece of cardboard, his daughter asleep on the ground under the cardboard.

Sleep had eluded him on that night: around him thin chests collapsing in an oblique light, apparitions of limp bodies, arms, legs dangling, being carted away by shadowed figures. A night of death in mime.

Just before dawn, the man lying next to him – a stranger of familiar clothes and unfamiliar dialect – very quietly pressed a six-inch knife into his own side, up to the wooden hilt and then beyond. He made no sound; there was little blood. He sighed as if in satisfaction and a thin trickle of red crept from the left corner of his mouth, slashed rapidly down across his cheek, like a wound opening itself.

He had watched, had made no attempt to interfere, had offered a mute compassion which, he knew, denied his profession. It had been a private act, silent, relieving, like the swallowing of a pill.

He had watched as the rain eased, then stopped, and the sun, creating steam, sliced more deeply into the churchyard, the ground black with people stirring tentatively, in disbelief of life.

His neighbor, drained, already shrunken, one hand still clutching what was left of the knife hilt, attracted no attention.

Safety. It provided no answers. They had to be made.

He remembered, but no longer really cared to, the trek through the city solidified with refugees in search of further flight. Papers, stamps, signatures; documents newly printed, crackling with the fresh and the official he could have believed no longer existed; tiny pleasures that surprised him, like being asked to sign his name and discovering that once more, in some miraculous way, it counted for something beyond the simplest of identification. He was asked for his medical papers. He didn't have them. But he was a doctor, he had a profession. It struck him as extraordinary, and he wondered, but only for a moment, that he could have watched with equanimity the suicide of his churchyard neighbor. That this could be construed as a denial of his profession seemed to him now only a passing fancy.

He managed, through contacts, to get the necessary papers. Everything could be managed somehow, even from a country still convulsed against itself—everything but his wife. Paper, if not destroyed, stayed put, could be traced, retrieved; but a person moved, was driven by spasm beyond human control like a piece of meat moving through intestine. Her rescue was the one thing he couldn't manage. She was too distant, out of his reach.

Wait, they said, wait for the war to end.

Wait for things to settle down. Settle yourself first.

Here's your visa. Take your daughter. Go. Wait.

One man, an official in white shirt with sleeves rolled stylishly, incongruously, to his elbow, meaning to be kind but in the hurried way survival demanded, said, "You've lost everything. You've lost your wife. Count her for dead. Take your daughter and go."

And he had thought: Yes.

So he had emigrated, got himself accredited, begun to build a base in a land alien to him. Here, the war was remote, a small item on the world-news page of the local newspaper. Then the war ended and the land he had left, quickly grown alien, withdrew into itself, became hermetic. It sealed his wife in.

He noted the withdrawal with calm. He was building his base. Much of the period he recalled only through a haze, as of fatigue, and it was this eviscerating effort that now offered itself as myth to him. His wife, the memory of her, began to evade him and after a while—he didn't know how long; time revealed its man-made fragility, divested itself of context—he stopped the unconscious calculation of time's breach. It had become pointless in every way.

His daughter grew quickly and, in a way that he found inexplicable, began to slip from his grasp. She was, he realized one evening, no longer an asexual being. She was becoming aware of differences, and his clumsiness only increased her apprehension. He was a doctor, he knew the technical details. But how to explain them to his daughter? For a time, he thought of his wife, as of a stranger, with blame. And then he thought of her no more.

Back then, the city which had become his had been grey and stolid.

Nothing sparkled. The foreign was distrusted. People kept to themselves. They worked and, afterwards, retreated to family, to a privacy that was itself hermetic.

So it surprised him when, at the hospital, Marya began seeking him out to talk: about her flight from Soviet armies at the end of the war, about the family she had had to abandon, about the man who had brought her here then discarded her for a middle-aged artist who promised mothering and an Oedipal sexuality. She went, from the first, to the heart of the personal.

No reply came to him; he felt a sense of caution, a wariness. He asked, with unmerited rudeness, why she had singled him out.

It was, she said, because she recognized in him someone who might understand: they shared a quality, a quality of absorption. In the grey city, it marked him.

He remained guarded.

She talked, and as she talked, weaving images, conjuring horror, his reserve broke.

He told her about his flight, his daughter, his problems, his wife, too, but almost incidentally: she was just another element.

Marya offered to help with his daughter.

He hesitated; he was a doctor, she a floor-cleaner. He often passed her in the corridor, he clasping a chart, she a mop, each acknowledging the other only by the merest of pauses, the way a bee might react before an artificial flower, with surprise and a mild confusion. Then, after a night of thought, he accepted her offer.

At first, his daughter resisted, but Marya was persistent. Over time they grew close, Marya, his daughter, and him. And the first time he slept with Marya he was surprised at the warmth and pliability of her flesh. Every day at the hospital he touched patients, but with her his fingers trembled, lost their professional edge, offered a thrill without memory, and culminated in an act that was, to him, startling in its exclusiveness. He discovered in his hands a set of abilities he thought he had lost. It was like a gift.

When, eventually, Marya moved in — she had only two suitcases and a box of assorted papers, pictures, mementoes, knick-knacks that assumed value only to an attenuated life — it seemed the natural thing to do, even, yet especially, in the grey city.

One evening he took a mental step outside his life and gazed back at it with what he thought was objectivity, and he was struck by what a perfect family they made. He thought with a gentle awe: I am happy.

I am happy. Yet, with lucidity, he refused to indulge the thought. It was an attitude not only of the present but also of the future; it reached beyond the graspable to the uncertainties of hope, dream, and expectation. He had seen too much, been through too much, been too much the pawn of the unpredictable. He would deal with what he could see, feel, smell, touch, hear, understand. He rejected the nebulous; he would not speculate.

His life then, to his relief, became uneventful. He worked. He bought a house. Marya became a housewife. His daughter grew. Years passed in unthinking contentment. His base expanded. His hair thinned, he took on a squat appearance.

When the letter arrived bearing stamps of a familiar style, yet less lyrical than those he'd known, extolling now the virtues of trains and pick-axes, it was as if some unexplored part of his mind had always known it would. He was not surprised. He was angered. Not at his wife: that she was alive after so many years was just a fact. His anger was, rather, at the unpredictable, at those elements that fitted no pattern, that came at random to disrupt. For his wife he felt no sorrow, no pity, a little relief. It had been too long.

Her letter told of hardship and distress, of years of physical labor on the farm to which she had been banished. Her words, unadorned, shorn of stylistic flourish, impressed him as would a relic. The country in which she was caught remained so remote; the letter was like a communication from the distantly dead.

His reply was passionless. He could not pretend. He gave her, briefly, the details of autobiography. He sent her some money, as he would continue to do every month for years even as the country, sealed, convulsed once more unto itself. He didn't mention Marya; there was no point. The two would never meet, they could never affect one another. To mention her might simply have caused an unnecessary distress.

The letters — fragments of self, in the style of the memo — continued to come, if infrequently. He replied, also in the style of the memo, communication of the flimsiest kind, reminders of existence rather than exchanges of thought.

His daughter grew. Marya continued to live as his wife. The letters, with their intricate, colorful stamps, continued to come. He sent her money, automatically, as if paying the telephone bill; it was no hardship, he saw it not as duty but simply as something that had to be done, like a household chore.

Sometimes he would read the letters to his daughter, translating from the language of which she had, over the years, retained only a few words. The daughter never made a comment, just asked at the end for the stamp. Once she said, "I wish she'd use different stamps, I have lots of these red ones already." He felt her attitude was correct.

After his daughter had moved into her own apartment, he continued ripping out the stamps for her. She never asked to hear the letters. After a while she stopped collecting stamps.

Marya took over the collection.

Of course, in the end, it had all been a matter of choice. "You had no choice": the words formed of themselves in his mind.

But he'd wanted to avoid such preparation. It hinted at self-defence, at justification of action in a time that had made thought, will, decision absurd.

He sought distraction. A crowd had gathered at the exit of the Customs Hall. In front of the doors — of an opaque glass that revealed the movements of shadowed ghosts — was a small old man in a casual blue and white uniform that lent him little air of authority. He faced the crowd, his blue peaked cap pushed to the back of his head. What was he? A guard? A guide? A porter? He joked with people in the crowd, he looked stern, he stood at attention, he leaned loosely on the wrought-iron rail that marked off the path from the doors; he was like a man who couldn't decide on a function, on an appropriate image, as if, despite himself, he was infected by those around him.

He felt sorry for the little old man in his anonymous uniform: he looked lost.

"You had no choice." The words formed once again, like a chant of response in the church he had attended for a time every Sunday morning twenty-two years before in order to improve his comprehension of English. And the thought pursued itself: "You had no choice. I did. For myself. For our daughter. Should I have refused? What is this loyalty that would deny life? To what does it aspire?" Words. Forming in his mind, they thickened the saliva in his mouth: he wanted to spit. Words now could only confuse.

He had long accepted that he would never again see his wife, and that she was here now affected him only in that it revealed his essential insignificance: man as plaything, life as mockery.

He had had no hesitation in bringing her out, not, he knew, from love but from duty, unquestioned, unquestioning, the way one lays flowers on the grave of a relative dead twenty years. His action carried no moral weight; the automatic never could. It had just been, just was.

He slipped his hands, suddenly cold, into his coat pockets.

Nervousness: he caught it, slipped momentarily into confusion. In that eternity of seconds he lost his name, his memory, his place in the world; his very existence seemed to slip from him. His fingers, grasping at the rough cloth of the coat pocket, seeking stability, brushed the picture. He took hold of it between two fingers, withdrew it.

But then a face that had changed little in its essence, much in its detail, slid past the little old man. His mind took a step backwards so that, observing her advance towards him, he observed himself and, on yet another level—not that of the observer of self but of another, less photographic, more judgmental—he remarked on his composure. She was here, he was greeting her, like an appointed official fulfilling duty.

The second level of his mind persisted, observing her with what the third level thought an interesting dispassion. She wore a plain coat, light grey, with no pretension to style. She was smaller now than before but less soft, with a rigidity in her forehead, her eyes, her mouth. Her skin was bronzed and a single thought—the picture, the past, the present—fused the levels of his mind: she used to be proud of her pure, unblemished skin, her only vanity.

In her left hand, the arm crooked at the elbow to accommodate a cheap plastic handbag, she held, like an amulet, a blue air-letter, his own, he guessed, probably the last he had sent, the one in which he had told her what to do, what to expect, on arrival at the airport. He supposed she made a touching sight.

With a tremor of panic, he clutched the photograph into his left fist, now gone moist.

Then she was before him, looking somehow tragically short.

They shook hands.

Hers was small, dry, rough, with a strong grip, a hand that no longer knew the syringe, that had been transformed by plough and hoe and shovel. He held it for a few unthinking seconds while her eyes—revealing a reserve, a puzzle, blank yet questioning, signalling a sense of betrayal yet a compassion he couldn't grasp—looked frankly into his own.

He knew, then, that she knew about Marya. And he knew, too, that he felt no guilt, no shame: relief, rather, and an enigmatic gratitude.

She took her hand away with a masculine briskness.

He said, "How are you?" After twenty-two years, in a language so long unused, the words, simplistic, meaningless, without weight, offered a measure of himself: he couldn't pretend.

"I am well, thank you, and how are you?"

"I am well."

"And how is our daughter?"

"She is well." Then: "She is longing to see you."

He sensed her unasked question and was grateful for her tact. Or was it fear? No, he decided, she was not a weak woman, she was a survivor in a way that he had never been. Could he, a doctor, who took a pure pride in the intellect, have survived those years in the fields as she had? Millions had died; starvation and execution had raked the ranks of their generation. Survival demanded a skill that was not his. He needed to see a future. He could build, but merely to survive: for this, strength evaded him.

"She had to work. She couldn't come with me." Transparent, he knew: this too revealed his weakness. But she said nothing, in no way acknowledged his lies, and once more he was grateful. He said, too hurriedly, "We have a lot to talk about."

"There is nothing to talk about."

"I have rented an apartment for you. I will take care of all your needs." Like an invalid, he thought, regretting his words.

"You owe me nothing."

He took her suitcase — of cheap plastic, like her handbag — tipped the porter, led her in silence to the exit. The doors slipped open. Outside, the air was cool, given bite by the wind. The sky was once more grey. There was no sun: the carpark across the way took on the aspect of monolith.

"Is she beautiful?"

His calm pleased him, but he couldn't look at her: "No, but she is a good woman. She has been a good mother to our daughter."

"I meant our daughter." Her voice did not change, was neutral.

Stupid, he thought. He had answered the two unstated questions, had revealed all in a manner more abrupt, more crushing, than he'd intended.

But she was a survivor.

"Yes," he said, "our daughter is beautiful."

The wind fingered down his neck, struck his chest. He shivered. The suitcase in his hand was light, the photograph in his left a more onerous weight. With an effort of will, he opened his palm. The photograph fluttered out. The wind picked it up, flung it into a gutter. He picked up his pace: there were things to do.

Presently not long after they had driven off, the old man in white coveralls, carrying a broom and a garbage bag, came along on yet another turn past the carpark. He saw the photograph, the outlines of black, white, and grey blurred into a desperate fuzziness, so that there was no distinction, no sharpness to the image, like an ink drawing on cheap paper. His mind couldn't sharpen the lines, couldn't define the contours.

He swept it into the garbage bag and went off in his unsteady shuffle after a fluttering candy-wrapper.

# Gerry Bostock

## Here Comes the Nigger

*Gerry Bostock's* Here Comes the Nigger *was first performed at the Black Theatre, Redfern, in 1976. Portions of the original playscript were printed in* Meanjin *in December 1977, although the entire text has never been published. The excerpt reproduced below is taken from a revised version of the play, transformed by the author into a draft filmscript.*

SAM: But the government's spending millions of dollars on Aborigines. Why isn't something being done?

VERNA: I'll tell ya why. Most of the money that's earmarked for blacks ends up in white pockets; it goes to pay the wages of the white bureaucrats who control the black affairs; hardly anything gets to the people who really need it. Just look at the money that's returned to Treasury every year because the bureaucrats say it isn't used; Millions of dollars! And if they do happen to fund Aboriginal development programmes they make damn sure there's a white man in control of the money; and if that white man mismanages the money and the programme goes bust, it's not him that gets in the shit, it's always the blacks who work in government departments, Them black bureaucrats are nothing but window dressing for the Government: shop-front niggers, good little jackey-jackies, little black puppets dancing to the white man's tune. Do you know what they remind me of? Coconuts: brown on the outside and white on the inside!

SAM: They're not all sell-outs. Not all of them have been bought off. Some of them get out and meet with the people. Some of them try to do things as best they can.

VERNA *(smiles):* Yeah, sure they do. They visit Aboriginal reserves and communities, they shoot in for a day or two in their big, black government cars. But do they live with the grass-roots people, and experience conditions for themselves? No they don't! Instead, they stay in the nearest posh hotel where they can go to buffet luncheons, and have room service with hot and cold running white girls. And why not? They've got their expense accounts. If they can't get their little white girls to give it away, they can always pay for it; and if that doesn't work they can always accuse the girls of being racist, appeal to their guilt complex. Why should they worry about the blacks? They've got it made, the bastards!

*(He places a comforting arm around her.)*

SAM *(softly):* It's okay kid. You're home now.

*(She sobs uncontrollably.)*

JIMMY: Anyone for a charge?

*(Billy looks broodingly as Jimmy hands out the beer. Cut to Odette.)*

ODETTE: Enjoying yourself, Sam?

SAM: I always do. How about you?

*(Sam flinches as a half filled can of beer, flung by Billy, lands at their feet. Billy stands out and confronts Odette.)*

BILLY: Bitch! You bloody shits. You can't leave us alone, can ya . . . !

*(She is obviously surprised by the attack but remains calm.)*

BILLY: Ya rip us off every chance ya get, don't ya! Ya've been kickin' us in the teeth for two hundred bloody years an ya still doing it, and we still have to put up with it!

ODETTE: I'm not responsible for anything my father or my forefathers did to your people, and I'm certainly not responsible for anything that happened tonight.

BILLY: You're not responsible? That's a cop-out and you know it. You are responsible! You're responsible for the two thousand black lepers in this country, you're responsible for the infant mortality rate of black babies being amongst the highest in the world, you're responsible for every old aged pensioner in this country who has to rummage through garbage cans to get something to eat, you're responsible for every unemployed person who has to steal to survive. Us blacks are the minority, we're two percent of the population. You're the majority; you can make changes so don't sit there and say you're not responsible for everything that happens in this country, so don't give me that cop-out about not being bloody responsible!

*(Verna prods Johnny. Billy holds up his hands for silence.)*

BILLY: Awright, you fellas. Give him a go.

LUCY: Come on, brothers. Show these buggers what ya made of!

SAM: I don't know?

BILLY: The white man settled this vast country;
  Cleared the land;
  Built a great nation democratic and free,
  And they looked after you, their friends,
  Our brothers, the Aborigine.

*(During the recital Billy walks in among the crowd using all the emotion at his command.)*

BILLY *(cont.):* They had to protect you, care for you,
　　They gave you a home
　　Or you would have died of disease
　　Or starved if they left you to roam.
*(From time to time Billy directs his recital at individual blacks as well as Odette.)*

BILLY *(cont.):* They educated you, employed you
　　And gave you a trade
　　They fed you and looked after your health
　　You had it made
　　They gave you a life of ease and leisure,
　　Your only want was for more pleasure
　　And they fought two bloody wars
　　For that happy treasure.
*(Verna and Ari seem anxious about the two brothers. Sometimes they are seen in the background, and sometimes the camera cuts to them, capturing their concerned facial expressions.)*

BILLY *(cont.):* These are the lies
　　Of our white Judas brother;
　　He has taught us deceit
　　And contempt for one another
　　And watched amused
　　As we grovelled for fresh air
　　Under his racist care;
　　Derelict and abused.
　　What about our infant mortality!
　　Where is his morality?
　　This patronising white
　　Has murdered our people in hateful spite
　　And bloody thirst
　　Because we lay claim to this land first!
*(Two blacks hang on Billy's every word. From time to time they make the odd comment but generally remain silent.)*

BILLY *(cont.):* Our land, our culture and our women
　　He rapes with a lecherous grin,
　　While society turns its back on his immoral sin
　　And whispers an apathetic sigh
　　While our people are left to starve and die.

He stares and glares and loves to gloat
This white beast frocked in an angelic cloak
Who laughs at our woeful plight
From which we have no respite
And no weapons to fight his aggressive might.

How long must we wait for justice
And freedom to be won?
The time has come
to fight this racist-scum!

Rise up Black children
And tell society what it's all about.
Stand together
And stamp black persecution out.
Remember our infant mortality!
Wake up to reality
The fascist monger
Has murdered our people by racism and hunger.

Society has cast you aside
And you've been made to hide
And grovel in the gutter
And all you've done is sit and mope
And mutter
About life without hope.

Rise up Black Children
With your anguish cry
And from the rooftops
How your babies die
From government neglect
And society's inaudible outcry.

For years our land
Has been subjected to pillage and rape;
While our people faced corrupt politicians,
Police persecution
And government red tape
And whites who care not for our plight;
The time is coming for us to fight!

Rise up Black Children
And stand as one,
Shoulder to shoulder 'til freedom's won;
Brace your back,
Dig in your heel
Arid if need be,
Prepare for the onslaught of cold steel!

Rise up and face society's might,
For justice for our people
And for our birthright,
Our land!
This land
In which we've suffered aggression
And known nothing but oppression,
By our conquerors,
The invaders
Who have lowered us
To the blackest depths of depression.

Prepare, Black Children,
For the Land Rights fight,
Our cause is true,
Our aim's in sight,
Unite, my people, unite.

Come on, Black Children,
Rise on your feet!
Get out of the gutter and onto the street;
United together, hand in hand,
Heads raised high we stand
Then, march as one,
Surging forward and onward
For justice, for freedom and for our land!
*(The blacks applaud and shout comments of approval.)*

BILLY:  That's your poetry, Sam. Keep writing that sorta stuff, brother.
SAM *(thoughtful):*  Yes, but that one's just a little bit strong.
    *(Billy gives up and sits down. Verna rises and walks slowly over to
    Sam as Billy rips open a can of beer.)*
VERNA:  A bit strong? A bit bloody strong! They're your words, Sam not

Billy's. You wrote *Black Children,* not him. A bit strong, ya say? God, man. You've been mixin' with whites too long!

ODETTE:   Now, just a damn minute. You've got no right to talk to him like that . . .

VERNA: *(coldly)*   You shut ya white mouth or I'll get Mother Palmer and her five daughters *(gesticulates)* and shove them down your throat!
   *(She turns to Sam.)*

VERNA *(softly):*   Now, look here, bundji; this warraluman, this whaa-zhin of yours says I shouldn't talk to you like this. I'm talking to you like this because you're Billy's brother, and I love you just as much as he does. You know how we feel, how most blacks feel about white society; *Black Children* expresses exactly how we feel and you wrote those words. Don't lose sight of that. Don't lose your values or change your way of thinking 'cause some whaa-zhin spreads her legs for a couple of minutes and shows you a good time. Don't change because of that.

BILLY *(rising):*   Anyway, it's a party time! Who wants to hear a blackfella yarn? *(pause)* This is a schoolboy yarn. It's a true story, too. It happened to me when I was going to school; as a matter of fact, it was the first day I met Ari. Remember that, Ari?
   *(Cut to Ari who seems uneasy and turns to Sam.)*

BILLY *(cont.):*   Ari and me was at one end of the schoolground when we heard this big commotion all the gubbah kids were making. Ya see, it was playtime and all the gubbahs formed themselves into this big procession; just like little soldiers. Everyone was marchin' and singing an clapping their hands; just havin' so much fun me and Ari decided to join in with them.

   We raced over to some garbage tins. Ari picked up a tin and a stick and I grabbed two tin lids, then we joined the gubbahs — and there we were, me and Ari: I was clangin' these two lids together as hard as I could, and Ari was beltin' shit outta the garbage tin with his stick — an we were singin' "Wallah-wallah-blackfella, wallah-wallah-blackfella, wallah-wallah-blackfella . . ."
   *(Billy moves around the room clapping his hands and emotionally chanting. The crowd, with the notable exception of Sam, Ari and Odette stamp their feet, clap their hands and pick up the chant.*

   *SUPERIMPOSE children in a procession in a school yard singing the chant. INTERCUT facial CLOSEUP of Sam and WIDE ANGLE of children. VOICE OVER of party crowd's chanting comes up and takes over from the children's track.*

   *CUT TO WIDE ANGLE. Billy and his followers chant.)*

BILLY: Wallah wallah blackfella, Wallah wallah blackfella, Wallah wallah blackfella.

*(Billy raises his hands for silence. The chanting stops and he goes over to Sam.)*

BILLY *(softly):* And you know what, my brother? When we looked everyone was laughing at you — 'cause you was the blackfella, Sam. You was the blackfella.

*(CLOSE to Sam. FAST INTERCUT between Sam and the jeering children, ending with Sam sitting rigid as the party crowd look on. FADE OUT.)*

*INTERIOR. DAY. FLAT.*

*The bed sitting room is small, comfortable, and economically furnished. Against the far wall, beneath a wide curtained window is a double bed covered with a Batik bedspread. Against the right hand wall is a small book-shelf with assorted books, magazines and a framed photograph of Odette's parents; a small stereo and assorted records; a small tape-recorder and cassettes; above are two posters of reproductions of famous paintings and two glass-framed Norman Lindsay prints; in the corner is a settee. The floor is covered by seagrass matting. In a corner by the far and the left-hand wall are two bean bags. Built in to the left-hand wall is a wardrobe, next to which is a door leading to the bathroom. The kitchen, situated in an alcove by the left of the front door, is separated from the main room by a serving bench; on the bench is small glass fish-tank containing two goldfish, a large corked bottle containing earth and a tropical plant. In the centre of the room is a small table with a lace table cloth and two chairs.*

*(Sam sits at the table reading a Braille book and Odette is on the settee reading and making notes.*

*SOUND FX TELEPHONE.)*

SAM *(looking up):* Are you going to answer that or what?

*(She continues to read as she rises.)*

ODETTE: You just keep working.

*(She crosses to the phone and Sam goes back to his book.)*

ODETTE *(answering phone):* Hullo? *(uncomfortably)* Hi, what are you doing in town? How did you get my number? I'm sorry. I'm fine. How are you? *(pause)* No, that's no good . . . Look, where are you? I'll drop by. *(looks at her watch)* About half and hour, okay? Right see you then.

*(CLOSE TO Odette. She hangs up and appears thoughtful. Sam looks over to her.)*

SAM: Everything okay?

ODETTE *(pondering):* Huh? Oh yes, everything's just fine.

*(She goes over and sits next to him.)*

SAM *(smiles):*
>One of your old flames, hey?

ODETTE:  Huh?

SAM:  On the phone? Was that one of your old boyfriends?
>*(She pats his hand.)*

ODETTE:  I have to go out for awhile. Can we finish this lesson tomorrow?

SAM:  Is our date still on for tonight?

ODETTE:  I don't know how long I'll be *(looks at her watch)*. Why don't I meet you at the railway station and we can go on from there?

SAM: *(Rising. He closes the book and puts it on the bookshelf.)*  Good. I'll walk you to the corner.

ODETTE:  Thanks. I'll get my coat . . .

# Dionne Brand

## *Return*

I
So the street is still there, still melting with sun
still the shining waves of heat at one o'clock
the eyelashes scorched, staring the distance of the
park to the parade stand, still razor grass burnt and
cropped, everything made indistinguishable from dirt
by age and custom, white washed, and the people . . .
still I suppose the scorpion orchid by the road, that
fine red tongue of flamboyant and orange lips
muzzling the air, that green plum turning fat and
crimson, still the crazy bougainvillea fancying and
nettling itself purple, pink, red, white, still the trickle of
sweat and cold flush of heat raising the smell of
cotton and skin . . . still the dank rank of breadfruit milk,
their bash and rain on steps, still the bridge this side
the sea that side, the rotting ship barnacle eaten still
the butcher's blood staining the walls of the market,
the ascent of hills, stony and breathless, the dry
yellow patches of earth still threaten to swamp at the
next deluge . . . so the road, that stretch of sand and
pitch struggling up, glimpses sea, village, earth
bare-footed hot, women worried, still the faces,
masked in sweat and sweetness, still the eyes
watery, ancient, still the hard, distinct, brittle smell of
slavery.

# . . . *Seen*

The day was threatening to be a real scorcher. If she didn't have to go to work, she'd lie there on the floor where it was cool or go to the beach. She knew that by one o'clock she'd be sleepy and harrassed and hot. She took a cold shower and put on the lightest garment that she could find. As she walked the ten minutes to the office, water from her wet hair fell to her forehead and shoulders. She said good morning to someone. There were so few people on the island that you had to say good morning to everyone or else they would be offended. It was impossible to look at the sun. This island was amazing, she remarked to herself, as she took the lane with houses only to one side.

The earth smell, acrid and thick, was always in the nostrils. Every living thing here went to extremes. There wasn't one good reason why flowers should be so red and leaves so green. The pressing sky and the fecund earth were sometimes unbearable. Insistent almost on a life where difficulty marked the body and finally the face. Every morning, facing the sky and the earth was a present challenge.

Looking at the faces passing her, she recognized the excuses for her continual thoughts of flight. The island threw her, them, into a battle against fear and hope. They hacked the land with machetes and footfalls, only to see it grow over come the rainy season and the sky changing faces, reflecting opposite impressions to the place below.

In the rainy season the sky is not as flamboyant. But no less dangerous. Deluged, the rain's water washes all colour out of it. The blues are lighter, the pinks, less bloody. It is no longer at arm's length and, in the evenings, the sun sinks, docile from the day's rivalry with the clouds. Some days, her mouth would drop open at the sight of the sky. She could spend all day looking at it, hoping that it would unravel something of its purpose.

Here, the inevitable conflict was with the sky It seemed closer, red as a hot-veined kiss. The face you'd turn to, to find an answer.

She had come home to work and work she had. Every day, awake at five, office by eight, working late, beach, then home by eight, sleep, if she could, by twelve. When the work took her up the islands, she'd sit in the eight-seater island hopper, so small against the sky. Her severity eased — was forced, coaxed to ease with the waiting in lines, the walking for miles, the rub and smell of market women, the trail and skip of children, the patient sun, the custom of everyone living by the day and the night and not by the artifice of wealth or superiority.

Sometimes at night, sitting at her small table with the lamp, the most exotic of insects passed in her presence. Beetles with anteater heads and antlers, mosquitoes with fat bellies of blood and sharp bites, the greenest, smallest and softest of grasshoppers, slow, small-winged, heavy-bottomed fruitflies, all the most absurd shaped and coloured creatures this island had to offer. Sometimes she spared their lives. At other times she killed them and thought that she would be punished in another life. So she tried to kill them without malice. But there was a closeness in their appearance, a humility in a place where pesticides could not be purchased cheaply and fecundity rose in the smell of all things rotten and decaying and ripening to be eaten. Such noises at night, such singing, neither gay nor sad. Frogs and crickets and indescribably green and crawling, flying beasts. Singing, for nothing, just to pass the night. Like her not singing, listening, coming home.

The night, whose morning found her on the floor, a bird woke her up. It screamed at around one a.m. Screamed and beat its wings across the top of the house. She jumped out of bed, thinking that it was a burglar and stayed awake all night. It was not long since she had fallen asleep. Another one of her long nights. Her nights were hardest, had always been, at home. Their blackness could be mistaken for smoke, so thick and billowing, and the mornings took long to come. What was she doing on the island, why had she come?

In the mornings she was still awake. The beasts outside stopped crying or singing and she fell asleep until the sun heated up and the flies began their buzzing around her face and left ear. Day noises did not startle her or fill her with as much wonder and fear. The sun blazed through the intermittent rain. Then, in the evenings, it sank below the level of the eyes signalling the singing and crying. At night, she locked the doors and the windows upon the first sound of singing. Suddenly the area between the door and the yard became wild, without order or control. All the things which she knew in the day, their positions, their shapes, became unknown. In the mornings, she would find them in their day places. The sugar apple tree, the corn, the breadfruit tree with its massive fruit and leaves. There, where they had been the day before. She laughed at herself each morning. Each morning, science and logic asserted themselves. At night they faded into fear and superstition.

A candle, a box of matches lay on the table with the lamp. The bottle of rum half empty stood next to them. She had drunk half of it and still had not slept after the bird had frightened her awake. She and the dogs barking at their shadows had kept vigil all night long.

She had come home. A year ago now. To live here, to understand this.

# Edward Kamau Brathwaite

## Red Rising

### 1

When the earth was made
when the wheels of the sky were being fashioned
when my songs were first heard in the voice of the coot of the owl
hillaby soufriere and kilimanjaro were standing towards me with
    water with fire

at the centre of the air

there
in the keel of the blue
the son of my song, father-giver, the sun/sum
walks the four corners of the magnet, caught in the wind, blind

in the eye of ihs own hurricane

and the trees on the mountain become mine: living eye of my branches
of bone; flute
where is my hope hope where is my psalter

my children wear masks dancing towards me the mews of their
    origen earth

so that this place which is called mine
which will never know that cold scalpel of skull, hill of dearth

*brain corals ignite and ignore it*

and that this place which is called now
which will never again glow: coal balloon anthracite: into cross-

roads of hollows

black spot of my life: *jah*
blue spot of my life: *love*
yellow spot of my life: *iises*
red spot of my dream that still flowers flowers flowers

*let us give thanks*

when the earth was made
when the sky first spoke with the voice of the rain/bow
when the wind gave milk to its music
when the suns of my morning walked out of their shallow
    thrill/dren

2

So that for centuries now have i fought against these opposites
how i am sucked from water into air
how the air surrounds me blue all the way

    from ocean to the other shore
    from halleluja to the black hole of hell

    from this white furnace where i burn
    to those green sandy ant-hills where you grow your yam

you would think that i would hate eclipses
    my power powdered over as it were

but it's hallucination my fine friend
    a fan a feather; some

    one else's breath of shadow
    the moon's cool or some plan/et's

    but can you ever guess how i
    who have wracked

    you wrong
    long too to be black

    be
    come part of that hool that shrinks us all to stars

    how i
    with all these loco

    motives in me
    would like to straighten

    strangle eye/self out

    grow a beard wear dark glasses
    driving the pack straight far

    ward into indigo and vi
    olet and on into ice like a miss

ile

rather than this surrendered curve
this habit forming bicycle of rains and seasons
weathers when i tear my hair

i will never i now know make it over the atlantic of that nebula

but that you may live my fond retreating future
i will accept i will accept the bonds that blind me
turning my face down/wards to my approaching past these
      morning chill/dren


## Author's Notes

*Red Rising*: dawn, the first voice of the rainbow.

### Stanza I

**l.4.** *hillaby soufriere and kilimanjaro*: mountain landmarks of the
Third World: Hillaby, Barbados (though less than 1,000 ft!);
Soufriere, St Vincent, active volcano; Kilimanjaro, Tanzania.
**l.9.** *sun/sum: sunsum*: Akan word for soul, origin of spiritual life.
**l.11.** *ihs*: natural/divine version of its/his
**l.16.** *mews*: sound-word (news/mews)
**l.17.** *origen*: origin, *originem,* and the Early Christian (Neo-platonist)
theologian of Alexandria (c. 155-253). The "rainbow" sense
(literal, moral, mystical) of "origin."
**l.26.** *iises*: Rastafarian version of 'praises'. *Jah, love* and *thanks* are
also Rasta ritual words, juxtaposed here with N. American Indian
sacred colours: black, blue, yellow, red.

### Stanza 2

**l.19.** *hool*: hole, whirlpool, galactic black hole.

# Dennis Brutus

## I Am Alien in Africa and Everywhere

I am alien in Africa and everywhere:

in Europe, outside Europe I stand and assess them
— find French racial arrogance and Teuton superiority,
moldering English humbug:

and in Africa one finds
chafing, through bumbling,
at the restraints of restraint,
brushing impatiently through varied cultures
in fruitless search of depths:
only in myself, occasionally, am I familiar.

*Paris-Algiers*

## I Am Out of Love with You for Now

I am out of love with you for now;
cold-sodden in my misery
your contours and allurements
cannot move me:

I murmur old endearments to revive
our old familiar glow again
— like sapless autumn leaves
they rasp in vain.

You have asked too much of me:
fond-fool, bereft I cling
unloving, to remembered love
and the spring.

*Johannesburg*

# Buhkwujjenene

## Nanaboozhoo Creates the World

Nanaboozhoo . . . had a son. He loved his son. He told his son never to go near the water lest evil should come to him. The son disobeyed his father, he went out in a canoe and was never seen or heard of more. Nanaboozhoo then vowed vengeance against the gods of the water who had destroyed his son. There were two of these gods and one day they lay sleeping on the shore. Nanaboozhoo was looking everywhere for them, determined to kill them. A loon offered to show him where they were sleeping. He followed the loon till he found them, and then he made short work of them with his tomahawk and his war-club. But lo and behold no sooner were the gods dead than the waters of the great lake rose up in vengeance; they pursued Nanaboozhoo up on to the dry land, and he had to run for his life. He sought the highest mountain and climbed to the top of the highest pine tree. Still the waters pursued him. They rose higher and higher. What could he do! He broke off a few of the topmost branches and made a raft upon which he got and saved himself. He saved also a number of the animals that were kicking and struggling in the water all around him. At length he bethought himself of making a new world. How should he do it? Could he but procure a little of the old world he might manage it. He selected the beaver from among the animals, and sent it to dive after some earth. When it came up it was dead. He sent the otter, but it died also. At length he tried the muskrat. The muskrat dived. When it came up it was dead. But in its claws was clenched a little earth. Nanaboozhoo carefully took this earth, rubbed it in his fingers till it was dry, then placed it in the palm of his hand, and blew it gently over the surface of the water. A new world was thus formed, and Nanaboozhoo and all the animals landed. Nanaboozhoo sent out a wolf to see how big the world was. He was gone a month. Again he sent him out and he was gone a year. Then he sent out a very young wolf. This young wolf died of old age before it could get back. So Nanaboozhoo said the world was big enough, and might stop growing.

# Willi Chen

## Assam's Iron Chest

A dull moon glowed in the country-night darkness. They came out of hiding from behind the caimette tree, avoiding the crackle of dead leaves underfoot. Into the pale light stepped big, loudmouthed Mathias, Boyo, with his matted dreadlocks wrapped up in a "Marvingay" hat, and laglee-chewing Sagamouth, so nicknamed because of his grotesque lips and the smattering noises they made.

In the little clearing overlooking Assam's shopyard, they waited patiently behind large tannia leaves that shielded them from the light of passing motorists. They waited for the last bus to rattle by on its return journey to town and for the soft glow of Assam's Coleman lamp, whirring moths and beetles striking against the lampshade, to go out.

Boyo puffed at the carmine-tipped stick of ganja that brightened his face as he slapped at mosquitoes. Sagamouth's lips continued slurping noisily.

"Keep quiet, man. Christ! You goh wake up the whole damn village," Mathias hissed between clenched teeth.

" Look, the light out," Sagamouth whispered excitedly.

"Yea, but keep your flapping mouth shut. I could see. Who in charge here?"

"Boyo, put out that weed. Whole place stink ah grass," Mathias warned.

At the galvanised paling surrounding the shop-yard, a flimsy steel sheet suddenly loosened in the moonlight and fell aside, allowing three figures to squeeze through the narrow space into the shop-yard. They were confronted by stacks of empty soft drink crates, discarded cartons, pitch oil tins and, against the shed, bundles of stacked crocus bags.

Remembering the action in the motion picture *Bataan*, and with the dramatic invasion in *Desert Fox* still fresh in his mind, Mathias crouched on all fours, leading his platoon across the yard.

"Sssh," he cautioned them as he sat on his buttocks before the big door. They paused in the darkness. Mathias' hands felt for the door frame. He inserted a pig foot into the crevice. With both feet against the wall he pried the door, throwing his whole weight on it. A slow cracking noise erupted as the nails lifted off the hinges and the door came up. A dank odour of wet oilmeal, soap and stale mackerel greeted them. They crawled in, feeling their way between the stacks of packaged goods. Further inside, they saw a table with a lighted lamp and a red spot of mosquito coil under it. A big square mosquito net hung over a four-poster bed out of which floated Assam's snores in grating spasms.

Convinced that Assam was sound asleep, Mathias struck a match and immediately shadows jumped across the walls, on the shelves of bottles and over tinned stuffs. On the floor, crowding the aisles, was the paraphernalia of jumbled haberdashery, pots and pans, and bags of peas and beans. Moving in the crowded interior, Mathias came to the room where, over a small table, bills hung pinned to the wall, next to a Chinese calendar. Cupping the lighted match in his hand, Mathias tiptoed further inside. More bags, packed in rows, and bales of macaroni and cornmeal. Flagons of cider and an old rum cask stood on the floor. In the corner, the square block of metal stood on a rough framework of local timber; a squat, dull hunk of iron with a circular dial of brass. It was the iron chest. Mathias came up to it and tested its weight. Boyo braced himself in readiness.

With Sagamouth holding the light, Mathias and Boyo heaved at the heavy hulk of iron. They pushed until the wooden stand inched along the floor.

"Damn thing must be full," Boyo said.

"Canefarmer pay, choopid," Sagamouth replied, spraying them with his spittle.

"All you keep quiet," Mathias entreated.

Pitting themselves against the heavy load, they worked with caution. Twice they heard Assam cough. Their hands glided, slipped over the smooth surface of the chest. After some strenuous efforts, they managed to push the chest to the doorway. Finally the whole bulk of metal was heaved outside, catapulting, digging into the yard with a dull thud.

The cool night breeze invigorated their bodies. The sight of the chest inspired their minds with the promise of new things in life. Sagamouth disappeared into the bushes and returned with a crocus bag containing a crowbar, a sledge hammer and a flambeau. Behind him he dragged a large piece of board, the underside of which was lined with plain galvanised sheeting. At one end was tied a long piece of rope.

They eased their cargo on to the wooden contraption. Mathias again directed the operations. Standing before the metal chest, he tied the end of the rope around his waist and leant forward. Boyo and Sagamouth were pushing at the rear.

They hauled the makeshift sledge along the grassy side tracks. With the heavy iron chest strapped to it, it skidded and scuttled across the bare ground. Their backs shone like their faces, which streamed with perspiration. Boyo puffed like a trace mule. Sagamouth's mouth continued its feeble movements. They halted behind a silk cotton tree. Mathias swung the axe in long, measured strokes against the chest. The sounds echoed deep into the woods. The heavy blows ricocheted over the door. Now and then he stopped to inspect the shallow indentations. The brass handle had fallen off, the dial long warped under the punishing blows. Yet the door remained sealed. They persevered, taking turns with the sledge hammer and the crowbar, until Mathias, bringing the heavy hammer from high overhead, struck the chest with such force that they heard a loud cracking noise.

Instantly they sprang forward, their eager hands reached out for the door. Three pairs of hands churned inside the chest, as their eyes opened in anticipation. Then Sagamouth withdrew exclaiming, " Empty."

"Christ, you mean the damn thing en't have a cent, boy."

"All dis damn trouble," Boyo said.

Mathias stood up wearily and looked at the others, his arms sore and wet, as he whispered, "Dat damn Chinese smart like hell! Ah never cud believe it. You mean he move out all de damn money, boy?"

Sagamouth's dribbling stopped. Boyo looked up at the sky.

One day, some three months afterwards, when the notorious episode was almost forgotten in the little village and the blue police van had long completed its trips to Assam's on investigation, Sagamouth came into Assam's shop. He stood at the counter and called for a pound of saltbeef. There was no one in the shop except for a well-dressed man. A briefcase was on the counter and he was busily scribbling on a pad.

"Yes, please sign on this, Mr. Assam," the man said in his mellow voice. Assam, spectacles tied to his ear with a piece of flour-bag string, leant over the counter and scrawled on the pad.

"Have everything dong, Mister Blong?"

"Yes, all that you have told me," Mr. Brown replied. "$1,000 in US, $15,000 in Canadian and $2,100 in TT cash. $89 in silver and that solid gold chain from China. But as I said, I'm not sure that the company will pay the foreign money."

Assam placed a large brown paper bag containing two bottles of rum on the counter before Mr. Brown.

"Well, check all in TT dollars then," Assam said, taking out another brown bag from below the counter.

Mr. Brown smiled and pointed to the last item on the list. "Ah — that is the iron chest, Mr. Assam. The company will pay you the $8,000 you have claimed."

"Yes, sah," Assam said smiling, "velly goot," his eyes two narrow slits behind thick lenses.

Sagamouth stood dumb, rooted in front of the counter, unmoving, as he listened to the conversation. His lips had suddenly lost all sense of movement. They hung droopily over the counter, nearly falling into the shop-scale pan.

# Austin Clarke

## *The Man*

The man passes the five open doors on two floors that shut as he passes, moving slowly in the dark, humid rooming house. Slowly, pausing every few feet, almost on every other step, he climbs like a man at the end of a double shift in a noisy factory, burdened down also by the weight of time spent on his feet, and by the more obvious weight of his clothes on his fat body, clothes that were seldom cleaned and changed. Heavy with the smell of his body and the weight of paper which he carries with him, in all nine pockets of trousers and jacket and one in his shirt, he climbs, leaving behind an acrid smell of his presence in the already odorous house.

When he first moved into this house, to live in the third-floor room, the landlady was a young wife. She is widowed now, and past sixty. The man smells like the oldness of the house. It is a smell like that which comes off fishermen when they come home from the rum shop after returning from the deep sea. And sometimes, especially in the evening, when the man comes home, the smell stings you and makes you turn your head, as your nostril receives a tingling sensation.

The man ascends the stairs. Old cooking rises and you think you can touch it on walls that have four coats of paint on them, put there by four different previous owners of the house. Or in four moods of decoration. The man pauses again. He inhales. He puts his hands on his hips. Makes a noise of regained strength and determination. And climbs again.

The man is dressed in a suit. The jacket is from a time when shoulders were worn wide and tailored broad. His shoulders are padded high, as his pockets are padded wide by the letters and the pieces of paper with notes on them, and clippings from the *Globe and Mail*, and envelopes with scribbling on them: addresses and telephone numbers. And the printed words he carries in his ten pockets make him look stuffed and overweight and important, and also like a man older than he really is. His hips are like those of a woman who has not always followed her diet to reduce. He meticulously puts on the same suit every day, as he has done for years. He is a man of some order and orderliness. His shirt was once white. He wears only shirts that were white when they were bought. He buys them second-hand from the bins of the Goodwill store on Jarvis Street and wears them until they turn grey. He changes them only when they are too soiled to be worn another day; and then he buys another one from the same large picked-over bins of the Goodwill store.

He washes his trousers in a yellow plastic pail only if a stain is too conspicuous, and presses them under his mattress; and he puts them on before they are completely dry. He walks most of the day, and at eight each night he sits at his stiff, wooden, sturdy-legged table writing letters to men and women all over the world who have distinguished themselves in politics, in government and in universities.

He lives as a bat. Secret and self-assured and self-contained as an island, high above the others in the rooming house; cut off from people, sitting and writing his important personal letters, or reading, or listening to classical music on the radio and the news on shortwave until three or four in the morning. And when morning comes, at eight o'clock he hits the streets, walking in the same two square miles from his home, rummaging through libraries for British and American newspapers, for new words and ideas for letters; then along Bloor Street, Jarvis Street, College Street, and he completes the perimeter at Bathurst Street. His room is the centre of gravity from which he is spilled out at eight each morning in all temperatures and weather, and from which he wanders no farther than these two square miles.

The man used to work as a mover with Maislin Transport in Montreal. Most of the workers came from Quebec and spoke French better than they spoke English. And one day he and a young man dressed in jeans and a red-and-black checkered shirt, resembling a man ready for the woods of lumberjacks and tall trees, were lifting a refrigerator that had two doors; and the man said "Left." He misunderstood the man's English and began to turn left through the small apartment door. He turned old suddenly. His back went out, as the saying goes. And he developed "goadies," a swelling of the testicles so large that they can never be hidden beneath the most restraining jockstrap. That was the end of his moving career.

This former animal of a man, who could lift the heaviest stove if only he was given the correct word, was now a shadow of his former muscle and sinews, with sore back and callused hands, moving slowly through a literary life, with the assistance of a private pension from Maislin Transport. He has become a different kind of animal now, prowling during the daytime through shelves of books in stores and in libraries, and visiting slight acquaintances as if they were friends whenever he smelled a drink or a meal; and attending public functions.

His pension cheque came every month at the same time, written in too much French for the rude bank teller, who said each time he presented it, even after two years, "Do you have some *identification?*"

He used to be sociable. He would nod his head to strangers, flick his eyes on the legs of women and at the faces of foreign-language men on College Street, all the way west of Spadina Avenue. He would even stop to ask for a light, and once or twice for a cigarette, and become confused in phrase-book phrases of easy, conversational Greek, Portuguese and Italian.

Until one evening. He was walking on a shaded street in Forest Hill Village when a policeman looked through the window of his yellow cruiser, stopped him in his wandering tracks and said, "What the hell're you doing up here, *boy?*" He had been walking and stopping, unsure along this street, looking at every mansion which seemed larger than the one before, when he heard the brutal voice. "Git in! Git your black ass in here!"

The policeman threw open the rear door of the cruiser. The man looked behind him, expecting to see a delinquent teenager who had earned the policeman's raw hostility. The man was stunned. There was no other person on the street. But somehow he made the effort to walk to the cruiser. The door was slammed behind him. The policeman talked on a stuttering radio and used figures and numbers instead of words, and the man became alarmed at the policeman's mathematical illiteracy. And then the cruiser sped off, scorching the peace of Forest Hill, burning rubber on its shaded quiet streets.

The cruiser stopped somewhere in the suburbs. He thought he saw Don Mills on a sign post. It stopped here, with the same temperamental disposition as it had stopped the first time in Forest Hill Village. The policeman made no further conversation of numerals and figures with the radio. He merely said,"*Git!*" The man was put out three miles from any street or intersection that he knew.

It was soon after this that he became violent. He made three pillows into the form of a man. He found a second-hand tunic and a pair of trousers that had a red stripe in them, and a hat that had a yellow band instead of a red one, and he dressed up the pillows and transformed them into a dummy of a policeman. And each morning at seven when he woke up, and late at night before he went to bed, after he washed out his mouth with salt water, he kicked the "policeman" twice — once in the flat feathery section where a man's testicles would be, and again at the back of the pillow in the dummy's ass. His hatred did not disappear with the blows. But soon he forgot about the effigy and the policeman.

Today he had been roaming the streets, like every day, tearing pieces of information from the *Globe and Mail* he took from a secretary's basket at the CBC, from *Saturday Night* and *Canadian Forum* magazines. And the moment he reached his attic room, he would begin to compose letters to great man and women around the world, inspired by the bits of information be had gathered.

And now, as he climbs, the doors of the roomers on each floor close as he passes, like an evil wind. But they close too late, for his scent and the wind of his presence have already touched them.

With each separation and denial, he is left alone in the dim light to which he is accustomed, and in the dust on the stairs; and he guides his hand along the shining bannister, the same sheen as the wallpaper, stained with the smells and specks of cooking. He walks slowly because the linoleum on the stairs is shiny too, and dangerous and tricky under the feet.

Now, on his last flight to his room for the night, his strength seems to leave his body, and he pauses and rests his hands, one on the bannister and the other on his right hip.

The cheque from Montreal will arrive tomorrow.

He feels the bulkiness of the paper in his pockets, and the weight of his poverty in this country he never grew to love. There was more love in Barbados. On many a hot afternoon, he used to watch his grandfather rest his callused hand on his hip as he stood in a field of endless potatoes, a field so large and quiet and cruel that he thought he was alone in the measureless sea of green waves, and not on a plantation. Alone perhaps now too, in the village, in the country, because of his unending work of bending his back to pull up the roots, and returning home when everyone else is long in bed.

And now he, the grandson, not really concerned with that stained ancestry, not really comparing himself with his grandfather, stands for a breath-catching moment on this landing in this house in which he is a stranger. He regards his room as the country. It is strange and familiar. It is foreign, yet it is home. It is dirty. And at the first signs of summer and warmth, he would go down on his hands and knees in what would have been an unmanly act and scrub the small space outside his door, and the four or five steps he had to climb to reach it. He would drop soap into the water, and still the space around the door remained dirty.

The house had passed that stage when it could be cleaned. It had grown old like a human body. And not even ambition and cleanliness could purify it of this scent. It could be cleaned only by burning. But he had become accustomed to the dirt, as he was accustomed to the thought of burning. In the same way, he had become accustomed to the small room which bulged, like his ten pockets, with the possessions of his strange literary life.

He is strong again. Enough to climb the last three or four steps and take out his keys on the shining ring of silver, after putting down the plastic bag of four items he had bought through the express check-out of Dominion around the corner, and then the collection of newspapers — two morning and two afternoon and two evening editions. He flips each key over, and it makes a dim somersault, until he reaches the last key on the ring which he knows has to be the key he's looking for.

Under the naked light bulb he had opened and shut, locked and unlocked this same blue-painted door when it was painted green and red and black, so many times that he thought he was becoming colour-blind. But he could have picked out the key even if he was blind; for it was the only key in the bunch which had the shape of the fleur de lys at its head. He went through all the keys on the ring in a kind of elimination process. It was his own private joke. A ritual for taking up time.

He spent time as if he thought it would not end: walking along College Street and Spadina Avenue when he was not thinking of letters to be written; looking at the clusters of men and women from different countries at the corner of Bathurst and Bloor; at the men passing their eyes slowly over the breasts and backsides of the women; at the women shopping at Dominion and the open-air stalls, or amongst the fibres of cheap materials and dresses, not quite pure silk, not one hundred percent cotton, which they tore as they searched for and tore from each other's hands to get at cheaper prices than those advertised at Honest Ed's bargain store. And he would watch how these women expressed satisfaction with their purchases in their halting new English.

And now in the last few months, along those streets he had walked and known, all of a sudden the names on stores and the signs on posts appeared in the hieroglyphics of Chinese. Or Japanese? He no longer felt safe, tumbling in the warmth and shouts of a washing machine in a public laundromat in this technicoloured new world of strangers.

He had loved those warm months and those warm people before their names and homes were written in signs. They were real until someone turned them into Chinese characters which he could not read. And he spent the warm months of summer writing letters to the leaders of the world, in the hope of getting back a reply, no matter how short or impersonal, with their signatures, which he intended to sell to the highest bidder.

He came from a colony, a country and a culture where the written word spelled freedom. An island where the firm touch of the pen on paper meant freedom. Where the pen gripped firmly in the hand was sturdier than a soldier holding a gun, and which meant liberation. And the appearance of words on paper, the meaning and transformation they gave to the paper, and the way they rendered the paper priceless, meant that he could now escape permanently from the profuse sweat and the sharp smell of perspiration on the old khaki trousers and the thick-smelling flannel worn next to the skin. This sweat was the uniform, and had been the profession of poor black grandfathers. Now pen and paper mean the sudden and unaccountable and miraculous disappearance from a colonial tradition where young bodies graduated from the play and games and beaches of children into the dark, steamy and bee-droning caverns and caves of warehouses in which sat white men in white drill suits and white cork hats, their white skin turning red from too much rum and too much sun, and from their too-deep appetites for food and local women. For years before this graduation, he could find himself placed like a lamp post, permanent and blissful in one job, in one spot, in one position, until perhaps a storm came, or a fierce hurricane, and felled him like the chattels of houses and spewed him into the gutter.

So he learned the power of the *word*. And kept close to it. When others filled the streets and danced in a Caribana festival and wore colours hot as summer in a new spring of life, this man remained in his isolation; and he cut himself off from those frivolous, ordinary pleasures of life that had surrounded his streets for years, just as the immigrants surrounded the open-air Kensington Market. He thought and lived and expressed himself in this hermitage of solitary joy, writing letters to President de Gaulle, President Carter, Willy Brandt (whose name he never learned to spell), to Mao Tse Tung, Dr. Martin Luther King and Prime Minister Indira Gandhi.

The few acquaintances he called friends and met for drinks on the eighteenth-floor bar of the Park Plaza Hotel, and those he visited and talked with and drank with in their homes, all thought he was mad. And perhaps he was mad. Perhaps his obsession with the word had sent him off.

The persons to whom he wrote were all unknown to him. He did not care for their politics or their talent. But he made a fortune out of time spent in addressing them. It was an international intrusion on their serious lives: *Dear Prime Minister, I saw your name and picture in the Toronto Globe and Mail this morning. I must say I was most impressed by some of the things you have said. You are one of the most indispensable personages in this western world. This western world would come to its end of influence were it not for you. You and you alone can save it and save us. Long may you have this power. Yours very sincerely, William Jefferson.*

"Look what I pulled off!" he told Alonzo. He held the glass of cold beer bought for him on the account of friendship, and a smile came to his face. The smile was the smile of literary success. He had just promised Alonzo that he would defray all his loans with the sale of his private correspondence. A smile came to Alonzo's face. It was the smile of accepted social indebtedness. "The university would just *love* to get its hands on this!" *This* was the reply from the Prime Minister: a plain white post card on which was written, *Thank you very much, Mr. Jefferson, for your thoughtfulness.*

He would charge the university one hundred dollars for the reply from Prime Minister Gandhi. Perhaps he could sell them his entire correspondence! Why not? Even publish them in *The Private Correspondence of William Jefferson with the Great Men and Great Women of the Twentieth Century.*

Alonzo did not know whether to continue smiling or laugh right out. He could not decide if his friend was slightly off the head. He needed more proof. The letter from Mrs. Gandhi, which he did not show, could supply the proof. But it was a man's private business, a man's private correspondence; and not even the postman who delivered it had the right to see it. If this correspondence went on, Alonzo thought, who knows, perhaps one day he may be drinking beer and associating with a man of great fame, a famous man of letters, hounded by universities to get a glimpse of this correspondence. . . .

While the man is trying to unlock his door, the urge overtakes him. The keyhole had not answered the key. And the urge to pee swells over his body like a high wave. This urge would overcome him almost always when a porcelain oval hole was not immediately available. It would take him into its grip and turn his entire body into a cramping, stuttering muscle-bound fist. Always on the wrong side of the street, too.

He was on Bloor Street once, in that stretch of shops and stores and restaurants where women wear furs and carry merchandise in shopping bags with Creeds and Holt Renfrew and Birks proclaimed on them, where the restaurants look like country clubs and the shops like chapels and banks, where he could not get the nerve to enter the stained-glass door with heraldry on it, jerk a tense glance in *that* direction and receive the direction to *there* or get a sign to show him the complicated carpeted route to *washrooms* printed on a brass plate. Not dressed the way he was. Not without giving some explanation. Not without alarming the waitresses dressed more like nurses and the waiters who looked like fashion models.

Once he dashed into Holt Renfrew. It was the last desperate haven. The water was heavy on his nerves, on his bladder. His eyes were red and watery. He barely had strength to speak his wish. Experience with this urge had cautioned him, as he stood before the glass case of ladies' silk underwear, that to open his mouth at that moment, when the association of this urge with ladies' panties was in full view, meant a relaxation of his grip on the water inside him. Then it would pour out onto the carpeted floor of Persian silence, perhaps even dribble onto the feet of the young clerk whose legs he could see beneath the thinness of her almost transparent dress.

The young woman saw his stiffness and posture, and with a smile and a wave, showed him the nearest haven. It had *Employees Only* inscribed on the shining brass. When he was finished, he could not move immediately. The loss of weight and water was like the loss of energy. "Have a good day, sir!" Her smile was brighter then.

He was still outside his room. The key was still in the hole. He did not have the strength to go down two flights of stairs to the second-floor bathroom beside the room of the woman who lived on welfare.

To have to go down now, with this weight making his head heavier, did something with his hand and the key turned.

He was safe inside his room. Relieved and safe. He did it in the pail. He keeps this pail in a corner, under the table, on which is a two-ringed hot plate. In times of urgency, he uses it, and in times of laziness and late at night. He adds soap flakes to the steaming liquid to hide its smell and composition, and when he carries the plastic pail down, the woman on welfare cannot smell or detect his business. He relishes his privacy.

Sometimes he has no flakes of soap, so he drops a pair of soiled underwear into the urine and walks with it, pretending there is no smell; and if the coast is clear, he bolts the lock on the bathroom door and does his business and laundry like a man hiding from his superstition.

He had heard that a famous Indian politician used to drink his own pee. And it overcame him.

He is safe inside his room. He breathes more easily now. He is home. His room relaxes him. It is like a library of a man obsessed with books and eccentric about the majesty of books.

Red building blocks which he stole two at a time are placed in fours at each end of the white-painted three-ply shelves. And the shelves end, as a scaffold should, at the end of available space, the ceiling. The same construction occupies all four walls. There are books of all sizes, all topics, all tastes.

The space between the bottom shelf and the floor is crammed with newspapers which are now yellow. There are magazines with their backs missing through frequent use. Each new magazine goes into the space which can get no larger. Statements of great political and international significance, the photograph of a man or a woman to be written to, are torn out from their sources and pinned to the three-ply shelves with common pins; and there are framed photographs of writers whom this man regards as the great writers of the world. No one else has heard of them.

He has collected relics of his daily passage throughout the city, in the same two square miles, not going beyond this perimeter. He has never again ventured into that part of the suburbs where the policeman had picked him up. Among his relics are jars and bottles, and one beautiful piece of pottery that looks as if it had been unearthed in an archaeological digging somewhere in the distant world. It is brown and has a mark like antiquity around its swelling girth; and where it stands on an old trunk that could have belonged to a sea captain, or to an immigrant from Europe or the West Indies, large enough to transport memories and possessions from a poorer life to this new country, this little brown jug gives age and seriousness to the other useless but priceless pieces in his room.

In all the jars and bottles, and in this brown "antique" jug, are dried branches of trees, flowers, sprigs and brambles. Dead beyond recognition.

The man collects dead things. Leaves and brambles and flowers and twigs. And he must like this death in things because there is nothing that lives in his room. Nothing but the man himself. He does not see them as dead things, or as meaning death.

He has five clocks. They are all miraculously set at the same, precise time, with not a second's difference. Every morning, using the time on the CBC radio as his standard and barometer, he checks and re-checks each of his five clocks; and when this is done, he sits on his old-fashioned, large and comfortable couch, upholstered in green velvet that now has patches like sores in the coat of a dog, with knobs of dull mahogany at the ends where the fingers touch, or rest, or agitate (if he is writing or thinking about a letter to an important personage in the world). He would sit here, now that he has set his time, and listen to the ticking, secure ordering of the meaning of time; pretending he is back home in the island that consumes time, where all the clocks ticked at various dispositions and carried different times. Canada has taught him important discipline. And he has learned about time. He has learned always to be *in* time.

Paper bags are stuffed between books, folded in their original creases and placed there, anxious for when they can be used a second time. A cupboard in the room is used as a clothes closet, a pantry and a storeroom. It contains more paper bags of all sizes, of all origins, from all supermarkets; but most are from Dominion. They are tied and made snug and tidy by elastic bands whose first use he has obviously forgotten. On the bottom shelf of the cupboard are plastic bags imprinted with barely visible names of stores and shops, folded in a new improvised crease and placed into a large brown paper bag.

All this time, he is walking the four short lengths of floor bordered by his books, stopping in front of one shelf, running his fingers absentmindedly over the titles of books. The linoleum floor is punctuated by the nails in his shoes that walk up and down, late into the night of thoughtfulness, of worrying about a correct address or a correct salutation. Now he stands beside a large wooden table made by immigrants or early settlers on farms, in the style of large sturdy legs the size and shape of their own husky peasant form. This table does not move. It cannot move. On it he has storeroomed his food and his drinks, his "eatables and drinkables," and it functions as his pantry of dishes and pots and pans. At one end of the table is the gas hot plate, the only implement for cooking that is allowed in this illegally-small living space.

On the hot plate is a shining aluminium saucepan battered around its girth by temper, hunger and burned rice.

He uncovers the saucepan. The food is old. Its age, two or three days, has thickened its smell, and makes it look like wet cement. The swollen black-eyed peas sit permanently among hunks of pig tails. He is hungry all of a sudden. These two urges, peeing and eating, come upon him without notice and with no regard to the last time he has eaten or peed. So he digs a "pot spoon" into the heart of the thick drying cement of food and uproots the swollen hunks of pig tails whose oily taste brings water and nostalgia to his eyes, and he half shuts his eyes to eat the first mouthful.

He replaces the lid. He puts the "pot spoon" between the saucepan rim and the lid, and pats the battered side of the saucepan the way a trainer would pat a horse that has just won on a long-shot bet.

He takes off his jacket. It is two sizes too large. Then he takes off his red woollen sweater, and another one of cotton, and long-sleeved; and then a third, grey, long-sleeved, round-necked and marked *Property of the Athletic Department, University of Toronto.*

He is a man of words, and the printed claim of ownership on his third pullover never ceases to amaze and impress him.

Stripped now of his clothes, he is left in a pair of grey long johns. And it is in these that he walks about the wordy room, ruminating as he struggles late into the night to compose the correct arrangement of words that would bring him replies from the pens of the great. Sometimes his own words do not flow as easily as he would wish. And this literary constipation aborts the urge to pee. At such times he runs to his Javex box, where he keeps all the replies he has ever received. He reads them now, praying for an easier movement of words from the bowels of his brain.

*Dear Mr. Jefferson, Thank you for your letter.*

That was all from one great personage, But it was good enough. It was a reply. And an official one at that. A rubber stamp of the signature tells you of the disinterest or the thick appointment book of the sender, that perhaps the sender does not understand the archival significance of the letter he has received from Mr. William Jefferson.

*This is to acknowledge receipt of your letter.*

Another reply from a great personage. Even the stamp, print and address are reproductions of the original. But the man believes that some value lies even in this impersonal reply.

*Dear Mr. Jefferson, We are very glad to know that, as a Barbadian, you have introduced us to the archives of the University of Toronto, which is considering maintaining a Barbados collection. We wish you every success in your significant venture.*

This is his most valuable letter. It is signed by someone who lives! A human hand has signed it. But he cannot untangle the name from its spidery script. He does not know who has replied to him. For typed beneath the script is only the person's official position: *Secretary.*

He understands more than any other living person the archival importance of these letters. And he treasures them within a vast imagination of large expectations, in this large brown box which contained Javex for bleaching clothes before it fell into his possession.

He has been nervous all week. And this nervousness erupted in strong urges to pee, strong and strange even for his weak bladder. The nervousness was linked to the price of his collection. This afternoon he had spoken to someone at the university. Over the telephone the voice told him, "Of course! Of course, Mr. Jefferson. We'll be interested in seeing your collection." It was a polite reply, like the written ones in his Javex box. But as a man obsessed by his relics, who attaches great significance to their esoteric value, he inflates that significance. He is also a man who would read an offer to purchase in a polite reply from the university. He is a man who hears more words than those that are spoken.

He starts to count his fortune. This letter to him from a living Prime Minister would be the basis of his fortune. His friend Alonzo would get a free round of beer at the Park Plaza roof bar. He would pay his rent six months in advance. He would have more time to spend on his private correspondence with the great men and women of the world.

He holds the Prime Minister's letter in his hand and examines the almost invisible water marks on which it is typed. He studies the quality of the official stationery made in Britain and used by the West Indies, and compares it to that of Canada and the United States. He decides that the British and West Indies knew more about prestigious stationery. He continues to feel the paper between big thumb and two adjoining fingers, rubbing and rubbing and feeling a kind of orgasm coming on; and in this trance, he reads another letter.

*Dear Mr. Jefferson, Thank you for your kind and thoughtful letter. Yours, Prime Minister's Office.*

Above this line, "Margaret Thatcher" is stamped in fading ink. Still, it is a mark on history; "a first" from a poor woman whom history had singled out to be great.

When he is in his creative mood, he moves like a man afraid to cause commotion in a room in which he is a guest, like a man moving amongst bric-a-brac, priceless mementos of glass and china and silver locked in a glass cabinet. He moves about his room soundlessly, preparing his writing materials and deepening his mood for writing.

His stationery is personalized. *William Jefferson, Esquire* is printed in bold letters at the top of the blue page. And below that, his address. He writes with a fountain pen. And when he fills it from the bottle of black ink, he always smiles when the pen makes its sucking noise. This sucking noise takes him back years to another room in another country when he formed his first letters. And he likes the bottle that contains the ink. It has a white label, with a squeezed circle like an alert eye; and through this eye, through the middle of this eye, is an arrow which pierces it. *Parker super quink ink. Permanent black.* It suggests strength and longevity. It is like his life: determined and traditional, poised outside the mainstream but fixed in habit and custom. Whenever he uses this fountain pen, his index finger and the finger next to that, and his thumb, bear the verdict and the evidence of this permanent blackness. This *noire.* He sometimes wishes that he could use the language of Frenchmen who slip words and the sounds of those words over their tongues like raw oysters going down the throat!

"What a remarkable use of the tongue the French have! That back of the throat sensation!" he told Alonzo one afternoon, but in such a way as if he were speaking to the entire room in the Park Plaza Hotel bar.

*Noire.*

Many years ago, in 1955, the minute his feet touched French soil at Dorval in Quebec, the first greeting he heard was "*Noire!*" The sound held him in its grip, and changed his view of ordinary things, and made him fastidious and proper and suspicious. The only word he retained was *noire.* It was not a new word to him. For years even before that greeting, and in Barbados on a Sunday afternoon after the heavy midday meal, he used to sit at the back door looking out onto the cackling of hens, one of which he had eaten earlier, inhaling with the freshness of stomach and glorious weather the strong smell of Nugget shoe polish as he lathered it on his shoes and on his father's shoes and his mother's shoes and his grandfather's shoes. So he had already dipped his hands into *noire* long before Canada.

He had known *noire* for years. But no one had addressed him as *noire.*

He likes the *noire* of the ink he uses, as he liked the *noire* in the Nugget which gave his shoes longer life and made them immortal and left its proud, industrious and indelible stain on his fingers.

Tomorrow the University of Toronto is coming to buy his papers. He runs his hands over his letters in the Javex box, hundreds of them, and thinks of money and certified cheques. He empties all his pockets and puts the papers on the table. He picks up each piece like a man picking flesh from a carcass of bones. Who should he write to tonight?

The silent books around him, their words encased in covers, do not offer advice. But he knows what they would answer. He finds it difficult to concentrate. Tomorrow is too near. The money from his papers, cash or certified cheque, is too close at hand. He spends time spending it in his mind. And the things contained in tomorrow, like the things contained in his Javex box, have at last delivered him, just as his articulate use of the pen confirmed the value of the word and delivered him from the raving crowds of new immigrants. He has gained peace and a respectable distance from those aggressive men and women because of his use of the word.

"Should I write to the President of Yale University?"

The books, thick in their shelves around him, and few of which he has read from cover to cover, all these books remain uncommunicative and have no words of advice.

"Should I write to President Reagan?"

His five electric clocks continue to keep constant time, and in their regulated determination, refuse to disclose a tick of assistance.

"The Prime Minister of Barbados?"

Barbados is no longer home. Home, he had told Alonzo ten years ago, "is where I pee and eat and write."

He gets up and turns on the flame of the hot plate under the saucepan. "While the grass is growing, the horse is starving," he tells the saucepan. He smiles at his own wisdom. The heat makes the saucepan crackle. "While the grass is growing . . ." The thin saucepan makes a smothered crackling sound. The hot plate seems to be melting the coagulated black-eyed peas and rice and pig tails. The hot plate is crackling as if it is intent upon melting the cheap alloy of the saucepan and turning the meal into soft hot lead, and then spreading its flame over the letters on the table, and then the table itself, and then the room. He lowers the flame.

"Fire cleans everything," he tells the hot plate. The saucepan stops laughing with the heat. His meal has settled down to being re-cooked.

But he is soon smelling things. The nostalgia of food and the perspiration from his mother's forehead as she cooked the food, and the strong, rich smell of pork. He smells also the lasting wetness of flannel shirts worn in the fields back on the small island.

He gets accustomed to these smells. And he thinks again of new correspondence since all these on the table before him would be gone by tomorrow, sold, archived among other literary riches. A hand-rubbing enthusiasm and contentment brings a smile to his face.

"I'll write the Prime Minister of Barbados!"

The smell comes up again. With the help of the smell, he is back on the small island, witnessing spires of blue smoke pouring out from each small castle of patched tin and rotting wood where his village stood. He can hear the waves and the turbulent sea, so much like the turbulence of water he boiled in the same thin-skin saucepan to make tea. As he thinks back, his eyes pass over used tea bags spread in disarray, an action caught in the midst of an important letter when he would sometimes drop a used tea bag into the yellow plastic pail.

*Dear Prime Minister . . .*

He reaches over to the hot plate and raises the flame. He sees it change from yellow to blue, and smiles. "The horse is starving . . ."

*Certain important universities have asked me to act as a liaison to encourage you to submit your . . .*

The fragile aluminium saucepan is losing its battle in the heat of warming the food. But it is the smell. The smell takes his mind off the letter, and off the great sums of money, cash and certified cheques. He is a boy again, running home from school, colliding with palings and dogs and the rising smells of boiled pork reddened in tomatoes and bubbling over rice like the thick tar which the road workers poured over a raw road under construction.

He can taste his country now. Clearly. And see the face of the Prime Minister, greedy to make a name for himself in a foreign institution of higher learning, and obtain foreign currency for his foreign account.

*. . . I have lived a solitary life, apart from the demonstrations and protests of the mainstream of immigrants. I have become a different man. A man of letters. I am more concerned with cultural things, radio, books and libraries, than with reports . . .*

Something is wrong with his pen. The flow is clogged and constricted, just like when he's caught with his pants up in a sudden urge to pee, and having forced it inwards, cannot get it outwards. And he gets up and heads downstairs. Just as he's moving away from his door, still on the first three or four steps going down, he turns back. "My pen is my penis," he tells the door.

He picks up the yellow plastic pail. He throws a shirt and underwear into the brown stagnant water. It looks like stale beer. Before he goes through the door again, he picks up the unfinished letter to the Prime Minister of Barbados, and in his long johns, armed with pail and paper, he creeps out.

The stairs are still dim. And he smiles. He moves down slowly, hoping that when he reaches the second floor the woman on welfare who occupies the toilet longer than any other tenant would not be there.

The saucepan has now begun to boil, although there are more solids than liquids within its thin frame. Popcorn comes into his mind. He doesn't even eat popcorn! He doesn't even go to the movies! The saucepan is turning red at the bottom. If he was in his room, he could not tell where the saucepan's bottom began and where the ring of the hot plate ended.

He thinks of roast corn as he reaches the closed door of the only bathroom in the house. He stands. He listens. He smells. He inhales. And he exhales. He puts his hand on the door and pushes gently, and the door opens with a small creak. He stands motionless, alarmed to see that the bathroom is indeed empty. Where is the woman on welfare?

. . . at night, back home, in the crop season when the sugar canes are cut and harvested, they burn the corn over coals. . . .

Right then, above his head, the saucepan explodes. He doesn't hear it. The black-eyed peas and rice burst out, pelting the cover before it, and the table top is splattered like careless punctuation marks. It falls on his fine blue stationery.

The explosion comes just as he holds the yellow pail at a tilt, over the growling toilet bowl. In the same hand as the pail is the unfinished letter. The urine is flowing into the bowl and he stands thinking, when he sees the first clouds of smoke crawling down the stairs, past the open bathroom door.

The smoke becomes heavier and makes tears come into his eyes. He is crying and passing his hands in front of his face, trying to clear a passage from the second floor, through the thickening smoke rising like high waves. Up and up he goes, no faster than when he entered the house that afternoon, struggling through the smoke until he reaches the steps in front of his door. And as he gets there, it seems as if all the books, all the letters, all the bags of plastic and paper shout at once in an even greater explosion.

Before he can get downstairs to call for help from the woman on welfare, he thinks he hears all five of his clocks alarming. And then, in the way a man who has been struck by a deadening blow waits for the second one to land, he stands, expecting the five clocks to do something else. It is then that he hears one clock striking the hour. He counts aloud until he reaches eight, and then he refuses to count any longer.

# Saros Cowasjee

## *His Father's Medals*

Ramu sat on the doorstep of his hut in a far corner of Thakur Madan Singh's compound, a good distance away from the quarters of the other servants better placed in life than himself. He spat on the silver medal and with the bottom edge of his shirt rubbed it hard till it shone with a dull lustre. "That's better," he said, dropping it gently into his shirt pocket and pulling out the other two—these of bronze. He again spat and polished them—in the same manner. If I had only dug my little finger in the polish on the lavatory shelf, he thought, these would have glittered like gold. And nobody would have suspected, for what has a sweeper boy to do with polish?

Three medals were all that his father, Ramji Lal, had left him. Dying, the medals still on his famished chest, he fought to keep back his last breath—not that life had much to give, but that death would take even the little he had. Ramji Lal died and the prized proof of a lifetime's devotion to duty passed on to Ramu, his only child. Ramu looked fondly at the medals. They were no mere tokens of affection—a link between a dead father and a living son—but a flaming ideal towards which he must strive. He pressed them to his heart and tears welled up in his eyes; his dear, dear father had left them in his care.

Three medals! The two large ones of bronze from the British Government for cleaning the officers' latrines through the Burma Campaign, and the little silver one from the Colonel himself as a mark of appreciation that they were well cleaned. He looked at the medals intently. Who was this bald, point-bearded man with the face of a butcher, waging wars and distributing medals? His father had often talked of him—a great king who ruled the world and did justice to all. Justice to all? What justice was done to his father? Two ribbons to decorate his breast while the heart beneath was starved of blood. Ah, but that was being too hard on the king. What could a king do but sit on a golden seat and empty his bowels in a silver pot? A silver pot—glistening like his little medal. How he would love to be a king's sweeper and handle silver pots!

Ramu shook himself. He was demanding too much from life. What God had given was good enough: it was not everybody who became a sweeper in the household of Thakur Madan Singh, BA. There were Goodan, Murari, Sona and Ravi and a horde of others sweeping the public streets from morning to night and envying him his honoured position.

The back door of the palatial house facing Ramu's quarters was flung open and Sultan Singh, the cook, clad in his yellow turban, called out: "Ramu! O Ramu! Come here and clean this."

Ramu dropped the medals in his pocket, jumped down the single step that led to his hut, and hurried towards the latrines. He lifted the lids off the commodes and expertly pulled out the pots. It was for the eleventh time this morning that he was cleaning them; yesterday he had had to attend to them some sixteen times, though only five people lived in this capacious house. God! What do they eat that they must go some twenty times a day? But it was good that they frequented the latrines, for were they habituated like the poor how could he have found full-time employment in a respectable home? As he gracefully carried the pots, his head thrown back to avoid the stink, he could not help musing that at least in this there was no difference between rich and poor except in its frequency; that whatever delicacies the rich might relish, it must come down to this, this that he carried at arm's length, and that kept him at arm's length from his fellow men.

Having done a good job, he sat down again on the doorstep. Once a sweeper, always a sweeper. He had given up all attempts to break through the social barrier. His life and his future must be decided by his own class, the Untouchable. Nothing could ever break through the rigid class system, no, not even love. There stood Kamala, now engaged to a lorry driver's son. He had loved her passionately, would have done anything to win her, but she had asked of him the impossible — to forget her. As children they had played together, planned together. He was not then a sweeper's son nor she a Rajput's daughter. But as Kamala grew to maidenhood, under the vigilance of her father Sultan Singh, and the providential care of Thakur Madan Singh, dignity and distance silenced her feeble pulse of love.

He remembered how he had once playfully caught her hand and the fear that had come into her eyes. "Leave me," she had begged. "Oh, let me go!" He had pulled back his hand, to see her rush back to her quarters. Through the half-open door he had seen her washing herself clean. He had turned his face aside, the humiliation sticking in his throat: he was an Untouchable. A sweeper holding the hand of a

Rajput's daughter! Did you ever hear of that?

No, he had never heard. He had given up all thought of possessing her, all thought and those rash promises of boyhood without a struggle. Love could live on, just as hope lives on, deep in the core of the poor man's heart. He would keep her memory alive, would keep the twisted hairpin and the broken bangles she had dropped into the litter bin close to his heart. And he would give her something: a little token that would remind her of Ramu and tell her that even a sweeper boy has a heart. A sweeper boy has a heart! Did you hear that?

A pathetic smile dissolved into anguish on his lips as he stood up and put his hands into the loose, patched trousers, which had once belonged to Thakur Madan Singh. He pulled out all the bits of copper and added them up. They made a little over two rupees. Enough to buy a handsome present, he said. If I run short I can sell off one of my father's medals. No, he would never sell his dear father's medals: not for love, not for this world — for what are love and a world to a sweeper boy?

He sauntered till he came to the market. He walked on, unable to decide where he should take his first peep. On the pavement Shivaji, notorious for his prices, had spread his fancy goods. He thought he could take a look; it would give him some idea of the things he could buy for Kamala. He came to the shop and stood in the midst of the little group that was examining the goods. His eager, boyish face beamed with excitement as he viewed the glittering array of bangles, hairpins, rings, bead necklaces, mirrors, till it came to rest on a pair of brilliant anklets. Shining silver anklets! He would put them round Kamala's ankles with his own hands, would give just a little press to her delicate feet; she would not object to that, no, not as long as he kept to her feet. But, ah, they must be expensive. Silver anklets cost a lot of money. Yet sometimes they are sold cheap, sometimes when they are false, sometimes when they are stolen. . . .

"How much do you want for these?" he asked hesitantly, pointing to the anklets.

"Fifteen rupees and nothing less," replied Shivaji.

Ramu stepped back. He felt as if somebody had given him a punch in the face. He turned to go.

"Wait," said Shivaji. "How much can you give?"

"I can't afford them. I don't want them," said Ramu.

"You do, you do. Give anything and take them."

Ramu blushed. "No, no."

"Can you give four rupees?" asked Shivaji, holding an anklet high to display it.

Ramu felt the weight of the copper in his pocket and taking courage said, "Two rupees."

Shivaji burst into a loud, coarse laugh. "Ha, ha, ha, ha. Silver anklets for two rupees!" And turning to the group of buyers he remarked, "Wants anklets for two rupees to put round the feet of some hussy!" Then with a malicious grin he swore at Ramu: "By God, how much do you pay her for a ride?"

The little crowd seemed to enjoy Shivaji's remarks and pressed closer to get a better view of Ramu. One from the crowd mockingly reprimanded Shivaji: "You mustn't be so hard on the poor fellow, Master. It may be for his mother!"

Burning rage gave him courage; the low jibe of Shivaji made him dare. He would teach him a lesson — and now. He looked to the left and then to the right. The street was surging with people. With one rush he snatched the anklet from Shivaji's hand and darted off to mingle in the crowd.

A hand lay on his shoulder. Two policemen tightly gripped him by the arms and stood on either side of him, while a jeering mob pressed around him.

"Move out of the way," yelled one of the policemen. "Let us take this son of a pig to the police station."

"The pimp," swore the other. "Thinks we police and justice are dead."

"That he will find out when the strap licks his bloody arse and leaves it as red as a monkey's bum," rejoined the first.

"As a monkey's bum," echoed one from the crowd. "Give him a monkey's bum. The fool is stealing in broad daylight, when nowadays it is not advisable even at night, because of our vigilant police."

The two policemen, sensing the irony in the remark, cut through the crowd and triumphantly marched away with their prey. Having got clear off the busy street, they began searching Ramu's pockets.

"Just two rupees! That's not much," said the first policeman. "What's in your shirt pocket?"

"Nothing, nothing," implored Ramu.

The second policeman dug his hand into Ramu's pocket and pulled out the medals. "Eh, where did you get these from?"

"I did not steal them, I did not steal them. They are my father's medals. Please give them back to me."

"Give them back to you, eh! Your father's medals! Where did he steal them from? Out with it, or my boot will be at your bottom. Quick."

"My father was not a thief. They were given to him for his services," wept Ramu, tears running down his cheeks.

"Services? What services? You and your father are not good enough to clean our latrines. Now march on fast," said the first policeman, hitting Ramu across the calves with his cane, "or you will find this creeping up your arse."

# Rienzi Crusz

## *Roots*

*For Cleta Marcellina Nora Serpanchy*

What the end usually demands
is something of the beginning,
and so
I conjure history from a cup
of warm Portuguese blood
from my forefathers,
black diamond eyes, charcoal hair
from my Sinhalese mothers;
the beached catamaran,
gravel voices of the fishermen,
the catch still beating like a heart
under the pelting sun;
how the pariah dogs looked urgent
with fish meal in their brains,
the children romped, sagged,
then melted into the sand.

A Portuguese captain holds
the soft brown hand of my Sinhala mother.
It's the year 1515 A.D.,
when two civilizations kissed and merged,
and I, burgher of that hot embrace,
write a poem of history
as if it were only the romance
of a lonely soldier on a crowded beach
in Southern Ceylon.

# Fred D'Aguiar

## *Home*

These days when I'm away too long,
anything I happen to clap eyes on,
that red phone box, somehow makes me
miss here like nothing I can name.

My heart performs its jazz drum solo
when the bared crow's feet on the 747
scrape down at Heathrow. H. M. Customs . . .
I'm resigned to the usual inquisition,

telling me with Surrey loam caked
on the tongue, home is always elsewhere.
I take it like an English middleweight
with a questionable chin, knowing

my passport photo's too open-faced,
haircut wrong (an afro) for the decade;
the stamp, British Citizen not bold enough
for my liking and too much for theirs.

The cockney cab driver begins chirpily
but can't or won't steer clear of race,
so rounds on Asians. I lock eyes with him
in the rearview when I say I'm one.

He settles to his task, grudgingly,
in a huffed silence. Cha! Drive man!
I have legal tender burning in my pocket
to move on, like a cross in Transylvania.

At my front door, why doesn't the lock
recognize me and budge? As I fight it,

I think intruder then see with the clarity
of a torture victim the exact detail:

in my case that extra twist necessary,
falling forward over the threshold
then mail or junk felicitations,
into a cool reception in the hall.

Grey light and close skies I love you.
Choky streets, roundabouts and streetlamps
with tires round them, I love you.
Police Officer, your boots need re-heeling.

Robin Redbreast; special request: burst
with calypso, bring the Michelin-rung worm
winding, carnival-style to the surface.
We must all sing for our suppers or else.

# Cyril Dabydeen

## *Señorita*

This Señorita from the Dominican
Republic flashes a smile;
she tells me she has attended school
in Canada, is interested in Lope de Vega
and extols the Golden Age of Spain.

I remind her of Pablo Neruda
and Nicolas Guillen,
both closer to her home.
She still smiles, professes
a dim acquaintance with the poetry

of both, talks about water imagery
in Neruda. I remind her about the latter's
fire of love, the Cuban's revolutionary
zeal. She's not impressed;
She still smiles however.

How about the poets
of the Dominican Republic?
She smiles once more. "Ah, do you
not see I have been educated
in Canada?" she protests innocently.

 "Five million people there —
surely there must be poets!"
I exclaim in silent rage.
Once more the Señorita smiles —
as bewitching as a metaphor.

## Elephants Make Good Stepladders

It isn't the same as growing up
On a different side of the tropics —

After all they are worlds apart,
Even though I've been accustomed to hearing

About India's tigers —
Not elephants.
How I wished for more than youthful
Visits to Circuses in a colonial town;

To hear a real elephant's grunt,
To watch its trunk come alive —

To climb with stepladder ease
As I am in the heart of the jungle:

This more than TV Wonderland or Disneyworld,
The trunk lifts up, lowers —

Water pours out as if from the clouds;
With Shakuntala innocence

I experience the thrill of monsoon magic
Hands folded, I contemplate the subcontinent's

Pastime flood; bending forward,
Water at my knees —

I meet the elephant eye to eye.

# David Dabydeen

## *Catching Crabs*

Ruby and me stalking savannah
Crab season with cutlass and sack like big folk.
Hiding behind stones or clumps of bush
Crabs locked knee-deep in mud mating
And Ruby seven years old feeling strange at the sex
And me horrified to pick them up
Plunge them into the darkness of bag,
So all day we scout to catch the lonesome ones
Who don't mind cooking because they got no prospect
Of family, and squelching through the mud,
Cutlass clearing bush at our feet,
We come home tired slow, weighed down with plenty
Which Ma throw live into boiling pot piece-piece.
Tonight we'll have one big happy curry feed,
We'll test out who teeth and jaw strongest
Who will grow up to be the biggest
Or who will make most terrible cannibal.

We leave behind a mess of bones and shell
And come to England and America
Where Ruby hustles in a New York tenement
And me writing poetry at Cambridge,
Death long catch Ma, the house boarded up
Breeding wasps, woodlice in its dark-sack belly:
I am afraid to walk through weed yard,
Reach the door, prise open, look,
In case the pot still bubbles magical
On the fireside, and I see Ma
Working a ladle, slow—
Limbed, crustacean-old, alone,
In case the woodsmoke and curry steam
Burn my child-eye and make it cry.

## The New Poetry

She wanted to be alone with her world, vexed
Always by his prehistoric eye,
The strange usurping tales of anthropophagi
And recitation of colonial texts.

Britannia is serviced by new machines
Humming and twinkling as they work,
The creak of mule-drawn punt or old slave feet,
The exhalation of the aborigines

Are esoteric notes in a scholar's curious book:
The new poetry quietly observes
The ways a leaf spirals neutrally to earth,
The shades of moon, the tides, the shepherd's timeless crook.

She forsook as tedious his confession,
His alien unbridgeable babble of words,
Settling comfortably on the sofa
She would turn the television on

And see confirmed the greetings beamed through space
Of natives singing by some runway,
The bone-shaped plane of fat white men and foreign aid
Met by loud spears and women jigging waist.

# Kamala Das

## *An Introduction*

I don't know politics but I know the names
Of those in power, and can repeat them like
Days of week, or names of months, beginning with
Nehru. I am Indian, very brown, born in
Malabar, I speak three languages, write in
Two, dream in one. Don't write in English, they said,
English is not your mother-tongue. Why not leave
Me alone, critics, friends, visiting cousins,
Every one of you? Why not let me speak in
Any language I like? The language I speak
Becomes mine, its distortions, its queernesses
All mine, mine alone. It is half English, half
Indian, funny perhaps, but it is honest,
It is as human as I am human, don't
You see? It voices my joys, my longings, my
Hopes, and it is useful to me as cawing
Is to crows or roaring to the lions, it
Is human speech, the speech of the mind that is
Here and not there, a mind that sees and hears and
Is aware. Not the deaf, blind speech
Of trees in storm or of monsoon clouds or of rain or the
Incoherent mutterings of the blazing
Funeral pyre. I was child, and later they
Told me I grew, for I became tall, my limbs
Swelled and one or two places sprouted hair. When
I asked for love, not knowing what else to ask
For, he drew a youth of sixteen into the
Bedroom and closed the door. He did not beat me
But my sad woman-body felt so beaten.

The weight of my breasts and womb crushed me. I shrank
Pitifully. Then . . . I wore a shirt and my

Brother's trousers, cut my hair short and ignored
My womanliness. Dress in sarees, be girl
Be wife, they said. Be embroiderer, be cook,
Be a quarreller with servants. Fit in. Oh,
Belong, cried the categorizers. Don't sit
On walls or peep in through our lace-draped windows.
Be Amy, or be Kamala. Or, better
Still, be Madhavikutty. It is time to
Choose a name, a role. Don't play pretending games.
Don't play at schizophrenia or be a
Nympho. Don't cry embarrassingly loud when
Jilted in love . . . I met a man, loved him. Call
Him not by any name, he is every man
Who wants a woman, just as I am every
Woman who seeks love. In him . . . the hungry haste
Of rivers, in me . . . the oceans' tireless
Waiting. Who are you, I ask each and everyone,
The answer is, it is I. Anywhere and,
Everywhere, I see the one who calls himself
If in this world, he is tightly packed like the
Sword in its sheath. It is I who drink lonely
Drinks at twelve, midnight, in hotels of strange towns,
It is I who laugh, it is I who make love
And then, feel shame, it is I who lie dying
With a rattle in my throat. I am sinner,
I am saint. I am the beloved and the
Betrayed. I have no joys which are not yours, no
Aches which are not yours. I too call myself I.


## The Looking Glass


Getting a man to love you is easy
Only be honest about your wants as
Woman. Stand nude before the glass with him
So that he sees himself the stronger one
And believes it so, and you so much more
Softer, younger, lovelier. . . . Admit your
Admiration. Notice the perfection

Of his limbs, his eyes reddening under
Shower, the shy walk across the bathroom floor,
Dropping towels, and the jerky way he
Urinates. All the fond details that make
Him male and your only man. Gift him all,
Gift him what makes you woman, the scent of
Long hair, the musk of sweat between the breasts,
The warm shock of menstrual blood, and all your
Endless female hungers. Oh yes, getting
A man to love is easy, but living
Without him afterward may have to be
Faced. A living without life when you move
Around, meeting strangers, with your eyes that
Gave up their search, with ears that hear only
His last voice calling out your name and your
Body which once under his touch had gleamed
Like burnished brass, now drab and destitute.

# Manoj Das

## *Encounters*

Along the Cantonment road a brief shower was welcome soon after the office hours. That gave such an excellent excuse to rush into the lone cafe at the middle of the long road!

I had my favourite seat at the window that overlooked the meadow. The cluster of *Krishnachura* trees teeming with flowers glowed blood-red in the rain and the small pool, although growing ever smaller encroached upon by the slum around it, had still enough frogs left in it to break into a chorus of croaks long forgotten in the other parts of the town.

There I met, every other time, the lean and lank gentleman with whom the erratic wind seemed to be very fond of playing pranks: it would turn the inside of his open umbrella out, but, undaunted, he would oblige the wind itself to set it right by holding the capsized thing like a rifle against the wind's course. With a triumphant smile he would then enter the cabin and hang the umbrella carefully from the window, its bottom projected at the pool below, and sit down facing me and make a comment, generally wise, on the weather or the way of the world. I took him seriously, because he resembled one of my primary teachers.

Some of the customers were used to occupying a few scattered stools on the veranda despite the chilling gusts. They were the ones in a hurry, excepting the dark and pock-marked man in bright livery who leaned against the wall and seemed to relish every drop of his tea. If he did not come in, it was because the imported car he had parked before the cafe was too precious to be left out of his sight.

"Do you mark that man?" the umbrella-owner asked me one day. His low tone was suggestive of mystery. "He is on his way to fetch his master, a 'somebody' in business, from that imposing office yonder."

"Yes?" I looked forward to some more significant disclosure about the man.

"He was my class-mate. That was long long ago, perhaps before you were born."

"I see."

"I recognise him all right. But I don't talk to him, lest he should feel embarrassed. I am a teacher and all he has become is a chauffeur. Although I have no complex about it — for me all work is work — but he might have," explained the teacher. I felt impressed.

A fortnight later it was a quieter day — a holiday for schools and Government offices. The chauffeur was out on his duty as usual, but today he was inside the cabin. Perhaps he feared no mischief to his car on a holiday.

He greeted me with a smile. After we had swapped our impressions about the changing quality of tea in the canteen, he asked me, "That gentleman who falters in with an ancient umbrella — he is a teacher, isn't he?"

"Right. How did you know?"

"Well, Babu, to be frank, I knew him rather well. We were once class-mates. He of course cannot recognise me now, unless I introduce myself. But I don't do it lest he should feel a bit embarrassed. He is a mere teacher — but I should say there is nothing wrong in it — while I sport a luxury limousine, although I've no complex about it . . ."

# Jack Davis

## *White Fantasy—Black Fact*

The bus driver was tired. He had been awakened several times during last night's hot summer hours, by the crying of the baby. His wife Anne had walked around with the child seemingly for hours. He hoped she had taken the child around to the Clinic today. After all it was the first summer of the child's existence, and it was really hot. Really hot.

The bus churned along the narrow bitumen road. He heard the slap, slap of the overhanging branches of roadside gums on the rooftop of the bus. His gaze fitted automatically to the approaching bus stop. He slowed the bus, but seeing nobody on the seat, he pushed the gear lever in a quick interchange of movement between foot on clutch pedal and hand on gear lever. The bus growled and surged ahead, sweeping back onto the centre of its laneway.

His mind slid back to the baby. They had called it Peggy Sue after Anne's mother. Anne had been so grateful when he had agreed with the name of their first child, Peggy Sue. He wondered what she would be like when she grew up. He knew she would be pretty. Blonde haired, blue eyed, and with a nice figure. Both him and Anne were well-built. He wondered what she would be character-wise. Anne was a calm practical even-tempered person. While he was almost the complete opposite. He hated untidiness, people with loud voices. He disliked violence, cruelty to animals. Both he and his wife sent money to overseas missions. He thought of the starving millions in Asia, and the resultant death and disease. Cholera, hook worm, sleeping sickness. His mind flitted through the explanatory brochures that he recalled to his mind, which were sent to him and his wife by the overseas mission people. He was glad that he lived in a country that was white, where there was plenty for all, where nobody starved, and everyone was equal. He saw the next bus stop ahead of him and he imperceptibly guided the bus off the bitumen. As he drew almost level with the stop he saw the small group of people. There were eight of them.

One man of indeterminate age, but old, was drunk and coughing, softly but violently. The paroxysms of his coughing shook his bony frame. He was accompanied by a man and woman and five children. The man was also affected by liquor. They were all scruffily dressed and untidy, and a faint whiff of body odour wafted into the interior of the empty bus. The bus driver stared blankly as the small group began gathering their belongings. The old man, his coughing subsiding into sporadic bursts, staggered forward and placed one hand on the bus door. The bus driver looked at the gnarled brown dirty broken finger-nailed hand. He had a mad kaleidoscopic vision of unparalleled sickness right there within the bus.

He thought of little Peggy Sue, her fair skin scabrous with sores. He thought of Anne her body broken, lying in the back-yard. He thought this must not happen, this cannot be. The old man began to heave himself onto the bus, the others ready to climb aboard behind him. The bus driver bent forward and spoke hoarsely, "You are not allowed on this bus, let go the door." The old man glowered at him, replying, "Why aren't I?" The woman lifted her head and stared at the bus driver, she spoke loudly, shrilly. "Why ain't we allowed, we're people ain't we?" The other man evidently her husband chipped in, saying: "Driver you can't stop us from gettin' on that bus. We got money don't worry about us," he opened his hand to show a crumpled two dollar note.

The bus driver rose from his seat and pushed the old man's hand quickly, but firmly, from the frame of the door and then grasping the lever he closed the door. He wrenched the gear stick downwards, and the engine snarled as if in protest against the unexpected call for power. The bus lurched back onto the bitumen sending a cloud of dust and leaves over the little Aboriginal group left standing at the side of the road.

Molly looked at the rapidly receding bus, tears of angry frustration in her eyes. She had to get the baby to the children's hospital that afternoon. She glanced at Peter, her husband, and the old man, her grandfather. She harangued them angrily, her voice rising high above their denunciation of the bus driver. "I told you to stop drinking," she said. "Now if the baby misses her appointment you'll be the one to blame, not the bus driver."

She looked at the long stretch of bitumen, it would be hours before another one traversed the road. The baby began to cry. Molly looked at the four other children. Three were her own. The eldest, Katey, a child of eight, was a parentless stray belonging to some distant relation who through circumstances had become part of her and Peter's brood. She had not wanted to bring them on the long journey from Geraldton to Perth. But as she had no one to leave them with she had been forced to bring them. They also had to bring the old man, grandfather Joshua. It had been his pension day when they had left Geraldton, and his money was needed to assist the group on the long journey. The old HR Holden had travelled well. But near Caversham in attempting a short cut to Guildford it had given up the mechanical ghost.

Peter and Joshua had pushed the car on to the side of the road. After gathering their essential belongings (Joshua carefully retrieved his remaining flagon) and locking the rickety doors, the small group had made their way to the Guildford road and the nearest bus stop. Two-years-old Tandy began whimpering for water. Molly surmised there would be water in the small creek some 159 metres down the road. The old man and Peter lay in the shade. She looked at them in disgust, disregarding her husband's half-hearted offer to obtain water. She emptied the collection of half-eaten food from a can and with the baby on her hip, and the children following, she made her way down the road where a small trickle of weed-covered water meandered slowly under a culvert then through the paddock bordering the road.

Molly and the children stood at the edge of the culvert. She looked dubiously down the sloping reed-covered bank. She spoke softly to Katey, "Looks like you'll have to get the water Katey Doll." The eight-year-old stepped forward eager to help. With the can in her hand she slithered agilely down the bank, her mother and the other children calling directions and encouragement. Katey stepped into the mud her feet making delicious squelching sounds as she wriggled her toes in its coolness. She looked up at the small group above her, white teeth flashing, brown eyes full of merriment, enjoying her endeavours. She stepped toward the roof of the culvert where the water underneath was cleaner, deeper. She placed one slim hand on the woodwork to steady herself, and glanced to find a place to grasp the culvert ledge.

Then for one terror filled second her fingers were a fraction of an inch away from the snake. Her reflexes were instant, but even as she snatched her hand away, it struck, and with such blinding speed and force that its fangs became embedded in the back of her tiny hand, and swinging off balance, Katey Doll screamed and flung the snake in an arc, where it landed some two metres away. Then slithering in the water it vanished among the reeds. Molly saw it all as if in slow motion. She tried to call out but her voice choked off. With the baby in her arms she leapt down the bank. She grabbed the trembling Katey who stood frozen clutching her hand to her crotch. Her eyes were enormous, dilated with fear. "Mummy," she cried, "it bit me, it bit me. Will I die? Oh, Mummy will I die?" And realising the horror and the enormity of it all, the woman and the child screamed together.

Peter heard the screaming. With one leap he was standing on the road. He saw the way the children were running towards him, something was amiss. "Gawd," he muttered. "What's happened?" he ran. Upon reaching the culvert he sprang down the bank grabbing Katey. He saw the two long tips in the skin of her hand. He did not hesitate. He pulled the now mute child to a sitting position, and knelt beside her and gripping her wrist tightly, he began sucking hard and deep over the ragged perforations.

Joshua stood on the road, looking at them aghast. Molly handed the baby up to him. She struggled up the bank, calling to the old man. "If a car comes flag it down." Even as she spoke they heard the hum of an approaching vehicle. Molly standing on the road stood waving her hands frantically. The car came fast. Behind it another. Molly screamed her plea. "Stop! Please! Help! Help!" Both cars roared past, the drivers looking at them with the curious detached look of the unconcerned.

Molly sank on her knees and cried, "O God, please help us." The children were all crying. Peter began pulling the trembling Katey up the bank, still endeavouring to suck the poison from the small frail body. They all knelt at the side of the road. They heard the purr of an engine. Joshua thrust the baby into Molly's arms. He stood almost in the centre of the road, his arms waving wildly. Molly breathed a gasping sigh of relief as she saw the car slow to a crawl. It came opposite the old man, who stepped forward to speak to the driver. Then with a screech of tortured tyres it leaped forward, and an epithet, mingling with the sound of laughter, sprang at them like barbed wire from the interior of the speeding car. The old man stood crouched at the side of the road crying hoarsely, "Aw, you bastards, you bloody, rotten mongrel bastards!" Tears of anger flowed down his thin checks.

It was obvious now that the poison and shock were having an effect on Katey Doll, her eyes were closed, her breathing shallow, and a small trace of vomit lingered at the corner of her mouth. Peter knew he had to keep her awake. He shook the child hard, her head, arms and legs were marionette like, limp and flaccid. The old man crouched on the road verge, his voice keeping low, in the beginning of a death chant. Molly turned to him and said fiercely, "Stop that! Do you hear me? She can hear you and that'll make her worse." Suddenly, the little group became aware of a sound, a strange almost frightening sound. Now the noise was around them. The motor bikes were black and gleaming and the riders helmeted, goggled and dressed in black leather. The whole thirty of them had the skull and crossbones emblem stenciled on their jackets. The roar of the bikes began to lessen, becoming staccato as if wolf-like they had to snap and snarl at one another. A thin blonde-haired youth was the first to dismount from his machine and he spoke to the frightened Molly. "What's wrong lady? Are you havin' trouble?" Pointing to the tableau of Peter and Katey Doll, Molly replied "My, my little girl, snake bite!" The youth swore softly and yelled: "Christ, where's the Doc? Get him someone, this kid's been bitten by a bloody snake."

A towering red-headed, red-bearded giant of two metres or more threaded his way swiftly through the mass of machines, he knelt beside the exhausted Peter sucking the back of the girl's hand. He clasped one huge paw on Katey Doll's wrist and spoke softly to Peter, "Come on let's have a look, mate." There were calls from the riders now watching intently. "How she doin' Red Doc?" The man called "Red Doc" (two years at medical school had given him that unofficial title) gently picked up the child. He spoke quickly, quietly. "We have to move fast. Go Bo, Slit Eyes, get going to the nearest phone box, and ring for an ambulance. Tell them to bring anti-venom and to meet us on the northern highway to Perth Hospital."

Three bikes leapt to life and with a full-throated roar, they swept down the road in a blinding acceleration of rising speed. Big Red Doc climbed onto his enormous Harley with Katey Doll cradled in his arms, her hand with a tourniquet applied, suspended by a belt tied around his neck. He looked at Peter, grinned and said, "Right mate, on the back." Red Doc spoke to the others. "OK you guys, you organise getting a car and get the rest of these people into town, better bring them to the hospital."

A half dozen of the bikies with Joshua and the children sat in the waiting room. Everybody was tense not knowing how Katey Doll was faring. The doctors had guessed correctly that the snake was a death adder, usually fatal. They saw the doctor with Peter and Molly walking toward them, and they knew suddenly, everything was alright. Peter spoke first, his hand groping for the massive paw of Big Red. "She gonna be OK. Thanks fellas, thanks a million." Molly began to cry quietly as reaction set in. The doctor smiling, spoke: "She's going to be alright. She is a lucky little girl, the only reason she is alive is because she had prompt attention."

Molly looked at the group of leather-jacketed men and smiling, spoke softly. "You know when you all came down the road this afternoon, I thought you were a pack of devils, but instead you were all angels on chariots, surely sent by God." Old Joshua looked up and cackled, "And it's the first time I reckon, they rode motor bikes."

Slit Eye spoke cheerfully, "Now that's why we got kicked out of Northam. It was all that 'upstairs guy's' fault." And in the late hour of the evening, the hospital waiting room echoed their laughter.

# Pay Back

Munda had been trailing the party of three whites since early morning. He hated them. Yet within this hate was a mixture of fear. There were reasons. At the last moon, a party of white men had poisoned one of their centuries old water holes and several members of his group had died in agony. But these were not the men actually responsible. He had photographed the heavy foot marks of the men in his mind of those who had killed, and those imprints would remain in his mind forever. But he knew they were the same type of man. He also knew the party was heading into waterless country.

The searing summer heat burnt into the very minds of the white men. Liles' party headed in the direction they were travelling four weeks before them. Although they had zig-zagged across the desert for nearly two weeks they had been unsuccessful in cutting across the other exploring party's tracks. Wargoton, the leader of the group, knew that to survive they would have to find water within the next twenty hours. He was a tall man, bearded, lean and sunburnt to a deep brown. The same description applied to his two companions, Lorrest and Wicknell.

One of their three camels had died a week ago. All their possessions, cut down to bare needs, were now being carried by their two remaining beasts. They made camp in the middle of the day's heat. They were wise in the ways of the desert, and knew it was better to conserve their energy, by travelling in the early morning and late afternoon.

Wargoton shook the canteen containing the last of their precious water. He looked at his two companions crouched together with him, in the six feet of shade thrown by the ledge of rock under which they crouched. He spoke hoarsely.

"Well we're down to about four mouthfuls of water each."

Wicknell replied, "I've had a feeling all morning that the blacks are trailing us, why the hell don't they show themselves."

"Why should they?" said Wargoton. "They'll trail and watch us keep watching until we perish then they'll spear the camels for food then share what we leave."

They lapsed into a moody silence. The sun began to move on its downward path, but the day was still viciously hot. The small patch of shade began to diminish.

Wargoton groaned between seared lips in his attempt to speak. "If we're going to sit in the sun, we might as well move." They struggled to their feet. Wargoton poured out three measures of water and said grimly. "Last drink until sundown and God help us tomorrow."

Even as he spoke, the three men saw the black, standing no more than twenty yards from them. At the sight of him they knew their immediate need was solved. He was of average height, thin build and stark naked. In one hand he held a hunting spear pointing carefully downwards. In the other he held a nulla nulla. In a hair belt around his left arm was a blade of quartz and around his forehead, was a belt of hair tied low. He stood looking at the three whites with an almost bovine expression on his bearded face.

It was Wicknell who broke the long sounds of silence. He raised one hand and pointed to the canteens strapped to one of their camels. "Water, where is water?" he said. Munda pointed to the sun then swept his arm half way down from its destination. "Good," said Lorrest. "The bastard understands us. That looks to be about two hours from here." "What if he's lying?" replied Wicknell. "No," said Wargoton. "He's telling the truth, but I think we should take care of ourselves, by the simple method of making him need water as much as we do."

Wargoton offered Munda the compass. His curiosity overcame his caution; he stepped forward, eager to take the offered object. They grabbed him. He offered little resistance, but moaned and jabbered in his own tongue as they bore him to his knees in the red desert sand.

Wicknell finding untapped energy ran to one of the camels. Rummaging quickly in the pack saddle he returned with a double cupped handful of salt.

Wargoton and Lorrest held the pitiful figure firmly, while Wicknell rammed the salt into the bearded mouth.

It was as if he realised their intentions, because he did not struggle. They let him go. He lay on his side in protest as the salt bit into his throat. He began retching, the spasms doubling him up in their intensity. Lorrest stepped forward, kicked him and pointing at the sun, said hoarsely, "Water, and bloody quick." Wicknell aimed his rifle in the black's direction. Munda climbed painfully to his feet clutching his throat, and the strange procession began.

The three whites finished the last of their water. They knew now that the black was their only chance of survival. Their victim was now nearly two hundred feet in advance of them. They let him lead. Once when he widened the distance, Wicknell slowed him with a rifle shot fired skyward.

They came to a claypan some quarter of a mile across. The black stumbling, headed across it with the men still trailing him. At the claypan's outer edge the black suddenly veered sideways. He stopped, then pointed left to a spot where long low sandhills ringed the claypan.

Wargoton spoke hoarsely jubilant. "We've won, we've won. I can see the ground damp from here." They ran forward eagerly. They saw the black running for the safety of the sandhill. Wicknell stopped and raised his rifle. Wargoton still running forward, called out, "Let him go we've got what we want."

The three men flung themselves down at the soak's edge gulping the tepid water greedily, and splashing it over their faces. They lay on their sides allowing the two camels to quench their thirst.

It was Wargoton who felt the first swordlike thrust of pain. Then agony struck Lorrest then Wicknell. Wargoton looked at his companions' eyes bulging. He gasped, "Liles, that bloody Liles has been here before us. He's always trying to wipe out the blacks, the soak has been poisoned."

Munda looked dispassionately at the scene below him. His woman came walking along the ridge of the sandhill, a kullamun of water balanced on her head. Munda drank and together, turning their backs on the scene of death below them, they walked down the sandhill and into the distance of their land.

# Anita Desai

## *Surface Textures*

It was all her own fault, she later knew—but how could she have helped it? When she stood, puckering her lips, before the fruit barrow in the market and, after sullen consideration, at last plucked a rather small but nicely ripened melon out of a heap on display, her only thought had been Is it worth a *rupee* and fifty *paise*? The lichees looked more poetic, in large clusters like some prickly grapes of a charming rose colour, their long stalks and stiff grey leaves tied in a bunch above them—but were expensive. Mangoes were what the children were eagerly waiting for—the boys, she knew, were raiding the mango trees in the school compound daily and their stomach-aches were a result, she told them, of the unripe mangoes they ate and for which they carried paper packets of salt to school in their pockets instead of handkerchiefs—but, leave alone the expense, the ones the fruiterer held up to her enticingly were bound to be sharp and sour for all their parakeet shades of rose and saffron; it was still too early for mangoes. So she put the melon in her string bag, rather angrily—paid the man his one *rupee* and fifty *paise* which altered his expression from one of promise and enticement to that of disappointment and contempt, and trailed off towards the vegetable barrow.

That, she later saw, was the beginning of it all, for if the melon seemed puny to her and boring to the children, from the start her husband regarded it with eyes that seemed newly opened. One would have thought he had never seen a melon before. All through the meal his eyes remained fixed on the plate in the centre of the table with its big button of a yellow melon. He left most of his rice and pulses on his plate, to her indignation. While she scolded, he reached out to touch the melon that so captivated him. With one finger he stroked the coarse grain of its rind, rough with the upraised criss-cross of pale veins. Then he ran his fingers up and down the green streaks that divided it into even quarters as by green silk threads, so tenderly. She was clearing away the plates and did not notice till she came back from the kitchen.

"Aren't you going to cut it for us?" she asked, pushing the knife across to him.

He gave her a reproachful look as he picked up the knife and went about dividing the melon into quarter-moon portions with sighs that showed how it pained him.

"Come on, come on," she said, roughly, "the boys have to get back to school."

He handed them their portions and watched them scoop out the icy orange flesh with a fearful expression on his face — as though he were observing cannibals at a feast. She had not the time to pay any attention to it then but later described it as horror. And he did not eat his own slice. When the boys rushed away, he bowed his head over his plate and regarded it.

"Are you going to fall asleep?" she cried, a little frightened.

"Oh no," he said, in that low mumble that always exasperated her — it seemed a sign to her of evasiveness and pusillanimity, this mumble — "Oh no, no." Yet he did not object when she seized the plate and carried it off to the kitchen, merely picked up the knife that was left behind and, picking a flat melon seed off its edge where it had remained stuck, he held it between two fingers, fondling it delicately. Continuing to do this, he left the house.

The melon might have been the apple of knowledge for Harish — so deadly its poison that he did not even need to bite into it to imbibe it: that long, devoted look had been enough. As he walked back to his office which issued ration cards to the population of their town, he looked about him vaguely but with hunger, his eyes resting not on the things on which people's eyes normally rest — signboards, the traffic, the number of an approaching bus — but on such things, normally considered nondescript and unimportant, as the paving stones on which their feet momentarily pressed, the length of wire in a railing at the side of the road, a pattern of grime on the windowpane of a disused printing press. . . . Amongst such things his eyes roved and hunted and, when he was seated at his desk in the office, his eyes continued to slide about — that was Sheila's phrase later: "slide about" — in a musing, calculating way, over the surface of the crowded desk, about the corners of the room, even across the ceiling. He seemed unable to focus them on a file or a card long enough to put to them his signature — they lay unsigned and the people in the queue outside went for another day without rice and sugar and kerosene for their lamps and Janta cookers. Harish searched — slid about, hunted, gazed — and at last found sufficiently interesting a thick book of rules that lay beneath a stack of files. Then his hand reached out — not to pull the book to him or open it, but to run the ball of his thumb across the edge of the pages. In their large number and irregular cut, so closely laid out like some crisp palimpsest, his eyes seemed to find something of riveting interest and his thumb of tactile wonder. All afternoon he massaged the cut edges of the book's seven hundred odd pages—tenderly, wonderingly. All afternoon his eyes gazed upon them with strange devotion. At five o'clock, punctually, the office shut and the queue disintegrated into vociferous grumbles and threats as people went home instead of to the ration shops, empty-handed instead of loaded with those necessary but, to Harish, so dull comestibles.

Although Government service is as hard to depart from as to enter—so many letters to be written, forms to be filled, files to be circulated, petitions to be made that it hardly seem worthwhile—Harish was, after some time, dismissed—time he happily spent judging the difference between white blotting paper and pink (pink is flatter, denser, white spongier) and the texture of blotting paper stained with ink and that which is fresh, that which has been put to melt in a saucer of cold tea and that which has been doused in a pot of ink. Harish was dismissed.

The first few days Sheila stormed and screamed like some shrill, wet hurricane about the house. "How am I to go to market and buy vegetables for dinner? I don't even have enough for that. What am I to feed the boys tonight? No more milk for them. The washerwoman is asking for her bill to be paid. Do you hear? Do you *hear*? And we shall have to leave this flat. Where shall we go?" He listened—or didn't—sitting on a cushion before her mirror, fingering the small silver box in which she kept the red *kum-kum* that daily cut a gash from one end of her scalp to the other after her toilet. It was of dark, almost blackened silver, with a whole forest embossed on it—banana groves, elephants, peacocks and jackals. He rubbed his thumb over its cold, raised surface.

After that, she wept. She lay on her bed in a bath of tears and perspiration, and it was only because of the kindness of their neighbours that they did not starve to death the very first week, for even those who most disliked and distrusted Harish—"Always said he looks like a hungry hyena," said Mr Bhatia who lived below their flat, "not human at all, but like a hungry, hunchbacked hyena hunting along the road"—felt for the distraught wife and the hungry children (who did not really mind as long as there were sour green mangoes to steal and devour) and looked to them. Such delicacies as Harish's family had never known before arrived in stainless steel and brass dishes, with delicate unobtrusiveness. For a while wife and children gorged on sweetmeats made with fresh buffalo milk, on pulses cooked according to grandmother's recipes, on stuffed bread and the first pomegranates of the season. But, although delicious, these offerings came in small quantities and irregularly and soon they were really starving.

"I suppose you want me to take the boys home to my parents," said Sheila bitterly, getting up from the bed. "Any other man would regard that as the worst disgrace of all—but not you. What is my shame to you? I will have to hang my head and crawl home and beg my father to look after us since you won't," and that was what she did. He was sorry, very sorry to see her pack the little silver *kum-kum* box in her black trunk and carry it away.

Soon after, officials of the Ministry of Works, Housing and Land Development came and turned Harish out, cleaned and painted the flat and let in the new tenants who could hardly believe their luck—they had been told so often they couldn't expect a flat in that locality for at least another two years.

The neighbours lost sight of Harish. Once some children reported they had seen him lying under the *pipal* tree at the corner of their school compound, staring fixedly at the red gashes cut into the papery bark and, later, a boy who commuted to school on a suburban train claimed to have seen him on the railway platform, sitting against a railing like some tattered beggar, staring across the criss-cross of shining rails. But next day, when the boy got off the train, he did not see Harish again.

Harish had gone hunting. His slow, silent walk gave him the appearance of sliding rather than walking over the surface of the roads and fields, rather like a snail except that his movement was not as smooth as a snail's but stumbling as if he had only recently become one and was still unused to the pace. Not only his eyes and his hands but even his bare feet seemed to be feeling the earth carefully, in search of an interesting surface. Once he found it, he would pause, his whole body would gently collapse across it and hours—perhaps days—would be devoted to its investigation and worship. Outside the town the land was rocky and bare and this was Harish's especial paradise, each rock having a surface of such exquisite roughness, of such perfection in shape and design, as to keep him occupied and ecstatic for weeks together. Then the river beyond the rock quarries drew him away and there he discovered the joy of fingering silk-smooth stalks and reeds, stems and leaves.

Shepherd children, seeing him stumble about the reeds, plunging thigh-deep into the water in order to pull out a water lily with its cool, sinuous stem, fled screaming, not certain whether this was a man or a hairy water snake. Their mothers came, some with stones and some with canes at the ready, but when they saw Harish, his skin parched to a violet shade, sitting on the bank and gazing at the transparent stem of the lotus, they fell back, crying, "Wah!" gathered closer together, advanced, dropped their canes and stones, held their children still by their hair and shoulders, and came to bow to him. Then they hurried back to the village, chattering. They had never had a Swami to themselves, in these arid parts. Nor had they seen a Swami who looked holier, more inhuman than Harish with his matted hair, his blue, starved skin and single-focused eyes. So, in the evening, one brought him a brass vessel of milk, another a little rice. They pushed their children before them and made them drop flowers at his feet. When Harish stooped and felt among the offerings for something his fingers could respond to, they were pleased, they felt accepted. "Swamiji," they whispered, "speak."

Harish did not speak and his silence made him still holier, safer. So they worshipped him, fed and watched over him, interpreting his moves in their own fashion, and Harish, in turn, watched over their offerings and worshipped.

# Eunice de Souza

## Catholic Mother

Francis X. D'Souza
father of the year.
Here he is top left
the one smiling.
By the Grace of God he says
we've had seven children
(in seven years)
We're One Big Happy Family
God Always Provides
India will Suffer for
her Wicked Ways
(these Hindu buggers got no ethics)

Pillar of the Church
says the parish priest
Lovely Catholic Family
says Mother Superior

the pillar's wife
says nothing.

## Return

I
The old wrought iron gate has gone
with the tall, tangled grass
and the mosquitoes.
The priest is chanting his blessings

on the stone of the new building.
Squirrels chase each other up and down
the two mango trees left standing.

My neighbours want to know,
did I enjoy?
Thinking of the old wrought iron gate
and the cotton flower tree
that managed only one flower every summer
I agree, perhaps enjoyment
should have no object.
        II
It was the sound of the shenai
in a London flat
that brought me scurrying back
to catch this train
to be again among
these old hills
stray bougainvillea
and the peasant women
with only a handful of berries to sell.
I want to touch this earth
and let its fierce sadness
blossom in my song.
        III
Tuka, forgive my familiarity.
I have loved your pithy verses
ever since that French priest
everyone thought mad
recited them, and told us
of his journey with your people.
They have broken down whole streets
of houses in Pandarpur, to widen
the road to the shrine.
The priests do not sound like you
but I'll offer a coconut anyway
for someone I love.
You made life hard for your wife
and I'm not sure I approve of that.
Nor did you heed her last request:
Come back soon.

# Nissim Ezekiel

## *Case Study*

Whatever he had done was not quite right.
The Masters never failed, however weak,
To know when they had sinned against the light.
Can their example purify his sight?
Ought he to practise Yoga, study Greek,
Or bluff his way throughout with brazen cheek?

Beginning with a foolish love affair
After common school and rotten college,
He had the patient will but not the flair
To climb with quick assault the envied stair;
Messed around instead with useless knowledge,
And staked on politics a fatal pledge.

His marriage was the worst mistake of all.
Although he loved his children when they came,
He spoilt them too with just that extra doll,
Or discipline which drove them to the wall.
His wife and changing servants did the same —
A man is damned in that domestic game.

He worked at various jobs and then he stopped
For reasons never clear or quite approved
By those who knew; some almost said he shopped
Around for dreams and projects later dropped
(Though this was quite untrue); he never moved
Unless he found something he might have loved.

He came to me and this is what I said:
"The pattern will remain, unless you break
It with a sudden jerk; but use your head.
Not all returned as heroes who had fled
In wanting both to have and eat the cake.
Not all who fail are counted with the fake."

# Lorna Goodison

## *Survivor*

The strangers passed through here
for years
  laying waste the countryside.
They took most living things
even some rare species
with half extended wings.
They took them all.
Now that genus is extinct
Lord, they were thorough
in their plunderings.
So, here the wind plays
mourning notes
on bones that once were ribs
(savages) they broke them
when they'd finished eating
and you know how creative
God is with ribs.
That survivor over there
with bare feet and bound hair
has some seeds stored
under her tongue
and one remaining barrel
of rain
She will go indoors
when her planting is done
loosen her hair
and tend to her son
and over the bone flute music
and the dead story it tells,
listen for grace songs
from her ankle bells.

# Nadine Gordimer

## *Is There Nowhere Else Where We Can Meet?*

It was a cool grey morning and the air was like smoke. In that reversal of the elements that sometimes takes place, the grey, soft, muffled sky moved like the sea on a silent day.

The coat collar pressed rough against her neck and her cheeks were softly cold as if they had been washed in ice water. She breathed gently with the air; on the left a strip of veld fire curled silently, flameless. Overhead a dove purred. She went on over the flat straw grass, following the trees, now on, now off the path. Away ahead, over the scribble of twigs, the sloping lines of black and platinum grass — all merging, tones but no colour, like an etching — was the horizon, the shore at which cloud lapped.

Damp burnt grass puffed black, faint dust from beneath her feet. She could hear herself swallow.

A long way off she saw a figure with something red on its head, and she drew from it the sense of balance she had felt at the particular placing of the dot of a figure in a picture. She was here: someone was over there.. . . Then the red dot was gone, lost in the curve of the trees. She changed her bag and parcel from one arm to the other and felt the morning, palpable, deeply cold and clinging against her eyes.

She came to the end of a direct stretch of path and turned with it round a dark-fringed pine and a shrub, now delicately boned, that she remembered hung with bunches of white flowers like crystals in the summer. There was a native in a red woollen cap standing at the next clump of trees, where the path crossed a ditch and was bordered by white-splashed stones. She had pulled a little sheath of pine needles, three in a twist of thin brown tissue, and as she walked she ran them against her thumb. Down; smooth and stiff. Up; catching in gentle resistance as the minute serrations snagged at the skin. He was standing with his back towards her, looking along the way he had come; she pricked the ball of her thumb with the needle-ends. His one trouser leg was torn off above the knee, and the back of the naked leg and half-turned heel showed the peculiarly dead, powdery black of cold.

She was nearer to him now, but she knew he did not hear her coming over the damp dust of the path. She was level with him, passing him; and he turned slowly and looked beyond her, without a flicker of interest, as a cow sees you go.

The eyes were red, as if he had not slept for a long time, and the strong smell of old sweat burned at her nostrils. Once past, she wanted to cough, but a pang of guilt at the red-weary eyes stopped her. And he had only a filthy rag — part of an old shirt? — without sleeves and frayed away into a great gap from underarm to waist. It lifted in the currents of cold as she passed. She had dropped the neat trio of pine needles somewhere, she did not know at what moment, so now, remembering something from childhood, she lifted her hand to her face and sniffed: yes, it was as she remembered, not as chemists pretend it in the bath salts, but a dusty green scent, vegetable rather than flower. It was clean, unhuman. Slightly sticky too; tacky on her fingers. She must wash them as soon as she got there. Unless her hands were quite clean, she could not lose consciousness of them, they obtruded upon her.

She felt a thudding through the ground like the sound of a hare running in fear and she was going to turn around and then he was there in front of her, so startling, so utterly unexpected, panting right into her face. He stood dead still and she stood dead still. Every vestige of control, of sense, of thought, went out of her as a room plunges into dark at the failure of power and she found herself whimpering like an idiot or a child. Animal sounds came out of her throat. She gibbered. For a moment it was Fear itself that had her by the arms, the legs, the throat; not fear of the man, of any single menace he might present, but Fear, absolute, abstract. If the earth had opened up in fire at her feet, if a wild beast had opened its terrible mouth to receive her, she could not have been reduced to less than she was now.

There was a chest heaving through the tear in front of her; a face panting; beneath the red hairy woollen cap the yellowish-red eyes holding her in distrust. One foot, cracked from exposure until it looked like broken wood, moved, only to restore balance in the dizziness that follows running, but any move seemed towards her and she tried to scream and the awfulness of dreams came true and nothing would come out. She wanted to throw the handbag and the parcel at him, and as she fumbled crazily for them she heard him draw a deep, hoarse breath and he grabbed out at her and — ah! It came. His hand clutched her shoulder.

Now she fought with him and she trembled with strength as they struggled. The dust puffed round her shoes and his scuffling toes. The smell of him choked her. — It was an old pyjama jacket, not a shirt — His face was sullen and there was a pink place where the skin had been grazed off. He sniffed desperately, out of breath. Her teeth chattered, wildly she battered him with her head, broke away, but he snatched at the skirt of her coat and jerked her back. Her face swung up and she saw the waves of a grey sky and a crane breasting them, beautiful as the figurehead of a ship. She staggered for balance and the handbag and parcel fell. At once he was upon them, and she wheeled about; but as she was about to fall on her knees to get there first, a sudden relief, like a rush of tears, came to her and instead, she ran. She ran and ran, stumbling wildly off through the stalks of dead grass, turning over her heels against hard winter tussocks, blundering through trees and bushes. The young mimosas closed in, lowering a thicket of twigs right to the ground, but she tore herself through, feeling the dust in her eyes and the scaly twigs hooking at her hair. There was a ditch, knee-high in blackjacks; like pins responding to a magnet they fastened along her legs, but on the other side there was a fence and then the road. . . . She clawed at the fence — her hands were capable of nothing — and tried to drag herself between the wires, but her coat got caught on a barb, and she was imprisoned there, bent in half, whilst waves of terror swept over her in heat and trembling. At last the wire tore through its hold on the cloth; wobbling, frantic, she climbed over the fence.

And she was out. She was out on the road. A little way on there were houses, with gardens, postboxes, a child's swing. A small dog sat at a gate. She could hear a faint hum, as of life, of talk somewhere, or perhaps telephone wires.

She was trembling so that she could not stand. She had to keep on walking, quickly, down the road. It was quiet and grey, like the morning. And cool. Now she could feel the cold air round her mouth and between her brows, where the skin stood out in sweat. And in the cold wetness that soaked down beneath her armpits and between her buttocks. Her heart thumped slowly and stiffly. Yes, the wind was cold; she was suddenly cold, damp-cold, all through. She raised her hand, still fluttering uncontrollably, and smoothed her hair; it was wet at the hairline. She guided her hand into her pocket and found a handkerchief to blow her nose.

There was the gate of the first house, before her.

She thought of the woman coming to the door, of the explanations, of the woman's face, and the police. Why did I fight, she thought suddenly. What did I fight for? Why didn't I give him the money and let him go? His red eyes, and the smell and those cracks in his feet, fissures, erosion. She shuddered. The cold of the morning flowed into her.

She turned away from the gate and went down the road slowly, like an invalid, beginning to pick the blackjacks from her stockings.

# Jessica Hagedorn

## *The Song of Bullets*

Formalized
by middle age
we avoid crowds
but still
love music.

Day after day
with less surprise
we sit
in apartments
and count
the dead.

Awake,
my daughter croons
her sudden cries
and growls
my new language.
While she sleeps
we memorize
a list of casualties:

The photographer's brother
the doctor is missing.
Or I could say:
"Victor's brother Oscar
has been gone for two years . . .
It's easier for the family
to think of him dead."

Victor sends
a Christmas card

from El Salvador:
"Things still the same."

And there are others
who don't play
by the rules —
someone else's brother
perhaps mine
languishes in a hospital;
everyone's grown tired
of his nightmares
and pretends
he's not there.

Someone else's father
perhaps mine
will be executed
when the time comes.
Someone else's mother
perhaps mine
telephones incessantly
her husband is absent
her son has gone mad
her lover has committed suicide
she's a survivor
who can't appreciate
herself.

The sight
of my daughter's
pink and luscious flesh
undoes me.
I fight
my weakening rage
I must remember
to commit
those names to memory
and stay angry.

Friends send postcards:
"Alternating between hectic

*social* Manila life & rural wonders
of Sagata . . . on to Hongkong and Bangkok —
Love . . ."

Assassins cruise the streets
in obtrusive limousines
sunbathers idle
on the beach

War is predicted
in five years
ten years
any day now
I always thought
it was already happening

snipers and poets locked
in a secret embrace
the country
my child may never see

a heritage
of women in heat
and men
skilled at betrayal

dancing
to the song
of bullets.

# Claire Harris

## *Framed*

She is in your painting     the one you bought when the taxi
snarled in market lines     you jumped out and grabbed
a picture of stilted wooden houses against the vivid island
even then there was recognition

She is the woman in a broken pair of men's shoes     her
flesh slipped down like old socks around her ankles     a tray
of laundry on her head     I am there too     but I would not
be like her     at supper she set the one plate and the whole
cup at my place     for herself a mug a bowl my leavings
they said I resembled her     I spent hours before the mirror
training my mouth to different lines

At night while I read     she folded the blanket on her
narrow board     coalfire smooth on her face     she boiled
scrubbed     ironed     musk of soap and others soil like
mist around her head     often she dreamed     I would have
a maid     like her     she laughed     I studied harder harder
she grieved     I was grown a woman     I was grown
without affinity

For the calling     her eroded hands     cupped like a chalice
she offered me the blasted world as if to say     this is our
sacrament     drink     I would not     this is all there is     I
could not     I left school     I left     she faded
the island faded     styles changed     you hid the dusty
painting in the attic     But I am still there     the one in
middle ground     my face bruising lines of soft white
sheets     my hand raised as if to push against the frame

# And So . . . Home

I walk the raw paths through winds that crowd me
now this autumn comes around before I'm ready
pulls at my slack time tautening
for a moment no existence at all

Behind the grave apartment towers clouds
pile up      rattle spare bones of rain      leaves
lift and twirl      among all that gold
the air is winged      crackling

Why now her song surprises me I'm not sure
memory spills from my lips      ribbons
crisp satin ribbons      grosgrain      so long ago

My mother      her fingers part my hair make
four neat plaits that dovetail on each side
become one that is crossed and pinned

She holds out a rainbow of ribbons says
*choose one*      ribbons hanging from her fingers
like paths      how can I choose when any choice
means a giving up      years later shucking the island

As painful as shucking skin      yet I left
weaving a new space to trap the voice
I thought I could      must return      my navel string

Buried where the rich fantasy      of peoples
stranded by empire jostled on those stunned hummocks
history's low road under the bruising sun

Now loving this chill autumn rain I know it has been too long
a memory of dark hands intelligent with a child's
ribbons      hands vulnerable among ruins
something to conjure with

# *Backstage at the Glenbow Museum, Calgary*

out of the pale life of northern streets into the hushed dim
of mausoleums      no need to rush      ideas suspended in silence
dead      and i can't quite believe i've come here knowing this
though i have a kind of duty i suppose      even to these shells

"Do come down . . . we have some wonderful things in the archives"
"I don't write on demand . . ."
"You can come down early . . . any day . . . I'll show you
around . . . these things should be seen . . ."

i have a kind of duty i suppose

        drop by drop i dive in
    where tall cupboards
      hold ancient
        other      music frozen
                     masks/gourds/stools
    other worlds into
                 feathered brilliances
                 boats/mats/statues
i float down aisles thru preserving light      temperature      humidity
ignoring ghostly canoes launched silent into corners the parrots'
muffled squawk and sigh      fat brown giggles clustering on window
sills fingers like roots weaving hailing      exotic      not mine not
mine   smoke   pots of red ochre   cedar leans cooking fires playing
ceilings      hooked on needs i bleed on must
    a kind of duty i suppose
        so      break water into
    musty silence      a dun beach behind
   which other silences should roll and tower
   should roll & tower in the usual endless peaks
                 but don't

     nothing

nothing here
nothing luminous
         here

perhaps behind the doors
      perhaps a cry racing entirely backwards
a space i can enter
      to find what?
   through murk and formless
                                        i
   wanting
come to the third cupboard on the third reef
      doors open    silence of sharks
or books
      i need
   a waterfall
                  africaafricaafricaafrica
                        AFRIC
                  africaAFRICAafrica
            af      af      af      afr
            ric     ric    ric    rica
                  A F R I C
                        Aaaaaa
brown rivers/plains/mountains/red earth/deserts/thorn
grass/forests/greatherds/beasts/red/white/black/brown
in flight and swarm/market places/drums/stamping feet
pestles/baskets/flutes/songs/peoples        staring through
it all       as through cloud drifts
            orisas
         challenge their fate
                  Oluwa wa Olu wa wa O lu
                                    wa wa
nothing

      shards      the past
   broken bits    ab/truth
a row of faces on a dusty shelf lean drunkenly cheek
      to cheek
   hanging with them that smell      bargaining

i have a kind of duty i suppose

                nothing but art
                                        it is May 1994 Calgary
        cold and sunny in the afternoon clouds rain High 13 Low 3
                how Africa eludes my every effort
            wraps itself in abysses
                in drums
                    in the terrible distances
                of pop  images
                            Serengetti
                                            Mandela
                            Buthelezi
                    Kenya
                                        Timbuktu


R(u)wanda        and i am here in this clear blue city        beached on
heads hacked off        Africa  dripping from the mouths of dogs
                                            the hands of men


i have a kind of duty i suppose

# Wilson Harris

## *Kanaima*

Tumatumari is a tiny dying village on the bank of the Potaro River, overlooking roaring rapids. The bursting stream foams and bunches itself into a series of smooth cascading shells enveloping backs of stone. Standing on the top of the hill one feels the gulley and river sliding treacherously and beautifully as though everything was slipping into its own curious violent inner concentration and energy, and one turns away and faces the tiny encampment and village with a sensation of loss — as of something alive and vibrant and wholehearted whose swift lure and summons one evades once again to return to the shell of this standing death.

A beaten trail that keeps its distance from the dangerous brink of the gorge winds its spirit over the hill, through the village, like the patient skin of a snake, lying on the ground with entrails hanging high as husks of vine, dangling and rotting in the ancient forest.

The village seems to hold its own against the proliferation of the jungle with great difficulty, dying slowly in a valiant effort to live, eternally addressed by the deep voice of the falls, conscious too of a high far witness across the slanting sky — a blue line of mountains upholding a fiction of cloud . . .

A tiny procession — about a dozen persons in all, mostly women and children — was making its way across the trail. The man who led them, a rather stocky Indian, had stopped. His face bore the mooning fateful look of the Macusi Indians, travelling far from home. They lived mostly in the high Rupununi savannahs stretching to Brazil, a long way off, and the village encampment at Tumatumari was composed of African and negro pork-knockers, most of whom were absent at this time, digging the interior creeks for diamonds. They had left a couple of old watchmen behind them at Tumatumari but otherwise the village (which they used as a base camp) was empty. The leader of the newcomers reconnoitred the situation, looking around him with brooding eyes, rolling a black globule and charm on his tongue and exhibiting this every now and then against his teeth — under his curling lips — with the inward defiance of an experienced hunter who watched always for the curse of men and animals.

The six o'clock parrots flew screeching overhead. The Indians looked at the sun and corrected their mental time-piece. It could not have been later than four. The sky was still glowing bright on the mountain's shoulder. In the bush the hour was growing dark, but here on the snake's trail — which coiled around the huts and the shattered houses — the air still swam with the yellow butter of the sun.

One of the old decrepit watchmen — left by the negro pork-knockers — was approaching the Macusis. He shambled along, eyeing the strangers in an inhospitable, barren way. "Is no use," he said, when he reached them, shaking his head at them with an ominous spirit, "Kanaima been here already." The Indians remained silent and sullen, but in reality they were deeply shaken by the news. They started chattering all of a sudden like the discordant premature parrots that had passed a few moments ago overhead. The sound of their matching voices rose and died as swiftly as it had begun. Their stocky leader — with the black fluid beetle on his tongue — addressed the old watchman, summoning all the resources of the pork-knocker's language he was learning to use. "When Kanaima," he spoke the dreadful name softly, hoping that its conversion into broken English utterance deprived it of calling all harm, and looking around as if the ground and the trees had black ears — "when Kanaima come here?" he asked. "And which way he pass and gone?" His eyes, like charms betokening all guarded fear, watched the watchman before him. They glanced at the sky as if to eclipse the sentence of time and looked to the rim of the conjuring mountains where the approach of sunset burned indifferently, as though it stood on the after-threshold of dawn, rather than against the closing window of night.

"He gone so — that way." The old negro pointed to the golden mountains of heaven. "He say to tell you . . ." his voice croaked a little . . . "he expect you here today and he coming tonight to get you. He know every step of the way you come since you run away from home and is no use you hiding any more now. I believe . . ." he dropped his voice almost to a whisper . . . "I believe if you can pass him and shake him off your trail in the forest tonight — you got your only chance."

The Indians had listened attentively and their chattering rose again, full of staccato, wounded cries above the muffled voice of the waterfall, dying into helpless silence and submersion at last. "We got take rest," the leader of the party declared heavily and slowly, pronouncing each word with difficulty. He pointed to everyone's condition, indicating that they stood on the very edge of collapse. They had come a long way—days and weeks—across steep ridges and through treacherous valleys. They must stop now—even if it was only for four or five hours of recuperative sleep. The burden of flight would be too great if they left immediately and entered the trail in the night.

"Is no use," the old man said. Nevertheless he turned and shambled towards a shattered hut which stood against the wall of the jungle. It was all he was prepared to offer them. The truth was he wanted them to go away from his village. His name was Jordan. Twenty years of pork-knocking—living on next to nothing—expending nearly every drop of heart's blood in the fever and lust of the diamond bush—had reduced him to a scarecrow of ill-omen always seeing doom, and Kanaima—the avenging Amerindian god, who could wear any shape he wished, man or bird or beast—had come to signify—almost without Jordan being aware of it—the speculative fantasy of his own life; the sight of strange Indians invariably disturbed him and reminded him of the uselessness of time like a photograph of ghosts animated to stir memories of injustice and misfortune. He always pictured them as bringing trouble or flying from trouble. They were a conquered race, were they not? Everybody knew that. It was best to hold them at arm's length though it seemed nothing could prevent their scattered fictions from trespassing on ground where he alone wanted to be.

The light of afternoon began to lose its last vivid shooting colour, the blazing gold became silver, and the resplendent silver was painted over by the haze of dusk. In the east the sky had turned to a deep purple shell, while an intensity of steel appeared in the west, against which—on the topmost ridge of the ghostly mountains—the trees were black smudges of valiant charcoal emphasising the spectral earth and the reflection of fury. A few unwinking stars stood at almost vanishing point in the changing spirit of heaven.

The Indians witnessed the drama of sunset, as if it were the last they would see, through the long rifts in the roof of the house, and out beyond the open places in the desolate walls. The stupor of their long day enveloped them, the ancient worship of the sun, the mirage of space and the curse of the generations.

Kanaima had been on their heels now for weeks and months. Their home and village—comprising about sixty persons—had been stricken. First, there had been an unexpected drought. Then the game had run away in the forest and across the savannahs. After that, people had started dropping down dead. Kanaima planted his signature clear at last in the fire he lit no one knew when and where; it came suddenly running along the already withered spaces of the savannahs, leaving great black charred circles upon the bitten grass everywhere, and snaking into the village-compound where it lifted its writhing self like a spiritual warning in the headman's presence before climbing up the air into space.

They knew then it was no use quarrelling with fate. Day after day they had travelled, looking for somewhere to set up a new encampment, their numbers dwindling all the time, and every situation they came to, it was always to find that Kanaima had passed through before them. If it was not nature's indifference—lack of water or poor soil—they stumbled upon barren human looks and evil counsel, the huts they saw were always tumbling down, and the signs upon the walls they visited were as arid and terrible as flame, as their own home had looked when they had left to search for a new place. It was as if the world they saw and knew was dying everywhere, and no one could dream what would take its place. The time had surely come to stop wherever they were and let whatever had to happen, happen.

It was a hot, stifling night that fell pitch-black upon them. Jordan and the other aged watchman the pork-knockers had left at Tumatumari had nevertheless lit a fire in the village, over which they roasted a bush cow they had shot that morning. It was rare good fortune at a time when the country was yielding little game. The flame blazed steadily, painting a screen on the trees and the shadows of the two men seemed to race hither and thither out of a crowded darkness and back into multitudes still standing on the edge of the forested night. It seemed all of a sudden that another man was there in the open, a sombre reticent spectator. His shadow might have been an illusion of a glaring moment on the earth, or a curious blending of two living shapes into the settlement of a third moving presence.

He was taller than the two blind watchmen over whom he stood. He studied them from behind a fence of flaming stakes, a volcanic hallucinated gateway that might have belonged to some ancient overshadowed primeval garden. It was as if—though he stood near—he always too far for anyone to see his flowing garb. It appeared as if his feet were buried in a voluminous cloak whose material swept into a black hole in the ground, yet when he moved it was with perfect freedom and without a sign of stumbling entanglement. He occasionally glided over the enfolding majestic snake of his garment that obeyed his footsteps.

All at once the sparks flew and his shadow seemed to part the two men in a rain of comets, despatching one with a great leg of beef to the hut where the Indians were, while with another imperious gesture his muffled hand turned the roasting cow into a comfortable position for the one who remained by the fire to slice a share of the breast for dinner. It was the tenderest part of the meat and the stranger devoured a ghostly portion. A distant breeze stirred the whole forest and the fire lifted a tongue up to heaven as though a nest of crucial stars remaining just above a mass of dark trees had finally blown down on earth's leaves.

All around the fire and under the stars the night had grown blacker than ever. The crowding phantoms of the bush had vanished turning faceless and impotent and one with Kanaima's cloak of trailing darkness: the strong meat of life over which the lord of death stood had satisfied them and driven them down into the blackest hole at his feet. The aged watchmen too had their fill and seemed unable to rise from their squatting heels, dreaming of a pile of diamonds under the waterfall. The Macusi headman came to the door of the hut and stood looking towards every hidden snake and trail in the jungle. His companions were sound asleep after their unexpected meal. They had picked the bone clean and then tossed it into the uncanny depths of the lost pit outside their window. Even if they had wanted to resume their journey, the headman felt, it was impossible to do so now. The sound of the Tumatumari Falls rose into the air like sympathetic magic and universal pouring rain. But not a drop descended anywhere out of a sky which was on fire, burning with powder and dust and choked with silver and gold, a great pork-knocker's blackboard and riddle, infinitely rich with the diamonds of space and infinitely poor with the wandering skeletons of eternity.

The headman let his chin drop slowly upon his breast, half-asleep in awe and with nameless fatigue and misery. It was no use complaining he said to himself. Tumatumari was the same as every other village through which they had come, uniform as the river's fall and the drought standing all over the forgotten land from which they had fled, insignificant as every buried grave over which they had crossed. All the trails were vanishing into a running hole in the ground and there was nothing more to do than wait for another joint of roasting meat to fall upon them from the stars that smoked over their head.

There was a movement in the hut behind him, the shaking of a hammock, and a woman appeared in the door beside him. He recognised her in the dim light. She was his wife. She said something to him and began descending the steps, rolling a little like a balloon and half-crouching like an animal feeling for sand before it defecates.

The headman suddenly raised an alarm. He realised she had taken the wrong direction, her eyes half-bandaged by sleep. She had misjudged the trail and had blundered towards the waterfall. His voice was hardly out of his throat when her answering shriek pierced him. She had come to the yawning blind gulley, had tried to scramble for the foothold she was losing, and had only succeeded in slipping deeper and deeper. The headman continued to shout, running forward at the same time. He perceived the cloud of unknowing darkness where the chasm commenced and far below he felt he saw the white spit of foam illumined by starshine, blue and treacherous as a devil. The voices of his companions had followed him and were flying around him like a chorus of shrieks, and it seemed their cry also came from below. The two village-watchmen had also been aroused and they were heaving at the low fire, squandering a host of sparks, until they had acquired flaming branches in their hands. They began to approach the gulley. The flaring billowing light forked into the momentous presence of their infused companion, the shadow of the god who had attended the feast. He had been crouching at the fire beside them as though he presided over each jealous spark, his being shaped by the curious flux of their own bodies which wove his shape on the ground. Now his waving cloak swirled towards the great pit and it seemed that no one realised he was there until the headman of the Macusis saw him coming at last, a vast figure and extension of the dense frightful trees shaking everywhere. and shepherding the watchmen along.

"Kanaima," he screamed. The whole company was startled almost out of their wits, and Jordan — who had met the Indians that afternoon when they arrived in the village — gasped, "I tell you so." He repeated like a rigmarole — "I tell you so."

Then indeed — as if they were proving what they had known all along — they perceived him, his head raised far in the burning sky and his swirling trunk and body sliding over the illuminated cloud above the waterfall. Yet — in spite of themselves — they were all drawn towards the precipice and the roaring invisible rainfall in the night. The flaring torches in their hands picked out the snaking garment which streamed upon the hideous glitter of the angry river, whose jaws gaped with an evil intent. They were lost in wonder at what they saw. The woman who had fallen hung against the side of the cliff, half-sitting upon a jutting nose of rock, her hands clasping a dark trailing vine that wreathed itself upwards along a ragged descending face in the wall. The torches lit up her blind countenance and her pinpoint terrified eyes were enabled to see grinning massive teeth in the face on the wall. Tremblingly holding the vine — as if it were a lock of beloved hair — she began to climb upon the staircased-teeth, brushing lips of stone that seemed to support her, and yet not knowing whether at any moment she would be devoured by falling into the roaring jaws of death.

The watchers waited and beheld the groping muse of all their humanity: Kanaima alone knew whether she would reach the cliff top.

# Bessie Head

## *The Collector of Treasures*

The long-term central state prison in the south was a whole day's journey away from the villages of the northern part of the country. They had left the village of Puleng at about nine that morning and all day long the police truck droned as it sped southwards on the wide, dusty cross-country track-road. The everyday world of ploughed fields, grazing cattle, and vast expanses of bush and forest seemed indifferent to the hungry eyes of the prisoner who gazed out at them through the wire mesh grating at the back of the police truck. At some point during the journey, the prisoner seemed to strike at some ultimate source of pain and loneliness within her being and, overcome by it, she slowly crumpled forward in a wasted heap, oblivious to everything but her pain. Sunset swept by, then dusk, then dark and still the truck droned on, impersonally, uncaring.

At first, faintly on the horizon, the orange glow of the city lights of the new independence town of Gaborone, appeared like an astonishing phantom in the overwhelming darkness of the bush, until the truck struck tarred roads, neon lights, shops and cinemas, and made the bush a phantom amidst a blaze of light. All this passed untimed, unwatched by the crumpled prisoner; she did not stir as the truck finally droned to a halt outside the prison gates. The torchlight struck the side of her face like an agonising blow. Thinking she was asleep, the policeman called out briskly:

"You must awaken now. We have arrived."

He struggled with the lock in the dark and pulled open the grating. She crawled painfully forward, in silence.

Together, they walked up a short flight of stairs and waited awhile as the man tapped lightly, several times, on the heavy iron prison door. The night-duty attendant opened the door a crack, peered out and then opened the door a little wider for them to enter. He quietly and casually led the way to a small office, looked at his colleague and asked: "What do we have here?"

"It's the husband murder case from Puleng village," the other replied, handing over a file.

The attendant took the file and sat down at a table on which lay open a large record book. In a big, bold scrawl he recorded the details: Dikeledi Mokopi. Charge: Man-slaughter. Sentence: Life. A night-duty wardress appeared and led the prisoner away to a side cubicle, where she was asked to undress.

"Have you any money on you?" the wardress queried, handing her a plain, green cotton dress which was the prison uniform. The prisoner silently shook her head.

"So, you have killed your husband, have you?" the wardress remarked, with a flicker of humour. "You'll be in good company. We have four other women here for the same crime. It's becoming the fashion these days. Come with me," and she led the way along a corridor, turned left and stopped at an iron gate which she opened with a key, waited for the prisoner to walk in ahead of her and then locked it with the key again. They entered a small, immensely high-walled courtyard. On one side were toilets, showers, and a cupboard. On the other, an empty concrete quadrangle. The wardress walked to the cupboard, unlocked it and took out a thick roll of clean-smelling blankets which she handed to the prisoner. At the lower end of the walled courtyard was a heavy iron door which led to the cell. The wardress walked up to this door, banged on it loudly and called out: "I say, will you women in there light your candle?"

A voice within called out: "All right," and they could hear the scratch-scratch of a match. The wardress again inserted a key, opened the door and watched for a while as the prisoner spread out her blankets on the floor. The four women prisoners already confined in the cell sat up briefly, and stared silently at their new companion. As the door was locked, they all greeted her quietly and one of the women asked: "Where do you come from?"

"Puleng", the newcomer replied, and seemingly satisfied with that, the light was blown out and the women lay down to continue their interrupted sleep. And as though she had reached the end of her destination, the new prisoner too fell into a deep sleep as soon as she had pulled her blankets about her.

The breakfast gong sounded at six the next morning. The women stirred themselves for their daily routine. They stood up, shook out their blankets and rolled them up into neat bundles. The day-duty wardress rattled the key in the lock and let them out into the small concrete courtyard so that they could perform their morning toilet.

Then, with a loud clatter of pails and plates, two male prisoners appeared at the gate with breakfast. The men handed each woman a plate of porridge and a mug of black tea and they settled themselves on the concrete floor to eat. They turned and looked at their new companion and one of the women, a spokesman for the group said kindly:

"You should take care. The tea has no sugar in it. What we usually do is scoop the sugar off the porridge and put it into the tea."

The woman, Dikeledi, looked up and smiled. She had experienced such terror during the awaiting-trial period that she looked more like a skeleton than a human being. The skin creaked tautly over her cheeks. The other woman smiled, but after her own fashion. Her face permanently wore a look of cynical, whimsical humour. She had a full, plump figure. She introduced herself and her companions: "My name is Kebonye. Then that's Otsetswe, Galeboe, and Monwana. What may your name be?"

"Dikeledi Mokopi."

"How is it that you have such a tragic name," Kebonye observed. "Why did your parents have to name you *tears*?"

"My father passed away at that time and it is my mother's tears that I am named after," Dikeledi said, then added: "She herself passed away six years later and I was brought up by my uncle."

Kebonye shook her head sympathetically, slowly raising a spoonful of porridge to her mouth. That swallowed, she asked next:

"And what may your crime be?"

"I have killed my husband."

"We are all here for the same crime," Kebonye said, then with her cynical smile asked: "Do you feel any sorrow about the crime?"

"Not really," the other woman replied.

"How did you kill him?"

"I cut off all his special parts with a knife," Dikeledi said.

"I did it with a razor," Kebonye said. She sighed and added: "I have had a troubled life."

A little silence followed while they all busied themselves with their food, then Kebonye continued musingly:

"Our men do not think that we need tenderness and care. You know, my husband used to kick me between the legs when he wanted that. I once aborted with a child, due to this treatment. I could see that there was no way to appeal to him if I felt ill, so I once said to him that if he liked he could keep some other woman as well because I couldn't manage to satisfy all his needs. Well, he was an education-officer and each year he used to suspend about seventeen male teachers for making school girls pregnant, but he used to do the same. The last time it happened the parents of the girl were very angry and came to report the matter to me. I told them: 'You leave it to me. I have seen enough.' And so I killed him."

They sat in silence and completed their meal, then they took their plates and cups to rinse them in the wash-room. The wardress produced some pails and a broom. This sleeping quarters had to be flushed out with water; there was not a speck of dirt anywhere, but that was prison routine. All that was left was an inspection by the director of the prison. Here again Kebonye turned to the newcomer and warned:

"You must be careful when the chief comes to inspect. He is mad about one thing — attention! Stand up straight! Hands at your sides! If this is not done you should see how he stands here and curses. He does not mind anything but that. He is mad about that."

Inspection over, the women were taken through a number of gates to an open, sunny yard, fenced in by high, barbed-wire where they did their daily work. The prison was a rehabilitation centre where the prisoners produced goods which were sold in the prison store; the women produced garments of cloth and wool; the men did carpentry, shoe-making, brick-making, and vegetable production.

Dikeledi had a number of skills — she could knit, sew, and weave baskets. All the women at present were busy knitting woollen garments; some were learners and did their work slowly and painstakingly. They looked at Dikeledi with interest as she took a ball of wool and a pair of knitting needles and rapidly cast on stitches. She had soft, caressing, almost boneless, hands of strange power — work of a beautiful design grew from those hands. By mid-morning she had completed the front part of a jersey and they all stopped to admire the pattern she had invented in her own head.

"You are a gifted person," Kebonye remarked, admiringly.

"All my friends say so," Dikeledi replied smiling. "You know, I am the woman whose thatch does not leak. Whenever my friends wanted to thatch their huts, I was there. They would never do it without me. I was always busy and employed because it was with these hands that I fed and reared my children. My husband left me after four years of marriage but I managed well enough to feed those mouths. If people did not pay me in money for my work, they paid me with gifts of food."

"It's not so bad here," Kebonye said. "We get a little money saved for us out of the sale of our work, and if you work like that you can still produce money for your children. How many children do you have?"

"I have three sons."

"Are they in good care?"

"Yes."

"I like lunch," Kebonye said, oddly turning the conversation. "It is the best meal of the day. We get samp and meat and vegetables."

So the day passed pleasantly enough with chatter and work and at sunset the women were once more taken back to the cell for lock-up time. They unrolled their blankets and prepared their beds, and with the candle lit continued to talk a while longer. Just as they were about to retire for the night, Dikeledi nodded to her new-found friend, Kebonye:

"Thank you for all your kindness to me," she said, softly.

"We must help each other," Kebonye replied, with her amused, cynical smile. "This is a terrible world. There is only misery here."

And so the woman Dikeledi began phase three of a life that had been ashen in its loneliness and unhappiness. And yet she had always found gold amidst the ash, deep loves that had joined her heart to the hearts of others. She smiled tenderly at Kebonye because she knew already that she had found another such love. She was the collector of such treasures.

* * *

There were really only two kinds of men in the society. The one kind created such misery and chaos that he could be broadly damned as evil. If one watched the village dogs chasing a bitch on heat, they usually moved around in packs of four or five. As the mating progressed one dog would attempt to gain dominance over the festivities and oust all the others from the bitch's vulva. The rest of the hapless dogs would stand around yapping and snapping in its face while the top dog indulged in a continuous spurt of orgasms, day and night until he was exhausted. No doubt, during that Herculean feat, the dog imagined he was the only penis in the world and that there had to be a scramble for it. That kind of man lived near the animal level and behaved just the same. Like the dogs and bulls and donkeys, he also accepted no responsibility for the young he procreated and like the dogs and bulls and donkeys, he also made females abort. Since that kind of man was in the majority in the society, he needed a little analysing as he was responsible for the complete breakdown of family life. He could be analysed over three time-spans. In the old days, before the colonial invasion of Africa, he was a man who lived by the traditions and taboos outlined for all the people by the forefathers of the tribe. He had little individual freedom to assess whether these traditions were compassionate or not—they demanded that he comply and obey the rules, without thought. But when the laws of the ancestors are examined, they appear on the whole to have been vast, external disciplines for the good of the society as a whole, with little attention given to individual preferences and needs. The ancestors made so many errors and one of the most bitter-making things was that they relegated to men a superior position in the tribe, while women were regarded, in a congenital sense, as being an inferior form of human life. To this day, women still suffered from all the calamities that befall an inferior form of human life. The colonial era and the period of migratory mining labour to South Africa was a further affliction visited on this man. It broke the hold of the ancestors. It broke the old, traditional form of family life and for long periods a man was separated from his wife and children while he worked for a pittance in another land in order to raise the money to pay his British Colonial poll-tax. British Colonialism scarcely enriched his life. He then became "the boy" of the white man and a machine-tool of the South African mines. African independence seemed merely one more affliction on top of the afflictions that had visited this man's life. Independence suddenly and dramatically changed the pattern of colonial subservience. More jobs became available under the new government's localization programme and salaries sky-rocketed at the same time. It provided the first occasion for family life of a new order, above the childlike discipline of custom, the degradation of colonialism. Men and women, in order to survive, had to turn inwards to their own resources. It was the man who arrived at this turning point, a broken wreck with no inner resources at all. It was as though he was hideous to himself and in an effort to flee his own inner emptiness, he spun away from himself in a dizzy kind of death dance of wild destruction and dissipation.

One such man was Garesego Mokopi, the husband of Dikeledi. For four years prior to independence, he had worked as a clerk in the district administration service, at a steady salary of R50.00 a month. Soon after independence his salary shot up to R200.00 per month. Even during his lean days he had had a taste for womanising and drink; now he had the resources for a real spree. He was not seen at home again and lived and slept around the village, from woman to woman. He left his wife and three sons—Banabothe, the eldest, aged four; Inalame, aged three; and the youngest, Motsomi, aged one—to their own resources. Perhaps he did so because she was the boring, semi-literate traditional sort, and there were a lot of exciting new women around.

Independence produced marvels indeed.

There was another kind of man in the society with the power to create himself anew. He turned all his resources, both emotional and material, towards his family life and he went on and on with his own quiet rhythm: like a river. He was a poem of tenderness.

One such man was Paul Thebolo and he and his wife, Kenalepe, and their three children, came to live in the village of Puleng in 1966, the year of independence. Paul Thebolo had been offered the principalship of a primary school in the village. They were allocated an empty field beside the yard of Dikeledi Mokopi, for their new home.

Neighbours are the centre of the universe to each other. They help each other at all times and mutually loan each other's goods. Dikeledi Mokopi kept an interested eye on the yard of her new neighbours. At first, only the man appeared with some workmen to erect the fence, which was set up with incredible speed and efficiency. The man impressed her immediately when she went around to introduce herself and find out a little about the newcomers. He was tall, large-boned, slow-moving. He was so peaceful as a person that the sunlight and shadow played all kinds of tricks with his eyes, making it difficult to determine their exact colour. When he stood still and looked reflective, the sunlight liked to creep into his eyes and nestle there; so sometimes his eyes were the colour of shade, and sometimes light brown.

He turned and smiled at her in a friendly way when she introduced herself and explained that he and his wife were on transfer from the village of Bobonong. His wife and children were living with relatives in the village until the yard was prepared. He was in a hurry to settle down as the school term would start in a month's time. They were, he said, going to erect two mud huts first and later he intended setting up a small house of bricks. His wife would be coming around in a few days with some women to erect the mud walls of the huts.

"I would like to offer my help too," Dikeledi said. "If work always starts early in the morning and there are about six of us, we can get both walls erected in a week. If you want one of the huts done in woman's thatch, all my friends know that I am the woman whose thatch does not leak."

The man smilingly replied that he would impart all this information to his wife, then he added charmingly that he thought she would like his wife when they met. His wife was a very friendly person; everyone liked her.

Dikeledi walked back to her own yard with a high heart. She had few callers. None of her relatives called for fear that since her husband had left her she would become dependent on them for many things. The people who called did business with her; they wanted her to make dresses for their children or knit jerseys for the winter time and at times when she had no orders at all, she made baskets which she sold. In these ways she supported herself and the three children but she was lonely for true friends.

All turned out as the husband had said — he had a lovely wife. She was fairly tall and thin with a bright, vivacious manner. She made no effort to conceal that normally, and every day, she was a very happy person. And all turned out as Dikeledi had said. The work-party of six women erected the mud walls of the huts in one week; two weeks later, the thatch was complete. The Thebolo family moved into their new abode and Dikeledi Mokopi moved into one of the most prosperous and happy periods of her life. Her life took a big, wide upward curve. Her relationship with the Thebolo family was more than the usual friendly exchange of neighbours. It was rich and creative.

It was not long before the two women had going one of those deep, affectionate, sharing-everything kind of friendships that only women know how to have. It seemed that Kenalepe wanted endless amounts of dresses made for herself and her three little girls. Since Dikeledi would not accept cash for these services — she protested about the many benefits she received from her good neighbours — Paul Thebolo arranged that she be paid in household goods for these services so that for some years Dikeledi was always assured of her basic household needs — the full bag of corn, sugar, tea, powdered milk, and cooking oil. Kenalepe was also the kind of woman who made the whole world spin around her; her attractive personality attracted a whole range of women to her yard and also a whole range of customers for her dressmaking friend, Dikeledi. Eventually, Dikeledi became swamped with work, was forced to buy a second sewing-machine and employ a helper. The two women did everything together — they were forever together at weddings, funerals, and parties in the village. In their leisure hours they freely discussed all their intimate affairs with each other, so that each knew thoroughly the details of the other's life.

"You are a lucky someone," Dikeledi remarked one day, wistfully. "Not everyone has the gift of a husband like Paul."

"Oh yes," Kenalepe said happily. "He is an honest somebody." She knew a little of Dikeledi's list of woes and queried: "But why did you marry a man like Garesego? I looked carefully at him when you pointed him out to me near the shops the other day and I could see at one glance that he is a butterfly."

"I think I mostly wanted to get out of my uncle's yard," Dikeledi replied. "I never liked my uncle. Rich as he was, he was a hard man and very selfish. I was only a servant there and pushed about. I went there when I was six years old when my mother died, and it was not a happy life. All his children despised me because I was their servant. Uncle paid for my education for six years, then he said I must leave school. I longed for more because as you know, education opens up the world for one. Garesego was a friend of my uncle and he was the only man who proposed for me. They discussed it between themselves and then my uncle said: "You'd better marry Garesego because you're just hanging around here like a chain on my neck." I agreed, just to get away from that terrible man. Garesego said at that time that he'd rather be married to my sort than the educated kind because those women were stubborn and wanted to lay down the rules for men. Really, I did not ever protest when he started running about. You know what the other women do. They chase after the man from one hut to another and beat up the girlfriends. The man just runs into another hut, that's all. So you don't really win. I wasn't going to do anything like that. I am satisfied I have children. They are a blessing to me."

"Oh, it isn't enough," her friend said, shaking her head in deep sympathy. "I am amazed at how life imparts its gifts. Some people get too much. Others get nothing at all. I have always been lucky in life. One day my parents will visit — they live in the south — and you'll see the fuss they make over me. Paul is just the same. He takes care of everything so that I never have a day of worry . . ."

The man Paul attracted as wide a range of male friends as his wife. They had guests every evening: illiterate men who wanted him to fill in tax forms or write letters for them, or his own colleagues who wanted to debate the political issues of the day — there was always something new happening every day now that the country had independence. The two women sat on the edge of these debates and listened with fascinated ears, but they never participated. The following day they would chew over the debates with wise, earnest expressions.

"Men's minds travel widely and boldly," Kenalepe would comment. "It makes me shiver the way they freely criticise our new government. Did you hear what Petros said last night? He said he knew all those bastards and they were just a lot of crooks who would pull a lot of dirty tricks. Oh dear! I shivered so much when he said that. The way they talk about the government makes you feel in your bones that this is not a safe world to be in, not like the old days when we didn't have governments. And Lentswe said that ten per cent of the population in

England really control all the wealth of the country, while the rest live at starvation level. And he said communism would sort all this out. I gathered from the way they discussed this matter that our government is not in favour of communism. I trembled so much when this became clear to me . . ." She paused and laughed proudly. "I've heard Paul say this several times: 'The British only ruled us for eighty years.' I wonder why Paul is so fond of saying that?"

And so a completely new world opened up for Dikeledi. It was so impossibly rich and happy that, as the days went by, she immersed herself more deeply in it and quite overlooked the barrenness of her own life. But it hung there like a nagging ache in the mind of her friend, Kenalepe.

"You ought to find another man," she urged one day, when they had one of their personal discussions. "It's not good for a woman to live alone."

"And who would that be?" Dikeledi asked, disillusioned. "I'd only be bringing trouble into my life whereas now it is all in order. I have my eldest son at school and I can manage to pay the school fees. That's all I really care about."

"I mean," said Kenalepe, "we are also here to make love and enjoy it."

"Oh I never really cared for it," the other replied. "When you experience the worst of it, it just puts you off altogether."

"What do you mean by that?" Kenalepe asked, wide-eyed.

"I mean it was just jump on and jump off and I used to wonder what it was all about. I developed a dislike for it."

"You mean Garesego was like that!" Kenalepe said, flabbergasted. "Why, that's just like a cock hopping from hen to hen. I wonder what he is doing with all those women. I'm sure they are just after his money and so they flatter him . . ." She paused and then added earnestly: "That's really all the more reason you should find another man. Oh, if you knew what it was really like, you would long for it, I can tell you! I sometimes think I enjoy that side of life far too much. Paul knows a lot about all that. And he always has some new trick with which to surprise me. He has a certain way of smiling when he has thought up something new and I shiver a little and say to myself: "Ha, what is Paul going to do tonight!"

Kenalepe paused and smiled at her friend, slyly.

"I can loan Paul to you if you like," she said, then raised one hand to block the protest on her friend's face. "I would do it because I have never had a friend like you in my life before whom I trust so much. Paul had other girls you know, before he married me, so it's not such an uncommon thing to him. Besides, we used to make love long before we got married and I never got pregnant. He takes care of that side too. I wouldn't mind loaning him because I am expecting another child and I don't feel so well these days . . ."

Dikeledi stared at the ground for a long moment, then she looked up at her friend with tears in her eyes.

"I cannot accept such a gift from you," she said, deeply moved. "But if you are ill I will wash for you and cook for you."

Not put off by her friend's refusal of her generous offer, Kenalepe mentioned the discussion to her husband that very night. He was so taken off-guard by the unexpectedness of the subject that at first he looked slightly astonished, and burst out into loud laughter and for such a lengthy time that he seemed unable to stop.

"Why are you laughing like that?" Kenalepe asked, surprised.

He laughed a bit more, then suddenly turned very serious and thoughtful and was lost in his own thoughts for some time. When she asked him what he was thinking he merely replied: "I don't want to tell you everything. I want to keep some of my secrets to myself."

The next day Kenalepe reported this to her friend.

"Now whatever does he mean by that? I want to keep some of my secrets to myself?"

"I think," Dikeledi said smiling, "I think he has a conceit about being a good man. Also, when someone loves someone too much, it hurts them to say so. They'd rather keep silent."

Shortly after this Kenalepe had a miscarriage and had to be admitted to hospital for a minor operation. Dikeledi kept her promise "to wash and cook" for her friend. She ran both their homes, fed the children and kept everything in order. Also, people complained about the poorness of the hospital diet and each day she scoured the village for eggs and chicken, cooked them, and took them to Kenalepe every day at the lunch-hour.

One evening Dikeledi ran into a snag with her routine. She had just dished up supper for the Thebolo children when a customer came around with an urgent request for an alteration on a wedding dress. The wedding was to take place the next day. She left the children seated around the fire eating and returned to her own home. An hour later, her own children asleep and settled, she thought she would check the Thebolo yard to see if all was well there. She entered the children's hut and noted that they had put themselves to bed and were fast asleep. Their supper plates lay scattered and unwashed around the fire. The hut which Paul and Kenalepe shared was in darkness. It meant that Paul had not yet returned from his usual evening visit to his wife. Dikeledi collected the plates and washed them, then poured the dirty dishwater on the still-glowing embers of the outdoor fire. She piled the plates one on top of the other and carried them to the third additional hut which was used as a kitchen. Just then Paul Thebolo entered the yard, noted the lamp and movement in the kitchen hut and walked over to it. He paused at the open door.

"What are you doing now, Mme-Banabothe?" he asked, addressing her affectionately in the customary way by the name of her eldest son, Banabothe.

"I know quite well what I am doing," Dikeledi replied happily. She turned around to say that it was not a good thing to leave dirty dishes standing overnight but her mouth flew open with surprise. Two soft pools of cool liquid light were in his eyes and something infinitely sweet passed between them; it was too beautiful to be love.

"You are a very good woman, Mma-Banabothe," he said softly.

It was the truth and the gift was offered like a nugget of gold. Only men like Paul Thebolo could offer such gifts. She took it and stored another treasure in her heart. She bowed her knee in the traditional curtsey and walked quietly away to her own home.

\* \* \*

Eight years passed for Dikeledi in a quiet rhythm of work and friendship with the Thebolos. The crisis came with the eldest son, Banabothe. He had to take his primary school leaving examination at the end of the year. This serious event sobered him up considerably as like all boys he was very fond of playtime. He brought his books home and told his mother that he would like to study in the evenings. He would like to pass with a "Grade A" to please her. With a flushed and proud face Dikeledi mentioned this to her friend, Kenalepe.

"Banabothe is studying every night now," she said. "He never really cared for studies. I am so pleased about this that I bought him a spare lamp and removed him from the children's hut to my own hut where things will be peaceful for him. We both sit up late at night now. I sew on buttons and fix hems and he does his studies . . ."

She also opened a savings account at the post office in order to have some standby money to pay the fees for his secondary education. They were rather high – R85.00. But in spite of all her hoarding of odd cents, towards the end of the year, she was short on R20.00 to cover the fees.

Midway during the Christmas school holidays the results were announced. Banabothe passed with a "Grade A". His mother was almost hysterical in her joy at his achievement. But what to do? The two youngest sons had already started primary school and she would never manage to cover all their fees from her resources. She decided to remind Garesego Mokopi that he was the father of the children. She had not seen him in eight years except as a passer-by in the village. Sometimes he waved but he had never talked to her or enquired about her life or that of the children. It did not matter. She was a lower form of human life. Then this unpleasant something turned up at his office one day, just as he was about to leave for lunch. She had heard from village gossip that he had eventually settled down with a married woman who had a brood of children of her own. He had ousted her husband, in a typical village sensation of brawls, curses, and abuse. Most probably the husband did not care because there were always arms outstretched towards a man, as long as he looked like a man. The attraction of this particular woman for Garesego Mokopi, so her former lovers said with a snicker, was that she went in for heady forms of love-making like biting and scratching.

Garesego Mokopi walked out of his office and looked irritably at the ghost from his past, his wife. She obviously wanted to talk to him and he walked towards her, looking at his watch all the while. Like all the new "success men," he had developed a paunch, his eyes were blood-shot, his face was bloated, and the odour of the beer and sex from the previous night clung faintly around him. He indicated with his eyes that they should move around to the back of the office block where they could talk in privacy.

"You must hurry with whatever you want to say," he said impatiently. "The lunch-hour is very short and I have to be back at the office by two."

Not to him could she talk of the pride she felt in Banabothe's achievement, so she said simply and quietly: "Garesego, I beg you to help me pay Banabothe's fees for secondary school. He has passed with a 'Grade A' and as you know, the school fees must be produced on the first day of school or else he will be turned away. I have struggled to save money the whole year but I am short by R20.00."

She handed him her post office savings book, which he took, glanced at and handed back to her. Then he smiled, a smirky know-all smile, and thought he was delivering her a blow in the face.

"Why don't you ask Paul Thebolo for the money?" he said. "Everyone knows he's keeping two homes and that you are his spare.

Everyone knows about that full bag of corn he delivers to your home every six months so why can't he pay the school fees as well?"

She neither denied this, nor confirmed it. The blow glanced off her face which she raised slightly, in pride. Then she walked away.

As was their habit, the two women got together that afternoon and Dikeledi reported this conversation with her husband to Kenalepe who tossed back her head in anger and said fiercely: "The filthy pig himself! He thinks every man is like him, does he? I shall report this matter to Paul, then he'll see something."

And indeed Garesego did see something but it was just up his alley. He was a female prostitute in his innermost being and like all professional prostitutes, he enjoyed publicity and sensation — it promoted his cause. He smiled genially and expansively when a madly angry Paul Thebolo came up to the door of his house where he lived with *his* concubine. Garesego had been through a lot of these dramas over those eight years and he almost knew by rote the dialogue that would follow.

"You bastard!" Paul Thebolo spat out. "Your wife isn't my concubine, do you hear?"

"Then why are you keeping her in food?" Garesego drawled. "Men only do that for women they fuck! They never do it for nothing."

Paul Thebolo rested one hand against the wall, half dizzy with anger, and he said tensely: "You defile life, Garesego Mokopi. There's nothing else in your world but defilement. Mma-Banabothe makes clothes for my wife and children and she will never accept money from me so how else must I pay her?"

"It only proves the story both ways," the other replied, vilely. "Women do that for men who fuck them."

Paul Thebolo shot out the other hand, punched him soundly in one grinning eye and walked away. Who could hide a livid, swollen eye? To every surprised enquiry, he replied with an injured air:

"It was done by my wife's lover, Paul Thebolo."

It certainly brought the attention of the whole village upon him, which was all he really wanted. Those kinds of men were the bottom rung of government. They secretly hungered to be the President with all eyes on them. He worked up the sensation a little further. He announced that he would pay the school fees of the child of his concubine, who was also to enter secondary school, but not the school fees of his own child, Banabothe. People half liked the smear on Paul Thebolo; he was too good to be true. They delighted in making him a part of the general dirt of the village, so they turned on Garesego and scolded: "Your wife might be getting things from Paul Thebolo but it's beyond the purse of any man to pay the school fees of his own children as well as the school fees of another man's children. Banabothe wouldn't be there had you not procreated him, Garesego, so it is your duty to care for him. Besides, it's your fault if your wife takes another man. You left her alone all these years."

So that story was lived with for two weeks, mostly because people wanted to say that Paul Thebolo was a part of life too and as uncertain of his morals as they were. But the story took such a dramatic turn that it made all the men shudder with horror. It was some weeks before they could find the courage to go to bed with women; they preferred to do something else.

Garesego's obscene thought processes were his own undoing. He really believed that another man had a stake in his hen-pen and like any cock, his hair was up about it. He thought he'd walk in and re-establish his own claim to it and so, after two weeks, once the swelling in his eye had died down, he espied Banabothe in the village and asked him to take a note to his mother. He said the child should bring a reply. The note read: "Dear Mother, I am coming home again so that we may settle our differences. Will you prepare a meal for me and some hot water that I might take a bath? Gare."

Dikeledi took the note, read it and shook with rage. All its overtones were clear to her. He was coming home for some sex. They had had no differences. They had not even talked to each other.

"Banabothe," she said. "Will you play nearby? I want to think a bit then I will send you to your father with the reply."

Her thought processes were not very clear to her. There was something she could not immediately touch upon. Her life had become holy to her during all those years she had struggled to maintain herself and the children. She had filled her life with treasures of kindness and love she had gathered from others and it was all this that she wanted to protect from defilement by an evil man. Her first panic-stricken thought was to gather up the children and flee the village. But where to go? Garesego did not want a divorce, she had left him to approach her about the matter, she had desisted from taking any other man. She turned her thoughts this way and that and could find no way out except to face him. If she wrote back, don't you dare put foot in the yard I don't want to see you, he would ignore it. Black women didn't have that kind of power. A thoughtful, brooding look came over her face. At last, at peace with herself, she went into her hut and wrote a reply: "Sir, I shall prepare everything as you have said. Dikeledi."

It was about midday when Banabothe sped back with the reply to his father. All afternoon Dikeledi busied herself making preparations for the appearance of her husband at sunset. At one point Kenalepe approached the yard and looked around in amazement at the massive preparations, the large iron water pot full of water with a fire burning under it, the extra cooking pots on the fire. Only later Kenalepe brought the knife into focus. But it was only a vague blur, a large kitchen knife used to cut meat and Dikeledi knelt at a grinding-stone and sharpened it slowly and methodically. What was in focus then was the final and tragic expression on the upturned face of her friend. It threw her into confusion and blocked their usual free and easy feminine chatter. When Dikeledi said: "I am making some preparations for Garesego. He is coming home tonight," Kenalepe beat a hasty retreat to her own home terrified. They knew they were involved because when she mentioned this to Paul he was distracted and uneasy for the rest of the day. He kept on doing upside-down sorts of things, not replying to questions, absent-mindedly leaving a cup of tea until it got quite cold, and every now and again he stood up and paced about, lost in his own thoughts. So deep was their sense of disturbance that towards evening they no longer made a pretence of talking. They just sat in silence in their hut. Then, at about nine o'clock, they heard those wild and agonized bellows. They both rushed out together to the yard of Dikeledi Mokopi.

* * *

He came home at sunset and found everything ready for him as he had requested, and he settled himself down to enjoy a man's life. He had brought a pack of beer along and sat outdoors slowly savouring it while every now and then his eye swept over the Thebolo yard. Only the woman and children moved about the yard. The man was out of sight. Garesego smiled to himself, pleased that he could crow as loud as he liked with no answering challenge.

A basin of warm water was placed before him to wash his hands and then Dikeledi served him his meal. At a separate distance she also served the children and then instructed them to wash and prepare for bed. She noted that Garesego displayed no interest in the children whatsoever. He was entirely wrapped up in himself and thought only of himself and his own comfort. Any tenderness he offered the children might have broken her and swerved her mind away from the deed she had carefully planned all that afternoon. She was beneath his regard and notice too for when she eventually brought her own plate of food and sat near him, he never once glanced at her face. He drank his beer and cast his glance every now and again at the Thebolo yard. Not once did the man of the yard appear until it became too dark to distinguish anything any more. He was completely satisfied with that. He could repeat the performance every day until he broke the mettle of the other cock again and forced him into angry abuse. He liked that sort of thing.

"Garesego, do you think you could help me with Banabothe's school fees?" Dikeledi asked at one point.

"Oh, I'll think about it," he replied casually.

She stood up and carried buckets of water into the hut, which she poured into a large tin bath that he might bathe himself, then while he took his bath she busied herself tidying up and completing the last of the household chores. Those done, she entered the children's hut. They played hard during the day and they had already fallen asleep with exhaustion. She knelt down near their sleeping mats and stared at them for a long while, with an extremely tender expression. Then she blew out their lamp and walked to her own hut. Garesego lay sprawled across the bed in such a manner that indicated he only thought of himself and did not intend sharing the bed with anyone else. Satiated with food and drink, he had fallen into a deep, heavy sleep the moment his head touched the pillow. His concubine had no doubt taught him that the correct way for a man to go to bed, was naked.

So he lay, unguarded and defenceless, sprawled across the bed on his back.

The bath made a loud clatter as Dikeledi removed it from the room, but still he slept on, lost to the world. She re-entered the hut and closed the door. Then she bent down and reached for the knife under the bed which she had merely concealed with a cloth. With the precision and skill of her hardworking hands, she grasped hold of his genitals and cut them off with one stroke. In doing so, she slit the main artery which ran on the inside of the groin. A massive spurt of blood arched its way across the bed. And Garesego bellowed. He bellowed his anguish. Then all was silent. She stood and watched his death anguish with an intent and brooding look, missing not one detail of it. A knock on the door stirred her out of her reverie. It was the boy, Banabothe. She opened the door and stared at him, speechless. He was trembling violently.

"Mother," he said, in a terrified whisper. "Didn't I hear father cry?"

"I have killed him," she said, waving her hand in the air with a gesture that said — well, that's that. Then she added sharply:

"Banabothe, go and call the police."

He turned and fled into the night. A second pair of footsteps followed hard on his heels. It was Kenalepe running back to her own yard, half out of her mind with fear. Out of the dark Paul Thebolo stepped towards the hut and entered it. He took in every detail and then he turned and looked at Dikeledi with such a tortured expression that for a time words failed him. At last he said: "You don't have to worry about the children, Mma-Banabothe. I'll take them as my own and give them all a secondary school education."

# Keri Hulme

## *Hooks and Feelers*

On the morning before it happened, her fingers were covered with grey, soft clay.

"Charleston," she says. "It comes from Charleston. It's really a modeller's clay, but it'll make nice cups. I envisage," gesturing in the air, "tall fluted goblets. I'll glaze them sea blue and we'll drink wine together, all of us."

I went out to the shed and knocked on the door. There's no word of welcome, but the kerosene lamp is burning brightly, so I push on in.

She's pumping the treadle potter's wheel with a terrible urgency, but she's not making pots. Just tall, wavery cones. I don't know what they are. I've never seen her make them before. The floor, the shelves, the bench — the place is spikey with them.

"They've rung," I say.

She doesn't look up.

"They said he'll be home tomorrow."

The wheel slowed, stopped.

"So?"

"Well, will you get him?"

"No."

The wheel starts purring. Another cone begins to grow under her fingers.

"What are you making those for?"

She still won't look at me.

"You go," she says, and the wheel begins to hum.

Well, you can't win.

I go and get him and come home, chattering brightly all the way.

He is silent.

I carry him inside, painting out that I've repainted everywhere, that we've got a new stove and did you like your present? And he ignores it all.

But he says, very quietly, to his ma, "Hello." Very cool.

She looks at him, over him, round him, eyes going up and down but always avoiding the one place where she should be looking. She says "Hello," back.

"Put me down please," he says to me then.

No "Thanks for getting me." Not a word of appreciation for the new clothes. Just that polite, expressionless, "Put me down please."

Not another word.

He went into his bedroom and shut the door.

"Well, it's just the shock of being back home, eh?"

I look at her, and she looks at me. I go across and slide my hands around her shoulders, draw her close to me, nuzzle her ear, and for a moment it's peace.

Then she draws away.

"Make a coffee," she says brusquely. "I'm tired."

I don't take offence. After grinding the beans, I ask, "What are you making the cones for?"

She shrugs.

"It's just an idea."

The smell from the crushed coffee beans is rich and heavy, almost sickening.

His door opens.

He has his doll in his hand. Or rather, parts of his doll. He's torn the head off, the arms and legs apart.

"I don't want this anymore," he says into the silence.

He goes to the fire, and flings the parts in. And then he reaches in among the burning coals and plucks out the head, which is melted and smoking. He says, "On second thoughts, I'll keep this."

The smoke curls round the steel and lingers, acridly.

Soon after, she went back to the shed.

I went down to the pub.

"Hey!" yells Mata, "c'mon over here!"

"Look at that," he says, grinning hugely, waving a crumpled bit of paper. It's a Golden Kiwi ticket. "Bugger's won me four hundred dollars." He sways. "Whatta yer drinking?"

I never have won anything. I reach across, grab his hand, shake it. It's warm and calloused, hard and real.

"Bloody oath, Mat, what good luck!"

He smiles more widely still, his eyes crinkling almost shut. "Shout you eh?"

"Too right you can. Double whisky."

And I get that from him and a jug and another couple of doubles and another jug. I am warm and happy until someone turns the radio up.

"Hands across the water, hands across the sea . . ." the voices thunder and beat by my ears, and pianos and violins wail and wind round the words.

The shed's in darkness.

I push the door open, gingerly.

"Are you there?"

I hear her move.

"Yes."

"How about a little light on the subject?" I'm trying to sound happily drunk, but the words have a nasty callous ring to them.

"The lamp is on the bench beside you."

I reach for it and encounter a soft, still wet, cone of clay. I snatch my fingers away hurriedly.

"Are you revealing to the world what the cones are for yet?"

I've found the lamp, fumble for my matches. My fingers are clumsy, but at last the wick catches a light, glows and grows.

She sniffs.

"Give me the matches please."

I throw the box across and she snatches them from the air.

She touches a match to a cigarette; the match shows blue and then flares bright, steady, gold. The cigarette pulses redly. The lamp isn't trimmed very well.

She sighs and the smoke flows thickly out of her month and nose.

"I put nearly all of them back in the stodge-box today."

What? Oh yes, the cones. The stodge-box is her special term for the pile of clay that gets reworked.

"Oh." I add after a moment, apologetically, "I sort of squashed one reaching for the lamp."

"It doesn't matter," she says, blowing out another stream of smoke.

"I was going to kill that one too."

I take my battered, old, guitar and begin to play. I play badly. I've never learned to play properly.

He says, out of the dark, "Why are you sad?"

"What makes you think I am?"

"Because you're playing without the lights on."

I sigh. "A man call play in the dark if he wants."

"Besides I heard you crying."

My dear cool son.

"... so I cry sometimes ..."

"Why are you sad?" he asks again.

Everlasting questions ever since he began to talk.

"Shut up."

"Because of me?" he persists. He pauses, long enough to check whether I'm going to move.

"Or because of her?"

"Because of me, now get out of here," I answer roughly, and bang the guitar down. It groans. The strings shiver.

He doesn't move.

"You've been to the pub?"

I prop the guitar against the wall and get up.

"You've been to the pub," he states, and drifts back into his room.

My mother came to visit the next day, all agog to see the wreckage. She has a nice instinct for disasters. She used to be a strong little woman but she's run to frailty and brittle bones now. Alas; all small and powdery, with a thick fine down over her face that manages, somehow, to protrude through her make-up. It'd look so much better if she didn't pile powder and stuff on, but I can't imagine her face without pink gunk clogging the pores. That much has never changed.

She brought a bag of blackballs for him. When he accepts them, reluctantly, she coos and pats him and strokes his hair. He has always hated that.

"Oh dear," she says, "your poor careless mother," and "You poor little man" and (aside to me) "It's just as well you didn't have a daughter, it'd be so much worse for a girl." (He heard that, and smiled blandly.)

She asks him, "However are you going to manage now? Your guitar and football and all? Hmmm?"

He says, steadily, "It's very awkward to wipe my arse now. That's all."

For a moment I like him very much.

My mother flutters and tchs, "Oh, goodness me, dear, you mustn't say ..."

He's already turned away.

As soon as my mother left, I went out to the shed.

"You could have come in and said hello," I say reproachfully.

"It would have only led to a fight." She sits hunched up on the floor.

Her face is in shadow.

I look round. The shed's been tidied up. All the stray bits and pieces are hidden away. There's an innovation, however, an ominous one. The crucifix she keeps on the wall opposite her wheel has been covered with black cloth. The only part that shows is a hand, nailed to the wooden cross.

"Is that a reminder for penitence? Or are you mourning?"

She doesn't reply.

Early in the morning, while it's still quite dark, I awake to hear him sobbing. I lift the bedclothes gently—she didn't stir, drowned in sleep, her black hair wreathed about her body like seaweed—and creep away to his room.

The sobbing is part stifled, a rhythmic choking and gasping, rough with misery.

"Hello?"

"E pa . . ." he turns over and round from his pillow and reaches out his arms. He doesn't do that. He hasn't done that since he was a baby.

I pick him up, cradling him, cuddling him.

"I call still feel it pa. I can feel it still." He is desperate in his insistence and wild with crying. But he is also coldly angry at himself.

"I know it's not there anymore," he struck himself a blow, "but I can *feel* it still . . ."

I kiss and soothe and bring a tranquilliser that the people at the hospital gave me. He sobs himself back to sleep, leaning, in the end, away from me. And I go back to bed.

Her ocean, her ocean, te moananui a Kiwa, drowns me. Far away on the beach I can hear him calling, but I must keep on going down into the greeny deeps, down to where her face is, to where the soft anemone tentacles of her fingers beckon and sway and sweep me onward to the weeping heart of the world.

He stays home from school for another week. It's probably just as well, for once, the first time he ventured outside the house, the next door neighbour's kids shouted crudities at him.

I watched him walk over to them, talk, and gesture, the hook flashing bravely in the sun. The next door neighbour's kids fell silent, drew together in a scared huddled group.

"What did you do to stop that?" I ask, after he has stalked proudly back inside.

He shook his head.

"Tell me."

"I didn't have to do anything." He smiles.

"Oh?"

"I don't imagine," he says it so coolly, "that anyone wants this in their eyes."

The hair on the back of my neck bristles with shock.

"Don't you dare threaten anybody like that! No matter what they say!" I shout at him in rage, in horror. "I'll beat you silly if you do that again."

He shrugs. "Okay, if you say so pa."

(Imagine that cruel, steel curve reaching for your eyes. That pincer of unfeeling metal gouging in.) The steel hook glints as he moves away.

How can he be my son and have so little of me in him? Oh, he has my colouring, fair hair and steel-grey eyes, just as he has her colour and bone structure; a brown thickset chunk of a boy.

But his strange cold nature comes from neither of us. Well, it certainly doesn't come from me.

Later on that day—we are reading in front of the fire—a coal falls out. He reaches for it.

"Careful, it's hot," I warn.

"I don't care how hot it is," he says, grinning.

The two steel fingers pick up the piece of coal and slowly crush the fire out of it.

It hasn't taken long for him to get very deft with those pincers. He can pluck up minute things, like pins, or the smallest of buttons. I suspect he practises doing so, in the secrecy of his bedroom. He can handle almost anything as skilfully as he could before.

At night, after he's had a shower, I ask, "Let me look?"

"No."

"Ahh, come on."

He holds it out, silently.

All his wrist bones are gone. There remains a scarred purplish area with two smooth, rounded knobs on either side. In the centre is a small socket. The hook, which is mounted on a kind of swivel, slots into there. I don't understand how it works, but it looks like a nice practical piece of machinery.

He is looking away.

"You don't like it?"

"It's all right . . . will you string my guitar backwards? I tried, and I can't do it."

"Of course."

I fetch his guitar and begin immediately.

"There is something quite new we can do, you know." The specialist draws a deep breath of smoke and doesn't exhale any of it.

The smell of antiseptic is making me feel sick. This room is painted a dull grey. There are flyspots on the light. I bring my eyes down to him and smile, rigidly.

"Ahh, yes?"

"Immediately after amputation, we can attach an undamaged portion of sinew and nerve to this nyloprene socket."

He holds out a gadget, spins it round between his lean fingers, and snatches it away again, out of sight.

"It is a permanent implant, with a special prosthesis that fits into it, but the child will retain a good deal of control over his, umm, hand movements."

He sucks in more smoke and eyes me beadily, eagerly. Then he suddenly lets the whole, stale lungful go, right in my face.

"So you agree to that then?"

"Ahh, yes."

Later, at night, she says, "Are you still awake too?"

"Yes."

"What are you thinking of."

"Nothing really. I was just listening to you breathe." Her hand creeps to my side, feeling along until it finds a warm handful.

"I am thinking of the door," she says thoughtfully.

You know the way a car door crunches shut, with a sort of definite, echoing thunk?

Well, there was that. Her hurried footsteps. A split second of complete silence. And then the screaming started, piercing, agonized, desperate. We spun round. He was nailed, pinioned against the side of the car by his trapped hand.

She stood, going, "O my god! O my god!" and biting down on her hand. She didn't make another move, frozen where she stood, getting whiter and whiter and whiter.

I had to open the door.

"I know it's silly," she continues, still holding me warmly, "but if we hadn't bought that packet of peanuts, we wouldn't have spilled them. I wouldn't have got angry. I wouldn't have stormed out of the car. I wouldn't have slammed the door without looking. Without looking."

"You bought the nuts, remember?" she adds irrelevantly.

I don't answer.

There are other things in her ocean now. Massive black shadows that loom up near me without revealing what they are. Something glints. The shadows waver and retreat.

They stuck a needle attached to a clear, plastic tube into his arm. The tube filled with blood. Then, the blood cleared away and the dope ran into his vein. His eyelids dragged down. He slept, unwillingly, the tears of horror and anguish still wet on his face.

The ruined hand lay on a white, shiny bench, already apart from him. It was like a lump of raw, swollen meat with small, shattered, bluish bones through it.

"We'll have to amputate that, I'm afraid. It's absolutely unsalvageable."

"Okay," I say. "Whatever you think best."

They say that hearing is the last of the senses to die, when you are unconscious.

They are wrong, at least for me. Images, or what is worse, not-quite images, flare and burst and fade before I sink into the dreamless sea of sleep.

I went out to the shed.

"Tea is nearly ready," I call through the open door.

"Good," she replies. "Come in and look."

She has made a hundred, more than a hundred, large shallow wine cups. "Kraters," she says, smiling to me briefly.

I grin back, delighted.

"Well, they should sell well."

She bends her head, scraping at a patch of dried clay on the bench.

"What were the cones?"

She looks up at me, the smile gone entirely. "Nothing important," she says. "Nothing important."

When she's washing the dishes, however, the magic happens again. For the first time since the door slammed shut, I look at her, and she looks willingly back and her eyes become deep and endless dark waters, beckoning to my soul. Drown in me . . . find yourself. I reach out flailing, groping for her hard, real body. Ahh, my hands encounter tense muscles, fasten on to them. I stroke and knead, rousing the long-dormant woman in her. Feel in the taut, secret places, rub the tender moist groove, caress her all over with sweet, probing fingers.

"Bait," says a cold, sneering voice.

She gasps and goes rigid again.

"Get away to bed with you," she says without turning round.

"I'm going to watch."

An overwhelming anger floods through me. I whip around and my erstwhile gentle hands harden and clench.

"No," she says, "no," touching me, warning me.

She goes across and kneels before him.

(I see he's trembling.)

She kisses his face.

She kisses his hand.

She kisses the hook.

"Now go to bed e tama."

He stands, undecided, swaying in the doorway.

Then, too quickly for it to be stopped, he lashes out with the hook. It strikes her on her left breast.

I storm forward, full of rage, and reach for him.

"No," she says again, kneeling there, motionless. "No," yet again.

"Go to bed, tama," she says to him.

Her voice is warm and friendly. Her face is serene.

He turns obediently, and walks away into the dark.

At the weekend, I suggested we go for a picnic.

"Another one?" she asks, her black eyebrows raised.

"Well, we could gather pauas, maybe some cress, have a meal on the beach. It'd be good to get out of the house for a while. This hasn't been too good a week for me, you know."

They both shrugged.

"Okay," he says.

"I will get the paua," she says, and begins stripping off her jeans.

"You get the cress," she says to him.

"I'll go with you and help," I add.

He just looks at me. Those steely eyes in that brown face. Then he pouted, picked up the kete, and headed for the stream.

He selects a stalk and pinches it suddenly. The plant tissue thins to nothing. It's like he's executing the cress. He adds it to the pile in the kete. He doesn't look at me, or talk. He is absorbed in killing cress.

There's not much I can do.

So I put on my mask and flippers and wade into the water, slide down under the sea. I spend a long peaceful time there, detaching whelks and watching them wobble down to the bottom. I cruise along the undersea rock shelf, plucking bits of weed and letting them drift away. Eventually, I reach the end of the reef, and I can hear the boom and mutter of the real ocean. It's getting too close; I surface.

One hundred yards away, fighting a current that is moving him remorselessly out, is my son.

When I gained the beach, I was exhausted.

I stand, panting, him in my arms.

His face is grey and waxy and the water runs off us both, dropping constantly on the sand.

"You were too far out . . ."

He cries.

"Where is she?"

Where is she? Gathering paua somewhere . . . but suddenly I don't know if that is so. I put my mask back on, leave him on the beach, and dive back under the waves, looking.

When I find her, as I find her, she is floating on her back amidst bullkelp. The brown weed curves sinuously over her body, like dark limp hands.

I splash and slobber over, sobbing to her. "God, your son nearly died trying to find you. Why didn't you tell us,"

She opens her brown eyes lazily.

No, not lazily: with defeat, with weariness.

"What on earth gave you the idea I was going to drown?" She rubs the towel roughly over her skin.

I say, haltingly, "Uh well, he was sure that . . . "

(He is curled up near the fire I've lit, peacefully asleep.)

"Sure of what?"

"I don't know. He went looking for you, got scared. We couldn't see you anywhere."

A sort of shudder, a ripple runs through her.

"The idea was right," she says, very quietly. She lets the towel fall. She cups her hand under her left breast and points.

"Feel there."

There is a hard, oval, clump amidst the soft tissue.

"God, did he do . . ."

"No. It's been growing there for the past month. Probably for longer than that, but I have only felt it recently." She rubs her armpit, thoughtfully. "It's there too and under here," gesturing to her jaw. "It'll have to come out." I can't stop it. I groan.

Do you understand that if I hadn't been there, both of them would have drowned?

There was one last thing.
    We were all together in the living room.
    I am in the lefthand chair, she is opposite me.
    He is crooning to himself, sprawled in front of the fire.
    "Loo-lie, loo-lay, loo-lie, loo-lay, the falcon hath borne my make away,"
he sings. He pronounces it, "the fawcon have borne my make away."
    "What is that?" I ask.
    "A song."
    He looks across to his ma and they smile slyly, at one another, smiles
like invisible hands reaching out, caressing secretly, weaving and touching.

I washed my hands.
    I wept.
    I went out to the shed and banged the door finally shut.
    I wept a little longer.
    And then, because there was nothing else to do, I went down to the
pub.
    I had been drinking double whiskies for more than an hour when
Mata came across and laid his arm over my shoulder.
    He is shaking.
    "E man," he whispers. His voice grows a little stronger. "E man,
don't drink by yourself. That's no good eh?" His arm presses down.
"Come across to us?"
    The hubbub of voices hushes.
    I snivel.
    "Mat, when I first knew, her fingers were covered in clay, soft grey
clay. And she smiled and said it's Charleston, we'll call him Charleston.
It's too soft really, but I'll make a nice cup from it. Cups. Tall fluted
goblets she said."
    His hand pats my shoulder with commiseration, with solicitude.
    His eyes are dark with horror.
    "I'll glaze them sea blue and we'll drink red wine together, all three
of us."
    We never did.

# Witi Ihimaera

## *A Game of Cards*

The train pulled into the station. For a moment there was confusion: a voice blaring over the loudspeaker system, people getting off the train, the bustling and shoving of the crowd on the platform.

And there was Dad, waiting for me. We hugged each other. We hadn't seen each other for a long time. Then we kissed. But I could tell something was wrong.

—Your Nanny Miro, he said. She's very sick.

Nanny Miro . . . among all my nannies, she was the one I loved most. Everybody used to say I was her favourite mokopuna, and that she loved me more than her own children who'd grown up and had kids of their own.

She lived down the road from us, right next to the meeting house in the big old homestead which everybody in the village called "The Museum" because it housed the prized possessions of the whanau, the village family. Because she was rich and had a lot of land, we all used to wonder why Nanny Miro didn't buy a newer, more modern house. But Nanny didn't want to move. She liked her own house just as it was.

—Anyway, she used to say, what with all my haddit kids and their haddit kids and all this haddit whanau being broke all the time and coming to ask me for some money, how can I afford to buy a new house?

Nanny didn't really care about money though. Who needs it? she used to say. What you think I had all these kids for, ay? To look after me, I'm not dumb!

Then she would cackle to herself. But it wasn't true really, because her family would send all their kids to her place when they were broke and she looked after them! She liked her mokopunas, but not for too long. She'd ring up their parents and say:

—Hey! When you coming to pick up your hoha kids! They're wrecking the place!

Yet, always, when they left, she would have a little weep, and give them some money. . . .

I used to like going to Nanny's place. For me it was a big treasure house, glistening with sports trophies and photographs, pieces of carvings and greenstone, and feather cloaks hanging from the walls.

Most times, a lot of women would be there playing cards with Nanny. Nanny loved all cards games—five hundred, poker, canasta, pontoon, whist, euchre—you name it, she could play it.

The sitting room would be crowded with the kuias, all puffing clouds of smoke, dressed in their old clothes, laughing and cackling and gossiping about who was pregnant—and relishing all the juicy bits too!

I liked sitting and watching them. Mrs Heta would always be there, and when it came to cards she was both Nanny's best friend and worst enemy. And the two of them were the biggest cheats I ever saw.

Mrs Heta would cough and reach for a hanky while slyly slipping a card from beneath her dress. And she was always reneging in five hundred! But her greatest asset was her eyes, which were big and googly. One eye would look straight ahead, while the other swivelled around, having a look at the cards in the hands of the women sitting next to her.

—Eeee! You cheat! Nanny would say. You just keep your eyes to yourself, Maka tiko bum!

Mrs Heta would look at Nanny as if she were offended. Then she would sniff and say:

—You cheat yourself, Miro Mananui. I saw you sneaking that ace from the bottom of the pack.

—How do you know I got an ace Maka? Nanny would say. I know you! You dealt this hand, and you stuck that ace down there for yourself, you cheat! Well, ana! I got it now! So take that!

And she would slap down her hand.

—Sweet, ay? she would laugh. Good? Kapai lalelale? And she would sometimes wiggle her hips, making her victory sweeter.

—Eeee! Miro! Mrs Heta would say. Well, I got a good hand too!

And she would slap her hand down and bellow with laughter.

—Take that!

And always, they would squabble. I often wondered how they ever remained friends. The names they called each other!

Sometimes, I would go and see Nanny and she would be all alone, playing patience. If there was nobody to play with her, she'd always play patience. And still she cheated! I'd see her hands fumbling across the cards, turning up a jack or queen she needed, and then she'd laugh and say:

—I'm too good for this game!

She used to try to teach me some of the games, but I wasn't very interested, and I didn't yell and shout at her like the women did. She liked the bickering.

—Aue . . . she would sigh. Then she'd look at me and begin dealing out the cards in the only game I ever knew how to play.

And we would yell snap! all the afternoon. . . .

Now, Nanny was sick.

I went to see her that afternoon after I'd dropped my suitcases at home. Nanny Tama, her husband, opened the door. We embraced and he began to weep on my shoulder.

—Your Nanny Miro, he whispered, She's . . . she's . . . .

He couldn't say the words. He motioned me to her bedroom.

Nanny Miro was lying in bed. And she was so old looking. Her face was very grey, and looked like a tiny wrinkled doll in that big bed. She was so thin now, and seemed all bones.

I walked into the room. She was asleep. I sat down on the bed beside her, and looked at her lovingly.

Even when I was a child, she must have been old. But I'd never realized it. She must have been over seventy now. Why do people you love grow old so suddenly?

The room had a strange, antiseptic smell. Underneath the bed was a big chamber pot, yellow with urine. . . . And the pillow was flecked with small spots of blood where she had been coughing.

I shook her gently.

—Nanny . . . Nanny, wake up.

She moaned. A long, hoarse sigh grew on her lips. Her eyelids fluttered, and she looked at me with blank eyes . . . and then tears began to roll down her cheeks.

—Don't cry, Nanny, I said. Don't cry. I'm here.

But she wouldn't stop.

So I sat beside her on the bed and she lifted her hands to me.

—Haere mai, mokopuna. Haere mai. Mmm. Mmm.

And I bent within her arms and we pressed noses.

After a while, she calmed down. She seemed to be her own self.

—What a haddit mokopuna you are, she wept. It's only when I'm just about in my grave that you come to see me.

—I couldn't see you last time I was home, I explained. I was too busy.

—Yes, I know you fullas, she grumbled. It's only when I'm almost dead that you come for some money.

—I don't want your money, Nanny.

—What's wrong with my money! she said. Nothing's wrong with it! Don't you want any?

—Of course I do, I laughed. But I know you! I bet you lost it all on poker!

She giggled. Then she was my Nanny again. The Nanny I knew.

We talked for a long time. I told her about what I was doing in Wellington and all the neat girls who were after me.

—You teka! she giggled. Who'd want to have you!

And she showed me all her injection needles and pills and told me how she wanted to come home from the hospital, so they'd let her.

—You know why I wanted to come home? she asked. I didn't like all those strange nurses looking at my bum when they gave me those injections. I was so sick, mokopuna, I couldn't even go to the lav, and I'd rather wet my own bed not their neat bed. That's why I come home.

Afterwards, I played the piano for Nanny. She used to like *Me He Manurere* so I played it for her, and I could hear her quavering voice singing in her room.

*Me he manurere aue. . . .*

When I finally left Nanny I told her I would come back in the morning.

But that night, Nanny Tama rang up.

—Your Nanny Miro, she's dying.

We all rushed to Nanny's house. It was already crowded. All the old women were there. Nanny was lying very still. Then she looked up and whispered to Mrs Heta:

—Maka . . . Maka tiko bum . . . I want a game of cards. . . .

A pack of cards was found. The old ladies sat around the bed, playing. Everybody else decided to play cards too, to keep Nanny company. The men played poker in the kitchen and sitting room. The kids played snap in the other bedrooms. The house overflowed with card players, even onto the lawn outside Nanny's window, where she could see. . . .

The women laid the cards out on the bed. They dealt the first hand. They cackled and joked with Nanny, trying not to cry. And Mrs Heta kept saying to Nanny:

—Eee! You cheat Miro. You cheat! And she made her googly eye reach far over to see Nanny's cards.

—You think you can see, ay, Maka tiko bum? Nanny coughed. You think you're going to win this hand, ay? Well, take that!

She slammed down a full house.

The other women goggled at the cards. Mrs Heta looked at her own cards. Then she smiled through her tears and yelled:

—Eee! You cheat Miro! I got two aces in my hand already! Only four in the pack. So how come you got three aces in your hand?

Everybody laughed. Nanny and Mrs Heta started squabbling as they always did, pointing at each other and saying: You the cheat, not me! And Nanny Miro said: I saw you, Maka tiko bum, I saw you sneaking that card from under the blanket.

She began to laugh. Quietly. Her eyes streaming with tears.

And while she was laughing, she died.

Everybody was silent. Then Mrs Heta took the cards from Nanny's hands and kissed her.

—You the cheat, Miro, she whispered. You the cheat yourself. . . .

We buried Nanny on the hill with rest of her family. During her tangi, Mrs Heta played patience with Nanny, spreading the cards across the casket.

Later in the year, Mrs Heta, she died too. She was buried right next to Nanny, so that they could keep on playing cards. . . .

And I bet you they're still squabbling up there. . . .

—Eee! You cheat Miro. . . .

—You the cheat, Maka tiko bum. You, you the cheat. . . .

# Sally Ito

## Sisters of the Modern Mind

### Of the Wave

Do you remember
when in my muddled baby English,
I called you,
"Pretty blonde fair eyes princess"
and you smiled, toothless,
without an inkling of a frown
on your five year old face?

We had laughed
high pitched peals,
in our simple nakedness once
when we were six.
Do you remember my touching you there,
when we'd thrown feather pillows
at one another, fast and furious;
hurling, hitting
as if in a blind rage,
until the white down settled onto our skin
where it lay like snow petals
on our childish cracks and curves?

We had splashed
in the bathtub once
when we were seven.
It was after our talk
about the Whelan boys across the street.
We sat prim in the tub
(for mother had put buns in our hair)
until we began to play.
Do you remember the frenzy

of white froth and bubbles
we created, crouching
like spawning pond frogs?

We grew up
congregated by telephone.
our lipstick a new weapon
heralding the moon
and her cycles of creation.   And yet,
ours was a bold red scrape on white tile and mirror;
graffiti about small socialism in bathrooms
once preserved for *"Jane is a slut"* tiles.

Then we sought after knowledge,
you and I.
Our painted nails carved deep crescents
into musty bindings.
Our hands jingled with bracelets and rings
as wrinkled pages were turned, over and over,
by wetted fingertip.
Discourse passed through our reddened lips
in enthused soprano voices.      Cheeks flushed
to each temperament of thought.
The knowledge became
as those pages of our skin
that we sought to caress with our own hands       too often
we could not,
though our ideas
urged us on, like heavy, masculine whispers
hot upon our lobes.

Our precious knowledge did not move
the precious opinion of the others.
Then, you were sad because Descartes was wrong
and I was happy because faith was free.
You left me then, to find perfect answers.
I waited for you.   I stopped wondering.
And when you returned, you were older.
And I was with child.

You wondered at the skin of my belly,

bloated and large,
a woman's disfigured testament of love,
a prophecy generations old.
And I marvelled at the sharpness of your mind
filled with the birthing of knowledge
from the belly of experience — the new womb
in successful trial.

We have worshipped different gods,
you and I.      Yet,
time and anatomy still wear
at our bones like the tide upon the sand
that tosses the jewelled shells,
you and I,      sisters,
of the wave.

# Arnold Itwaru

## *arrival*

this is the place
mark its name
the streets you must learn to remember

there are special songs here
they do not sing of you
in them you do not exist
but to exist you must learn to love them
you must believe them when they say
there are no sacrificial lambs here

the houses are warm
there's bread there's wine

bless yourself
you have arrived

    listen
keys     rattle
locks    click
doors   slam
    silence

## *roomer*

here i cower
from the day's
drain and glare

a shadow
a wrinkled skin
cover me gently
night's linen
prepare me
prepare me


## separate ways


stranger in the sunset
i long to know you
to touch the poem of your presence
to dispel this loneliness
but the sun darkens
and we go our separate ways

# Sunita Jain

## *Fly the Friendly Skies*

It was again the hurry-home time—the time most difficult for an outsider or alien in a foreign country. The buildings belched out men and women as if out of compulsion, and New York's Fifth Avenue, as were the other streets at that hour, was a veritable escalator of moving traffic. Arjun sat near the window inside the cafe and watched the Whites, Blacks and peoples of every description cluttering the sidewalk in their simultaneous onslaught.

He felt lonesome sitting by himself while all around him New York moved to get home. Arjun could not have moved even if he had wanted. All day he had window-shopped, gazing gaga eyed at the mannequins in the windows, the automatic toys, the gadgets galore. He had no money to buy anything yet, and he was in no hurry to possess any of the wealth that littered the shops. Instead he had felt extremely tired and alone. The excitement with which he had left India and reached New York three days ago, had disappeared.

A group of smartly dressed young women went past his window. *America is incredibly erotic. Too many legs make all these streets sexy . . .* Whose lines were these? Too many legs, but not erotic. Nothing stirred in Arjun except the vague evenings near Regal or Janpath and the sway of some Indian girl's body baling out the hypnotic scent of jasmine *gajaras*. The girls outside his window were shadows on a screen and distant. He was too ignorant and unbearably scared.

The new world around him had expanded into the multitude outside, and the sounds enveloping him were unfamiliarly harsh. He understood now why his elder brother had not left the small village in Panjab to which his family belonged.

"What does a man need . . ." his brother had said in answer to Arjun's pleading to shift to New Delhi, "what does a man need to live out his life happily except a small place he can belong to and a known face? I'll never belong to anything in your New Delhi . . ."

Nonsense. Arjun stiffened himself. A small place stinks and stagnates—it chokes you by degrees. Even New Delhi got too small;

there weren't any jobs anymore or decent houses within the reach of one's income. One had to, one must, enlarge one's world in order to fully unfold — Joyce did it, and Henry James . . .

It was getting dark outside. The shadows struggled with the glare of lights. He paid for his coffee and stepped out. "Don't loiter in NY after seven . . . stay indoors. There is too much crime these days . . ." An old friend settled in Washington had advised him through letters. A close-cropped young man ran swiftly past Arjun. His heart dropped a beat. "It's not healthy to be so scared." Arjun chastised himself. "I am starting a new chapter of my life in America, the beautiful. I'll get used to it just as I got used to the IIT hostel life in Delhi."

The air grew slightly chilly. He walked close to the warmth of the walls that glowed with electric lights. He was ravenously hungry. For three days now he had eaten more sweet dishes and fruits than at any other time in his life. The few vegetable and cheese preparations he tried had strange tastes, and were unable to satisfy his hunger. His stomach growled for spicy food, for peas thick with large chunks of *panir*, for potatoes fried whole before they were curried, and for a plate of rich rice *pillao* . . . The aroma of the food he hungered for assailed his memory and he felt weak in the knees. The thought of sandwiches with milk for dinner revolted him.

He stopped involuntarily outside the large show window of a shop which was now closed for business. Several Indian carpets rioted in color behind the bright glass. Here and there a strategically placed large brass tabletop accented the flavor of the handknotted Mirzapurs, Kashmirs, and Agras.

"Aren't they beautiful!" Someone said to him, making him jolt out of his reverie. He turned around. An aged white woman carrying a heavy grocery bag in the cradle of her left arm stood by the window. She too had stopped to look at the carpets.

"You know," she smiled, "I can't go past this window without slowing down. Tell me, how long does it take to make one of those?" She pointed to a sharp velvet blue Kashmir. "I am told they are *actually* hand made . . ."

He mumbled a reply, for he himself did not know how long it takes to knot a Kashmir carpet, big or small. In just the few days away from home, Arjun had learned how little he knew about India, and how much he had taken for granted, or had never bothered to know the statistics of. Whenever people asked him *when* or *how* or *where* of something or an event — he had uttered confused answers.

The two moved away from the window. The lady walked rather

slowly as if her feet or legs hurt. He realized then that she was actually very old. She was telling him about how once when she was in high school she had wanted to go to India.

The woman grew nostalgic and sentimental about her past. Her voice sounded glad to have an audience. She pointed out the names of buildings and places that could be of interest to a newcomer. Arjun's mind began to wander, looking for an excuse to excuse himself. The friend in Washington had written: you will meet a very large number of lonely elders in this country. Avoid cultivating their friendship even if you are lonesome, for you will end up hurting their feelings . . .

The two had drifted away from the business section, and he had a feeling he was lost. But somehow it did not bother him. Home-sickness had made him reckless. "I'll hail a taxi back to my hotel," he assured himself.

"I live in that building." The lady indicated one of the several red brick buildings sectioned into layers of apartments. "Have you had your supper?" she asked.

"Not yet." He tried to disengage himself. A tall, dark Indian appeared on the other side of the street. "Excuse me, Mam, there's a friend I want to say hello to . . ." Waving a hurried goodbye he crossed over to the other side.

Arjun was very eager to catch up with the Indian. He had seen other Indian men and women on the streets during the day; but right now he wanted to be able to talk to one. To have a chat about *home* over a cup of tea!

"Hello . . ." His voice was as eager as his manner.

"Yes?" The man looked at him. The expression in the man's eye however, made Arjun stammer suddenly.

"Are you from India?" he asked, but felt very foolish in asking it.

"Yes," the man answered.

"I am also from India."

"So?" The man stared at Arjun.

The lash of the insult flushed his face. The man relented.

"Look, young man," he said to Arjun in a cryptic voice, "you are probably new here, but you did not travel ten thousand miles to know another Indian, nor did I. Good-night."

The street light changed. The elderly woman had entered her apartment building. The revolving door swallowed her. In the distance the neon sign flashed rhythmically, fly the friendly skies — of United . . .

# Ruth Prawer Jhabvala

## *The Old Lady*

She woke up, as she did every morning, very early and very happy. The sky was still grey, and only here and there a bird stirred in a tree and gave its first, fresh twitter. She stood on her veranda and looked out at this quiet dawn and smiled with happiness. She was strong and calm and at peace. Still smiling, she turned back into her bedroom and sat on the floor before the little table on which stood the small brass image of Vishnu and an incense holder and a framed photograph of her guru. She sat there with her legs crossed under her and her hands laid palm upwards on her knees. She sat like that for quite a long time, though she did not know for how long, because she was too happy to be aware of any time.

Then the bearer came in with her morning tea, set out on her silver tray, and she smiled and was happy at that too, because she always enjoyed her morning tea. Munni, her grand-daughter, came with her tumbler of milk, and they sat drinking together. Munni told her dream — she had a dream every night — this time about how a big white horse had come for her and carried her off to a blue cloud. "How beautiful," said her grandmother admiringly, and Munni said in a complacently off-hand way that yes, it was. Sometimes Munni's dreams were beautiful and fantastic, and sometimes they were very stern and tragic, as when she dreamed that both her parents had been condemned to be hanged and she had watched the execution. Her grandmother was always the first person to be informed of these dreams, and afterwards they sat and discussed them together. Nobody else in the house would listen to Munni's dreams, but her grandmother told her they were serious and important.

Leila and Bobo always liked to sleep a long time, so the old lady had time to go round and see that everything was being properly cleaned and dusted. The whole house was alive with cleaning: marble floors were washed, brass ornaments rubbed, rugs beaten, cushions shaken, door handles polished, fresh flowers put in vases. The old lady walked around sprinkling rosewater out of a long-handled silver sprinkler; she sang as she did so, she was feeling so happy and lighthearted—like a bird, she thought, she felt just like a bird singing from green trees and lawns on a dewy morning.

But her daughter Leila was feeling cross. She suffered from some stomach trouble, and that always made her irritable in the mornings. She had consulted many doctors, but they all said that there was nothing wrong. "It is nerves," they told her. So now Leila often referred to her nerves .

"I can't bear it," was the first thing she said, and her mother asked: "What, daughter?" full of sympathy. Leila's face was an unhealthy colour and it was screwed up with irritation and her breath did not smell very nice. Looking at her, the old lady was a little ashamed that she herself was feeling so fresh and gay.

"Not today," said Leila, shutting her eyes. "I can't bear it today. He will talk, and we will all talk, and what will be the good of it?"

"Krishna?" said her mother. Leila nodded, her eyes still painfully shut. Her mother clicked her tongue in sympathy but nevertheless offered, "It will be nice to see him." Leila laughed hollowly.

Munni asked, "Daddy is coming today?"

"Go away and play," Leila told her; Munni saw that her mother was in her morning mood, so she went without comment.

"And it will be nice to see him eat," the old lady said, a trifle sadly. She never could help feeling sorry for her son-in-law. "I don't know *what* they give him in that hotel." She added, "Poor boy," and could not suppress a very gentle sigh.

"Oh, Mother," said Leila in exasperation.

"I know, I know," said the old lady. "It is not your fault." Now she felt sorry for both of them, for Krishna and for Leila. How sad it was for people to be unhappy in their marriage. She sighed, and picked up a plate of biscuits. She took the plate into the drawing-room and put it on a table beside her son Bobo, who lay stretched out on the sofa, reading an art magazine. She enjoyed feeding biscuits to Bobo—she had baked them herself, with such love—but she wished he were not getting so fat. His stomach bulged through his silk shirt, his cheeks were round and puffed. It was not a healthy fatness, and one could see that he often had pimples and boils.

The old lady hurried out into the garden. She had to hurry because she felt waves of happiness passing over her: not really happiness, but that was what she called it to herself, because she knew no other word for it. She stood in the garden, sheltered from the morning sun by the tall old trees, and the birds' twittering trickled like water, and the gardener's hose gurgled softly in the grass, and she could hear the gardener snipping with his shears. She stood there with her eyes shut, seeing nothing, yet feeling everything, while ecstasy held her and carried her. She did not mind the gardener seeing her like this — though she did mind her children seeing. That was why she always hurried away from them when she felt her happiness coming over her. She did not want them to know about it. Perhaps because she felt guilty for having something so precious and not being able to share it with them.

Munni came running across the lawn, with her doll pushed carelessly under her arm; one finger was stuck in her mouth and she was warbling a war song. She ran straight into her grandmother and, clasping her arms round the old lady's legs, buried her face in the sari, which smelled of jasmine scent and camphor. The old lady laughed happily. Once the transition from her states of ecstasy had been very difficult for her, but now it was easy and effortless. Everything now was easy and effortless. Gay as a young girl, she went back to the house and into the kitchen, where the cook sat squatting on the floor and vigorously ground spices on a stone. "Quickly now!" the old lady cried in her bright voice. "Cut up the onions!" and she began to melt fat in a pan, deftly shaking it round with sharp little jerks. She had always loved cooking.

The cook let his knife slice through an onion with precision, his head laid critically to one side. "Have you heard?" he said. "Yesterday they killed a snake outside Mathur Sahib's bungalow."

"A snake!" she cried.

"A cobra," he said with relish, handing her the onions which she slid into the fat while clicking her tongue over the cobra. "It was so long," he told her, showing her with his hands; he pursed his mouth and said in a judicious voice, "It must have been some evil spirit."

"Yes," she said, "it is difficult to know in what shape an evil spirit may not come to visit us. Are the spices ready?"

"Mother!" Leila called from the drawing-room and was annoyed when her mother failed to hear her. "She must be gossiping with the servants again," she told Bobo who smiled indulgently and said, "Why not, if it makes her happy?"

"I know," said Leila, "but it is hardly dignified."

Bobo was looking at some Rajput miniatures. "Lovely," he murmured with sensuousness, trying to enjoy them like a taste.

"Mother is often not dignified," Leila said. "For instance, with Krishna. It is very awkward for me when she is so soft with Krishna."

"Lovely," said Bobo, "but probably fake." He looked up to ask: "Why awkward?"

"It might make Krishna think — you see," she said with emphasis, "I want it to be *quite* clear that everything is finished and there can be no reconciliation."

"But isn't that obvious? When you and Munni are living here — "

"But Mother keeps calling him!" Leila cried in exasperation. "When none of us is at home, she goes quietly to the telephone and says Krishna, come and eat a meal with us."

"Poor fellow," murmured Bobo, who had inherited some part of his mother's sympathy.

"Yes, but what about me!" Leila demanded. "Because you and Mother feel sorry for him, you want me always to be tied to an incompatible husband?"

Bobo yawned (how he hated argument! and his sister was very argumentative) but politely tried to cover it up.

"It is very difficult for me," sighed Leila, and then she said, "I am going to telephone."

Her mother, emerging from the kitchen, was glad to see her telephoning. She knew that Leila's mood always improved at the telephone. Already her voice was quite cheerful: "We shall just have to call an Extraordinary Meeting, that's all," she was saying. Her telephone conversations were full of references to meetings, sub-committees, resolutions, agendas. She was an enthusiastic committee woman and had many committee friends, to whom she telephoned and with whom she exchanged, several times a day, important notes and papers, which were carried to and fro by a scared young clerk specially hired for the purpose.

"Leila was complaining that you gossip too much with the servants," Bobo told the old lady. He said it with good humour, but nevertheless in the patronizing tone which all her children used towards her. The old lady did not mind. On the contrary, she rather liked being patronized by her children. They were so much cleverer than she had ever been.

"Yes," she said, smiling radiantly, "I talk too much. Shall I bring your milk?" And then she said, "Oh son, why won't you get married?" She did so want him to. But Bobo only smiled, showing his pointed wide-spaced little teeth and his gums. She sat down and said dreamily, "I wish one of you two boys would get married. I could arrange so nicely for you." She could talk like this to Bobo, though not to her other son. If she diffidently mentioned marriage to Satish, he only clicked his tongue and made a movement of irritation.

"And you would be happy," she told Bobo, looking at him with appealing eyes. "With a wife and children you would be so happy." And maybe with a wife and children he would become more active and would no longer lie all day on a sofa, reading and looking at *objets d'art*. Of course, she realized that was his work, and she was always proud when an article of his appeared in one of the art magazines or in the Sunday edition of the *Statesman*. But still, she did wish he would *move* a little more; if only to stop him from getting too fat.

"Why not talk to Satish?" Bobo teased her.

She shrugged. "He is so busy, poor boy," she murmured.

"So busy making money and a name," Bobo said, a trifle acidly. The two brothers did not get on well together. Satish had taken very much after his father; like his father, he had gone in for law and had already established a very remunerative practice for himself. He was hardworking and ambitious, which Bobo decidedly was not.

Krishna turned up punctually at lunchtime. He was nervous, and so was giggling in that rather silly way he had. The old lady glanced apprehensively at Leila and saw, as she had feared and expected, that Leila was already looking irritated. Krishna must also have noticed, for he giggled more; and then, feeling obliged to make some remark, made this: "Hot again today, no?"

"Yes!" cried the old lady, so eager that her voice trembled. "Yes, hot!" Now Leila was frowning at her mother too. Bobo, still lying on the sofa with a big, glossy art magazine, said, "Are we going to discuss the weather?" Krishna laughed out loud. Munni came in and said, "Oh look, Daddy has come." Her grandmother would have liked to see her greet him more warmly, but Munni made no further move towards him. Krishna looked over his daughter's head, pretending in his shyness not to see her.

They were already seated round the huge, heavy-legged dining-table when Satish came in, saying briskly "Sorry I'm late." This briskness and his hasty entrance, combined with a frowning air of preoccupation, were enough to make them all feel ashamed of their idleness, which had allowed them to sit down, spaciously and in good time, for their lunch. The old lady got up, flustered and hurried; she seized the tray from the bearer who was serving them and began herself to fill her son's plate. Satish let her serve him but said, "Why do you fuss so, Mother?" in a calm, patronizing voice.

"Allow me, son," she said, her hands shaking a little as she piled food on to his plate, "it is my pleasure." Satish was so much like his father that she even felt towards him as she used to feel towards her husband: inadequate, that is, and as if she had neglected some part of her duty. Only then, in her youth and middle age, this feeling had penetrated her completely, so that she had felt dissatisfied and unhappy, whereas now it was only a kind of surface disturbance, which left her great depths of calm unrippled. Perhaps she was even glad of this disturbance, and tended slightly to exaggerate it; because it made her feel that she was still sufficiently in touch with her children and had not yet given herself over to her own happiness alone.

After a while Satish said, "Well, if you want to file your divorce papers, you had better make up your minds."

Leila said at once, "How long have I been telling you that my mind *is* made up." So then they all looked at Krishna, who became so confused that he giggled, and that confused him further, so that with flushed face he bent close over his plate and ate. The old lady called quite sharply to the bearer, "Give Krishna Sahib water! Don't you see his glass is empty?"

"It is better to get these things over and done with," said Satish in his brisk, busy voice.

Bobo drawled in deliberate contrast: "Don't hurry them into something they might not wish to do."

"There is no question," said Leila, "of *not* wishing."

Bobo shrugged and waved his hand to the bearer to bring the rice round again.

"What are divorce papers?" Munni whispered to her grandmother.

Leila said in a loud voice, "Mother, please don't encourage Munni to speak before everything on her plate is finished."

"Eat, child, eat," the old lady obediently murmured. She remembered so many meals in this room round this table: her husband stern and domineering like Satish, her children tense with conflict. And she herself full of unhappiness, because she did not know what to do or what to say. She still did not know what to do or what to say; but now she was only gently sad because she could not show her children the way to her own peace.

"Anywhere else," said Leila fiercely, "everything would have been settled and finished long ago."

"Now we shall hear about poor oppressed Indian womanhood," Bobo said with a smile.

"For you everything is a joke," Leila accused him. "But it is true. In Europe and America —"

"Why don't we remain to the point?" said Satish shortly.

"It *is* the point!" Leila said. "Our attitude of mind is wrong. We don't understand that divorce is a natural thing in any enlightened society."

And Krishna was shy and embarrassed as a young girl, picking at his food with the point of his fork, his eyes lowered.

"Yes, yes," said Satish, "but what is it you want to *do*?"

Munni looked up from her plate. She was a little afraid of her uncle Satish, but she found him interesting. For instance, she found it interesting that he should suggest doing something; she liked to hear such talk, it offered possibilities. Nothing of what the others talked ever offered possibilities — that was why she usually did not bother to listen to them.

"But I have told you," Leila said.

"Oh no, not again," said Bobo, peering into the bowl of dessert the bearer was offering to him, and then casting an accusing look at his mother.

"Tomorrow I will make carrot halwa," she promised him.

"And you, Krishna?" Satish said, now looking directly at his brother-in-law who, thus forced to commit himself, glanced first helplessly round the table. His mother-in-law smiled at him encouragingly, but he was too nervous to smile back.

"Yes," he said at last. "Of course."

There was a silence. The old lady tried hard to think of something suitable to interpose, but it was Leila who spoke first. "Really!" she said in an exasperation which was however half triumphant, for after all her point was being proved.

"Of course," said Krishna with a heroic effort, "if Leila wants . . ." He looked distressed. "Of course," he said again, "if she wants," and then he giggled and quickly continued to eat. The old lady felt that she loved him terribly. Leila put both her hands to her forehead and said, "This is frightful for my nerves."

Afterwards Satish paced up and down the drawing-room, looking at his watch and saying, "I have just half an hour." Bobo, replete and drowsy with food, was again lying on the sofa and leafing through a magazine with a dreamy smile on his lips. A note had just come for Leila and she sat on the edge of a chair and opened it; she frowned and pursed her lips and looked busy, while the young clerk who had brought it stood in front of her with his head bent. Everybody seemed to be waiting for something.

The old lady got up and hurried to her room. Only for one minute, she promised herself. She sat in front of the little table with the image of Vishnu and the photograph of her guru, and — God forgive her — at once forgot all about her children sitting puzzled in the drawing-room. Everything now was clear and serene. Her guru looked at her out of his silver frame: he had large burning eyes and an ugly mouth with thick unshaped lips. The very first time she had seen him, she had known that he was the man who would guide her. Not much had been said. She had gone to see him with a friend. He sat in a little room over a sweetmeat shop. There were several other people in the room, sitting around, not doing anything much. Out on the veranda, which overlooked the street, a woman sat cooking and a fat naked little boy sat beside her and watched. Her friend had asked the guru several questions, but he had only smiled instead of replying. Then suddenly he had turned, not to her friend but to her, and his eyes burned as he looked at her and he said, "If you look for it, peace is not hard to find." So now she sat crosslegged before her little table, surrounded by vast fields of peace in which her spirit frisked like a lamb. While downstairs in the drawing-room Bobo yawned and said, "Where is Mother?" hard put to it to suppress a burp.

"Why does she always disappear like that?" Leila said. She licked the flap of the envelope in an efficient way and handed it to the clerk, who still stood humbly before her; she said, "Now see that you deliver this at once, but at *once*," sharply.

"Perhaps she is resting?" Krishna diffidently suggested.

"Poor Mother," Bobo said. They often said "poor Mother," for they felt she ought to be in need of pity. Their father had always been the strong force in the family, and it was only to be expected that after his death she should be lost and broken. That was why they said "poor Mother" and, when they remembered, were kind and considerate to her.

"Yes, but since we are here to *discuss*," Leila said, and Krishna again looked embarrassed. Satish flicked out his wrist to look at his watch; he frowned, and managed to look pressed for time. Bobo, observing him, put on a deliberate gentleman-of-leisure act, crossing his plump legs one over the other as he lay on the sofa.

Munni quietly crept up the stairs and into her grandmother's room. She came up behind the old lady and put her arms round her neck and whispered into her ear, "They are all waiting for you." But Grandmother did not move. Maybe she was dead. Munni peered round into her face. Grandmother's eyes were wide open, and her mouth too was slightly open, with the tip of the tongue showing. She looked very strange. What if she really was dead? They would put a red cloth over her and carry her on a board down to the Jumna and there they would burn her till there was nothing left of her but ashes. "Grandmother!" Munni suddenly cried. The old lady said, "Yes, Munni" in a quiet voice.

After a while Munni said, "When people get very, very, *very* old, do they die?"

"Yes," said the old lady cheerfully, "they die."

There was another pause, and then Munni asked: "Grandmother, are you very, very, *very* old?"

"Oh yes," said the old lady, even more cheerfully.

"No!" Munni cried angrily. "The cook's mother is much older than you are! I know!"

The old lady smiled and began to stroke Munni's hair. They sat like that together, and the guru looked at them from out of the photograph.

"When people die," the old lady said, "they become happy."

"But they are burnt, how can they be happy?"

"Their spirit is happy," the old lady explained; and she smiled, her eyes looking far into the distance as if she saw there vast flowering plains for spirits to be happy in.

When they got downstairs, Satish said with an air of finality, "Well, I have to be going," and slapped his pocket to see if his car key was in it.

"Already?" said the old lady in a somewhat dazed manner. She was blinking her eyes as if she had just woken up, which made Leila say, "Really, Mother, you could have postponed your nap for *one* afternoon." Her mother at once looked contrite and blamed herself for selfishness.

"Nothing settled, as usual," Satish said. "If only you people would let me know what you want."

"But I have told you!" Leila cried. Krishna bent his head and pretended to be engrossed in the back page of a folded newspaper.

The old lady ventured to say, "Perhaps it would be better to wait." Her voice was cracked and nervous, and after she had spoken there was a silence, so that she wished she had not spoken.

"Mother doesn't understand," Leila at last said. "She still thinks the marriage bond is sacred"; and she made a school-girl face of distaste to show how completely she dissociated herself from such an attitude.

Bobo said, "You can't expect Mother to give up the ideas of her generation so easily."

"No," said Leila, "but that is no reason why she should criticize *our* ideas."

The old lady sat humbly with her hands folded in her lap and listened to them talking about her. She thought they were right and that she was old-fashioned, with no conception of the modern ideas and principles which guided their lives. She admired her children for being so much more advanced and intelligent than she was; but that did not prevent her from feeling sorry for them. If only she could have shown them — opened the way for them as it had been opened for herself that day in the shabby little room where people sat around casually and the smell of cooking came from the veranda.

"You can give me a lift in your car," Leila told Satish. "I have a meeting."

Krishna got up at once and said, "Let me." His eyes and voice begged quite without shame. But Leila turned away from him and followed Satish. Krishna sat down again, looking unhappy.

Perhaps she could show Krishna. She looked at him tenderly and thought that perhaps she loved him best of all. Bobo had gone to sleep on the sofa. His heavy head had dropped sideways and his mouth was slightly open to allow big regular breaths to escape. The old lady put out one finger and laid it on Krishna's wrist. What she had to communicate could not be said in words. But she felt him to be ready for it: he was unhappy and tender and lost. She could feel him seeking for something, straining for something, without himself knowing it. She wanted to pray to be able to help him. Slowly she stroked his wrist with her finger. Come with me, she wanted to say.

"Grandmother," Munni said sternly, watching the old lady stroke Krishna's wrist, "you know very well Mummy says we mustn't be too kind to Daddy."

# Jamaica Kincaid

## *My Mother*

Immediately on wishing my mother dead and seeing the pain it caused her, I was sorry and cried so many tears that all the earth around me was drenched. Standing before my mother, I begged her forgiveness, and I begged so earnestly that she took pity on me, kissing my face and placing my head on her bosom to rest. Placing her arms around me, she drew my head closer and closer to her bosom, until finally I suffocated. I lay on her bosom, breathless, for a time uncountable, until one day, for a reason she has kept to herself, she shook me out and stood me under a tree and I started to breathe again. I cast a sharp glance at her and said to myself, "So." Instantly I grew my own bosoms, small mounds at first, leaving a small, soft place between them, where, if ever necessary, I could rest my own head. Between my mother and me now were the tears I had cried, and I gathered up some stones and banked them in so that they formed a small pond. The water in the pond was thick and black and poisonous, so that only unnameable invertebrates could live in it. My mother and I now watched each other carefully, always making sure to shower the other with words and deeds of love and affection.

\* \* \*

I was sitting on my mother's bed trying to get a good look at myself. It was a large bed and it stood in the middle of a large, completely dark room. The room was completely dark because all the windows had been boarded up and all the crevices stuffed with black cloth. My mother lit some candles and the room burst into a pink-like, yellow-like glow. Looming over us, much larger than ourselves, were our shadows. We sat mesmerised because our shadows had made a place between themselves, as if they were making room for someone else. Nothing filled up the space between them, and the shadow of my mother sighed. The shadow of my mother danced around the room to a tune that my own shadow sang, and then they stopped. All along, our shadows had grown thick and thin, long and short, had fallen at every angle, as if they were controlled by the light of day. Suddenly my mother got up and blew out the candles and our shadows vanished. I continued to sit on the bed, trying to get a good look at myself.

* * *

My mother removed her clothes and covered thoroughly her skin with a thick gold-coloured oil, which had recently been rendered in a hot pan from the livers of reptiles with pouched throats. She grew plates of metal-coloured scales on her back, and light, when it collided with this surface, would shatter and collapse into tiny points. Her teeth now arranged themselves into rows that reached all the way back to her long white throat. She uncoiled her hair from her head and then removed her hair altogether. Taking her head into her large palms, she flattened it so that her eyes, which were by now ablaze, sat on top of her head and spun like two revolving balls. Then, making two lines on the soles of each foot, she divided her feet into crossroads. Silently, she had instructed me to follow her example, and now I too travelled along on my white underbelly, my tongue darting and flickering in the hot air. "Look," said my mother.

* * *

My mother and I were standing on the seabed side by side, my arms laced loosely around her waist, my head resting securely on her shoulder, as if I needed the support. To make sure she believed in my frailness, I sighed occasionally—long soft sighs, the kind of sigh she had long ago taught me could evoke sympathy. In fact, how I really felt was invincible. I was no longer a child but I was not yet a woman. My skin had just blackened and cracked and fallen away and my new impregnable carapace had taken full hold. My nose had flattened; my hair curled in and stood out straight from my head simultaneously; my many rows of teeth in their retractable trays were in place. My mother and I wordlessly made an arrangement—I sent out my beautiful sighs, she received them; I leaned ever more heavily on her for support, she offered her shoulder, which shortly grew to the size of a thick plank. A long time passed, at the end of which I had hoped to see my mother permanently cemented to the seabed. My mother reached out to pass a hand over my head, a pacifying gesture, but I laughed and, with great agility, stepped aside. I let out a horrible roar, then a self-pitying whine. I had grown big, but my mother was bigger, and that would always be so. We walked to the Garden of Fruits and there ate to our hearts' satisfaction. We departed through the southwesterly gate, leaving as always, in our trail, small colonies of worms.

* * *

With my mother, I crossed, unwillingly, the valley. We saw a lamb grazing and when it heard our footsteps it paused and looked up at us. The lamb looked cross and miserable. I said to my mother, "The lamb is cross and miserable. So would I be, too, if I had to live in a climate not suited to my nature." My mother and I now entered the cave. It was the dark and cold cave. I felt something growing under my feet and I bent down to eat it. I stayed that way for years, bent over eating whatever I found growing under my feet. Eventually, I grew a special lens that would allow me to see in the darkest of darkness; eventually, I grew a special coat that kept me warm in the coldest of coldness. One day I saw my mother sitting on a rock. She said, "What a strange expression you have on your face. So cross, so miserable, as if you were living in a climate not suited to your nature." Laughing, she vanished. I dug a deep, deep hole. I built a beautiful house, a floorless house, over the deep, deep hole. I put in lattice windows, most favoured of windows by my mother, so perfect for looking out at people passing by without her being observed; I painted the house itself yellow, the windows green, colours I knew would please her. Standing just outside the door, I asked her to inspect the house. I said, "Take a look. Tell me if it's to your satisfaction." Laughing out of the corner of a mouth I could not see, she stepped inside. I stood just outside the door, listening carefully, hoping to hear her land with a thud at the bottom of the deep, deep hole. Instead, she walked up and down in every direction, even pounding her heel on the air. Coming outside to greet me, she said, "It is an excellent house. I would be honoured to live in it," and then vanished. I filled up the hole and burnt the house to the ground.

* * *

My mother has grown to an enormous height. I have grown to an enormous height also, but my mother's height is three times mine. Sometimes I cannot see from her breasts on up, so lost is she in the atmosphere. One day, seeing her sitting on the seashore, her hand reaching out in the deep to caress the belly of a striped fish as he swam through a place where two seas met, I glowed red with anger. For a while then I lived alone on the island where there were eight full moons and I adorned the face of each moon with expressions I had seen on my mother's face. All the expressions favoured me. I soon grew tired of living in this way and returned to my mother's side. I remained, though glowing red with anger, and my mother and I built houses on opposite banks of the dead pond. The dead pond lay between us; in it, only small invertebrates with poisonous lances lived. My mother behaved towards them as if she had suddenly found herself in the same room with relatives we had long since risen above. I cherished their presence and gave them names. Still I missed my mother's close company and cried constantly for her, but at the end of each day when I saw her return to her house, incredible and great deeds in her wake, each of them singing loudly her praises, I glowed and glowed again, red with anger. Eventually, I wore myself out and sank into a deep, deep sleep, the only dreamless sleep I have ever had.

* * *

One day my mother packed my things in a grip and, taking me by the hand, walked me to the jetty, placed me on board a boat, in care of the captain. My mother, while caressing my chin and cheeks, said some words of comfort to me because we had never been apart before. She kissed me on the forehead and turned and walked away. I cried so much my chest heaved up and down, my whole body shook at the sight of her back turned towards me, as if I had never seen her back turned towards me before. I started to make plans to get off the boat, but when I saw that the boat was encased in a large green bottle, as if it were about to decorate a mantelpiece, I fell asleep, until I reached my destination, the new island. When the boat stopped, I got off and I saw a woman with feet exactly like mine, especially around the arch of the instep. Even though the face was completely different from what I was used to, I recognised this woman as my mother. We greeted each other at first with great caution and politeness, but as we walked along, our steps became one, and as we talked, our voices became one voice, and we were in complete union in every other way. What peace came over me then, for I could not see where she left off and I began, or where I left off and she began.

* * *

My mother and I walk through the rooms of her house. Every crack in the floor holds a significant event: here, an apparently healthy young man suddenly dropped dead; here a young woman defied her father and, while riding her bicycle to the forbidden lovers' meeting place, fell down a precipice, remaining a cripple for the rest of a very long life. My mother and I find this a beautiful house. The rooms are large and empty, opening on to each other, waiting for people and things to fill them up. Our white muslin skirts billow up around our ankles, our hair hangs straight down our backs as our arms hang straight at our sides. I fit perfectly in the crook of my mother's arm, on the curve of her back, in the hollow of her stomach. We eat from the same bowl, drink from the same cup; when we sleep, our heads rest on the same pillow. As we walk through the rooms, we merge and separate, merge and separate; soon we shall enter the final stage of our evolution.

* * *

The fishermen are coming in from sea; their catch is bountiful, my mother has seen to that. As the waves plop, plop against each other, the fishermen are happy that the sea is calm. My mother points out the fishermen to me, their contentment is a source of my contentment. I am sitting in my mother's enormous lap. Sometimes I sit on a mat she has made for me from her hair. The lime trees are weighed down with limes—I have already perfumed myself with their blossoms. A hummingbird has nested on my stomach, a sign of my fertileness. My mother and I live in a bower made from flowers whose petals are imperishable. There is the silvery blue of the sea, crisscrossed with sharp darts of light, there is the warm rain falling on the clumps of castor bush, there is the small lamb bounding across the pasture, there is the soft ground welcoming the soles of my pink feet. It is in this way my mother and I have lived for a long time now.

# On Seeing England for the First Time

When I saw England for the first time, I was a child in school sitting at a desk. The England I was looking at was laid out on a map gently, beautifully, delicately, a very special jewel; it lay on a bed of sky blue — the background of the map — its yellow form mysterious, because though it looked like a leg of mutton, it could not really look like anything so familiar as a leg of mutton because it was England — with shadings of pink and green, unlike any shadings of pink and green I had seen before, squiggly veins of red running in every direction. England was a special jewel all right, and only special people got to wear it. The people who got to wear England were English people. They wore it well and they wore it everywhere: in jungles, in deserts, on plains, on top of the highest mountains, on all the oceans, on all the seas. When my teacher had pinned this map up on the blackboard, she said, "This is England" — and she said it with authority, seriousness, and adoration, and we all sat up. It was as if she had said, "This is Jerusalem, the place you will go to when you die but only if you have been good." We understood then — we were meant to understand then — that England was to be our source of myth and the source from which we got our sense of reality, our sense of what was meaningful, our sense of what was meaningless — and much about our own lives and much about the very idea of us headed that last list.

At the time I was a child sitting at my desk seeing England for the first time, I was already very familiar with the greatness of it. Each morning before I left for school, I ate a breakfast of half a grapefruit, an egg, bread and butter and a slice of cheese, and a cup of cocoa; or half a grapefruit, a bowl of oat porridge, bread and butter and a slice of cheese, and a cup of cocoa. The can of cocoa was often left on the table in front of me. It had written on it the name of the company, the year the company was established, and the words "Made in England." Those words, "Made in England," were written on the box the oats came in too. They would also have been written on the box the shoes I was wearing came in; the bolt of gray linen cloth lying on the shelf of a store from which my mother had bought three yards to make the uniform that I was wearing had written along its edge those three words. The shoes I wore were made in England; so were my socks and cotton undergarments and the satin ribbons I wore tied at the end of two plaits of my hair. My father, who might have sat next to me at breakfast, was a carpenter and cabinetmaker. The shoes he wore to work would have been made in England, as were his khaki shirt and trousers, his underpants and undershirt, his socks and brown felt hat. Felt was not the proper material from which a hat that was expected to provide shade from the hot sun should have been made, but my father must have seen and admired a picture of an Englishman wearing such a hat in England, and this picture that he saw must have been so compelling that it caused him to wear the wrong hat for a hot climate most of his long life. And this hat — a brown felt hat — became so central to his character that it was the first thing he put on in the morning as he stepped out of bed and the last thing he took off before he stepped back into bed at night. As we sat at breakfast, a car might go by. The car, a Hillman or a Zephyr, was made in England. The very idea of the meal itself, breakfast, and its substantial quality and quantity, was an idea from England; we somehow knew that in England they began the day with this meal called breakfast, and a proper breakfast was a big breakfast. No one I knew liked eating so much food so early in the day; it made us feel sleepy, tired. But this breakfast business was "Made in England" like almost everything else that surrounded us, the exceptions being the sea, the sky, and the air we breathed.

At the time I saw this map — seeing England for the first time — I did not say to myself, "Ah, so that's what it looks like," because there was no longing in me to put a shape to those three words that ran through every part of my life no matter how small; for me to have had such a longing would have meant that I lived in a certain atmosphere, an atmosphere in which those three words were felt as a burden. But I did not live in such an atmosphere. When my teacher showed us the map, she asked us to study it carefully, because no test we would ever take would be complete without this statement: "Draw a map of England." I did not know then that the statement "Draw a map of England" was something far worse than a declaration of war, for a flat-out declaration of war would have put me on alert. In fact, there was no need for war — I had long ago been conquered. I did not know then that this statement was part of a process that would result in my erasure — not my physical erasure, but my erasure all the same. I did not know then that this statement was meant to make me feel awe and small whenever I heard the word "England":

awe at the power of its existence, small because I was not from it.

After that there were many times of seeing England for the first time. I saw England in history. I knew the names of all the kings of England. I knew the names of their children, their wives, their disappointments, their triumphs, the names of people who betrayed them. I knew the dates on which they were born and the dates they died. I knew their conquests and was made to feel good if I figured in them; I knew their defeats.

This view—the naming of the kings, their deeds, their disappointments — was the vivid view, the forceful view. There were other views, subtler ones, softer, almost not there—but these softer views were the ones that made the most lasting impression on me, the ones that made me really feel like nothing. "When morning touched the sky" was one phrase, for no morning touched the sky where I lived. The morning where I lived came on abruptly, with a shock of heat and loud noises. "Evening approaches" was another. But the evenings where I lived did not approach; in fact, I had no evening—I had night and I had day, and they came and went in a mechanical way: on, off, on, off. And then there were gentle mountains and low blue skies and moors over which people took walks for nothing but pleasure, when where I lived a walk was an act of labor, a burden, something only death or the automobile could relieve. And the weather there was so remarkable because the rain fell gently always, and the wind blew in gusts that were sometimes deep, and the air was various shades of gray, each an appealing shade for a dress to be worn when a portrait was being painted; and when it rained at twilight, wonderful things happened: People bumped into each other unexpectedly and that would lead to all sorts of turns of events—a plot, the mere weather caused plots.

The reality of my life, the life I led at the time I was being shown these views of England for the first time, for the second time, for the one hundred millionth time, was this: The sun shone with what sometimes seemed to be a deliberate cruelty; we must have done something to deserve that. My dresses did not rustle in the evening air as I strolled to the theater (I had no evening, I had no theater; my dresses were made of a cheap cotton, the weave of which would give way after not too many washings). I got up in the morning, I did my chores (fetched water from the public pipe for my mother, swept the yard), I washed myself, I went to a woman to have my hair combed freshly every day (because before we were allowed into our classroom our teachers would inspect us, and children who had not bathed that day, or had dirt under their fingernails, or whose hair had not been combed anew that day might not be allowed to attend class). I ate that breakfast. I walked to school. At school we gathered in an auditorium and sang a hymn, "All Things Bright and Beautiful," and looking down on us as we sang were portraits of the queen of England and her husband; they wore jewels and medals and they smiled. I was a Brownie. At each meeting we would form a little group around a flagpole, and after raising the Union Jack, we would say, "I promise to do my best, to do my duty to God and the queen, to help other people every day and obey the scouts' law."

But who were these people and why had I never seen them? I mean, really seen them, in the place where they lived? I had never been to England. England! I had seen England's representatives. I had seen the governor-general at the public grounds at a ceremony celebrating the queen's birthday. I had seen an old princess and I had seen a young princess. They had both been extremely not beautiful, but who among us would have told them that? I had never seen England, really seen it. I had only met a representative, seen a picture, read books, memorized its history. I had never set foot, my own foot, in it.

The space between the idea of something and its reality is always wide and deep and dark. The longer they are kept apart — idea of thing, reality of thing — the wider the width, the deeper the depth, the thicker and darker the darkness. This space starts out empty, there is nothing in it, but it rapidly becomes filled up with obsession or desire or hatred or love — sometimes all of these things, sometimes some of these things. That the idea of something and its reality are often two completely different things is something no one ever remembers; and so when they meet and find that they are not compatible, the weaker of the two, idea or reality, dies.

And so finally, when I was a grown-up woman, the mother of two children, the wife of someone, a person who resides in a powerful country that takes up more than its fair share of a continent, the owner of a house with many rooms in it and of two automobiles, with the desire and will (which I very much act upon) to take from the world more than I give back to it, more than I deserve, more than I need, finally then, I saw England, the real England, not a picture, not a painting, not through a story in a book, but England, for the first time. In me, the space between the idea of it and its reality had become filled with hatred, and so when at last I saw it I wanted to take it into my hands and tear it into little pieces and then crumble it up as if it were clay, child's clay. That was impossible, and so I could only indulge in not-favorable opinions.

If I had told an English person what I thought, that I find England ugly, that I hate England; the weather is like a jail sentence; the English are a very ugly people; the food in England is like a jail sentence; the hair of English people is so straight, so dead-looking; the English have an unbearable smell so different from the smell of people I know, real people, of course, I would have been told that I was a person full of prejudice. Apart from the fact that it is I—that is, the people who look like me—who would make that English person aware of the unpleasantness of such a thing, the idea of such a thing, prejudice, that person would have been only partly right, sort of right: I may be capable of prejudice, but my prejudices have no weight to them, my prejudices have no force behind them, my prejudices remain opinions, my prejudices remain my personal opinion. And a great feeling of rage and disappointment came over me as I looked at England, my head full of personal opinions that could not have public, my public, approval. The people I come from are powerless to do evil on a grand scale.

The moment I wished every sentence, everything I knew, that began with England would end with "and then it all died, we don't know how, it just all died" was when I saw the white cliffs of Dover. I had sung hymns and recited poems that were about a longing to see the white cliffs of Dover again. At the time I sang the hymns and recited the poems, I could really long to see them again because I had never seen them at all, nor had anyone around me at the time. But there we were, groups of people longing for something we had never seen. And so there they were, the white cliffs, but they were not that pearly, majestic thing I used to sing about, that thing that created such a feeling in these people that when they died in the place where I lived they had themselves buried facing a direction that would allow them to see the white cliffs of Dover when they were resurrected, as surely they would be. The white cliffs of Dover, when finally I saw them, were cliffs, but they were not white; you could only call them that if the word "white" meant something special to you; they were steep; they were so steep, the correct height from which all my views of England, starting with the map before me in my classroom and ending with the trip I had just taken, should jump and die and disappear forever.

# Thomas King

## *Coyote Goes to Toronto*

Coyote went to Toronto
    to become famous.
It's TRUE
    that's what she said.

She walked up and down those
    FAMOUS streets.
And she stood on those
    FAMOUS corners.

Waiting.

But nothing happened.

SO.
Coyote got hungry and went
    into a restaurant
    to EAT.

But there was a long line
    and Coyote could see it was
    because the restaurant was
    painted a BEAUTIFUL green.

SO.
Coyote painted herself GREEN
    and she went back to the rez
    to show the people what an
    UP-TO-DATE Coyote she was.

And she STOOD on the rez
    and waited.

So that RAIN came along.
So that WIND came along.
So that HAIL came along.
So that SNOW came along.

And that PAINT began to peel
  and pretty soon the people
  came along and says,
HEY, that's Coyote, by golly
  she's not looking too good.

And the women brought her FOOD.
And the men brushed her COAT
  until it was shiney.
And the children PLAYED with
  their friend.

I been to Toronto Coyote tells
  the people.
Yes, everybody says,
We can SEE that.

# Joy Kogawa

## *What Do I Remember of the Evacuation*

What do I remember of the evacuation?
I remember my father telling Tim and me
About the mountains and the train
And the excitement of going on a trip.
What do I remember of the evacuation?
I remember my mother wrapping
A blanket around me and my
Pretending to fall asleep so she would be happy
Though I was so excited I couldn't sleep
(I hear there were people herded
Into the Hastings Park like cattle.
Families were made to move in two hours
Abandoning everything, leaving pets
And possessions at gun point.
I hear families were broken up
Men were forced to work. I heard
It whispered late at night
That there was suffering) and
I missed my dolls.
What do I remember of the evacuation?
I remember Miss Foster and Miss Tucker
Who still live in Vancouver
And who did what they could
And loved the children and who gave me
A puzzle to play with on the train.
And I remember the mountains and I was
Six years old and I swear I saw a giant
Gulliver of Gulliver's Travels scanning the horizon
And when I told my mother she believed it too
And I remember how careful my parents were
Not to bruise us with bitterness
And I remember the puzzle of Lorraine Life

Who said "Don't insult me" when I
Proudly wrote my name in Japanese
And Tim flew the Union Jack
When the war was over but Lorraine
And her friends spat on us anyway
And I prayed to the God who loves
All the children in his sight
That I might be white.

## When I Was a Little Girl

When I was a little girl
We used to walk together
Tim, my brother who wore glasses,
And I, holding hands
Tightly as we crossed the bridge
And he'd murmur, "You pray now"
— being a clergyman's son —
Until the big white boys
Had kicked on past.
Later we'd climb the bluffs
Overhanging the ghost town
And pick the small white lilies
And fling them like bombers
Over Slocan.

# Shirley Geok-lin Lim

## *Ah Mah*

Grandmother was smaller
than me at eight. Had she
been child forever?

Helpless, hopeless, chin sharp
as a knuckle, fan face
hardly half-opened, not a scrap

of fat anywhere: she tottered
in black silk, leaning on
handmaids, on two tortured

fins. At sixty, his sons all
married, grandfather bought her,
Soochow flower song girl.

Every bone in her feet
had been broken, bound tighter
than any neighbor's sweet

daughter's. Ten toes and instep
curled inwards, yellow petals
of chrysanthemum, wrapped

in gold cloth. He bought the young
face, small knobby breasts
he swore he'd not dress in sarong

of maternity. Each night
he held her feet in his palms,
like lotus in the tight

hollows of celestial lakes.
In his calloused flesh, her
weightless soles, cool and slack,

clenched in his stranger's fever.

## *To Li Poh*

I read you in a stranger's tongue,
Brother whose eyes were slanted also.
But you never left to live among
Foreign devils. Seeing the rice you ate grow
In your own backyard, you stayed on narrow
Village paths. Only your mind travelled
Easily: east, north, south, and west
Compassed in observation of field
And family. All men were guests
To one who knew traditions, the best
Of race. Country man, you believed to be Chinese
No more than a condition of human history.
Yet I cannot speak your tongue with ease,
No longer from China. Your stories
Stir griefs of dispersion and find
Me in simplicity of kin.

# Jayanta Mahapatra

## *The Abandoned British Cemetery at Balasore*

This is history.
I would not disturb it: the ruins of stone and marble,
the crumbling wall of brick, the coma of alienated decay.
How exactly should the archaic dead make me behave?

A hundred and fifty years ago
I might have lived. Now nothing offends my ways.
A quietness of bramble and grass holds me to a weed.
Will it matter if I know who the victims were, who survived?

And, if awed by the forgotten dead,
I walk around them: thirty-nine graves, their legends
floating in a twilight of baleful littoral,
the flaking history my intrusion does not animate.

Awkward in the silence, a scrawny lizard
watches the drama with its shrewd, hooded gaze.
And a scorpion, its sting drooping,
two eerie arms spread upon the marble, over an alien name.

In the circle the epitaphs run: Florence R — — , darling wife
of Captain R — — R — — , aged nineteen, of cholera . . .
Helen, beloved daughter of Mr. & Mrs. — — , of cholera,
aged seventeen, in the year of our Lord, eighteen hundred . . .

Of what concern to me is a vanished Empire?
Or the conquest of my ancestors' timeless ennui?
It is the dying young who have the power to show
what the heart will hide, the grass shows no more.

Who watches now in the dark near the dead wall?
The tribe of grass in the cracks of my eyes ?

It is the cholera still, death's sickly trickle,
that plagues the sleepy shacks beyond this hump of earth,

moving easily, swiftly, with quick power
through both past and present, the increasing young,
into the final bone, wearying all truth with ruin.
This is the iron

rusting in the vanquished country, the blood's unease,
the useless rain upon my familiar window;
the tired triumphant smile left behind by the dead
on a discarded anchor half-sunk in mud beside the graves:

out there on the earth's unwavering gravity
where it waits like a deity perhaps
for the elaborate ceremonial of a coming generation
to keep history awake, stifle the survivor's issuing cry.

# Lee Maracle

## *Charlie*

Charlie was a quiet boy. This was not unusual. His silence was interpreted by the priests and catholic lay teachers as stoic reserve – a quality inherited from his pagan ancestors. It was regarded in the same way the religious viewed the children's tearless response to punishment: a quaint combination of primitive courage and lack of emotion. All the children were like this and so Charlie could not be otherwise.

Had the intuitive sense of the priesthood been sharper they might have noticed the bitter look lurking in the shadows of the children's bland faces. The priests were not deliberately insensitive. All of their schooling had taught them that even the most heathen savage was born in the image of their own sweet lord. Thus, they held to the firm conviction that the sons and daughters of the people they were convinced were God's lowliest children were eternally good. Blinded by their own teaching they could not possibly be called upon to detect ill in the warm broad faces of their little charges.

Charlie did not do much schoolwork. He daydreamed. Much standing in the corner, repeated thrashings and the like had convinced him that staring out the window at the trees beyond the schoolyard was not the way to escape the sterile monotony of school. While the window afforded him the luxury of sighting a deer or watching the machinations of a bluejay trying to win the heart of his lady-bird fair, the thrashing he knew could be counted on for committing the crime of daydreaming was not worth the reward. So, like the other children, he would stare hard at his work, the same practiced look of bewilderment used by his peers on his face, while his thoughts danced around the forest close to home – far away from the arithmetic sums he was sure had nothing to do with him.

He learned to listen for the questions put to him by the brother over the happy daydream. He was not expected to know the answer; repeating the question sufficed. Knowing the question meant that, like the others, he was slow to learn but very attentive. No punishment was meted out for thickheadedness.

"What is three multiplied by five, Charlie?" The brother's brisk, clipped English accent echoed hollowly in the silence.

Charlie's eyes fixed on the empty page. His thoughts followed the manoeuvres of a snowshoe hare scampering ahead of himself and his half-wild dog. The first snow had fallen. It was that time of year. The question reached out to him over the shrieks of joy and the excited yelping of his dog, but it did not completely pluck him from the scene of his snow-capped, wooded homeland.

"Three . . . times . . . five?" muttered Charlie, the sounds coming out as though his voice were filled with air. A tense look from the brother. A quizzically dull look on Charlie's face. All the children stared harder at their pages — blank from want of work. He was still staring at the teacher but his mind was already following the rabbit. Did the brother's shoulders heave a sigh of disappointment?

"Thomas," the boredom of the teacher's voice thinly disguised.

"Fifteen," clearly and with volume. Poor Thomas, he always listened.

The bell rang. The class dutifully waited for dismissal. The brother sighed. The sound of scholarly confidence carefully practiced by all pedagogues left his voice at each bell. Exasperation permeated his dismissal command. It was the only emotion he allowed himself to express.

As he stood by the doorway watching the bowed heads slink by, his thoughts wandered about somewhat. *Such is my lot, to teach a flock of numbskulls . . . Ah, had I only finished and gotten a degree. Then, I could teach in a real school with eager students.* Each day his thoughts read thus and every time he laid out plans to return to university, but he never carried them out. At home every night a waiting bottle of Seagram's drowned out his self-pity and steadied him for the morrow.

\* \* \*

Charlie was bothered at meal times. The food was plain and monotonously familiar: beef stew on Monday, chicken stew on Tuesday — the days with their matching meal plan never varied. Unvarying menus did not bother Charlie though. Nor was it the plain taste of domestic meat as opposed to the sharp taste of wild meat that bothered him. He was bothered by something unidentifiable, tangible but invisible. He couldn't figure it out and that, too, bothered him.

From the line-up, he carried his plate to the section of the eating hall reserved for sixth grade boys. He looked up to watch the teenaged boys exchanging flirtatious glances with the young girls in a line opposite them. In the segregated classes of the school, boys and girls weren't permitted to mingle with, talk to, or touch one another. They sat in the same eating hall, but ate on separate sides. Charlie bored quickly of watching the frustrated efforts of youth struggling to reach each other through the invisible walls of rigid moral discipline erected by the priesthood.

His eyes began wandering about the eating room of his own home. The pot of stew was on the stove. It always had something warm and satisfying to the taste in it. He scarcely acknowledged its existence before he came to residential school. Now he saw it each day at meal time.

At home no one served you or stopped you from ladling out some of the pot's precious contents. Here at school, they lined you up to eat. Each boy at each age level got exactly the same portion. A second plate was out of the question. He felt ashamed to eat.

A stiff-backed white man appeared in the room and the low murmuring of voices stopped.

"EAT EVER-Y-THING ON YOUR PLATE!" he bellowed, clicking out the last *t* on the word plate. His entrance never varied. He said the same thing every day, careful to enunciate each word perfectly and loudly, in the manner he was sure best befitted the station of principal of a school. He marched up and down the aisles between tables in a precise pattern that was designed to impress on the boys that he was, indeed, the principal of the school. Finished with the last aisle, he marched stiff-legged out the door.

The boys were more than impressed. They were terrified. They likened the stiff-legged walk to the walk of an angry wolf. They had come to believe that whites were not quite human, so often did they walk in this wolf-like way. They knew the man who had just pranced about the eating hall to be the principal, not by the superiority of his intellect as compared to the other instructors, but by virtue of his having the stiffest walk and, hence, the fiercest temperament of the pack.

Night came and Charlie prepared for the best part of his incarceration. Between prayers and lights out, the children were left alone for fifteen minutes. Quickly into pyjamas and to the window.

The moon and the stars spread a thin blue light over the whitening ground below. Crystal flake after crystal flake draped the earth in a frock of glittering snow. As always, a tightness arose in his small boy-chest. He swallowed hard.

"LIGHTS OUT!"

Darkness swallowed the room and his little body leapt for the bunk with a willingness that always amazed him. He did not sleep right away.

"Hay, Chimmy, you got your clothes on?"

"Yeh."

"Ah-got the rope."

"Keh."

Runaway talk! Charlie hurriedly grabbed some clothes from the cupboard beneath the top of the night-table he shared with another boy.

"Ah'm comin' too," he hissed, struggling to snap up his jeans and shirt.

"Hurry, we're not waitin'."

He rushed breathless to the closet and grabbed a jacket. The older boys had already tied the rope to the metal latticing that closed the window. Each boy squeezed through the square created by one missing strip of metal lattice, and, hanging on to the rope, swung out from the window, then dropped to the ground below.

Safe in the bosom of the forest, after a tense but joyous run across the yard, the boys let go the cramped spirit that the priesthood so painstakingly tried to destroy in them. They whooped, they hollered, bayed at the moon and romped about chucking snow in loose, small balls at each other.

Jimmy cautioned them that that was enough. The faster they moved the greater the head start. They had to get through the forest to the railroad tracks by night cover.

The trek was uneventful. The older boys had run away before and knew exactly where they were going and how to get there. Stars and a full moon reflected against white snow provided them with enough light to pick their way along. As time wore by, the excited walk became dull plodding. They reached the tracks of the railroad sometime near daylight. All were serious now. They cast furtive glances up and down the track. The shelter of darkness was gone. Discovery became real in the bright light of day. Surely the priest had sent the police in search of them by now.

The boys trod light-footed and quickly along the trackline, fear spurring them on. A thin wisp of smoke curling upward from the creaking pines on their right brought the boys to a halt.

"It's mah uncle's house," Jimmy purred with contentment. The empty forest carries sound a long way in winter, so the boys spoke in whispers. It never occurred to the other boys to ask Jimmy what his uncle's reaction to their visit would be. They assumed it would be the same as their own folks' response.

A short trek through the woods brought them to the cabin's door. Uncle and aunt were already there to greet them. They were now used to the frequent runaway boys that always stopped for a day or two, then not knowing how to get home, trudged the nine and some miles back to school. The holiday, uncle mused to aunt, would do them no harm. Besides which, they enjoyed the company of happy children.

A good meal . . . a day's play . . . nightfall . . . heavenly sleep in this cabin full of the same sweet smells of his own cabin brought sentimental dreams to Charlie.

Charlie's dreams followed the familiar lines of his home. In the centre stood his mama quietly stirring the stew. Above her head, hanging from the rafters, were strips of dried meat. Hundreds of them, dangling in mute testimony to his father's skill as hunter and provider. A little ways from the stove hung mama's cooking tools. Shelving and boxes made of wood housed such food stuffs as flour, sugar, oatmeal, salt and the like. All here was hewn from the forest's bounty by Charlie's aging grandfather.

Crawling and toddling about were his younger brother and sister, unaware of Charlie's world or his dream of them. Completing the picture was his dad. He stood in the corner, one leg perched on a log stump used as a kindling split. He had a smoke in his hand.

No one but his wife knew how his thoughts ran. How he wondered with a gnawing tightness why it was he had to send his little ones, one after the other, far away to school.

Daily, he heard of young ones who had been to school and not returned. More often, he would come across the boys who recently finished school, hanging about the centre of the village, unwilling and poorly equipped to take care of themselves. Without hunting or trapping skills, the boys wasted away, living from hand-to-mouth, a burden on their aging parents. One by one they drifted away, driven by the shame of their uselessness.

It was not that they could not learn to hunt or trap. But it takes years of boyhood to grow accustomed to the ways of the forest, to overcome the lonely and neurotic fear it can sometimes create in a man. A boy who suddenly becomes a man does not want to learn what he is already supposed to know well. No man wants to admit his personal fear of his home.

The pull of years of priestly schooling towards the modern cities of a Canada that hardly touched their wilderness village grew stronger. For a while, family and city pulled with equal strength, gripping the youth in a listless state of paralysis. For some, the city won out and they drifted away. Charlie's father worried about the fate of his young ones.

His private agony was his own lack of resistance. He sent his son to school. It was the law. A law that he neither understood nor agreed to, but he sent them. His willingness to reduce his son to a useless waster stunned him. He confided none of his self-disgust to his wife. It made him surly but he said nothing.

In his dream, Charlie did not know his father's thoughts. He saw his father standing, leg-on-log, as he usually stood while he awaited breakfast, and he awoke contented.

Jimmy's uncle had given up wondering about the things that plagued Charlie's father. His children had grown up and left, never to return. He did not even know if there were grandchildren.

He lived his life without reflection now. Jimmy was the eldest son of his youngest brother. It was enough for his life's labours that this boy called him grandfather out of respect for the man's age.

"I'm going to check the short lines," he said, biting into his bannock and not looking at the boys.

"Can we help?" The older boys looked at their plates, studiously masking their anxiety.

"Sure." Staring at them carefully, he added, "but the small one must stay." The old man was unwilling to risk taking the coatless boy with him.

Charlie followed them to the edge of the woods. He knew that no amount of pleading would change the old man's mind and crying would only bring him shame. He watched them leave and determined to go home where his own grandfather would take him to check his short lines.

The old aunt tried to get him to stay. She promised him a fine time. It was a wasted effort. He wanted the comfort and dignity of his own cabin, not a fine time.

Charlie knew the way home. It had not taken him long to travel the distance from the tracks near his home to the school. He had marked the trail in the way that so many of his ancestors might have: a rocky crag here, a distorted, lone pine there. He gave no thought to the fact that the eight-hour trip had been made by rail and not on foot.

The creaking pines, straining under the heavy snowfall of the night before, brought Charlie the peace of mind that school had denied him. A snow-bird feeding through the snow curled Charlie's mouth into a delighted smile. A rabbit scampered across the tracks and disappeared into the forest. He had half a mind to chase it.

"Naw, better just go home." His voice seemed to come from deep within him, spreading itself out in a wide half-circle and meeting the broad expanse of hill and wood only to be swallowed by nature's huge majesty somewhere beyond his eyes. The thinness of his voice against the forest made him feel small.

The day wore by tediously slow. Charlie began to worry. He had not seen his first landmark.

"Am I going the right way?" What a terrible trick of fate to trek mile after mile only to arrive back at school. The terror of it made him want to cry.

Around the bend, he recognized a bare stone cliff. Assured, he ran a little. He coughed and slowed down again. He tired a little. He felt sleepy. He touched his bare hands. Numb.

"Frostbite," he whispered.

In his rush to leave the dormitory he had grabbed his fall jacket. The cold now pierced his chest. Breathing was difficult. His legs cried out for rest. Charlie fought the growing desire to sleep.

The biscuits aunt had given him were gone. Hunger beset him. He trudged on, squinting at the sprays of sunlight that cast a reddish hue on the snow-clad pines in final farewell to daylight.

Darkness folded itself over the land with a cruel swiftness. It fell upon the landscape, swallowing Charlie and the thread of track connecting civilization to nature's vastness, closing with maddening speed the last wisps of light from Charlie's eyes.

Stars, one by one, woke from their dreamy sleep and filled the heavens. Charlie stumbled. He rose reluctantly. His legs wobbled forward a few more steps, then gave in to his defeated consciousness that surrendered to the sparkling whiteness that surrounded him. He rolled over and lay face up scanning the star-lit sky.

Logic forsook him. His heart beat slower. A smile nestled on his full purple lips. He opened his eyes. His body betrayed him. He felt warm again. Smiling he welcomed the Orion queen — not a star constellation but the great Wendigo — dressed in midnight blue, her dress alive with the glitter of a thousand stars. Arms outstretched, he greeted the lady that came to lift his spirit and close his eyes forever to sleep the gentle sleep of white death.

# Dambudzo Marechera

## *Black Skin What Mask*

My skin sticks out a mile in all the crowds around here. Every time I go out I feel it tensing up, hardening, torturing itself. It only relaxes when I am in shadow, when I am alone, when I wake up early in the morning, when I am doing mechanical actions, and, strangely enough, when I am angry. But it is coy and self-conscious when I draw in my chair and begin to write.

It is like a silent friend: moody, assertive, possessive, callous — sometimes.

I had such a friend once. He finally slashed his wrists. He is now in a lunatic asylum. I have since asked myself why he did what he did, but I still cannot come to a conclusive answer.

He was always washing himself — at least three baths every day. And he had all sorts of lotions and deodorants to appease the thing that had taken hold of him. He did not so much wash as scrub himself until he bled.

He tried to purge his tongue too, by improving his English and getting rid of any accent from the speaking of it. It was painful to listen to him, as it was painful to watch him trying to scrub the blackness out of his skin.

He did things to his hair, things which the good lord never intended any man to do to his hair.

He bought clothes, whole shops of them. If clothes make the man, then certainly he was a man. And his shoes were the kind that make even an elephant lightfooted and elegant. The animals that were murdered to make those shoes must have turned in their graves and said Yeah, man.

But still he was dissatisfied. He had to have every other African within ten miles of his person follow his example. After all, if one chimpanzee learns not only to drink tea but also to promote that tea on TV, what does it profit it if all the other god-created chimpanzees out there continue to scratch their fleas and swing around on their tails chattering about Rhodes and bananas?

However, he was nice enough to put it more obliquely to me one day. We were going to the New Year Ball in Oxford Town Hall.

"Don't you ever change those jeans?" he asked.

"They're my only pair," I said.

"What do you do with your money, man, booze?"

"Yes," I said searching through my pockets. Booze and paper and ink. The implements of my trade.

"You ought to take more care of your appearance, you know. We're not monkeys."

"I'm all right as I am."

I coughed and because he knew what that cough meant he tensed up as though for a blow.

"If you've got any money," I said firmly, "lend me a fiver."

That day he was equally firm:

"Neither a lender nor a borrower be," he quoted.

And then as an afterthought he said:

"We're the same size. Put on this other suit. You can have it if you like. And the five pounds."

That is how he put it to me. And that is how it was until he slashed his wrists.

But there was more to it than that.

Appearances alone — however expensive — are doubtful climbing-boots when one hazards the slippery slopes of social adventure. Every time he opened his mouth he made himself ridiculous. Logic — that was his magic word: but unfortunately that sort of thing quickly bored even the most thick-skinned anthropologist-in-search-of-African attitudes. I was interested in the booze first and then lastly in the company. But he — god help me — relied on politics to get on with people. But who in that company in their right mind gives a shit about Rhodesia? He could never understand this.

And Christ! when it came to dancing he really made himself look a monkey. He always assumed that if a girl accepted his request for a dance it meant that she had in reality said Yes to being groped, squeezed, kissed and finally screwed off the dance floor. And the girls were quite merciless with him. The invitations would stop and all would be a chilly silence.

I did not care for the type of girl who seemed to interest him. He liked them starched, smart and demure, and with the same desperate conversation:

"What's your college?"

"__.What's yours?"

"__."

Pause.

"What's your subject?"

"__.What's yours?"

"__."

Pause. Cough.

"I'm from Zimbabwe."

"What's that?"

"Rhodesia."

"O. I'm from London. Hey (with distinct lack of interest), Smith's a bastard, isn't he?"

And he eagerly:

"As a matter of fact, I have just addressed the Africa Society on the thesis that Ian Smith blah blah blah blah blah blah blah . . ."

(Yawning) "Interesting. Very interesting."

"Smith blah blah blah blah blah blah . . . (Suddenly) Would you like to dance?"

Startled:

"Well . . . I . . . yes, why not."

And that's how it was. Yes, that's how it was, until he slashed his wrists.

But there was more to it than that.

A black tramp accosted him one night as we walked to the University Literary Society party. It was as if he had been touched by a leper. He literally cringed away from the man, who incidentally knew me from a previous encounter when he and I had sat Christmas Eve through on a bench in Carfax drinking a bottle of whisky. He was apoplectic with revulsion and at the party could talk of nothing else:

"How can a black man in England let himself become a bum? There is much to be done. Especially in Southern Africa. What I would like to see blah blah blah . . ."

"Have a drink," I suggested.

He took it the way God accepts anything from Satan.

"You drink too much, you know," he sighed.

"You drink too little for your own good," I said.

The incident of the tramp must have gnawed him more than I had thought because when we got back in college he couldn't sleep and came into my room with a bottle of claret which I was glad to drink with him until breakfast when he did stop talking about impossible black bastards; he stopped talking because he fell asleep in his chair.

And that's how it was until he slashed his wrists.

But there were other sides to the story.

For example: he did not think that one of his tutors "liked" him.

"He doesn't have to like anyone," I pointed out, "and neither do you."

But he wasn't listening. He cracked his fingers and said:

"I'll send him a Christmas and New Year card, the best money can buy."

"Why not spend the money on a Blue Nun?" I suggested.

The way he looked at me, I knew I was losing a friend.

For example: he suggested one day that if the Warden or any of the other tutors asked me if I was his friend I was to say no.

"Why?" I asked.

"You do drink too much, you know," he said looking severe, "and I'm afraid you do behave rather badly, you know. For instance, I heard about an incident in the beercellar and another in the dining room and another in Cornmarket where the police had to be called, and another on your staircase . . ."

I smiled.

"I'll have your suit laundered and sent up to your rooms," I said firmly, "and I did give you that five pounds back. So that's all right. Are you dining in Hall, because if you are then I will not, it'd be intolerable. Imagine it. We're the only two Africans in this college. How can we possibly avoid each other, or for that matter . . ."

He twisted his brow. Was it pain? He had of late begun to complain of insomnia and headaches, and the lenses of his spectacles did not seem to fit the degree of his myopia. Certainly something cracked in his eyes, smarting:

"Look, I say, what, forget what I said. I don't care what they think. It's my affair, isn't it, who I choose to be friends with?"

I looked him squarely in the eye:

"Don't let them stuff bullshit into you. Or spew it out right in their faces. But don't ever puke their gut-rot on me."

"Let's go play tennis," he said after a moment.

"I can't. I have to collect some dope from a guy the other end of town," I said.

"Dope? You take that — stuff?"

"Yes. The Lebanese variety is the best piss for me."

He really was shocked.

He turned away without another word. I stared after him, hoping he wouldn't work himself up into telling his moral tutor — who was actually the one who didn't like him. And that's how it was. That's how it was, until he slashed his wrists.

But there had to be another side to it: sex.

The black girls in Oxford—whether African, West Indian or American—despised those of us who came from Rhodesia. After all, we still haven't won our independence. After all, the papers say we are always quarrelling among ourselves. And all the other reasons which black girls choose to believe. It was all quite unflattering. We had become—indeed we are—the Jews of Africa, and nobody wanted us. It's bad enough to have white shits despising us; but it's a more maddening story when one kettle ups its nose at another kettle . . . And this he had to learn.

I didn't care one way or the other. Booze was better than girls, even black girls. And dope was heaven. But he worried. And he got himself all mixed up about a West Indian girl who worked in the kitchen. Knowing him as I did, such a "comedown" was to say the least shattering.

"But we're all black," he insisted.

It was another claret being drunk until breakfast.

"You might as well say to a National Front thug that we're all human," I said.

"Maybe black men are not good enough for them," he protested. "Maybe all they do is dream all day long of being screwed nuts by white chaps. Maybe . . ."

"I hear you've been hanging around the kitchen every day."

He sat up.

I *was* finally losing a friend.

But he chose to sigh tragically, and for the first time—I had been waiting for this—he swore a sudden volley of earthy expletives.

"From now on, it's white girls or nothing."

"You've tried that already," I reminded him.

He gripped the arms of his chair and then let his lungs collapse slowly.

"Why don't you try men?" I asked, refilling my glass.

He stared.

And spat:

"You're full of filth, do you know that?"

"I have long suspected it," I said, losing interest.

But I threw in my last coin:

"Or simply masturbate. We all do."

Furiously, he refilled his glass.

We drank in silence for a long, contemplative hour.

"They're going to send me down," I said.

"What?"

It was good of him to actually sound surprised.

"If I refuse to go into Warneford as a voluntary patient," I added.

"What's Warneford?"

"A psychiatric care unit," I said. "I have until lunch this afternoon to decide. Between either voluntary confinement or being sent down."

I tossed him the Warden's note to that effect. He unfolded it.

He whistled.

The sound of his whistle almost made me forgive him everything, including himself. Finally he asked: "What have you decided to do?"

"Be sent down."

"But . . ."

I interrupted:

"It's the one decision in my life which I know will turn out right."

"Will you stay on in England?"

"Yes."

"Why not go to Africa and join our guerrillas? You've always been rather more radical than myself and this will be a chance blah blah blah blah blah."

I yawned.

"Your glass is empty," I said. "But take a good look anyway, a good look at me and all you know about me and then tell me whether you see a dedicated guerrilla."

He looked.

I refilled his glass and opened another bottle as he scrutinised me.

He lit up; almost maliciously.

"You're a tramp," he said firmly, "You're just like that nigger-tramp who accosted me the other day when we . . ."

"I know," I said belching.

He stared.

"What will you do?"

"Writing."

"How will you live?"

"Tomorrow will take care of itself. I hope," I said.

And that was the last time we made speech to each other over bottles of claret throughout the small hours until clean sunlight slivered lucidly through the long open windows and I left him sleeping peacefully in his chair and hurried to my last breakfast in college.

# Pauline Melville

## *The Truth is in the Clothes*

Later, much later, I came to the conclusion that she was a manipulator, this black woman from Soweto: powerful certainly, a shrewd entrepreneur and a hugely talented designer, but, finally, without those powers of sorcery that I initially attributed to her. The gifts of the genuine shaman overlap in places with the psychological wizardry of the charlatan. After a lapse of time, I became convinced that her powers were more akin to those of the confidence trickster.

This is the story.

Late one night, there was a knock on my door. Zephra, my singer friend from Trinidad, stood on the doorstep with a small group of people. She was radiant, bubbling with that energy performers get after a show. Whether it was the light falling on her from the doorway or the brightness of the outfit she wore, I couldn't tell, but she eclipsed the others:
  "Hi. Sorry to call so late." Her eyes shone with exuberance. "This is Kalimbo, a band from South Africa I've just been working with." Two shortish men, one with a pork-pie hat, the other bare headed, stepped shyly over the threshold. Behind them entered a tall woman with a headwrap.
  "Come in. Come in." The front room had that air of peaceful expectancy that rooms unaccountably acquire after being tidied. "I've only got rum in the house. Will that do everybody?" The woman asked for fruit juice.

Zephra trailed after me into the kitchen, chatting while I fixed rum drinks with ice, freshly squeezed limes and Cassis:
  "Old Oak rum!" she squealed. "I ain' seen that since I was home."
  It was good to see her so happy, Zephra, with her tremulous spirit and history of breakdowns. She was still thin, her eyes enormous in a gaunt, brown face. I ignored the remnants of a black eye, a tiny,

upturned crescent of crimson under her right eye.

"What are you wearing?" I asked. "It looks wonderful."

Under the bright kitchen lights, she held up her arms to show off the outfit. Shocking pink cotton cloth with great, batwing sleeves hung down to her mid-calves. Printed in black on the cloth were African heads and the occasional brilliant green banana tree set against a hot orange sun. Her hat was pill-box shaped, the same bright pink, edged with black and with two stiffened, black, batwing shapes on either side.

"Isn't it beautiful?" she said. "I tell you, girl, when I step out on that stage tonight, these clothes uplifted my spirit. My songs just took off like a flight of birds. You must check out this band. You will love their music. I know it."

We took the drinks back into the front room. It was darker in there, lit only by a table-lamp. The men were seated in a corner, talking quietly. The woman stood in the centre of the room.

"This is Maisie." Zephra introduced her.

"I am pleased to meet you." The voice was low and sweet as an underground river. She was a broad but lean-faced African woman with thin lips, her complexion charcoal black with patches of bronze on the cheekbones. I guessed she was about forty, tall and rangy. The light raincoat she held bunched round her was the colour of earth but in no way drab. Round her head, she had twisted, carelessly but with immense style, a rough piece of maroon cloth patterned with a diagram of white drumsticks.

Zephra plumped herself down on the sofa, took a packet of ganga from her bag and began to build a spliff. Maisie sat down in the armchair next to the four foot-high weeping-fig plant. I sat on the floor.

"Are you all from Soweto?" I asked.

"Yes," the man with the pork-pie hat and fat, brown eyelids replied. "We are from the Naledi township." The men exchanged words in their own language and laughed.

"They are telling you that I am from the Rockville area. One of the electrified areas," said Maisie.

"It was Maisie who made me these clothes," chimed in Zephra. "I needed something for the gig tonight and she ran this up for me in an hour!"

"That is what I do." Maisie spoke with soft intimacy. "I am a designer of clothes. I make the clothes for the band. In Africa I make clothes for many artists. Musicians come from far seeking my clothes.

They like to be photographed in them for the front of their albums. They know my clothes can make them successful. They can make people into stars. They can make people live long. My clothes can kill people. My clothes can heal people. I tell you, the truth is in the clothes."

She leaned towards me. Her eyes were a lighter brown than most African eyes. The ear-rings dangling from her ears were long, silver ones with tiny chains hanging from the bottom:

"When I make clothes for performing artists," she continued, "other artists become jealous. Competitive. They consult a witch-doctor for potions and herbs to take away the magic from my clothes. Powerful African mixtures," she muttered as though I would not understand. "When performers do that — try to bewitch another performer who is wearing my clothes — then I get sick, because they are trying to kill me at home. Twice I have been in the hospital vomiting blood. I carry on because I am guided. I see something about the person and I am guided to make the clothes. Are you a journalist?" she asked, unexpectedly. She must have seen the typewriter and clutter of papers on the table. "I want you to write something about me."

"I don't write that sort of thing. I write stories," I apologised. "I might write a story about you, about someone who makes clothes that can kill or heal people. That would make a good story."

"You must do that," she said.

Zephra rifled through the cassette tapes. She dug out some Cuban salsa music and slapped it in the machine. Then she began to dance. The men talked between themselves in location language.

"I like you," said Maisie. "I will make something for you. A beautiful jacket." I was flattered as if someone had offered to paint my portrait. Immediately, I wanted that jacket more than anything in the world.

"I will pay you, of course," I said. Payment did not seem enough. "But I will also write the story about you. I will make a story for you in exchange for the jacket."

The light from the table-lamp shone up through the weeping-fig and threw dappled shadows of leaves onto the ceiling over her head. Suddenly, I saw her quite clearly sitting on a wooden bench in Africa. She was leaning forward under the shade of a great, spreading tree. Behind her, on the other side of a chicken-wire fence, sprawled an estate of yellow, matchbox housing. I smelled a burning smell. Creosote or burning rubber. In her left hand she held a piece of corn. Fine, silky brown hair sprouted from the top. Maisie. The name itself reminded me of corn and fertility; roots growing in the earth that can be ground and made into nourishment. Maisie. A fermenting, bubbling name, golden like mead. Mealie meal. Finely ground maize. Maisie.

"I want to make a film." She was back sitting in the chair. "Can you help me to do that?" she asked, abruptly.

"I don't think so," I said. "Where? Here or in Africa?"

"Anywhere. I travel extensively." She paused, then added, "The United States."

"I'll try and think of someone who could help you. How are things in Soweto?" I enquired, respectfully sympathetic.

"I am not an oppressed woman," she snapped. "And my people are not oppressed."

Conversation in the room had ceased. The Cubans shouted gaily from the machine. My little black cat, Basil, strolled in, tail on high and rubbed himself around her legs.

Zephra switched off the cassette player:

"We have to go now," she announced. "Some people are expecting us."

I knew if I lost track of them I would lose my jacket:

"Where can I find you all?"

"I've got to go to Manchester tomorrow," said Zephra. "The band will be playing at the Club Sozo in the Seven Sisters Road. Go down there tomorrow night."

"Will you be there?" I asked Maisie.

"Yes. I will be there," she said.

We said our goodbyes. I showed them to the door.

Next evening I squeezed into the back of the Club Sozo. It was packed. Squinting in the dark, I tried reading the promo leaflet: "Kalimbo style—spirit of ancestors. Benda region. Benda people. Used by many tribes. Crossing of traditional with popular music of townships."

One of the men on stage had not been at my flat the night before, a thin man. The skin head of his drum was anchored by strings to the pegs round the outside. The rhythms vibrated through the crowd. But it was not his playing that attracted my attention. It was what he wore. He wore a most extraordinary suit, the shape of Africa. The suit was made of dark green cotton with fiery orange and yellow markings. The pants were baggy. The right sleeve made up the enormous bulge of the West Coast. The left sleeve cut away sharply, following the outline of the coast of Ethiopia, dipping up to Somaliland and the Horn of Africa. Stitched onto the front was a pocket, also shaped like Africa, in black with the same hectic markings. The southern part of the continent fell just below his knees. As he slapped the drum, fire crackled all over the cloth. I looked for Maisie in the audience. There was no sign of her.

The cramped dressing-room smelled of stale beer. Some kind of ruck was going on. The promoter, a thin-faced Englishman, was angry. The night before, the drummer had been drunk, too paralytic to perform. Now the promoter would not give them their full fee. Maisie sat sulking in a corner. The men were arguing but I could see they were subdued, depressed. The guitarist smiled a hello at me with sad eyes:

"We are homesick," he said. "The tour has been a long one."

I went over and crouched at Maisie's feet in the small space:

"When can I come and see you about my jacket?"

"I don't know," she said, then changed her mind. "Tomorrow. Give me a pen and paper. I will write down the address where I will be in the morning." She wrote down an address somewhere in Camberwell.

The address was difficult to find, nowhere near an underground station. The August morning was dull and overcast. I had to walk up the drives of several of the large Victorian houses because the numbers were either missing or not clear. When finally I found it, the front door was open. I walked in. The house was in the process of being renovated into flats, floorboards bare, wires sticking out from wall sockets. I called her name:

"Maisie." There was no reply. I walked up the stairs.

She was already at work on the third floor. The room stank of hot wax and vegetable oil. A welter of mainly brownish cloth festooned the place, draped over sofa, floor and chairs. Patches of the green cloth worn by the drummer lay here and there, jumbled with other fragments and scraps of material. Strung across the windows were swatches of cloth, the colour of caramel rivers. Beside an ancient, two-ring burner stood Maisie, stirring vigorously the wax in a rusty tin can. She wore a shift of the softest brushed cotton thinly striped in grey and pink, Arab style, and a headwrap of the same stuff.

"Come in and sit down."

I found a stool and squatted on it. She worked as she talked.

"You see how fast I work? When I was in America I made one thousand tie and dye pieces in five days, each one a different colour, a different design. They refused to believe I had done it." She sounded bitter. "They tried to cheat me. They said I only made seven hundred. I refused the money they were offering because it was less than what I had been promised. I do not make the clothes for money. Money is drawn to me but I do not make the clothes because of money. God speaks to me. I am guided by him. I follow whatever he says. In America they said I was a witch."

Metal buckets of dye gleamed dully on the floor, indigo, dark green, vermilion. As she spoke she dipped cloth, intricately tied with string, into one or another bucket. The liquid never spilled. Then she started to paint the hot wax onto the cotton in strong, bold patterns. She would crack the wax on other pieces of cloth, where it had dried, re-dip the cloth and force the new colour into the fissures and creases she formed constantly with her hands.

"How did you discover you had this gift?" I was impressed.

"Always, always I loved clothes. From when I was tiny. If my mother wanted to punish me she would forbid me to wear my favourite clothes. My mother was an Anglican. My father a Methodist. I ran from my mother and went to my father's church. That is where I heard the story of the coat of many colours. I knew I could make one. Wherever I go I borrow the equipment I need to make clothes. I cannot stop."

I watched her twist the cloth into special folds.

"When I was little I would put pebbles and stones, even bricks, into the cloth to make the shapes I needed. I stitched with raffia. I had to use tamarind water and indigo for dye. Now I use cold water dyes, but I use them hot. I use caustic soda to fix the colours and sodium sulphate to make the white more brilliant. God has helped me. I have three factories where people sew for me. I have two shops, one in the airport at Bophutaswanaland. You must help me find an outlet in England."

She strung up the cloth to dry. Curiously, no drips fell from it. She took up a length of material and began to cut. She cut boldly, sleeves and body of the wrap from a single piece of cloth. I tried to bring the conversation round to my jacket:

"Do you need to take my measurements for the jacket?"

"No. I have looked at you. That is enough."

I tried to resist asking but couldn't:

"What will it be like?"

"I shall make you a jacket of royal blue. I like working with royal blue. I shall line it with red. And there will be things on it. Things that are for you especially."

Excitement ground the pit of my stomach. Something else I wanted to know:

"How is it you say your clothes can kill people?"

"Whatever is done in the clothes affects the man himself. That is not my responsibility. God tells me what to do. The clothes can kill. The clothes can heal. That is God's will, not mine."

In the corner on a table rested an old treadle sewing-machine. She seated herself at it:

"One time when I could not find what it was I wanted to wear, I took down the curtains in my house and quickly made them into a new outfit." She laughed.

I took fifty pounds from my purse:

"Is fifty pounds enough for the jacket?"

She answered through the whirr of the machine:

"That is enough. Put it on the table. I do not pursue money but I do not like to be cheated. I do not make clothes for the money. "

I could hardly believe that. Three factories? Two shops? Business trips all over the world?

"I am leaving for Zimbabwe the day after tomorrow," she said. "When I am gone I want you to go to Harrods and tell them about my clothes."

"I'll try," I said, doubtfully. "Will you have time to make my jacket?"

"Write your name and address down on a piece of paper and leave it with me. The jacket will come to you."

I did as she asked.

"Thank you very much, Maisie." I got up to leave. She got up too. "Will you be coming back to England?"

"January. I will come back in January. Goodbye. Don't forget you must write a nice story about me."

I turned back in the doorway to wave goodbye. She stood facing me, her back to the window. Everywhere in the room the cloth had formed itself into a miniature landscape around her. A female Ozymandias, she bestrode the desert. Behind her were steep escarpments, grooved cliffs of brown sandstone. Tiny mountain ranges obscured her feet. In front of me stretched a panorama of dried-out river beds, dizzying whorls of sand, hillocks and dunes patched with green oases. All this I saw with the scale and clarity of detail as though from an ascending aeroplane. It lasted for a split second. Then the room returned to normal. I left, again the smell of burning rubber in my nostrils.

Four days later the jacket arrived, delivered by hand, in a brown paper parcel tied with string. I unpacked it. In length the garment was half way between a coat and a jacket, reaching to mid-thigh. It was cut, all in one, with wide sleeves like a kaftan. Outside, as she had promised, the colour was a magnificent royal blue. The lining was deep red. Round about the hem there alternated a golden bell and a pomegranate, the same around the hem of the sleeves. Strikingly printed all over the blue exterior and the red lining were black shapes. I examined them more closely. They were scarabs, the sacred beetle of ancient Egypt.

I went straight to the mirror to try it on. It fitted perfectly but somehow I was disappointed. It made me look pale and wasted. Several times over the next few months, I tried it on. The result was always the same. Either I looked ill or, when it did suit me, I could find nothing to wear with it. In the end I left it hanging in the cupboard.

January came and went. No sign of Maisie. Shortly after she left I tried to write a story about her but nothing came. I decided that it was my own suggestibility that had endowed her with supernatural powers and I felt foolish.

I forgot about her. A year later I was working on a collection of short stories. I needed three more. I remember that it was a Wednesday evening and I was sitting, browsing through old notebooks searching for ideas. I found a few notes on Maisie. Perhaps I could knock them into a story. I wrote the first unflattering paragraph, stating that she was no more than a con-woman. As I completed it, the telephone rang. I heard the blip and squeak of a long-distance call, then the voice, quite clear:

"Hello. This is Julia." I tried to think who it might be.

"Julia Legwabe," the voice said as if I should know it.

"Hi," I bluffed. "Where are you?"

"Bophutaswanaland," came the reply. "Maisie says you must meet her at the airport on Friday."

I glanced guiltily over at the page sticking out of the typewriter:

"I'm afraid I can't. I'm working on Friday." I lied.

"All right. Thank you very much. I will tell her. Goodbye." The receiver at the other end clicked down.

Unnerved by the timing of the call, I felt that she was heading over here to stop me writing the truth about her. I decided to go ahead and worked late that night and all through the next day. In the evening the telephone rang. This time it was her:

"Hello. This is Maisie," said the husky voice, intimate even at a distance of thousands of miles.

"Hello," I said with false delight. "Where are you?"

"Mafeking," she said. I had a picture of her flitting around the southern part of Africa, one minute in Bophutaswanaland, the next in Mafeking.

"I am coming to London on Sunday. I want to stay with you."

"Oh no. What a shame. I won't be in London. I'm working out of town." I hoped she mistook my hesitation for the normal time-lag of a long-distance call.

"That is a pity because I am having a show. I wanted you to see it."

"Maybe I can get back for a bit. Where is it?"

"The South African Embassy."

I was shocked.

"I can't go in there," I said. "There's a cultural boycott. There's a picket outside. There's a continuous twenty-four-hour demonstration in front of the Embassy."

"I know." She chuckled. "You should come with me. You might learn something."

"How long will you be in London?"

"Just for the show on Monday. Then I go to Belgium and Austria."

"Oh, I'm sorry. It looks as though I will miss you." I paused. "I haven't written that story about you yet."

It was not a lie. It was not the truth.

"A lot of people want to write about me. You must write a nice story about me."

"OK. Goodbye, Maisie." I hung up.

I returned to the typewriter. So far what I had written was a condemnation of her as a fraud, a sell-out, a reactionary, a collaborator. Now I decided I would not write about her at all. I would scrap the whole idea. I took the pages and chucked them in the bin.

I' d taken the jacket out and laid it open on the sofa to remind me of the style and feel of her work, hoping it would lead me into the story. I stared at it. The black scarab shapes on the scarlet lining appeared to shift. I blinked to clear my eyes. The second time I looked they shifted more violently. That happens sometimes with the juxtaposition of red and black. It is an optical illusion, something to do with the structure of the cells at the back of the retina. I shut my eyes for a full minute. When I looked again, both the blue exterior of the jacket and the red lining were completely plain. There was nothing on them at all. Slowly, I raised my eyes. The black shapes were all over the wall and half-way across the ceiling. I looked away and looked back. They were still there.

The cat started to use the leg of the table as a scratching post. I pushed him down. Immediately, he levitated, rotating upright, his four legs outspread. With a sudden change of speed and direction, he hurled himself against the back wall and buried himself in the plaster causing thin, jagged cracks. I went over for a closer inspection. There was, where he had sunk in, a wide, cork plug in the wall, the sort of stopper you see in glass jars in fashionable kitchens. I manoeuvred it out. Through the hole in the wall I could see dusty catacombs. I was able to hear footsteps in there, but I saw nobody. I pulled away enough bits of plaster and masonry to be able to squeeze through.

The yellow porous rock crumbled a little under my touch. Rough walls were pitted with holes containing grains of sand. Light came from somewhere but I couldn't discover the source. There was no trace of damp and the air was warm. To my left, in a hollowed-out cave, a man lay groaning on the ground, his shirt wrapped tightly round him. I approached. Over his head some letters were scratched in the wall. The letters were all constructed of straight lines. As I studied them they lit up as if someone had shone a torch from behind me. I read:

H . . . E . . . R . . . A . . . K . . . L . . . The last letters were indecipherable.

I did not go too close to the man because I knew his shirt was poisoned.

I passed through the honeycombed passages and came to the bottom of a staircase. It was familiar. I recognised it as the staircase of a London house where I had lived some years earlier in a flat on the top floor. I climbed the stairs. The house appeared to be unoccupied. Where there had been carpeting on the stairs, the boards were bare and dusty. I held onto the wooden banister and went up to the top. The flat was empty, the windows dirty, and my shoes made tapping noises on the floorboards. I opened the door to what used to be the living room.

To my surprise I found myself at the back of an evangelical church hall. A phalanx of wooden chairs waited for a congregation. The only occupants were two women seated some way apart, one in a drab maroon coat, the other in dull green. A flush of embarrassment came over me. What would my friends think if they discovered I had a functioning church in my front room? There was no altar, just a high pulpit set in front of the chairs. An Anglican vicar entered from the back and made his way down the left-hand aisle to the pulpit. His white surplice hung limply over the black gown. Steel grey streaked the hair on the back of his head. He mounted the pulpit:

"Today's sermon is taken from two readings of the Old Testament:

the first from Exodus, Chapter 39, verses 24-26 and the second from Ecclesiastes, Chapter 3, verses 1-3."

The voice was weary:

*"'And they made upon the hems of the robe, pomegranates of blue and purple, and scarlet, and twined linen.*

*And they made bells of pure gold and put the bells between the pomegranates upon the hem of the robe, round about between the pomegranates;*

*A bell and a pomegranate, a bell and a pomegranate round about the hem of the robe.'*

The church smelled musty. He continued with monotonous intonation:

*'To everything there is a season, and a time to every purpose under the heaven:*

*A time to be born and a time to die; a time to plant and a time to pluck up that which is planted;*

*A time to kill and a time to heal . . .'"*

I slipped out through the side door into the sunshine.

The grass beneath my feet was dry and brown, the heat overpowering. Dolores was hanging out clothes on the line strung between the mango tree and Mr Elliot's house. Water glistened on her brown hands. As she reached for the pegs her dress rode up round her strong thighs. I couldn't believe that I had lived in my ground floor London flat for five years without ever realising that Jamaica was just on the other side of my back wall. Relief flooded me. Now I would be able to return whenever I wanted, by going through the hole in the wall:

"Hi there, Dolores."

She turned, smiling:

"Hi there to you too. 'Ave you seen Mr Elliot? 'Im say 'im a soon come but 'im don' reach yet." She spoke in her slow, country accent.

"I ain' seen him."

Every day Dolores walked three miles across Kingston to look after Mr Elliot's children while his wife was in America:

"Thirta dollars 'im say 'im woudda give me today. Thirta dollars."

She sprinkled some Coldpower from a packet into a tin tub full of white washing. The clothes squeaked as she rubbed them. Another tub on the ground contained the clean water for rinsing. Heat prickled the back of my neck. A bird was cursing in the hedge.

"How are the children?" I knew that the father of her two children had deserted her for a rich man's daughter.

"They doin' fine. Is me mudda raise dem now. She don' barn dem but she do raise dem."

"Do you ever hear from Fat-Boy?"

"Not one word. Not one dollar. But ah washin' this for 'im now." She held up a long, dazzling white robe. The brilliance of the white hurt my eyes. It reminded me of the garb worn for the pocomania ritual.

"I'm surprised you're doing anything for him," I said.

She convulsed with laughter:

"It's the media," she said. I must have looked confused. She laughed again, this time astonished at my lack of comprehension.

"You don' hunnerstan'? It's the MEEDEEA." She doubled up, clutching the robe to her chest, creased with laughter.

I left her and went into the house. In Mr Elliot's bedroom lay the jumble and clutter of a man whose wife is away. The room was stuffy. I turned the handle of a door to the right of the bed. It opened onto a room which I recognised immediately as the place where I was supposed to be.

The ceiling was high. The walls were built of great, square, yellow stone slabs. The room was no bigger than a cell. I shut the door gently behind me. Everything was peaceful. The only furniture was a small wooden table with a wooden chair set by it. The wood was rough and white and reminded me of the wooden draining-board we had at home which my mother used to scrub with parazone. On the table stood a typewriter. Sunlight fell on it from a window that was no more than a slit in the enormously thick walls. Placed next to the typewriter was an opened packet of plain foolscap paper.

I took out a sheet of paper and inserted it in the typewriter. I barely needed to touch the keys. The typewriter wrote of its own accord:

THE TRUTH IS IN THE CLOTHES

# Sudesh Mishra

## The Black Pagoda: Konarak

*The Statesman* on Nicolae Ceausescu.
Another brute, another revolution.
Always we favour the grenade-solution.
A tour of the Sun Temple won't stop a coup
In some piddling Calypso Republic.
All our monuments are monstrosities;
The blood of serfs sustains our royal trees.
So what if each plinth is in precise cubic
Feet? I have learnt to measure human Art
Through the eyes of slaves in a carrion cart.

## Mt. Abu: St. Xavier's Church

There is an Anglican Church at Bazaar
With broken stained-glass windows and a belfry
That will crumble in less than two or three
Years, if the rajah or ruling salkaar
Continues to tread the path of negligence.
Should I be indifferent after the fact,
Being one with many axes to grind? What
Perverted sense, what religious romance
Gave rise to this house — while in Calcutta
They sold you, Father, across the water?

# Rohinton Mistry

## *Swimming Lessons*

The old man's wheelchair is audible today as he creaks by in the hallway: on some days it's just a smooth whirr. Maybe the way he slumps in it, or the way his weight rests has something to do with it. Down to the lobby he goes, and sits there most of the time, talking to people on their way out or in. That's where he first spoke to me a few days ago. I was waiting for the elevator, back from Eaton's with my new pair of swimming-trunks.

"Hullo," he said. I nodded, smiled.

"Beautiful summer day we've got."

"Yes," I said, "it's lovely outside."

He shifted the wheelchair to face me squarely. "How old do you think I am?"

I looked at him blankly, and he said, "Go on, take a guess."

I understood the game; he seemed about seventy-five although the hair was still black, so I said, "Sixty-five?" He made a sound between a chuckle and a wheeze: "I'll be seventy-seven next month." Close enough.

I've heard him ask that question several times since, and everyone plays by the rules. Their faked guesses range from sixty to seventy. They pick a lower number when he's more depressed than usual. He reminds me of Grandpa as he sits on the sofa in the lobby, staring out vacantly at the parking lot. Only difference is, he sits with the stillness of stroke victims, while Grandpa's Parkinson's disease would bounce his thighs and legs and arms all over the place. When he could no longer hold the *Bombay Samachar* steady enough to read, Grandpa took to sitting on the veranda and staring emptily at the traffic passing outside Firozsha Baag. Or waving to anyone who went by in the compound: Rustomji, Nariman Hansotia in his 1932 Mercedes-Benz, the fat ayah Jaakaylee with her shopping-bag; the *kuchrawalli* with her basket and long bamboo broom.

The Portuguese woman across the hall has told me a little about the old man. She is the communicator for the apartment building. To gather and disseminate information, she takes the liberty of unabashedly throwing open her door when newsworthy events transpire. Not for Portuguese Woman the furtive peerings from thin cracks or spyholes. She reminds me of a character in a movie, *Barefoot In The Park* I think it was, who left empty beer cans by the landing for anyone passing to stumble and give her the signal. But PW does not need beer cans. The gutang-khutang of the elevator opening and closing is enough.

The old man's daughter looks after him. He was living alone till his stroke, which coincided with his youngest daughter's divorce in Vancouver. She returned to him and they moved into this low-rise in Don Mills. PW says the daughter talks to no one in the building but takes good care of her father.

Mummy used to take good care of Grandpa, too, till things became complicated and he was moved to the Parsi General Hospital. Parkinsonism and osteoporosis laid him low. The doctor explained that Grandpa's hip did not break because he fell, but he fell because the hip, gradually growing brittle, snapped on that fatal day. That's what osteoporosis does, hollows out the bones and turns effect into cause. It has an unusually high incidence in the Parsi community, he said, but did not say why. Just one of those mysterious things. We are the chosen people where osteoporosis is concerned. And divorce. The Parsi community has the highest divorce rate in India. It also claims to be the most westernized community in India. Which is the result of the other? Confusion again, of cause and effect.

The hip was put in traction. Single-handed, Mummy struggled valiantly with bedpans and dressings for bedsores which soon appeared like grim spectres on his back. *Mamaiji*, bent double with her weak back, could give no assistance. My help would be enlisted to roll him over on his side while Mummy changed the dressing. But after three months, the doctor pronounced a patch upon Grandpa's lungs, and the male ward of Parsi General swallowed him up. There was no money for a private nursing home. I went to see him once, at Mummy's insistence. She used to say that the blessings of an old person were the most valuable and potent of all, they would last my whole life long. The ward had rows and rows of beds; the din was enormous, the smells nauseating, and it was just as well that Grandpa passed most of his time in a less than conscious state.

But I should have gone to see him more often. Whenever Grandpa went out, while he still could in the days before parkinsonism, he would bring back pink and white sugar-coated almonds for Percy and me.

Every time I remember Grandpa, I remember that; and then I think: I should have gone to see him more often. That's what I also thought when our telephone-owning neighbour, esteemed by all for that reason, sent his son to tell us the hospital had phoned that Grandpa died an hour ago.

*The postman rang the doorbell the way he always did and continuous; Mother went to open it, wanting to give him a piece of her mind but thought better of it, she did not want to risk the vengeance of postmen, it was so easy for them to destroy letters; workers nowadays thought no end of themselves, strutting around like peacocks, ever since all this Shiv Sena agitation about Maharashtra for Maharashtrians, threatening strikes and Bombay* bundh *all the time, with no respect for the public; bus drivers and conductors were the worst, behaving as if they owned the buses and were doing favours to commuters, pulling the bell before you were in the bus, the driver purposely braking and moving with big jerks to make the standees lose their balance, the conductor so rude if you did not have the right change.*

*But when she saw the airmail envelope with a Canadian stamp her face lit up, she said wait to the postman, and went in for a fifty paisa piece, a little* baksheesh *for you, she told him, then shut the door and kissed the envelope, went in running, saying my son has written, my son has sent a letter, and Father looked up from the newspaper and said, don't get too excited, first read it, you know what kind of letters he writes, a few lines of empty words, I'm fine, hope you are all right, your loving son—that kind of writing I don't call letter-writing.*

*Then Mother opened the envelope and took out one small page and began to read silently, and the joy brought to her face by the letter's arrival began to ebb; Father saw it happening and knew he was right, he said read aloud, let me also hear what our son is writing this time, so Mother read: My dear Mummy and Daddy, Last winter was terrible, we had record-breaking low temperatures all through February and March, and the first official day of spring was colder than the first official day of winter had been, but it's getting warmer now. Looks like it will be a nice warm summer. You asked about my new apartment. It's small, but not bad at all. This is just a quick note to let you know I'm fine, so you won't worry about me. Hope everything is okay at home.*

*After Mother put it back in the envelope, Father said everything about his life is locked in silence and secrecy, I still don't understand why he bothered to visit us last year if he had nothing to say; every letter of his has been a quick note so we won't worry—what does he think we worry about, his health, in that country everyone eats well whether they work or not, he should be worrying about us with all the black market and rationing, has he forgotten already how he used to go to the ration-shop and wait in line every week; and what kind of apartment description is that, not bad at all; and if it is a Canadian weather report I need from him, I can go with Nariman Hansotia from A Block to the Cawasji Framji Memorial Library and read all about it, there they get newspapers from all over the world.*

The sun is hot today. Two women are sunbathing on the stretch of patchy lawn at the periphery of the parking lot. I can see them clearly from my kitchen. They're wearing bikinis and I'd love to take a closer look. But I have no binoculars. Nor do I have a car to saunter out to and pretend to look under the hood. They're both luscious and gleaming. From time to time they smear lotion over their skin, on the bellies, on the inside of the thighs, on the shoulders. Then one of them gets the other to undo the string of her top and spread some there. She lies on her stomach with the straps undone. I wait. I pray that the heat and haze make her forget, when it's time to turn over, that the straps are undone.

But the sun is not hot enough to work this magic for me. When it's time to come in, she flips over, deftly holding up the cups, and reties the top. They arise, pick up towels, lotions and magazines, and return to the building.

This is my chance to see them closer. I race down the stairs to the lobby. The old man says hullo. "Down again?"

"My mailbox," I mumble.

"It's Saturday," he chortles. For some reason he finds it extremely funny. My eye is on the door leading in from the parking lot.

Through the glass panel I see them approaching. I hurry to the elevator and wait. In the dimly lit lobby I can see their eyes are having trouble adjusting after the bright sun. They don't seem as attractive as they did from the kitchen window. The elevator arrives and I hold it open, inviting them in with what I think is a gallant flourish. Under the fluorescent glare in the elevator I see their wrinkled skin, aging hands, sagging bottoms, varicose veins. The lustrous trick of sun and lotion and distance has ended.

I step out and they continue to the third floor. I have Monday night to look forward to, my first swimming lesson. The high school behind the apartment building is offering, among its usual assortment of macramé and ceramics and pottery classes, a class for non-swimming adults.

The woman at the registration desk is quite friendly. She even gives me the opening to satisfy the compulsion I have about explaining my non-swimming status.

"Are you from India?" she asks. I nod. "I hope you don't mind my asking, but I was curious because an Indian couple, husband and wife, also registered a few minutes ago. Is swimming not encouraged in India?"

"On the contrary," I say. "Most Indians swim like fish. I'm an exception to the rule. My house was five minutes walking distance from Chaupatty beach in Bombay. It's one of the most beautiful beaches in Bombay, or was, before the filth took over. Anyway, even though we lived so close to it, I never learned to swim. It's just one of those things."

"Well," says the woman, "that happens sometimes. Take me, for instance. I never learned to ride a bicycle. It was the mounting that used to scare me, I was afraid of falling." People have lined up behind me. "It's been very nice talking to you," she says, "hope you enjoy the course."

The art of swimming had been trapped between the devil and the deep blue sea. The devil was money, always scarce, and kept the private swimming clubs out of reach; the deep blue sea of Chaupatty beach was grey and murky with garbage, too filthy to swim in. Every so often we would muster our courage and Mummy would take me there to try and teach me. But a few minutes of paddling was all we could endure. Sooner or later something would float up against our legs or thighs or waists, depending on how deep we'd gone in, and we'd be revulsed and stride out to the sand.

Water imagery in my life is recurring. Chaupatty beach, now the high-school swimming pool. The universal symbol of life and regeneration did nothing but frustrate me. Perhaps the swimming pool will overturn that failure.

When images and symbols abound in this manner, sprawling or rolling across the page without guile or artifice, one is prone to say, how obvious, how skilless; symbols, after all, should be still and gentle as dewdrops, tiny, yet shining with a world of meaning. But what happens when, on the page of life itself, one encounters the ever-moving, all-engirdling sprawl of the filthy sea? Dewdrops and oceans both have their rightful places; Nariman Hansotia certainly knew that when he told his stories to the boys of Firozsha Baag.

The sea of Chaupatty was fated to endure the finales of life's everyday functions. It seemed that the dirtier it became, the more crowds it attracted: street urchins and beggars and beachcombers, looking through the junk that washed up. (Or was it the crowds that made it dirtier? – another instance of cause and effect blurring and evading identification.)

Too many religious festivals also used the sea as repository for their finales. Its use should have been rationed, like rice and kerosene. On Ganesh Chaturthi, clay idols of the god Ganesh, adorned with garlands and all manner of finery, were carried in processions to the accompaniment of drums and a variety of wind instruments. The music got more frenzied the closer the procession got to Chaupatty and to the moment of immersion.

Then there was Coconut Day, which was never as popular as Ganesh Chaturthi. From a bystander's viewpoint, coconuts chucked into the sea do not provide as much of a spectacle. We used the sea, too, to deposit the leftovers from Parsi religious ceremonies, things such as flowers, or the ashes of the sacred sandalwood fire, which just could not be dumped with the regular garbage but had to be entrusted to the care of Avan Yazad, the guardian of the sea. And things which were of no use but which no one had the heart to destroy were also given to Avan Yazad. Such as old photographs.

After Grandpa died, some of his things were flung out to sea. It was high tide; we always checked the newspaper when going to perform these disposals; an ebb would mean a long walk in squelchy sand before finding water. Most of the things were probably washed up on shore. But we tried to throw them as far out as possible, then waited a few minutes; if they did not float back right away we would pretend they were in the permanent safekeeping of Avan Yazad, which was a comforting thought. I can't remember everything we sent out to sea, but his brush and comb were in the parcel, his *kusti*, and some Kemadrin pills, which he used to take to keep the parkinsonism under control.

Our paddling sessions stopped for lack of enthusiasm on my part. Mummy wasn't too keen either, because of the filth. But my main concern was the little guttersnipes, like naked fish with little buoyant penises, taunting me with their skills, swimming underwater and emerging unexpectedly all around me, or pretending to masturbate – I think they were too young to achieve ejaculation. It was embarrassing. When I look back, I'm surprised that Mummy and I kept going as long as we did.

I examine the swimming-trunks I bought last week. Surf King, says the label, Made in Canada – Fabriqué Au Canada. I've been learning bits and pieces of French from bilingual labels at the supermarket too.

These trunks are extremely sleek and streamlined hipsters, the distance from waistband to pouch tip the barest minimum. I wonder how everything will stay in place, not that I'm boastful about my endowments. I try them on, and feel that the tip of my member lingers perilously close to the exit. Too close, in fact, to conceal the exigencies of my swimming lesson fantasy: a gorgeous woman in the class for non-swimmers, at whose sight I will be instantly aroused, and she, spying the shape of my desire, will look me straight in the eye with her intentions; she will come home with me, to taste the pleasures of my delectable Asian brown body whose strangeness has intrigued her and unleashed uncontrollable surges of passion inside her throughout the duration of the swimming lesson.

I drop the Eaton's bag and wrapper in the garbage can. The swimming-trunks cost fifteen dollars, same as the fee for the ten weekly lessons. The garbage bag is almost full. I tie it up and take it outside. There is a medicinal smell in the hallway; the old man must have just returned to his apartment.

PW opens her door and says, "Two ladies from the third floor were lying in the sun this morning. In bikinis."

"That's nice," I say, and walk to the incinerator chute. She reminds me of Najamai in Firozsha Baag, except that Najamai employed a bit more subtlety while going about her life's chosen work.

PW withdraws and shuts her door.

*Mother had to reply because Father said he did not want to write to his son till his son had something sensible to write to him, his questions had been ignored long enough, and if he wanted to keep his life a secret, fine, he would get no letters from his father.*

*But after Mother started the letter he went and looked over her shoulder, telling her what to ask him, because if they kept on writing the same questions, maybe he would understand how interested they were in knowing about things over there; Father said go on, ask him what his work is at the insurance company, tell him to take some courses at night school, that's how everyone moves ahead over there, tell him not to be discouraged if his job is just clerical right now, hard work will get him ahead, remind him he is a Zoroastrian:* manashni, gavashni, kunashni, *better write the translation also: good thoughts, good words, good deeds—he must have forgotten what it means, and tell him to say prayers and do* kusti *at least twice a day.*

*Writing it all down sadly, Mother did not believe he wore his* sudra *and* kusti *anymore, she would be very surprised if he remembered any of the prayers; when she had asked him if he needed new* sudras *he said not to take any trouble because the Zoroastrian Society of Ontario imported them from Bombay for their members, and this sounded like a story he was making up, but she was leaving it in the hands of God, ten thousand miles away there was nothing she could do but write a letter and hope for the best.*

*Then she sealed it, and Father wrote the address on it as usual because his writing was much neater than hers, handwriting was important in the address and she did not want the postman in Canada to make any mistake; she took it to the post office herself, it was impossible to trust anyone to mail it ever since the postage rates went up because people just tore off the stamps for their own use and threw away the letter, the only safe way was to hand it over the counter and make the clerk cancel the stamps before your own eyes.*

Berthe, the building superintendent, is yelling at her son in the parking lot. He tinkers away with his van. This happens every fine-weathered Sunday. It must be the van that Berthe dislikes because I've seen mother and son together in other quite amicable situations.

Berthe is a big Yugoslavian with high cheekbone. Her nationality was disclosed to me by PW. Berthe speaks a very rough-hewn English, I've overheard her in the lobby scolding tenants for late rents and leaving dirty lint screens in the dryers. It's exciting to listen to her, her words fall like rocks and boulders, and one can never tell where or how the next few will drop. But her Slavic yells at her son are a different matter, the words fly swift and true, well-aimed missiles that never miss. Finally, the son slams down the hood in disgust, wipes his hands on a rag, accompanies mother Berthe inside.

Berthe's husband has a job in a factory. But he loses several days of work every month when he succumbs to the booze, a word Berthe uses often in her Slavic tirades on those days, the only one I can understand, as it clunks down heavily out of the tight-flying formation of Yugoslavian sentence. He lolls around in the lobby, submitting passively to his wife's tongue-lashings. The bags under his bloodshot eyes, his stringy moustache, stubbled chin, dirty hair are so vulnerable to the poison-laden barbs (poison works the same way in any language) emanating from deep within the powerful watermelon bosom. No one's presence can embarrass or dignify her into silence.

No one except the old man who arrives now. "Good morning," he says, and Berthe turns, stops yelling, and smiles. Her husband rises, positions the wheelchair at the favourite angle. The lobby will be peaceful as long as the old man is there.

It was hopeless. My first swimming lesson. The water terrified me. When did that happen, I wonder, I used to love splashing at Chaupatty, carried about by the waves. And this was only a swimming pool. Where did all that terror come from? I'm trying to remember.

Armed with my Surf King I enter the high school and go to the pool area. A sheet with instructions for the new class is pinned to the bulletin board. All students must shower and then assemble at eight by the shallow end. As I enter the showers three young boys, probably from a previous class, emerge. One of them holds his nose. The second begins to hum, under his breath: Paki Paki, smell like curry. The third says to the first two: pretty soon all the water's going to taste of curry. They leave.

It's a mixed class, but the gorgeous woman of my fantasy is missing. I have to settle for another, in a pink one-piece suit, with brown hair and a bit of a stomach. She must be about thirty-five. Plain-looking.

The instructor is called Ron. He gives us a pep talk, sensing some nervousness in the group. We're finally all in the water, in the shallow end. He demonstrates floating on the back, then asks for a volunteer. The pink one-piece suit wades forward. He supports her, tells her to lean back and let her head drop in the water.

She does very well. And as we all regard her floating body, I see what was not visible outside the pool: her bush, curly bits of it, straying out at the pink Spandex V. Tongues of water lapping against her delta, as if caressing it teasingly, make the brown hair come alive in a most tantalizing manner. The crests and troughs of little waves, set off by the movement of our bodies in a circle around her, dutifully irrigate her; the curls alternately wave free inside the crest, then adhere to her wet thighs, beached by the inevitable trough. I could watch this forever, and I wish the floating demonstration would never end.

Next we are shown how to grasp the rail and paddle, face down in the water. Between practising floating and paddling, the hour is almost gone. I have been trying to observe the pink one-piece suit, getting glimpses of her straying pubic hair from various angles. Finally, Ron wants a volunteer for the last demonstration, and I go forward. To my horror he leads the class to the deep end. Fifteen feet of water. It is so blue, and I can see the bottom. He picks up a metal hoop attached to a long wooden stick. He wants me to grasp the hoop, jump in the water, and paddle, while he guides me by the stick. Perfectly safe, he tells me. A demonstration of how paddling propels the body.

It's too late to back out; besides, I'm so terrified I couldn't find the words to do so even if I wanted to. Everything he says I do as if in a trance. I don't remember the moment of jumping. The next thing I know is, I'm swallowing water and floundering, hanging on to the hoop for dear life. Ron draws me to the rails and helps me out. The class applauds.

We disperse and one thought is on my mind: what if I'd lost my grip? Fifteen feet of water under me. I shudder and take deep breaths. This is it. I'm not coming next week. This instructor is an irresponsible person. Or he does not value the lives of non-white immigrants. I remember the three teenagers. Maybe the swimming pool is the hangout of some racist group, bent on eliminating all non-white swimmers, to keep their waters pure and their white sisters unogled.

The elevator takes me upstairs. Then gutang-khutang. PW opens her door as I turn the corridor of medicinal smells. "Berthe was screaming loudly at her husband tonight," she tells me.

"Good for her," I say, and she frowns indignantly at me.

The old man is in the lobby. He's wearing thick wool gloves. He wants to know how the swimming was, must have seen me leaving with my towel yesterday. Not bad, I say.

"I used to swim a lot. Very good for the circulation." He wheezes. "My feet are cold all the time. Cold as ice. Hands too."

Summer is winding down, so I say stupidly, "Yes, it's not so warm any more."

The thought of the next swimming lesson sickens me. But as I comb through the memories of that terrifying Monday, I come upon the straying curls of brown pubic hair. Inexorably drawn by them, I decide to go.

It's a mistake, of course. This time I'm scared even to venture in the shallow end. When everyone has entered the water and I'm the only one outside, I feel a little foolish and slide in.

Instructor Ron says we should start by reviewing the floating technique. I'm in no hurry. I watch the pink one-piece pull the swim-suit down around her cheeks and flip back to achieve perfect flotation. And then reap disappointment. The pink Spandex triangle is perfectly streamlined today, nothing strays, not a trace of fuzz, not one filament, not even a sign of post-depilation irritation. Like the airbrushed parts of glamour magazine models. The barrenness of her impeccably packaged apex is a betrayal. Now she is shorn like the other women in the class. Why did she have to do it?

The weight of this disappointment makes the water less manageable, more lung-penetrating. With trepidation, I float and paddle my way through the remainder of the hour, jerking my head out every two seconds and breathing deeply, to continually shore up a supply of precious, precious air without, at the same time, seeming too anxious and losing my dignity.

I don't attend the remaining classes. After I've missed three, Ron the instructor telephones. I tell him I've had the flu and am still feeling poorly, but I'll try to be there the following week.

He does not call again. My Surf King is relegated to an unused drawer. Total losses: one fantasy plus thirty dollars. And no watery rebirth. The swimming pool, like Chaupatty beach, has produced a stillbirth. But there is a difference. Water means regeneration only if it is pure and cleansing. Chaupatty was filthy, the pool was not. Failure to swim through filth must mean something other than failure of rebirth — failure of symbolic death? Does that equal success of symbolic life? death of a symbolic failure? death of a symbol? What is the equation?

*The postman did not bring a letter but a parcel, he was smiling because he knew that every time something came from Canada his* baksheesh *was guaranteed, and this time because it was a parcel Mother gave him a whole rupee, she was quite excited, there were so many stickers on it besides the stamps, one for Small Parcel, another Printed Papers, a red sticker saying Insured; she showed it to Father, and opened it, then put both hands on her cheeks, not able to speak because the surprise and happiness was so great, tears came to her eyes and she could not stop smiling, till Father became impatient to know and finally got up and came to the table.*

*When he saw it he was surprised and happy too, he began to grin, then hugged Mother saying our son is a writer, and we didn't even know it, he never told us a thing; here we are thinking he is still clerking away at the insurance company, and he has written a book of stories, all these years in school and college he kept his talent hidden, making us think he was just like one of the boys in the Baag, shouting and playing the fool in the compound, and now what a surprise; then Father opened the book and began reading it, heading back to the easy chair, and Mother so excited, still holding his arm, walked with him, saying it was not fair him reading it first, she wanted to read it too, and they agreed that he would read the first story, then give it to her so she could also read it, and they would take turns in that manner.*

*Mother removed the staples from the padded envelope in which he had mailed the book, and threw them away, then straightened the folded edges of the envelope and put it away safely with the other envelopes and letters she had collected since he left.*

The leaves are beginning to fall. The only ones I can identify are maple. The days are dwindling like the leaves. I've started a habit of taking long walks every evening. The old man is in the lobby when I leave, he waves as I go by. By the time I'm back, the lobby is usually empty.

Today I was woken up by a grating sound outside that made my flesh crawl. I went to the window and saw Berthe raking the leaves in the parking lot. Not in the expanse of patchy lawn on the periphery, but in the parking lot proper. She was raking the black tarred surface. I went back to bed and dragged a pillow over my head, not releasing it till noon.

When I return from my walk in the evening, PW, summoned by the elevator's gutang-khutang, says, "Berthe filled six big black garbage bags with leaves today."

"Six bags!" I say. "Wow!"

Since the weather turned cold, Berthe's son does not tinker with his van on Sundays under my window. I'm able to sleep late.

Around eleven, there's a commotion outside. I reach out and switch on the clock radio. It's a sunny day, the window curtains are bright. I get up, curious, and see a black Olds Ninety-Eight in the parking lot, by the entrance to the building. The old man is in his wheelchair, bundled up, with a scarf wound several times round his neck as though to immobilize it, like a surgical collar. His daughter and another man, the car-owner, are helping him from the wheelchair into the front seat, encouraging him with words like: that's it, easy does it, attaboy. From the open door of the lobby, Berthe is shouting encouragement too, but hers is confined to one word: yah, repeated at different levels of pitch and volume, with variations on vowel-length. The stranger could be the old man's son, he has the same jet black hair and piercing eyes.

Maybe the old man is not well, it's an emergency. But I quickly scrap that thought — this isn't Bombay, an ambulance would have arrived. They're probably taking him out for a ride. If he is his son, where has he been all this time, I wonder.

The old man finally settles in the front seat, the wheelchair goes in the trunk, and they're off. The one I think is the son looks up and catches me at the window before I can move away, so I wave, and he waves back.

In the afternoon I take down a load of clothes to the laundry room. Both machines have completed their cycles, the clothes inside are waiting to be transferred to dryers. Should I remove them and place them on top of a dryer, or wait? I decide to wait. After a few minutes, two women arrive, they are in bathrobes, and smoking. It takes me a while to realize that these are the two disappointments who were sunbathing in bikinis last summer.

"You didn't have to wait, you could have removed the clothes and carried on, dear," says one. She has a Scottish accent. It's one of the few I've learned to identify. Like maple leaves.

"Well," I say, "some people might not like strangers touching their clothes."

"You're not a stranger, dear," she says, "you live in this building, we've seen you before."

"Besides, your hands are clean," the other one pipes in. "You can touch my things any time you like."

Horny old cow. I wonder what they've got on under their bathrobes. Not much, I find, as they bend over to place their clothes in the dryers.

"See you soon," they say, and exit, leaving me behind in an erotic wake of smoke and perfume and deep images of cleavages. I start the washers and depart, and when I come back later, the dryers are empty.

PW tells me, "The old man's son took him out for a drive today. He has a big beautiful black car."

I see my chance, and shoot back: "Olds Ninety-Eight."

"What?"

"The car," I explain, "it's an Oldsmobile Ninety-Eight."

She does not like this at all, my giving her information. She is visibly nettled, and retreats with a sour face.

*Mother and Father read the first five stories, and she was very sad after reading some of them, she said he must be so unhappy there, all his stories are about Bombay, he remembers every little thing about his childhood, he is thinking about it all the time even though he is ten thousand miles away, my poor son, I think he misses his home and us and everything he left behind, because if he likes it over there why would he not write stories about that, there must be so many new ideas that his new life could give him.*

*But Father did not agree with this, he said it did not mean that he was unhappy, all writers worked in the same way, they used their memories and experiences and made stories out of them, changing some things, adding some, imagining some, all writers were very good at remembering details of their lives.*

*Mother said, how can you be sure that he is remembering because he is a writer, or whether he started to write because he is unhappy and thinks of his past, and wants to save it all by making stories of it; and father said that is not a sensible question, anyway it is now my turn to read the next story.*

The first snow has fallen, and the air is crisp. It's not very deep, about two inches, just right to go for a walk in. I've been told that immigrants from hot countries always enjoy the snow the first year, maybe for a couple of years more, then inevitably the dread sets in, and the approach of winter gets them fretting and moping. On the other hand, if it hadn't been for my conversation with the woman at the swimming registration desk, they might now be saying that India is a nation of non-swimmers.

Berthe is outside, shovelling the snow off the walkway in the parking lot. She has a heavy, wide pusher which she wields expertly.

The old radiators in the apartment alarm me incessantly. They continue to broadcast a series of variations on death throes, and go from hot to cold and cold to hot at will, there's no controlling their temperature. I speak to Berthe about it in the lobby. The old man is there too, his chin seems to have sunk deeper into his chest, and his face is a yellowish grey.

"Nothing, not to worry about anything," says Berthe, dropping rough-hewn chunks of language around me. "Radiator no work, you tell me. You feel cold, you come to me, I keep you warm," and she opens her arms wide, laughing. I step back, and she advances, her breasts preceding her like the gallant prows of two ice-breakers. She looks at the old man to see if he is appreciating the act: "You no feel scared, I keep you safe and warm."

But the old man is staring outside, at the flakes of falling snow. What thoughts is he thinking as he watches them? Of childhood days, perhaps, and snowmen with hats and pipes, and snowball fights, and white Christmases, and Christmas trees? What will I think of, old in this country, when I sit and watch the snow come down? For me, it is already too late for snowmen and snowball fights, and all I will have is thoughts about childhood thoughts and dreams, built around snowscapes and winter-wonderlands on the Christmas cards so popular in Bombay; my snowmen and snowball fights and Christmas trees are in the pages of Enid Blyton's books, dispersed amidst the adventures of the Famous Five, and the Five Find-Outers, and the Secret Seven. My snowflakes are even less forgettable than the old man's, for they never melt.

It finally happened. The heat went. Not the usual intermittent coming and going, but out completely. Stone cold. The radiators are like ice. And so is everything else. There's no hot water. Naturally. It's the hot water that goes through the rads and heats them. Or is it the other way around? Is there no hot water because the rads have stopped circulating it? I don't care, I'm too cold to sort out the cause and effect relationship. Maybe there is no connection at all.

I dress quickly, put on my winter jacket, and go down to the lobby. The elevator is not working because the power is out, so I take the stairs. Several people are gathered, and Berthe has announced that she has telephoned the office, they are sending a man. I go back up the stairs. It's only one floor, the elevator is just a bad habit. Back in Firozsha Baag they were broken most of the time. The stairway enters the corridor outside the old man's apartment, and I think of his cold feet and hands. Poor man, it must be horrible for him without heat.

As I walk down the long hallway, I feel there's something different but can't pin it down. I look at the carpet, the ceiling, the wallpaper: it all seems the same. Maybe it's the freezing cold that imparts a feeling of difference.

PW opens her door: "The old man had another stroke yesterday. They took him to the hospital."

The medicinal smell. That's it. It's not in the hallway any more.

*In the stories that he'd read so far Father said that all the Parsi families were poor or middle-class, but that was okay; nor did he mind that the seeds for the stories were picked from the sufferings of their own lives; but there should also have been something positive about Parsis, there was so much to be proud of: the great Tatas and their contribution to the steel industry, or Sir Dinshaw Petit in the textile industry who made Bombay the Manchester of the East, or Dadabhai Naoroji in the freedom movement, where he was the first to use the word* swaraj, *and the first to be elected to the British Parliament where he carried on his campaign; he should have found some way to bring some of these wonderful facts into his stories, what would people reading these stories think, those who did not know about Parsis—that the whole community was full of cranky, bigoted people; and in reality it was the richest, most advanced and philanthropic community in India, and he did not need to tell his own son that Parsis had a reputation for being generous and family-oriented. And he could* have written something also about the historic background, how Parsis came to India from Persia because of Islamic persecution in the seventh century, and were the descendants of Cyrus the Great and the magnificent Persian Empire. He could have made a story of all this, couldn't he?

Mother said what she liked best was his remembering everything so well, how beautifully he wrote about it all, even the sad things, and though he changed some of it, used his imagination, there was truth in it.

My hope is, Father said, that there will be some story based on his Canadian experience, that way we will know something about our son's life there, if not through his letters then in his stories; so far they are all about Parsis and Bombay, and the one with a little bit about Toronto, where a man perches on top of the toilet, is shameful and disgusting, although it is funny at times and did make me laugh, I have to admit, but where does he get such an imagination from, what is the point of such a fantasy; and Mother said that she would also enjoy some stories about Toronto and the people there; it puzzles me, she said, why he writes nothing about it, especially since you say that writers use their own experience to make stories out of.

Then Father said this is true, but he is probably not using his Toronto experience because it is too early; what do you mean, too early, asked Mother and Father explained it takes a writer about ten years time after an experience before he is able to use it in his writing, it takes that long to be absorbed internally and understood, thought out and thought about, over and over again, he haunts it and it haunts him if it is valuable enough, till the writer is comfortable with it to be able to use it as he wants; but this is only one theory I read somewhere, it may or may not be true.

That means, said Mother, that his childhood in Bombay and our home here is the most valuable thing in his life just now, because he is able to remember it all to write about it, and you were so bitterly saying he is forgetting where he came from; and that may be true, said Father, but that is not what the theory means, according to the theory he is writing of these thing because they are far enough in the past for him to deal with objectively, he is able to achieve what critics call artistic distance, without emotions interfering; and what do you mean emotions, said Mother, you are saying he does not feel anything for his characters, how can he write so beautifully about so many sad things without any feelings in his heart?

But before father could explain more, about beauty and emotion and inspiration and imagination, Mother took the book and said it was her turn now and too much theory she did not want to listen to, it was *confusing and did not make as much sense as reading the stories, she would read them her way and father could read them his.*

My books on the windowsill have been damaged. Ice has been forming on the inside ledge, which I did not notice, and melting when the sun shines in. I spread them in a corner of the living-room to dry out.

The winter drags on. Berthe wields her snow pusher as expertly as ever, but there are signs of weariness in her performance. Neither husband nor son is ever seen outside with a shovel. Or anywhere else, for that matter. It occurs to me that the son's van is missing, too.

The medicinal smell is in the hall again, I sniff happily and look forward to seeing the old man in the lobby. I go downstairs and peer into the mailbox, see the blue and magenta of an Indian aerogramme with Don Mills, Ontario, Canada in Father's flawless hand through the slot.

I pocket the letter and enter the main lobby. The old man is there, but not in his usual place. He is not looking out through the glass door. His wheelchair is facing a bare wall where the wallpaper is torn in places. As though he is not interested in the outside world any more, having finished with all that, and now it's time to see inside. What does he see inside, I wonder? I go up to him and say hullo. He says hullo without raising his sunken chin. After a few seconds his grey countenance faces me. "How old do you think I am?" His eyes are dull and glazed; he is looking even further inside than I first presumed.

"Well, let's see, you're probably close to sixty-four."

"I'll be seventy-eight next August." But he does not chuckle or wheeze. Instead, he continues softly, "I wish my feet did not feel so cold all the time. And my hands." He lets his chin fall again.

In the elevator I start opening the aerogramme, a tricky business because a crooked tear means lost words. Absorbed in this while emerging, I don't notice PW occupying the centre of the hallway, arms folded across her chest: "They had a big fight. Both of them have left."

I don't immediately understand her agitation. "What . . . who?"

"Berthe. Husband and son both left her. Now she is all alone."

Her tone and stance suggest that we should not be standing here talking but do something to bring Berthe's family back. "That's very sad," I say, and go in. I picture father and son in the van, driving away, driving across the snow-covered country, in the dead of winter, away from wife and mother; away to where? how far will they go? Not son's van nor father's booze can take them far enough. And the further they go, the more they'll remember, they can take it from me.

*All the stories were read by Father and Mother, and they were sorry when the book was finished, they felt they had come to know their son better now, yet there was much more to know, they wished there were many more stories; and this is what they mean, said Father, when they say that the whole story can never be told, the whole truth can never be known; what do you mean, they say, asked Mother, who they, and Father said writers, poets, philosophers. I don't care what they say, said Mother, my son will write as much or as little as he wants to, and if I can read it I will be happy.*

*The last story they liked the best of all because it had the most in it about Canada, and now they felt they knew at least a little bit, even if it was a very little bit, about his day-to-day life in his apartment; and Father said if he continues to write about such things he will become popular because I am sure they are interested there in reading about life through the eyes of an immigrant, it provides a different viewpoint; the only danger is if he changes and becomes so much like them that he will write like one of them and lose the important difference.*

The bathroom needs cleaning. I open a new can of Ajax and scour the tub. Sloshing with mug from bucket was standard bathing procedure in the bathrooms of Firozsha Baag, so my preference now is always for a shower. I've never used the tub as yet; besides, it would be too much like Chaupatty or the swimming pool, wallowing in my own dirt. Still, it must be cleaned.

When I've finished, I prepare for a shower. But the clean gleaming tub and the nearness of the vernal equinox give me the urge to do something different today. I find the drain plug in the bathroom cabinet, and run the bath.

I've spoken so often to the old man, but I don't know his name. I should have asked him the last time I saw him, when his wheelchair was facing the bare wall because he had seen all there was to see outside and it was time to see what was inside. Well, tomorrow. Or better yet, I can look it up in the directory in the lobby. Why didn't I think of that before? It will only have an initial and a last name, but then I can surprise him with: hullo Mr Wilson, or whatever it is.

The bath is full. Water imagery is recurring in my life: Chaupatty beach, swimming pool, bathtub. I step in and immerse myself up to the neck. It feels good. The hot water loses its opacity when the chlorine, or whatever it is, has cleared. My hair is still dry. I close my eyes, hold my breath, and dunk my head. Fighting the panic, I stay under and count to thirty. I come out, clear my lungs and breathe deeply.

I do it again. This time I open my eyes under water, and stare blindly without seeing, it takes all my will to keep the lids from closing. Then I am slowly able to discern the underwater objects. The drain plug looks different, slightly distorted; there is a hair trapped between the hole and the plug, it waves and dances with the movement of the water. I come up, refresh my lungs, examine quickly the overwater world of the washroom, and go in again. I do it several times, over and over. The world outside the water I have seen a lot of, it is now time to see what is inside.

The spring session for adult non-swimmers will begin in a few days at the high school. I must not forget the registration date.

The dwindled days of winter are now all but forgotten; they have grown and attained a respectable span. I resume my evening walks, it's spring, and a vigorous thaw is on. The snowbanks are melting, the sound of water on its gushing, gurgling journey to the drains is beautiful. I plan to buy a book of trees, so I can identify more than the maple as they begin to bloom.

When I return to the building, I wipe my feet energetically on the mat because some people are entering behind me, and I want to set a good example. Then I go to the board with its little plastic letters and numbers. The old man's apartment is the one on the corner by the stairway, that makes it number 201. I run down the list, come to 201, but there are no little white plastic letters beside it. Just the empty black rectangle with holes where the letters would be squeezed in. That's strange. Well, I can introduce myself to him, then ask his name.

However, the lobby is empty. I take the elevator, exit at the second floor, wait for the gutang-khutang. It does not come: the door closes noiselessly, smoothly. Berthe has been at work, or has made sure someone else has. PW's cue has been lubricated out of existence.

But she must have the ears of a cockroach. She is waiting for me. I whistle my way down the corridor. She fixes me with an accusing look. She waits till I stop whistling, then says: "You know the old man died last night."

I cease groping for my key. She turns to go and I take a step towards her, my hand still in my trouser pocket. "Did you know his name?" I ask, but she leaves without answering.

*Then Mother said, the part I like best in the last story is about Grandpa, where he wonders if Grandpa's spirit is really watching him and blessing him, because you know I really told him that, I told him helping an old suffering person who is near death is the most blessed thing to do, because that person will ever after watch over you from heaven, I told him this when he was disgusted with Grandpa's urine-bottle and would not touch it, would not hand it to him even when I was not at home.*

*Are you sure, said Father, that you really told him this, or you believe you told him because you like the sound of it, you said yourself the other day that he changes and adds and alters things in the stories but he writes it all so beautifully that it seems true, so how can you be sure; this sounds like another theory, said Mother, but I don't care, he says I told him and I believe now I told him, so even if I did not tell him then it does not matter now.*

*Don't you see, said Father, that you are confusing fiction with facts, fiction does not create facts, fiction can come from facts, it can grow out of facts by compounding, transposing, augmenting, diminishing, or altering them in any way; but you must not confuse cause and effect, you must not confuse what really happened with what the story says happened, you must not loose your grasp on reality, that way madness lies.*

*Then Mother stopped listening because, as she told Father so often, she was not very fond of theories, and she took out her writing pad and started a letter to her son; Father looked over her shoulder, telling her to say how proud they were of him and were waiting for his next book, he also said, leave a little space for me at the end, I want to write a few lines when I put the address on the envelope.*

# Timothy Mo

## *One of Billy's Boys: A Memoir*

When I think of Hong Kong all those years ago, it's the diminutive but formidable figure of Billy Tingle which strides through my insomniac reveries, much as Blind Pew must have through those of the grown-up Jim Hawkins, while the cable drums of the upper Peak tram station (those tarry windmills of the mind) whine and Billy chases me through the dancing mists of a February evening, brandishing a cricket bat instead of a crutch or white stick, and crying not "Pieces of Eight!" but rather "Sportsmen and a gentleman! Sportsman and a gentleman!"

Am I the only one who remembers Mr Tingle? Am I the sole surviving Tingle boy in what used to be called the Crown Colony? Billy Tingle was as much a part of the expat Brit family's life here 35 years ago as taking the kids to the PG Farm and throwing streamers down from the decks of a P & O liner at the beginning of a leave.

Those were the days when you could walk under shaded granite arches the whole length of Nathan Road and Mody Road was splashed bright red with expectorated betel juice from the mouths of the Indian leather workers, and when the pug marks of confused tigers could be seen in the New Territories. The days, too, when you could still hear people speak of the waterfront as the Praya, of lunch as tiffin, and—with a strange affection—of "Camp," internment under the Japanese on Stanley peninsula.

Mr Tingle had been flyweight champion of the Australian goldfields in the early part of the century, or it might have been the dying years of the previous one. He looked, in 1957, much like a spry, elderly, weight-trained and cross-countried version of that other Billy, Bunter. At the age of nine, when I left Mr Tingle's academy of self-defence, I could look him straight in the eye, so I deduce he must have been about 4ft 11ins tall. Mr Tingle was physical instructor and character builder extraordinary by appointment to the children of the expatriate gentry. He taught the Noble Art to a select few after lessons had finished at Quarry Bay School and the Peak School. On Saturday mornings droves of red and white capped boys took over the grounds of the HK Cricket

Club—now concreted over as Ghater Garden—in what was known simply as Billy Tingle's.

In the summer I dreaded those Saturday mornings; tedium unmitigated from nine till twelve, interspersed with moments of fright and angst. We wore white shirts and shorts, our school summer uniforms, so the only extra item of expense was the caps—always an important consideration for the parent, as Mr Tingle well knew. He wore one, too.

We'd troop out from the pavilion in 20-strong squads for callisthenics under the supervision of young Englishmen. There was a lot of aimless standing around. I think these off-duty schoolmasters and shipping clerks were at a loss to know what to occupy us with weekend in and weekend out. We had to call them "Sir," which was novel and unsettling, as the teachers at my coed primary school were female and to be addressed as "Mrs Penman" (shrewd New Zealander) or "Miss Archer" (strapping English girl).

I had Mr Partridge at Billy Tingle's, he of the handlebar moustache. For some reason we genuinely had trouble with his name, few of us being familiar with English gamebirds but all devotees of *Blackhawk* and *Superman* comics, the *77th Bengal Lancers* and *The Naked City* on black and white television (we even tried to speak with American accents, as I don't doubt they still do at KGV), so he became Mr Cartridge to his mild irritation. "My name's Partridge, not Cartridge. Cartridge is what you fire from a gun, OK?" And he pulled out a brassy .303 case confiscated from an Andrew Jackson, who'd obtained the trophy from the firing range below Lugard Road. "Yes, Mr Cartridge." "Right-o. You're all going to call me sir from now on."

Over to the long jump pit, a dog-defiled minefield of broken sand clods opposite what is now the front door of the Furama-Kempinski. Break, eagerly looked forward to, probably by Mr Cartridge as well, was in the Pavilion and consisted of Kit Kats, for which we had brought our 20 cents. No dried beef, no *chan pei mui* (preserved plum with orange and licorice essence). And, of course, there wasn't a Chinese boy in sight, not even a rich one, like Donald Hardoon or Raymond Woo, the only Chinese boys in class 5. Or a girl for that matter (those creatures seen outside school hours at the Ladies Recreation Club — another bastion of half-witted Anglo would be exclusiveness—where a mob of boys and girls by lofty, high-minded, but deeply misconceived adult decree had to change for the swimming-pool in the same tiny shack. Denunciation to turn the blood cold before one's guardians. "We saw Timmy looking at Kerrie's wee-wee.")

Nor were American boys to be seen at Billy Tingle's either. They, lucky chaps—like Jimmy McDonough whose father had the most glamorous job in the world short of being a filmstar (a Pan Am pilot)—were roaming Repulse Bay or Bowen Path in their jeans and basketball boots, while we were buckling musty cricket pads round our bare legs.

Cricket, unlike the callisthenics, was no lack-lustre activity. Mr Tingle himself umpired on a no-concessions 22-yard pitch. The intensity of the attention bestowed upon you by the fielders to the sides, the wicket-keeper to the rear, the bowler charging towards you, and not least by Mr Tingle himself, glaring behind his spectacles down a bee-line from the other wicket, would have been sufficient to shrink my own balls, had they already descended. I never lasted longer than an over and was terrified of being hit by the little red grenade of spite. Rounders with Mrs Penman was more my line, or even the baseball games the American boys ran, with the catchers mitts to take the sting from a catch. If it was a really dire weekend, there was a Tingle official ramble, commencing at the KCR station by the Star Ferry, over the then virgin hills of the New Territories.

But for all the high-minded pep talks about keeping a straight bat in life (sincere on Mr Tingle's part), the institution was basically a ploy for getting the kids out of your hair on Saturday mornings. As an Italian once remarked to me: "It's not that the English hate children, it's just that they love animals."

Boxing, in the winter terms, was another matter. I loved that. From the start, flurries of fists held no terrors for me. It does have to be said that Mr Tingle's method of teaching boxing, even in 1956, was already hopelessly outmoded. He coached by numbers: "Ready now. One: Left lead to the head. Two: left lead to the body. Three: knock-knock, double left lead to the head. Four: Straight right to the head. Five: straight right to the body. Six: right uppercut." That was the Tingle offence in all its rectilinear classicism. Defence was: "One: block with the right. Two: parry with the right. Three: duck."

Mr Tingle's left lead involved shooting out the glove while taking a stormtrooper's goosestep forward, digging the heel into the ground, chin well up with shoulders thrown back like a guardsman. In its way it was the boxing equivalent of a cavalry charge into machine-gun fire.

Some 20 years previously, Joe Louis had perfected the jab, sliding pantherishly forward on the ball of his left foot, the right rear foot dragged as if it had been placed in a bucket, the chin tucked down into the hunched left shoulder, and knees well flexed. The left hook, combination punching—Mr Tingle had the same attitude to these as admirals of the battleship era had for the aircraft carrier.

Before engaging in sparring, we would touch gloves. Mr Tingle explained this as meaning: "I will conduct myself at all times like a sportsman and gentleman," his exact words, still echoing in my mind after nearly 40 years. Naturally, the most heinous offence in the Tingle canon was to punch one's opponent while he offered to shake hands.

Mr Tingle wasn't a humbug. He practised what he preached. Kids penetrate adult flannel with ease—you forget you did as you get older yourself—and it was obvious to us that he was a tough old boy but both kindly and upright.

I was the only one who knew of his goldfield days—I think my stepfather had an Australian connection—and Mr Tingle had reacted with asperity, while still confirming this information. A grimace came over the stubbly face. With hindsight, I think it hadn't all been sportsmanship and Queensberry rules among the prospectors. I think the fights were desperate bareknuckle affairs, with big bets going down. And, of course, what makes me smile now is the reflection that the capped, short back and sides, deeply conservative cherubs receiving the Tingle sermon would in under ten years be many of them long-haired, pot-smoking, acid-dropping hippies. And probably stockbrokers ten years after that.

Funnily enough, with all its limitations in the ring, I think now that Tingle-style boxing would be a lot safer in a street-fight than modern bob and weave. What's drummed into a kick-boxer from day one is always to stand upright with your hands up; never duck, it'll only be into a knee butt. I suspect Billy Tingle of having been a very tasty customer indeed in his day.

Came the time to examine the student and I had my first ever contest over three one-minute rounds against one Anthony Maine in a raised ring pitched in the centre of the cricket ground. The red corner was for the usual Tingle boys, the blue for Chinese boys from a less educationally advantaged institution where Mr Tingle probably coached free. I suppose they should have put me in ring centre, with the referee.

I was given a blue sash. Without exception every boxer from this corner had lost. In the interval before the third and final round, breathless on my stool, blood leaking from my nose, I asked the two garrison sergeants who had been the blue seconds throughout, "How am I doing?" A burst of urgent instructions followed—they'd been silent till then, as had I—mostly about keeping sticking out one's left (that's what British amateur corner men always say). I think they were more pleased than I was when I scraped home on points.

Whatever the travails and eccentricities of Tingle's, it was a holiday camp compared with the Convent of the Precious Blood, the Roman Catholic school I had attended a couple of years earlier and which I called Bloody Blood. I wasn't trying to be funny. This was dominated by ferocious Chinese nuns who thought RC meant Rebarbative Confucianism.

I was the dunce of the calligraphy class who managed the characters for one, two, and three but balked at four. I got put in the corner with sticking-plaster over my mouth for asking questions. I got hit in the face ten times, very, very lightly, but still ten times. (Unfortunately Billy Tingle had yet to drill me in his one, two, three defensive routine.) The nuns instructed my amahs to feed me just white rice, without soya sauce. Little did they know it was fish fingers and chips on the menu at home.

Lord, how I hated that old-style Chinese education. Taunting and ostracism were the weapons used to break young spirits, to make them obedient to parents and, in due course, rulers, frightened to be different from all the other sniggering conformists. It was the essence of small-mindedness and Tingle, with all his ingenuousness, was large-minded.

I bade farewell to Mr Tingle in 1959, the last time I saw him alive. He gave me a warm handshake and prophesied I'd startle the boxing coaches in England. With my Corinthian style, I did, of course, but not in the way he meant.

# Tololwa Marti Mollel

## A Night Out

For a long moment, Mika sat awkwardly without his usual self-assurance, despite the alcohol singing in his veins. But suddenly, feeling a fool for his unease, he cleared his throat, a trifle too loudly, and ventured: "What's your name?"

"Mama Tumaini." (Mother of Tumaini)

She did not lift her eyes but went on busying herself with putting the child to sleep on the mat on the floor. Quite unexpectedly, the child began to cough, a violent, racking outburst that threw his little body into spasms.

Mika leaned forward and felt the child. His brow was damp and hot with fever. "Has he had treatment?" he asked, relieved to find something neutral to say.

She replied, "There isn't an aspirin to be had at the dispensary."

Under the mother's soothing, the child Tumaini eventually lay still, asleep, his breath rasping in and out. Mama Tumaini wrapped herself in a *khanga*, then lit a mosquito coil. Smoke rose in spiral, spreading over the mat. The child stirred and sneezed. The mother, squatting, gently patted him to sleep.

"God grant you health, my little one," she murmured, "God grant you health and strength, good little mama's soldier!"

"Why soldier . . . ?" Mika asked, rather pointlessly.

"Yes, soldiers don't starve, or get sick." She spoke with such toneless simplicity, it could have been a child talking.

"Yes, they don't starve," Mika said, "they get killed!"

"Better to die than this nameless misery of ours," she shot back. "Better a quick clean bullet in the head than this slow dying and burning from hunger and disease!"

"Oh, soldiers starve too, you know, when there is nothing to eat . . ." Mika said hard-heartedly.

But she was sunk deep in her thoughts, she might not have heard. Then as if to herself, alone in the room, she said, "Tumaini's father was a soldier . . ."

"Was . . . ?" went Mika.

" . . . a real bull of a man he was, with none to equal him. Life was easier then, with him around. He was like a father to me, to my mother, to all of us. Now living has become such a task. You have to struggle for each small thing. Everything, everything, you have to pay for in blood, if you can find it! If Tumaini's father were around still . . . " She seemed almost on the point of bursting into tears, but she didn't.

"Why, is he dead?" Mika asked, but purely out of curiosity, his voice too loud and untouched by the woman's dull sorrow.

"I don't want to talk, don't ask me, please . . . " she pleaded, then she began to cry and said through her tears. "He went off to Uganda, to war. He might be alive, he might be dead . . . "

Mika said nothing. The child Tumaini was still again, his mother's hand on him, still patting, absently. At last Mama Tumaini straightened up and turned off the small tin lamp in the room. In the dark, she submitted herself, silently, dutifully, and professionally. But, afterwards, when Mika rolled his body off her, there wasn't the usual feeling of having conquered; though fully sated, he lay back less than happy, vaguely unsettled, the laboured breathing from the mat adding to his sense of deflation.

He did not know when he finally fell asleep and woke up with the panic of one who does not know where he is. It was not until he felt Mama Tumaini's body by his side that he remembered where he was.

He got out of bed and lit a cigarette. The coil had burnt out and mosquitoes buzzed angrily. He sat frowning in the dark, something troubling him, though he didn't know what. Suddenly he was aware of the silence in the room.

Mouth dry and head faintly throbbing, he got up, putting out his cigarette, and went to the mat. There was no sound from the child and in the darkness he could only make out a mute, still haze, but he dared not strike a match to light the lamp. He put his hand out towards the child, and his eyes, gradually used to the dark, gazed down fascinated at the little body, lifeless and cold to his touch, its form now becoming distinct under the first stabs of dawnlight.

Mama Tumaini stirred, mumbled something, then went back to sleep. Mika waited until her breathing grew deep and even again before he sat on the bed, gingerly, and lit another cigarette, his mind busy.

Then, moving softly, he picked up his clothes from the floor where he had dumped them in a drunken pile. Dressed, he paused awhile, his eyes involuntarily seeking the child's body. No, he must leave immediately, he urged himself. It wouldn't do to get caught in the mourning and the funeral ceremonies. There was no point and it would delay him further. And anyway, he found himself thinking, what was the child to him, or the mother for that matter? Mechanically, he took out his wallet, peeled off several notes, and with no attempt to make out the amount, placed the money on a stool by the bed, and set the lamp on it as weight.

The door squeaked as he unbolted it. He paused, his heart pounding, his ear strained towards the bed.

Mama Tumaini stirred. "You're going already?" she asked him.

"Yes," he answered.

"This early?"

"You know that transport is a problem, and I have to travel today."

\* \* \*

Come what may, he just had to get out today, and try and make it to Dar es Salaam by nightfall. For two days now, he had been sunk in this dreary little town, because petrol shortage had crippled transportation and inundated the small town with stranded travellers. It was to get away from the sweating hordes hopelessly milling all over the town in search of transport, that on the previous day he had decided on an evening of entertainment and action. Drink had appealed to him as just the antidote he needed for his despondence. But the search for beer, which he preferred, was doomed from the start. There had been no beer in town, he was told at the first bar he stopped in, since the day the beer truck went crashing over a bridge leading into town. The truck was still here, a useless wreck of scrap metal. Mika did not want to believe this although he suspected it was probably the truth. He would have given his little finger for a drop of beer, and he went all over town, which didn't take long as there was little of it besides the bus stop.

A couple of depressing, dusty, narrow lanes made up the backbone of the town and beyond that was only a patchwork of slums. But he had no luck whatever in his search and had to make do with the local *pombe* which was in abundance. He had little stomach for local stuff, but even though he imbibed it slowly and grudgingly, gradually the booze took hold and he felt some of his despair lift. He even felt cheerful enough to join a group of local drinkers at a nearby table. But just as the evening seemed to be taking off, he suddenly found himself abandoned, his fellow drinkers having left for other bars or their homes. He had left too, and gone stumbling through the night. He would never remember how he ended up in Mama Tumaini's place, or why he decided he could not spend the night alone in his bed in the room he had rented at the lodging house. Funny, he thought aimlessly, paying for a room then sleeping elsewhere; wasteful, he concluded grimly.

Mama Tumaini was talking. "Even so," she said, "won't you wait for me to make you a cup of tea at least, to start you off?" That was the last thing he wanted, her getting up and finding out about the baby. He had to get away first. "No, no," he said quickly, "my things are at the lodging house, I've to get ready. I'll eat somewhere."

"Suit yourself," she said, turning over. Then faintly, almost inaudibly, as if it was an afterthought, she wished him a safe journey.

He thanked her, then limply, guiltily, he mumbled, "Your money . . . I've put the money . . . your money . . . on the stool." But she might have gone back to sleep or she might have had enough of him, as she made no response.

Mika opened the door and walked away in quick, tense steps, as light broke out over the rooftops and wisps of smoke from the early morning cooking lazed over the slums, announcing the start of another day.

# Toshio Mori

## *Slant-Eyed Americans*

My mother was commenting on the fine California weather. It was Sunday noon, December 7. We were having our lunch, and I had the radio going. "Let's take the afternoon off and go to the city," I said to Mother.

"All right. We shall go," she said dreamily. "Ah, four months ago my boy left Hayward to join the army, and a fine send-off he had. Our good friends – ah, I shall never forget the day of his departure."

"We'll visit some of our friends in Oakland and then take in a movie," I said. "Care to come along, Papa?"

Father shook his head. "No, I'll stay home and take it easy."

"That's his heaven," Mother commented. "To stay home, read the papers over and over, and smoke his Bull Durham."

I laughed. Suddenly the musical program was cut off as a special announcement came over the air: At 7:25 a.m. this morning a squadron of Japanese bombing planes attacked Pearl Harbour. The battle is still in progress.

"What's this? Listen to the announcements," I cried, going to the radio.

Abruptly the announcement stopped and the musicale continued.

"What is it?" Mother asked. "What has happened?"

"The radio reports that the Japanese planes attacked Hawaii this morning," I said incredulously. "It couldn't be true."

"It must be a mistake. Couldn't it have been a part of a play?" asked Mother.

I dialled other stations. Several minutes later one of the stations confirmed the bulletin.

"It must be true," Father said quietly.

I said,"Japan has declared war on the United States and Great Britain."

The room became quiet but for the special bulletin coming in every now and then.

"It cannot be true, yet it must be so," Father said over and over.

"Can it be one of those programs scaring the people about invasion?" Mother asked me.

"No. I'm sure this is a news report," I replied.

Mother's last ray of hope paled and her eyes became dull. "Why did it have to happen? The common people in Japan don't want war, and we don't want war. Here the people are peace-loving. Why cannot the peoples of the earth live together peacefully?"

"Since Japan declared war on the United States it'll mean that you parents of American citizens have become enemy aliens," I said.

"Enemy aliens," my mother whispered.

Night came but sleep did not come. We sat up late in the night hoping against hope that some good news would come, retracting the news of vicious attack and open hostilities.

"This is very bad for the people with Japanese faces," I said.

Father slowly shook his head.

"What shall we do?" asked Mother.

"What can we do?" Father said helplessly.

At the flower market next morning the growers were present but the buyers were scarce. The place looked empty and deserted. "Our business is shot to pieces," one of the boys said.

"Who'll buy flowers now?" another called.

Don Haley, the seedsman, came over looking bewildered. "I suppose you don't need seeds now."

We shook our heads.

"It looks bad," I said. "Will it affect your business?"

"Flower seed sale will drop but the vegetable seeds will move quicker," Don said. "I think I'll have to put more time on the vegetable seeds."

Nobu Hiramatsu who had been thinking of building another greenhouse joined us. He had plans to grow more carnations and expand his business.

"What's going to happen to your plans, Nobu?" asked one of the boys.

"Nothing. I'm going to sit tight and see how things turn out," he said.

"Flowers and war don't go together," Don said. "You cannot concentrate too much on beauty when destruction is going about you."

"Sure, pretty soon we'll raise vegetables instead of flowers," Grasselli said.

A moment later the market opened and we went back to the table to sell our flowers. Several buyers came in and purchased a little. The flowers didn't move at all. Just as I was about to leave the place I met Tom Yamashita, the Nisei gardener with a future.

"What are you doing here, Tom? What's the matter with your work?" I asked as I noticed his pale face.

"I was too sick with yesterday's news so I didn't work," he said. "This is the end. I am done for."

"No, you're not. Buck up, Tom," I cried. "You have a good future, don't lose hope."

"Sometimes I feel all right. You are an American, I tell myself. Devote your energy and life to the American way of life. Long before this my mind was made up to become a true American. This morning my Caucasian American friends sympathized with me. I felt good and was grateful. Our opportunity has come to express ourselves and act. We are Americans in thought and action. I felt like leaping to work. Then I got sick again because I got to thinking that Japan was the country that attacked the United States. I wanted to bury myself for shame."

I put my hand on his shoulder. "We all feel the same way, Tom. We're human so we flounder around awhile when an unexpected and big problem confronts us, but now that situation has to be passed by. We can't live in the same stage long. We have to move along, face the reality no matter what's in store for us."

Tom stood silently.

"Let's go to my house and take the afternoon off," I suggested. "We'll face a new world tomorrow morning with boldness and strength. What do you say, Tom?"

"All right," Tom agreed.

At home Mother was anxiously waiting for me. When she saw Tom with me her eyes brightened. Tom Yamashita was a favorite of my mother's.

"Look, a telegram from Kazuo!" she cried to me, holding up an envelope. "Read it and tell me what he says."

I tore it open and read. "He wants us to send $45 for train fare. He has a good chance for a furlough."

Mother fairly leaped in the air with the news. She had not seen my brother for four months. "How wonderful! This can happen only in America."

Suddenly she noticed Tom looking glum, and pushed him in the house.

"Cheer up, Tom. This is no time for young folks to despair. Roll up your sleeves and get to work. America needs you."

Tom smiled for the first time and looked at me.

"See, Tom?" I said. "She's quick to recover. Yesterday she was wilted and she's seventy three."

"Tom, did you go to your gardens today?" she asked him.

"No."

"Why not?" she asked, and then added quickly. "You young men should work hard all the more, keeping up the normal routine of life. You ought to know, Tom, that if everybody dropped their work everything would go to seed. Who's going to take care of the gardens if you won't?"

Tom kept still.

Mother poured tea and brought the cookies. "Don't worry about your old folks. We have stayed here to belong to the American way of life. Time will tell our true purpose. We remained in America for permanence — not for temporary convenience. We common people need not fear."

"I guess you are right," Tom agreed.

"And America is right. She cannot fail. Her principles will stand the test of time and tyranny. Someday aggression will be outlawed by all nations."

Mother left the room to prepare the dinner. Tom got up and began to walk up and down the room. Several times he looked out the window and watched the wind blow over the field.

"Yes, if the gardens are ruined I'll rebuild them," he said. "I'll take charge of every garden in the city. All the gardens of America for that matter. I'll rebuild them as fast as the enemies wreck them. We'll have nature on our side and you cannot crush nature."

I smiled and nodded. "Good for you. Tomorrow we'll get up early in the morning and work, sweat, and create. Let's shake on it."

We solemnly shook hands, and by the grip of his fingers I knew he was ready to lay down his life for America and for his gardens.

"No word from him yet," Mother said worriedly. "He should have arrived yesterday. What's happened to him?"

It was eight in the evening, and we had had no word from my brother for several days.

"He's not coming home tonight. It's too late now," I said. "He should have arrived in Oakland this morning at the latest."

Our work had piled up and we had to work late into the night. There were still some pompons to bunch. Faintly the phone rang in the house.

"The phone!" cried Mother excitedly. "It's Kazuo, sure enough."

In the flurry of several minutes I answered the phone, greeted my brother, and was on my way to San Leandro to drive him home. On the way I tried to think of the many things I wanted to say. From the moment I spotted him waiting on the corner I could not say the thing I wanted to. I took his bag and he got in the car, and for some time we did not say anything. Then I asked him how the weather had been in Texas and how he had been.

"We were waiting for you since yesterday," I said. "Mother is home getting the supper ready. You haven't eaten yet, have you?"

He shook his head. "The train was late getting into Los Angeles. We were eight hours behind time and I should have reached San Francisco this morning around eight."

Reaching home it was the same way. Mother could not say anything. "We have nothing special tonight, wish we had something good."

"Anything would do, Mama," my brother said.

Father sat in the room reading the papers but his eyes were over the sheet and his hands were trembling. Mother scurried about getting his supper ready. I sat across the table from my brother, and in the silence which was action I watched the wave of emotions in the room. My brother was aware of it too. He sat there without a word, but I knew he understood. Not many years ago he was the baby of the family, having never been away from home. Now he was on his own, his quiet confidence actually making him appear larger. Keep up the fire, that was his company's motto. It was evident that he was a soldier. He had gone beyond life and death matter, where the true soldiers of war or peace must travel, and had returned.

For five short days we went about our daily task, picking and bunching the flowers for Christmas, eating heavy meals, and visiting the intimates. It was as if we were waiting for the hour of his departure, the time being so short. Every minute was crowded with privacy, friends, and nursery work. Too soon the time for his train came but the family had little to talk.

"Kazuo, don't worry about home or me," Mother said as we rode into town.

"Take care of yourself," my brother told her.

At the 16th Street Station Mother's close friend was waiting for us. She came to bid my brother good-bye. We had fifteen minutes to wait. My brother bought a copy of *The Coast* to see if his cartoons were in.

"Are you in this month's issue?" I asked.

"I haven't seen it yet," he said, leafing the pages. "Yes, I'm in. Here it is."

"Good!" I said. "Keep trying hard. Someday peace will come, and when you return laughter will reign once again."

My mother showed his cartoon to her friend. The train came in and we got up. It was a long one. We rushed to the Los Angeles-bound coach.

Mother's friend shook hands with my brother. "Give your best to America. Our people's honor depend on you Nisei soldiers."

My brother nodded and then glanced at Mother. For a moment her eyes twinkled and she nodded. He waved good-bye from the platform. Once inside the train we lost him. When the train began to move my mother cried, "Why doesn't he pull up the shades and look out? Others are doing it."

We stood and watched until the last of the train was lost in the night of darkness.

# Mervyn Morris

## *To an Expatriate Friend*

Colour meant nothing. Anyone
who wanted help, had humour or was kind
was brother to you; categories of skin
were foreign; you were colour-blind.

And then the revolution. Black
and loud the horns of anger blew
against the long oppression; sufferers
cast off the precious values of the few.

New powers re-enslaved us all:
each person manacled in skin, in race.
You could not wear your paid-up dues;
the keen discriminators typed your face.

The future darkening, you thought it time
to say good-bye. It may be you were right.
It hurt to see you go; but, more,
it hurt to see you slowly going white.

# Family Pictures

In spite of love
desire to be alone
haunts him like prophecy.

Observe: the baby chuckles,
gurgles his delight
that daddy-man is handy,
to be stared at, clawed at,
spitted-up upon;
the baby's elder brother
laughs, or hugs, and nags
for popcorn or a pencil
or a trip.

And see: the frazzled wife
who jealously
protects the idol infant
from the smallest chance
of harm, and anxious
in the middle of the night
wakes up to coughs; and checks
and loves, and screams
her nerves; but loves him
patient still: the wife
who sweets the bigger boy
and teases him through homework,
bright as play.

But you may not observe
(it is a private sanctuary)
the steady glowing power
that makes a man feel loved,
feel needed, all of time;
yet frees him, king of her
emotions, jockey of her

flesh, to cherish
his own corner
of the cage.

In spite of love
this dream:
to go alone
to where
the fishing boats are empty
on the beach
and no one knows
which man is
father, husband, victim,
king, the master of one cage.

# Es'kia Mphahlele

## *The Coffee-cart Girl*

The crowd moved like one mighty being, and swayed and swung like the sea. In front, there was the Metropolitan Steel Windows Ltd. All eyes were fixed on it. Its workers did not hear one another: perhaps they didn't need to, each one interested as he was in what he was saying—and that with his blood. All he knew was that he was on strike: for what? If you asked him he would just spit and say: "Do you think we've come to play?"

Grimy, oily, greasy, sweating black bodies squeezed and chafed and grated. Pickets were at work; the law was brandishing batons; cars were hooting a crazy medley.

"Stand back, you monkeys!" cried a black man pinned against a pillar. "Hey, you black son of a black hen!"

The coffee-cart girl was absorbed in the very idea of the Metropolitan Steel Windows strike, just as she was in the flood of people who came to buy her coffee and pancakes: she wasn't aware of the swelling crowd and its stray atoms which were being flung out of it towards her cart until she heard an ear-splitting crash behind her. One of the row of coffee-carts had tipped over and a knot of men fallen on it. She climbed down from her cart, looking like a bird frightened out of its nest.

A woman screamed. Another crash. The man who had been pinned against the pillar had freed himself and he found himself standing beside the girl. He sensed her predicament. Almost rudely he pushed her into the street, took the cart by the stump of a shaft and wheeled it across the street, shouting generally, "Give way, you black monkeys." Just then a cart behind him went down and caved in like matchwood.

"Oh, thank you so much, mister!"

"Ought to be more careful, my sister."

"How can I thank you! Here, take coffee and a pancake."

"Thank you, my sister."

"Look, they're moving forward, maybe to break into the factory!"

When next she looked back he was gone. And she hadn't even asked him his name: how unfriendly of her, she thought . . .

Later that winter morning the street was cleared of most people. The workers had gone away. There had been no satisfactory agreement. Strikes were unlawful for black people anyhow.

"Come back to work, or you are signed off, or go to gaol," had come the stock executive order. More than half had been signed off.

It was comparatively quiet now in this squalid West End sector of the city. Men and women continued their daily round. A dreary smoky mist lingered in suspension, or clung to the walls; black sooty chimneys shot up malignantly; there was a strong smell of bacon; the fruit and vegetable shops resumed trade with a tremulous expectancy; old men stood Buddha-like at the entrances with folded arms and a vague grimace on their faces, seeming to sneer at the world in general and their contemptible mercantile circle in particular; and the good earth is generous enough to contain all the human sputum these good suffering folk shoot out of their mouths at the slightest provocation. A car might tear down the cross-street and set up a squall and weep dry horse manure so that it circled in the air in a momentary spree, increasing the spitting gusto . . .

"Hullo."

"Hullo, want coffee?"

"Yes, and two hot buns."

\* \* \*

She hardly looked at him as she served him. For a brief spell her eyes fell on the customer. Slowly she gathered up the scattered bits of memory and unconsciously the picture was framed. She looked at him and found him scanning her.

"Oh!" She gave a gasp and her hand went to her mouth. "You're the good uncle who saved my cart!"

"Don't uncle me, please. My name is Ruben Lemeko. The boys at the factory call me China. Yours?"

"Zodwa."

His eyes travelled from her small tender fingers as she washed a few things, to her man's jersey which was a faded green and too big for her, her thin frock, and then to her peach-coloured face, not well fed, but well framed and compelling under a soiled black beret. As he ate hungrily she shot a side-glance at him occasionally. There was something sly in those soft, moist, slit eyes, but the modest stoop at the shoulders gave him a benign appearance; otherwise he would have looked twisted and rather fiendish. There was something she felt in his presence: a repelling admiration. She felt he was the kind of man who could be quite attractive so long as he remained more than a touch away from the contemplator; just like those wax figures she once saw in the chamber of horrors.

"Signed off at the Metropolitan?"

"Hm." His head drooped and she could read dejection in the oily top of his cap. "Just from the insurance fund office." She pitied him inwardly; a sort of pity she had never before experienced for a strange man.

"What to do now?"

"Like most of us," looking up straight into her eyes, "beat the road early mornings just when the boss's breakfast is settling nicely in the stomach. No work, no government papers, no papers, no work, then out of town."

"It's hard for everybody, I guess."

"Ja."

"I know. When you feel hungry and don't have money, come past here and I'll give you coffee and pancake."

"Thanks, er — let me call you Pinkie, shall I?"

"Hm," she nodded automatically.

He shook her hand. "Grow as big as an elephant for your goodness, as we say in our idiom." He shuffled off. For a long time, until he disappeared, she didn't take her eyes off the stooping figure, which she felt might set any place on fire. Strange man Pinkie thought idly as she washed up.

\* \* \*

China often paused at Pinkie's coffee-cart. But he wouldn't let her give him coffee and pancakes for nothing.

"I'm no poorer than you," he said. "When I'm really in the drain pipes you may come to my help."

As she got used to him and the idea of a tender playfellow who is capable of scratching blood out of you, she felt heartily sorry for him; and he detected it, and resented it and felt sorry for her in turn.

"Right, Pinkie, I'll take it today."

"You'll starve to death in this cruel city."

"And then? Lots of them starve; think of this mighty city, Pinkie. What are we, you and me? If we starved and got sick and died, who'd miss you and me?"

Days when China didn't come, she missed him. And then she was afraid of something; something mysterious that crawls into human relations, and before we know it it's there; and because it is frightening it does not know how to announce itself without causing panic and possibly breaking down bonds of companionship. In his presence she tried to take refuge in an artless sisterly pity for him. And although he resented it, he carried on a dumb show. Within, heaven and earth thundered and rocked, striving to meet; sunshine and rain mingled; milk and gall pretended friendship; fire and water went hand in hand; tears and laughter hugged each other in a fit of hysterics; the screeching of the hang-bird started off with the descant of a dove's cooling; devils waved torches before a chorus of angels. Pinkie and China panicked at the thought of a love affair and remained dumb.

"Pinkie, I've got a job at last!"

"I'm happy for you, China!"

"You'll get a present, first money I get. Ach, but I shouldn't have told you. I wanted to surprise you." He was genuinely sorry.

"Don't worry, China I'll just pretend I'm surprised really, you'll see." They laughed.

Friday came.

"Come, Pinkie, let's go."

"Where to?"

"I'll show you." He led her to the cheapjack down the street.

"Mister, I want her to choose anything she wants."

The cheapjack immediately sprang up and in voluble cataracts began to sing praises upon his articles.

"All right, mister, let me choose." Pinkie picked up one article after another, inspected it, and at last she selected a beautiful long bodkin, a brooch, and a pair of bangles. Naidoo, the cheapjack, went off into rhapsodies again on Pinkie's looks when China put the things on her himself, pinning the bodkin on her beret. He bought himself a knife, dangling from a fashionable chain. They went back to the coffee-cart.

From this day onwards, Naidoo became a frequent customer at Pinkie's coffee-cart. He often praised her cakes and coffee. Twice at lunch-time China found him relating some anecdotes which sent Pinkie off into peals of laughter.

"Where you work, my prend?" asked Naidoo one day.

He was one of the many Indians who will say "pore-pipty" for "four fifty," "pier foms" for "five forms," "werry wital" for "very vital."

"Shoe factory, Main Street."

"Good pay?"

"Where do you find such a thing in this city?"

"Quite right, my prend. Look at me: I was wanted to be a grocer, and now I'm a cheapjack."

"I'm hungry today, Pinkie," China said one day. He was clearly elated over something.

"It's so beautiful to see you happy, China, what's the news?"

"Nothing. Hasn't a man the right to be jolly sometimes?"

"Of course. Just wondered if anything special happened."

He looked at her almost transparent pink fingers as she washed the coffee things.

"Hey, you've a lovely ring on your finger, where's the mine?"

Pinkie laughed as she looked at the glass-studded ring, fingered it and wiped it.

"From Naidoo."

"It's nothing, China, Naidoo didn't have any money for food, so he offered me this for three days' coffee and cakes." She spoke as if she didn't believe her own self. She sensed a gathering storm.

"You lie!"

"Honestly China, now what would I be lying for?"

So! he thought, she couldn't even lie to keep their friendship: how distant she sounded. His fury mounted.

"Yes, you lie! Now listen Pinkie, you're in love with that cheapjack. Every time I found him here he's been damn happy with you, grinning and making eyes at you. Yes, I've watched him every moment."

He approached the step leading into the cart.

"Do you see me? I've loved you since I first saw you, the day of the strike." He was going to say more, but something rose inside him and choked him. He couldn't utter a word more. He walked slowly; a knife drawn out, with a menacing blade, pointed towards her throat. Pinkie retreated deeper into her cart, too frightened to plead her case.

At that very moment she realised fully the ghastliness of a man's jealousy, which gleamed and glanced on the blade and seemed to have raised a film which steadied the slit eyes. Against the back wall she managed to speak.

"All right, China, maybe you've done this many times before. Go ahead and kill me; I won't cry for help, do what you like with me."

She panted like a timid little mouse cornered by a cat. He couldn't finish the job he had set out to do. Why? He had sent two men packing with a knife before. They had tried to fight, but this creature wasn't resisting at all. Why, why, why? He felt the heat pounding in his temples; the knife dropped, and he sank on to a stool and rested his head on the wall, his hands trembling.

After a moment he stood up, looking away from Pinkie. "I'm sorry, Pinkie, I pray you never in your life to think about this day."

She looked at him, mystified.

"Say you forgive me." She nodded twice.

Then she packed up for the day, much earlier than usual.

The following day China did not visit Pinkie; nor the next. He could not decide to go there. Things were all in a barbed wire tangle in his mind. But see her he must, he thought. He would just go and hug her; say nothing but just press her to himself because he felt too mean even to tell her not to be afraid of him any more.

* * *

The third day the law came. It stepped up the street in goose-march fashion. The steel on its heels clanged on the pavement with an ominous echo. It gave commands and everything came to an end at once. Black man's coffee-cart was not to operate any more in the city. "...Makes the city look ugly," the city fathers said.

For several days China, unaware of what had happened, called on Pinkie, but always found the coffee-carts empty and deserted. At last he learned everything from Naidoo, the cheapjack.

He stepped into her coffee-cart and sat on the stool.

He looked into the cheerless pall of smoke. Outside life went on as if there had never been a Pinkie who sold coffee and pancakes.

Dare he hope that she would come back, just to meet him? Or was it going to turn out to have been a dream? He wondered.

We'll meet in town, some day, China thought. I'll tell her all about myself, all about my wicked past; she'll get used to me, not be afraid of me any more ...

And still he sat in the coffee-cart which was once Pinkie's all through the lunch-hour ...

# Bharati Mukherjee

## *Hindus*

I ran into Pat at Sotheby's on a Friday morning two years ago. Derek and I had gone to view the Fraser Collection of Islamic miniatures at the York Avenue galleries. It bothered Derek that I knew so little about my heritage. Islam is nothing more than a marauder's faith to me, but the Mogul emperors stayed a long time in the green delta of the Ganges, flattening and reflattening a fort in the village where I was born, and forcing my priestly ancestors to prove themselves brave. Evidence on that score is still inconclusive. That village is now in Bangladesh.

Derek was a filmmaker, lightly employed at that time. We had been married three hundred and thirty-one days.

"So," Pat said, in his flashy, plummy, drawn-out intonation, "you finally made it to the States!"

It was one of those early November mornings when the woodsy smell of overheated bodies in cloth coats clogged the public stairwells. Everywhere around me I detected the plaintive signs of over-preparedness.

"Whatever are you doing here?" He engulfed me in a swirl of Liberty scarf and cashmere lapels.

"Trying to get the woman there to sell me the right catalog," I said.

The woman, a very young thing with slippery skin, ate a lusty Granny Smith apple and ignored the dark, hesitant miniature-lovers hanging about like bats in the daytime.

"They have more class in London," Pat said.

"I wouldn't know. I haven't been back since that unfortunate year at Roedean."

"It was always New York you wanted," Pat laughed. "Don't say I didn't warn you. The world is full of empty promises."

I didn't remember his having warned me about life and the inevitability of grief. It was entirely possible that he had—he had always been given to clowning pronouncements—but I had not seen him in nine years and in Calcutta he had never really broken through the fortifications of my shyness.

"Come have a drink with me," Pat said.

It was my turn to laugh. "You must meet Derek," I said.

Derek had learned a great deal about India. He could reel off statistics of Panchayati Raj and the electrification of villages and the introduction of mass media, though he reserved his love for birds migrating through the wintry deserts of Jaisalmer. Knowledge of India made Derek more sympathetic than bitter, a common trait of decent outsiders. He was charmed by Pat's heedless, old-world insularity.

"Is this the lucky man?" he said to Derek. He did not hold out his hand. He waved us outside; a taxi magically appeared. "Come have a drink with me tomorrow. At my place."

He gave Derek his card. It was big and would not fit into a wallet made to hold Visa and American Express. Derek read it with his usual curiosity.

H.R.H. Maharajah Patwant Singh
of
Gotlah
Purveyor and Exporter

He tucked the card in the pocket of his raincoat. "I'll be shooting in Toronto tomorrow," he said, "but I'm sure Leela would like to keep it."

There was, in the retention of those final "h's" — even Indian maps and newspapers now referred to Gotla and to maharajas, and I had dropped the old "Leelah" in my first month in America — something of the reclusive mountebank. "I'm going to the Patels for dinner tomorrow," I said, afraid that Pat would misread the signs of healthy unpossessiveness in our marriage.

"Come for a drink before. What's the matter, Leela? Turning a prude in your old age?" To Derek he explained, "I used to rock her on my knee when she was four. She was gorgeous then, but I am no lecher."

It is true that I was very pretty at four and that Pat spent a lot of time in our house fondling us children. He brought us imported chocolates in beautiful tins and made a show of giving me the biggest. In my family, in every generation, one infant seems destined to be the repository of the family's comeliness. In my generation, I inherited the looks, like an heirloom, to keep in good condition and pass on to the next. Beauty teaches humility and responsibility in the culture I came from. By marrying well, I could have seen to the education of my poorer cousins.

Pat was in a third floor sublet in Gramercy Park South. A West Indian doorman with pendulous cheeks and unbuttoned jacket let me into the building. He didn't give me a chance to say where I was going as I moved toward the elevator.

"The maharaja is third floor, to the right. All the way down."

I had misunderstood the invitation. It was not to be an hour of wit and nostalgia among exotic knick-knacks squirreled into New York from the Gotla Palace. I counted thirty guests in the first quarter hour of my short stay. Plump young men in tight-fitting suits scuttled from living room to kitchen, balancing overfull glasses of gin and tonic. The women were mostly blondes, with luridly mascaraed, brooding eyes, blonde the way South Americans are blonde, with deep residual shading. I tried to edge into a group of three women. One of them said, "I thought India was spellbinding. Naresh's partner managed to get us into the Lake Palace Hotel."

"I don't think I could take the poverty," said her friend, as I retreated.

The living room walls were hung with prints of British East India Company officials at work and play, the vestibule with mirror-images of Hindu gods and goddesses.

"Take my advice," a Gujarati man said to Pat in the dim and plantless kitchen. "Get out of diamonds—emeralds *won't* bottom out. These days it *has* to be rubies and emeralds."

In my six years in Manhattan I had not entered a kitchen without plants. There was not even a straggly avocado pushing its nervous way out of a shrivelling seed.

I moved back into the living room where the smell of stale turmeric hung like yellow fog from the ceiling. A man rose from the brocade-covered cushions of a banquette near me and plumped them, smiling, to make room for me.

"You're Pat's niece, no?" The man was francophone, a Lebanese. "Pat has such pretty nieces. You have just come from Bombay? I love Bombay. Personally, Bombay to me is just like a jewel. Like Paris, like Beirut before, now like Bombay. You agree?"

I disclaimed all kinship to H.R.H. I was a Bengali Brahmin; maharajas—not to put too sharp a point on it—were frankly beneath me, by at least one caste, though some of them, like Pat, would dispute it. Before my marriage to Derek no one in my family since our initial eruption from Vishnu's knee had broken caste etiquette. I disclaimed any recent connection with India. "I haven't been home in ages," I told the Lebanese. "I am an American citizen."

"I too am. I am American," he practically squealed. He rinsed his glass with a bit of gin still left in the bottom, as though he were trying to dislodge lemon pulp stuck and drying on its sides. "You want to have dinner with me tonight, yes?" I know Lebanese places, secret and intimate. Food and ambiance very romantic."

"She's going to the Patels." It was Pat. The Gujarati with advice on emeralds was still lodged in the kitchen, huddling with a stocky blonde in a fuchsia silk sari.

"Oh, the Patels," said the Lebanese. "You did not say. Super guy, no? He's doing all right for himself. Not as well as me, of course. I own ten stores and he only has four."

Why, I often ask myself, was Derek never around to share these intimacies? Derek would have drawn out the suave, French-speaking, soulful side of this Seventh Avenue *shmattiste*.

It shouldn't have surprised me that the Lebanese man in the ruffled shirt should have known Mohan and Motibehn Patel. For immigrants in similar trades, Manhattan is still a village. Mohan had been in the States for eighteen years and last year had become a citizen. They'd been fortunate in having only sons, now at Cal Tech and Cornell; with daughters there would have been pressure on them to return to India for a proper, arranged marriage.

"Is he still in Queens?"

"No," I told him. "They've moved to a biggish old place on Central Park West."

"Very foolish move," said the Lebanese. "They will only spend their money now." He seemed genuinely appalled.

Pat looked at me surprised. "I can't believe it," he exclaimed. "Leela Lahiri actually going crosstown at night by herself. I remember when your Daddy wouldn't let you walk the two blocks from school to the house without that armed Nepali, what was his name, dogging your steps."

"Gulseng," I said. "He was run over by a lorry three years ago. I think his name was really something-or-other-Rana, but he never corrected us."

"Short, nasty and brutal," said Pat. "They don't come that polite and loyal these days. Just as likely to slit your throat as anyone else, these days."

The Lebanese, sensing the end of the brave New World overtures, the gathering of the darknesses we shared, drifted away.

"The country's changed totally, you know," Pat continued. "Crude rustic types have taken over. The *dhoti-wallahs*, you know what I mean, they would wrap themselves in loincloths if it got them more votes. No integrity, no finesse. The country's gone to the dogs, I tell you."

"That whole life's outmoded, Pat. Obsolete. All over the world."

"They tried to put me in jail," he said. His face was small with bitterness and alarm. "They didn't like my politics, I tell you. Those Communists back home arrested me and threw me in jail. Me. Like a common criminal."

"On what charges?"

"Smuggling. For selling family heirlooms to Americans who understand them. No one at home understands their value. Here, I can sell off a little Pahari painting for ten thousand dollars. Americans understand our things better than we do ourselves. India wants me to starve in my overgrown palace."

"Did you really spend a night in jail?" I couldn't believe that modernization had finally come to India and that even there, no one was immune from consequences.

"Three nights!" he fumed. "Like a common *dacoit*. The country has no respect anymore. The country has nothing. It has driven us abroad with whatever assets we could salvage."

"You did well, I take it." I did not share his perspective; I did not feel my country owed me anything. Comfort, perhaps, when I was there; a different comfort when I left it. India teaches her children: you have seen the worst. Now go out and don't be afraid.

"I have nothing," he spat. "They've stripped me of everything. At night I hear the jackals singing in the courtyard of my palace."

But he had recovered by the time I left for the crosstown cab ride to the Patels. I saw him sitting on the banquette where not too long before the Lebanese had invited me to share an evening of unwholesomeness. On his knee he balanced a tall, silver-haired woman who looked like Candice Bergen. She wore a pink cashmere sweater which she must have put through the washing machine. Creases, like worms, curled around her sweatered bosom.

I didn't see Pat for another two years. In those two years I did see a man who claimed to have bounced the real Candice Bergen on his knee. He had been a juggler at one time, had worked with Edgar Bergen on some vaudeville act and could still pull off card tricks and walk on his hands up and down my dining table. I kept the dining table when Derek and I split last May. He went back to Canada which we both realized too late he should never have left and the table was too massive to move out of our West 11th Street place and into his downtown Toronto, chic renovated apartment. The ex-juggler is my boss at a publishing house. My job is menial but I have a soothing title. I am called an Administrative Assistant.

In the two years I have tried to treat the city not as an island of dark immigrants but as a vast sea in which new Americans like myself could disappear and resurface at will. I did not avoid Indians, but without Derek's urging for me to be proud of my heritage, I did not seek them out. The Patels did invite me to large dinners where all the guests seemed to know with the first flick of their eyes in my direction that I had married a white man and was now separated, and there our friendships hit rock. I was a curiosity, a novel and daring element in the community; everyone knew my name. After a while I began to say I was busy to Motibehn Patel.

Pat came to the office with my boss, Bill Haines, the other day. "I wanted you to meet one of our new authors, Leela," Bill said.

"Leela, *dar-ling*!" Pat cried. His voice was shrill with enthusiasm, and he pressed me histrionically against his Burberry raincoat. I could feel a button tap my collarbone. "It's been years! Where have you been hiding your gorgeous self?"

"I didn't realize you two knew each other," Bill said.

All Indians in America, I could have told him, constitute a village.

"Her father bailed me out when the Indian government sought to persecute me," he said with a pout. "If it hadn't been for courageous friends like her daddy, I and my poor subjects might just as well have kicked the bucket."

"She's told me nothing about India," said Bill Haines. "No accent, Western clothes—"

"Yes, a shame, that. By the way, Leela, I just found a picture of Lahiri-*sahab* on an elephant when I was going through my official papers for Bill. If you come over for drinks—after getting out of those ridiculous clothes, I must insist—I can give it to you. Lahiri-*sahab* looks like Ernest Hemingway in that photo. You tell him I said he looks like Hemingway."

"Daddy's in Ranikhet this month," I said. "He's been bedridden for a while. Arthritis. He's just beginning to move around a bit again."

"I have hundred of good anecdotes, Bill, about her daddy and me doing *shikar* in the Sundarban forest. Absolutely *huge* Bengal tigers. I want to balance the politics—which as you rightly say are central—with some stirring bits about what it was like in the good old days."

"What are you writing?" I asked.

"I thought you'd never ask, my dear. My memoirs. At night I leave a Sony by my bed. Night is the best time for remembering. I hear the old sounds and voices. You remember, Leela, how the palace ballroom used to hum with dancing feet on my birthdays?"

*"Memoirs of a Modern Maharajah,"* Bill Haines said.

"I seem to remember the singing of jackals," I said, not unkindly, though he chose to ignore it.

"Writing is what keeps me from going through death's gate. There are nights . . ." He didn't finish. His posture had stiffened with self-regard; he communicated great oceans of anguish. He'd probably do well. It was what people wanted to hear.

"The indignities," he said suddenly. "The atrocities." He stared straight ahead, at a watercooler. "The nights in jail, the hyenas sniffing outside your barred window. I will never forget their smell, never! It is the smell of death, Leela. The new powers-that-be are peasants. Peasants! They cannot know, they cannot suspect how they have made me suffer. The country is in the hands of tyrannical peasants!"

"Look, Pat," Bill Haines said, leading the writer toward his office, "I have to see Bob Savage, the sub-rights man one floor down. Make yourself at home. Just pull down any book you want to read. I'll be back in a minute."

"Don't worry about me. I shall be all right, Bill. I have my Sony in my pocket. I shall just sit in a corner beside the daughter of my oldest friend, this child I used to bounce on my knee, and I shall let my mind skip into the nooks and crannies of Gotlah Palace. Did I tell you, when I was a young lad my mother kept pet crocs? Big, huge gents and ladies with ugly jaws full of nasty teeth. They were her pets. She gave them names and fed them chickens every day. Come to me, Padma. Come to me, Prem."

"It'll be dynamite," Bill Haines said. "The whole project's dynamite." He pressed my hand as he eased his stubby, muscular body past the stack of dossiers on my desk. "And *you'll* be a godsend in developing this project."

"And what's with you?" Pat asked me. I could tell he already knew the essentials.

"Nothing much." But he wasn't listening anyway.

"You remember the thief my security men caught in the early days of your father's setting up a factory in my hills? You remember how the mob got excited and poured acid on his face?"

I remembered. Was the Sony recording it? Was the memory an illustration of swift and righteous justice in a collapsed Himalayan princely state, or was it the savage and disproportionate fury of a people resisting change?

"Yes, certainly I do. Can I get you a cup of coffee? Or tea?" That, of course, was an important part of my job.

"No thanks," he said with a flutter of his wrinkled hands. "I have given up all stimulants. I've even given up bed-tea. It interferes with my writing. Writing is everything to me nowadays. It has been my nirvana."

"The book sounds dynamite," I assured him. An Indian woman is brought up to please. No matter how passionately we link bodies with our new countries, we never escape the early days.

Pat dropped his voice, and stooping conspiratorially, said to me in Hindi, "There's one big favor you can do for me, though. Bill has spoken of a chap I should be knowing. Who is this Edgar Bergen?"

"I think he was the father of a movie actress," I said. I too, had gone through the same contortion of recognition with Bill Haines. Fortunately, like most Americans, he could not conceive of a world in which Edgar Bergen had no currency. Again in Hindi, Pat asked me for directions to the facilities, and this time I could give a full response. He left his rolled-slim umbrella propped against my desk and walked toward the fountain.

"Is he really a maharaja?" Lisa leaned over from her desk to ask me. She is from Rhode Island. Brown hasn't cured her of responding too enthusiastically to each call or visit from a literary personage. "He's terrific. So suave and distinguished! Have you known him from way back when?"

"Yes," I said, all the way from when.

"I had no idea you spoke Hindu. It's eerie to think you can speak such a hard language. I'm having trouble enough with French. I keep forgetting that you haven't lived here always."

I keep forgetting it too. I was about to correct her silly mistake — I'd learned from Derek to be easily incensed over ignorant confusions — between Hindi and Hindu — but then I thought, why bother? Maybe she's right. That slight undetectable error, call it an accent, isn't part of language at all. I speak Hindu. No matter what language I speak it will come out slightly foreign, no matter how perfectly I mouth it. There's a whole world of us now, speaking Hindu.

The manuscript of *Memoirs* was not dynamite, but I stayed up all night to finish it. In spite of the arch locutions and the aggrieved posture that Pat had stubbornly clung to, I knew I was reading about myself, blind and groping conquistador who had come to the New World too late.

# V. S. Naipaul

## B. Wordsworth

Three beggars called punctually every day at the hospitable houses in Miguel Street. At about ten an Indian came in his dhoti and white jacket, and we poured a tin of rice into the sack he carried on his back. At twelve an old woman smoking a clay pipe came and she got a cent. At two a blind man led by a boy called for his penny.

Sometimes we had a rogue. One day a man called and said he was hungry. We gave him a meal. He asked for a cigarette and wouldn't go until we had lit it for him. That man never came again.

The strangest caller came one afternoon at about four o'clock. I had come back from school and was in my home-clothes. The man said to me, "Sonny, may I come inside your yard?"

He was a small man and he was tidily dressed. He wore a hat, a white shirt and black trousers.

I asked, "What you want?"

He said, "I want to watch your bees."

We had four small gru-gru palm trees and they were full of uninvited bees.

I ran up the steps and shouted, "Ma, it have a man outside here. He say he want to watch the bees."

My mother came out, looked at the man and asked in an unfriendly way, "What you want?"

The man said, "I want to watch your bees."

His English was so good, it didn't sound natural, and I could see my mother was worried.

She said to me, "Stay here and watch him while he watch the bees."

The man said, "Thank you, madam. You have done a good deed today."

He spoke very slowly and very correctly as though every word was costing him money.

We watched the bees, this man and I, for about an hour, squatting near the palm trees.

The man said, "I like watching bees. Sonny, do you like watching bees?"

I said, "I ain't have the time."

He shook his head sadly. He said, "That's what I do, I just watch. I can watch ants for days. Have you ever watched ants? And scorpions, and centipedes, and *congorees* – have you watched those?"

I shook my head.

I said, "What you does do, mister?"

He got up and said, "I am a poet."

I said, "A good poet?"

He said, "The greatest in the world."

"What your name, mister?"

"B. Wordsworth."

"B for Bill?"

"Black. Black Wordsworth. White Wordsworth was my brother. We share one heart. I can watch a small flower like the morning glory and cry."

I said, "Why you does cry?"

"Why, boy? Why? You will know when you grow up. You're a poet, too, you know. And when you're a poet you can cry for everything."

I couldn't laugh.

He said, "You like your mother?"

"When she not beating me."

He pulled out a printed sheet from his hip-pocket and said, "On this paper is the greatest poem about mothers and I'm going to sell it to you at a bargain price. For four cents."

I went inside and I said, "Ma, you want to buy a poetry for four cents?"

My mother said, "Tell that blasted man to haul his tail away from my yard, you hear."

I said to B. Wordsworth, "My mother say she ain't have four cents."

B. Wordsworth said, "It is the poet's tragedy."

And he put the paper back in his pocket. He didn't seem to mind.

I said, "Is a funny way to go round selling poetry like that. Only calypsonians do that sort of thing. A lot of people does buy?"

He said, "No one has yet bought a single copy."

"But why you does keep on going round, then?"

He said, "In this way I watch many things, and I always hope to meet poets."

I said, "You really think I is a poet?"

"You're as good as me," he said.

And when B. Wordsworth left, I prayed I would see him again.

About a week later, coming back from school one afternoon, I met him at the corner of Miguel Street.

He said, "I have been waiting for you for a long time."

I said, "You sell any poetry yet?"

He shook his head.

He said, "In my yard I have the best mango tree in Port of Spain. And now the mangoes are ripe and red and very sweet and juicy. I have waited here for you to tell you this and to invite you to come and eat some of my mangoes."

He lived in Alberto Street in a one-roomed hut placed right in the centre of the lot. The yard seemed all green. There was the big mango tree. There was a coconut tree and there was a plum tree. The place looked wild, as though it wasn't in the city at all. You couldn't see all the big concrete houses in the street.

He was right. The mangoes were sweet and juicy. I ate about six, and the yellow mango juice ran down my arms to my elbows and down my mouth to my chin and my shirt was stained.

My mother said when I got home, "Where was you? You think you is a man now and could go all over the place? Go cut a whip for me."

She beat me rather badly, and I ran out of the house swearing that I would never come back. I went to B. Wordsworth's house. I was so angry, my nose was bleeding.

B. Wordsworth said, "Stop crying, and we will go for a walk."

I stopped crying, but I was breathing short. We went for a walk. We walked down St Clair Avenue to the Savannah and we walked to the race-course.

B. Wordsworth said, "Now, let us lie on the grass and look up at the sky, and I want you to think how far those stars are from us."

I did as he told me, and I saw what he meant. I felt like nothing, and at the same time I had never felt so big and great in all my life. I forgot all my anger and all my tears and all the blows.

When I said I was better, he began telling me the names of the stars, and I particularly remembered the constellation of Orion the Hunter, though I don't really know why. I can spot Orion even today, but I have forgotten the rest.

Then a light was flashed into our faces, and we saw a policeman. We got up from the grass.

The policeman said, "What you doing here?"

B. Wordsworth said, "I have been asking myself the same question for forty years."

We became friends, B. Wordsworth and I. He told me, "You must never tell anybody about me and about the mango tree and the coconut tree and the plum tree. You must keep that a secret. If you tell anybody, I will know, because I am a poet."

I gave him my word and I kept it.

I liked his little room. It had no more furniture than George's front room, but it looked cleaner and healthier. But it also looked lonely.

One day I asked him, "Mister Wordsworth, why you does keep all this bush in your yard? Ain't it does make the place damp?"

He said, "Listen, and I will tell you a story. Once upon a time a boy and girl met each other and they fell in love. They loved each other so much they got married. They were both poets. He loved words. She loved grass and flowers and trees. They lived happily in a single room, and then one day, the girl poet said to the boy poet, 'We are going to have another poet in the family.' But this poet was never born, because the girl died, and the young poet died with her, inside her. And the girl's husband was very sad, and he said he would never touch a thing in the girl's garden. And so the garden remained, and grew high and wild."

I looked at B. Wordsworth, and as he told me this lovely story, he seemed to grow older. I understood his story.

We went for long walks together. We went to the Botanical Gardens and the Rock Gardens. We climbed Chancellor Hill in the late afternoon and watched the darkness fall on Port of Spain, and watched the lights go on in the city and on the ships in the harbour.

He did everything as though he were doing it for the first time in his life. He did everything as though he were doing some church rite.

He would say to me, "Now, how about having some ice-cream?"

And when I said yes, he would grow very serious and say, "Now, which café shall we patronize?" As though it were a very important thing. He would think for some time about it, and finally say, "I think I will go and negotiate the purchase with that shop."

The world became a most exciting place.

One day, when I was in his yard, he said to me, "I have a great secret which I am now going to tell you."

I said, "It really secret?"

"At the moment, yes."

I looked at him, and he looked at me. He said, "This is just between you and me, remember. I am writing a poem."

"Oh." I was disappointed.

He said, "But this is a different sort of poem. This is the greatest poem in the world."

I whistled.

He said, "I have been working on it for more than five years now. I will finish it in about twenty-two years from now, that is, if I keep on writing at the present rate."

"You does write a lot, then?"

He said, "Not any more. I just write one line a month. But I make sure it is a good line."

I asked, "What was last month's good line?"

He looked up at the sky, and said, *"The past is deep."*

I said, "It is a beautiful line."

B. Wordsworth said, "I hope to distil the experiences of a whole month into that single line of poetry. So, in twenty-two years, I shall have written a poem that will sing to all humanity."

I was filled with wonder.

Our walks continued. We walked along the sea-wall at Docksite one day, and I said, "Mr Wordsworth, if I drop this pin in the water, you think it will float?"

He said, "This is a strange world. Drop your pin, and let us see what will happen."

The pin sank.

I said, "How is the poem this month?"

But he never told me any other line. He merely said, "Oh, it comes, you know. It comes."

Or we would sit on the sea-wall and watch the liners come into the harbour.

But of the greatest poem in the world I heard no more.

I felt he was growing older.

"How you does live, Mr Wordsworth?" I asked him one day.

He said, "You mean how I get money?"

When I nodded, he laughed in a crooked way.

He said, "I sing calypsoes in the calypso season."

"And that last you the rest of the year?"

"It is enough."

"But you will be the richest man in the world when you write the greatest poem?"

He didn't reply.

One day when I went to see him in his little house, I found him lying on his little bed. He looked so old and so weak, that I found myself wanting to cry.

He said, "The poem is not going well."

He wasn't looking at me. He was looking through the window at the coconut tree, and he was speaking as though I wasn't there. He said, "When I was twenty I felt the power within myself." Then, almost in front of my eyes, I could see his face growing older and more tired. He said, "But that — that was a long time ago."

And then — I felt it so keenly, it was as though I had been slapped by my mother. I could see it clearly on his face. It was there for everyone to see. Death on the shrinking face.

He looked at me, and saw my tears and sat up.

He said, "Come." I went and sat on his knees.

He looked into my eyes, and he said, "Oh, you can see it, too. I always knew you had the poet's eye."

He didn't even look sad, and that made me burst out crying loudly.

He pulled me to his thin chest, and said, "Do you want me to tell you a funny story?" and he smiled encouragingly at me.

But I couldn't reply.

He said, "When I have finished this story, I want you to promise that you will go away and never come back to see me. Do you promise?"

I nodded.

He said, "Good. Well, listen. That story I told you about the boy poet and the girl poet, do you remember that? That wasn't true. It was something I just made up. All this talk about poetry and the greatest poem in the world, that wasn't true, either. Isn't that the funniest thing you have heard?"

But his voice broke.

I left the house, and ran home crying, like a poet, for everything I saw.

I walked along Alberto Street a year later, but I could find no sign of the poet's house. It hadn't vanished, just like that. It had been pulled down, and a big, two-storeyed building had taken its place. The mango tree and the plum tree and the coconut tree had all been cut down, and there was brick and concrete everywhere.

It was just as though B. Wordsworth had never existed.

# *Jasmine*

One day about ten years ago, when I was editing a weekly literary programme for the BBC's Caribbean Service, a man from Trinidad came to see me in one of the freelancers' rooms in the old Langham Hotel. He sat on the edge of the table, slapped down some sheets of typescript and said, "My name is Smith. I write about sex. I am also a nationalist." The sex was tepid, Maugham and coconut-water; but the nationalism was aggressive. Women swayed like coconut trees; their skins were the colour of the sapodilla, the inside of their mouths the colour of a cut star-apple; their teeth were as white as coconut kernels; and when they made love they groaned like bamboos in high wind.

The writer was protesting against what the English language had imposed on us. The language was ours, to use as we pleased. The literature that came with it was therefore of peculiar authority; but this literature was like an alien mythology. There was, for instance, Wordsworth's notorious poem about the daffodil. A pretty little flower, no doubt; but we had never seen it. Could the poem have any meaning for us? The superficial prompting of this argument, which would have confined all literatures to the countries of their origin, was political; but it was really an expression of dissatisfaction at the emptiness of our own formless, unmade society. To us, without a mythology, all literatures were foreign. Trinidad was small, remote and unimportant, and we knew we could not hope to read in books of the life we saw about us. Books came from afar; they could offer only fantasy.

To open a book was to make an instant adjustment. Like the medieval sculptor of the North interpreting the Old Testament stories in terms of the life he knew, I needed to be able to adapt. All Dickens's descriptions of London I rejected; and though I might retain Mr Micawber and the others in the clothes the illustrator gave them, I gave them the faces and voices of people I knew and set them in buildings and streets I knew. The process of adaptation was automatic and continuous. Dickens's rain and drizzle I turned into tropical downpours; the snow and fog I accepted as conventions of books.

Anything—like an illustration—which embarrassed me by proving how weird my own recreation was, anything which sought to remove the characters from the make-up world in which I set them, I rejected.

I went to books for fantasy; at the same time I required reality. The gypsies of *The Mill on the Floss* were a fabrication and a disappointment, discrediting so much that was real: to me gypsies were mythical creatures who belonged to the pure fantasy of Hans Christian Andersen and *The Heroes*. Disappointing, too, was the episode of the old soldier's sword, because I thought that swords belonged to ancient times; and the Tom Tulliver I had created walked down the street where I lived. The early parts of *The Mill on the Floss*, then; chapters of *Oliver Twist, Nicholas Nickleby, David Copperfield*; some of the novels of H. G. Wells; a short story by Conrad called "The Lagoon": all these which in the beginning I read or had read to me I set in Trinidad, accepting, rejecting, adapting, and peopling in my own way. I never read to find out about foreign countries. Everything in books was foreign; everything had to be subjected to adaptation; and everything in, say, an English novel which worked and was of value to me at once ceased to be specifically English. Mr Murdstone worked; Mr Pickwick and his club didn't. *Jane Eyre* and *Wuthering Heights* worked; *Pride and Prejudice* didn't. Maupassant worked; Balzac didn't.

I went to books for a special sort of participation. The only social division I accepted was that between rich and poor, and any society more elaborately ordered seemed insubstantial and alien. In literature such a society was more than alien; it was excluding, it made nonsense of my fantasies and more and more, as I grew older and thought of writing myself, it made me despairingly conscious of the poverty and haphazardness of my own society. I might adapt Dickens to Trinidad; but it seemed impossible that the life I knew in Trinidad could ever be turned into a book. If landscapes do not start to be real until they have been interpreted by an artist, so, until they have been written about, societies appear to be without shape and *embarrassing*. It was embarrassing to be reminded by a Dickens illustration of the absurdity of my adaptations; it was equally embarrassing to attempt to write of what I saw. Very little of what I read was of help. It would have been possible to assume the sensibility of a particular writer. But no writer, however individual his vision, could be separated from his society. The vision was alien; it diminished my own and did not give me the courage to do a simple thing like mentioning the name of a Port of Spain street.

Fiction or any work of the imagination, whatever its quality, hallows its subject. To attempt, with a full consciousness of established authoritative mythologies, to give a quality of myth to what was agreed to be petty and ridiculous—Frederick Street in Port of Spain, Marine Square, the districts of Laventille and Barataria—to attempt to use these names required courage. It was, in a way, the rejection of the familiar, meaningless word—the rejection of the unknown daffodil to put it no higher—and was as self-conscious as the attempt to have sapodilla-skinned women groaning like bamboos in high wind.

With all English literature accessible, then, my position was like that of the maharaja in *Hindoo Holiday*, who, when told by the Christian lady that God was here, there and everywhere, replied, "But what use is that to *me*?" Something of more pertinent virtue was needed, and this was provided by some local short stories. These stories, perhaps a dozen in all, never published outside Trinidad, converted what I saw into "writing." It was through them that I began to appreciate the distorting, distilling power of the writer's art. Where I had seen a drab haphazardness they found order; where I would have attempted to romanticize, to render my subject equal with what I had read, they accepted. They provided a starting-point for further observation; they did not trigger off fantasy. Every writer is, in the long run, on his own; but it helps, in the most practical way, to have a tradition. The English language was mine; the tradition was not.

Literature, then, was mainly fantasy. Perhaps it was for this reason that, although I had at an early age decided to be a writer and at the age of eighteen had left Trinidad with that ambition, I did not start writing seriously until I was nearly twenty-three. My material had not been sufficiently hallowed by a tradition; I was not fully convinced of its importance; and some embarrassment remained. My taste for literature had developed into a love of language, the word in isolation. At school my subjects were French and Spanish; and the pleasures of the language were at least as great as those of the literature. Maupassant and Moliere were rich; but it was more agreeable to spend an hour with the big Harrap French-English dictionary, learning more of the language through examples, than with Corneille or Racine. And it was because I thought I had had enough of these languages (both now grown rusty) that when I came to England to go to university I decided to read English.

This was a mistake. The English course had little to do with literature. It was a "discipline" seemingly aimed at juvenile antiquarians. It by-passed the novel and the prose "asides" in which so much of the richness of the literature lay. By a common and curious consent it concentrated on poetry; and since it stopped at the eighteenth century it degenerated, after an intensive study of Shakespeare, into a lightning survey of minor and often severely local talents. I had looked forward to wandering among large tracts of writing; I was presented with "texts". The metaphysicals were a perfect subject for study, a perfect part of a discipline; but, really, they had no value for me. Dryden, for all the sweet facility of his prose, was shallow and dishonest; did his "criticism" deserve such reverential attention? *Gulliver's Travels* was excellent; but could *The Tale of a Tub* and *The Battle of the Books* be endured?

The fact was, I had no taste for scholarship, for tracing the growth of schools and trends. I sought continuously to relate literature to life. My training at school didn't help. We had few libraries, few histories of literature to turn to; and when we wrote essays on *Tartuffe* we wrote out of a direct response to the play. Now I discovered that the study of literature had been made scientific, that each writer had to be approached through the booby-traps of scholarship. There were the bound volumes of the Publications of the Modern Language Association of America, affectionately referred to by old and knowing young as PMLA. The pages that told of Chaucer's knowledge of astronomy or astrology (the question came up every year) were black and bloated and furred with handling, and even some of the pencilled annotations *(No, Norah!)* had grown faint. I developed a physical distaste for these bound volumes and the libraries that housed them.

Delight cannot be taught and measured; scholarship can; and my reaction was irrational. But it seemed to me scholarship of such a potted order. A literature was not being explored; it had been codified and reduced to a few pages of "text", some volumes of "background" and more of "criticism"; and to this mixture a mathematical intelligence might have been applied. There were discoveries, of course: Shakespeare, Marlowe, Restoration comedy. But my distaste for the study of literature led to a sense of being more removed than ever from the literature itself.

The language remained  mine, and it was to the study of its development that I turned with pleasure. Here was enough to satisfy my love of language; here was unexpected adventure. It might not have been easy to see Chaucer as a great imaginative writer or to find in the *Prologue* more than a limited piece of observation which had been exceeded a thousand times; but Chaucer as a handler of a new, developing language was exciting. And my pleasure in Shakespeare was doubled. In Trinidad English writing had been for me a starting-point for fantasy. Now, after some time in England, it was possible to isolate the word, to separate the literature from the language.

Language can be so deceptive. It has taken me much time to realize how bad I am at interpreting the conventions and modes of English speech. This speech has never been better dissected than in the early stories of Angus Wilson. This is the judgment of today; my first responses to these stories were as blundering and imperfect as the responses of Professor Pforzheim to the stern courtesies of his English colleagues — in *Anglo-Saxon Attitudes*. But while knowledge of England has made English writing more truly accessible, it has made participation more difficult; it has made impossible the exercise of fantasy, the reader's complementary response. I am inspecting an alien society, which I yet know, and I am looking for particular social comment. And to re-read now the books which lent themselves to fantastic interpretation in Trinidad is to see, almost with dismay, how English they are. The illustrations to Dickens cannot now be dismissed. And so, with knowledge, the books have ceased to be mine.

It is the English literary vice, this looking for social comment; and it is difficult to resist. The preoccupation of the novelists reflects a society ruled by convention and manners in the fullest sense, an ordered society of the self-aware who read not so much for adventure as to compare, to find what they know or think they know. A writer is to be judged by what he reports on; the working-class writer is a working-class writer and no more. So writing develops into the private language of a particular society. There are new reports, new discoveries: they are rapidly absorbed. And with each discovery the society's image of itself becomes more fixed and the society looks further inward. It has too many points of reference; it has been written about too often; it has read too much. Angus Wilson's characters, for instance, are great readers; they are steeped in Dickens and Jane Austen. Soon there will be characters steeped in Angus Wilson; the process is endless. Sensibility will overlay sensibility: the grossness of experience will be refined away by self-awareness. Writing will become Arthur Miller's definition of a newspaper: a nation talking to itself. And even those who have the key will be able only to witness, not to participate.

All literatures are regional; perhaps it is only the placelessness of a Shakespeare or the blunt communication of "gross" experience as in Dickens that makes them appear less so. Or perhaps it is a lack of knowledge in the reader. Even in this period of "internationalism" in letters we have seen literatures turning more and more inward, developing languages that are more and more private. Perhaps in the end literature will write itself out, and all its pleasures will be those of the word.

A little over three years ago I was in British Guiana. I was taken late one afternoon to meet an elderly lady of a distinguished Christian Indian family. Our political attitudes were too opposed to make any discussion of the current crisis profitable. We talked of the objects in her veranda and of the old days. Suddenly the tropical daylight was gone, and from the garden came the scent of a flower. I knew the flower from my childhood; yet I had never found out its name. I asked now.

"We call it jasmine."

Jasmine! So I had known it all those years! To me it had been a word in a book, a word to play with, something removed from the dull vegetation I knew.

The old lady cut a sprig for me. I stuck it in the top buttonhole of my open shirt. I smelled it as I walked back to the hotel. Jasmine, jasmine. But the word and the flower had been separate in my mind for too long. They did not come together.

# Satendra Nandan

## *Return to a Certain Darkness*

It is 11 February 1993, and I am returning to Nadi, the place of my birth. It is exactly five years, two months and eight days since I left Fiji with my wife and two daughters. I came to Canberra, intending to live there for only a few months, but I stayed on.

Now I sit alone at Sydney's Kingsford Smith Airport. In Suva, I remember, there is a park named after that intrepid aviator. At one stage a crotch-scratching mayor of Suva tried to have the park renamed after himself, but howls of protest dissuaded him. Someone suggested that if he was so keen he should change his name to Kingsford Smith by deed poll. Soon afterwards he was voted out.

I feel no particular emotion waiting for QF 17, only a sense of melancholy deep down — not unlike the eldest son's feelings when he has to collect his father's charred bones and a handful of ashes to enshrine them in the sea or a river. This ancient rite gives grace and completeness to the dead so that the living can continue their lives, without ghosts. Except that the past, like our parents, lives on in us. Just now, my mind is full of ghosts.

It is 6 o'clock. There is just one person in the lounge: a plump, darkish Indian woman dressed in a white blouse, white skirt, pink stockings and black shoes. She reminds me of Josephine, the girl-woman who looked after our domestic affairs just before the coups. Whenever Josephine was fed up with the drudgery, she would threaten to migrate to Australia. Then one day she rang to say she wasn't coming to work; she was leaving for Australia as soon as she received a visa. I look at this woman again, but she isn't Josephine. Strange that Josephine should be my first connection with Fiji.

Josephine's double walks towards the cafeteria. Her gait reminds me of my two sisters, big, bountiful village women. My younger sister's crippled husband died in Auckland recently. His body was flown to Fiji for cremation. I did not attend his funeral, just as I did not attend Dr Timoci Bavadra's. So this journey is, in a sense, an atonement. My brother-in-law was cremated at the same Wailoaloa beach where my father had been cremated almost fifteen years before. The pyre must have been lit on the same spot, under the rusting corrugated iron shed. Another death, a different father, a different son, almost a different country. And my indifference.

I sit down not far from "Josephine." She is carrying two well-stuffed cabin bags, and a large pink plastic doll in a box. I flip through the first few pages of John Hewson's biography (dull reading) and then a book on Paul Keating (more interesting). I'm taking the two books for my brother; he's now in politics, or whatever shreds are left of it in Fiji. I thought he should know a bit about the Australian leaders, who are so important to Fiji, even in their calculated political callousness.

Around 7.30 p.m. we board the aircraft. As the plane takes off, tearing into the silence, I put the Keating biography in my satchel and take out a six-page story by Totaram Sanadhaya, "The Story of the Haunted Line," an autobiographical fragment of an indentured Indian's life. Nothing much survives of the thoughts, feelings and memories of the indentured Indians. Fiji had the highest suicide rate of any colony at the close of the nineteenth century. So Totaram's piece is priceless, like one or two surviving indenture agreements *(girmityas)*. It's a rare and moving narrative, offering a creative opening into one hundred years of servitude that remain unarticulated, buried like ancestral bones.

We are on our way to Nadi—pronounced Nandi—the name of a river, a village, a town, a district and now the international airport, two miles away from my home, where some people worshipped Nandi, Shiva's bull of plenty. Shiva is the god of the dance of life and death; Shiv was my father's first name. Shiva the god and my father Shiv were both fond of *nasha*, liquor on their breath. I adjust my watch to Fijian time.

Last Sunday I met Jairam Reddy, leader of the opposition in Fiji's new Parliament, elected on an apartheid constitution. This is the second time he has acquired the mantle of Leader of the Opposition, except that it is now a hollow position. He cannot become an alternative Prime Minister, and has to contend with thirteen opposition Indian MPs whose only parliamentary purpose seems to be to malign him.

Over dinner at a friend's place, Jairam talked frankly and quietly. I heard a deep fatigue in his voice. Burnt and bewildered by the tragedy of two unnecessary coups, betrayed by his community in the last elections, hemmed in by the vulgar and blatant racism of the *taukeis*, the Fijian extremists, he had few political options. He claimed to be a practical, pragmatic politician who was ready to accommodate and compromise, who played the politics of patience, persuasion and peace. His old, steely vision was tempered by the new menace of racism. There was disillusionment but not despair in his conversation; his tone was neither vengeful nor forgetful. He knew that it was an unprincipled election. Political expediency had its price, but political dispossession, he argued, would have more disastrous consequences. As a community lost its sense of identity, its response to the savagery of racism could destroy the vision of a multi-ethnic society. Once that happened, the racist elements would have won.

The lights are switched on: we are descending at Nadi airport. Still no flutter in the heart; just a momentary worry whether they'll let me in. We land soon after midnight, to be greeted by the claptrap of tourists, stamping of visas and clanking of duty-free liquor (you're now allowed *three* litres, the shop notice proclaims in garish colors). As I wait for my baggage my eyes are drawn to a touristic mural on the opposite wall. All the faces are of native Fijians, giving a collective hibiscus smile. I am struck by the absence of Indian faces on that grotesque piece of commercial art. Perhaps the Indians are lucky not to be so crudely used. Then I pick up my luggage and turn: most of the customs officials and taxi drivers *are* Indians. In the Qantas and tourist ads, the Indians remain nameless, faceless, voiceless; in Fiji they are landless, and are slowly becoming countryless. They are the invisible people of Fiji, the outsiders within.

I walk straight to the immigration official, a young woman with a blue cap. The young don't remember old politicians. My passport is stamped; a young Indian customs inspector whispers: "Doc, just walk through." I walk out into the balmy night: my youngest brother is there, along with my eldest brother and his three married sons. We drive to my youngest brother's home behind Nadi town. We sit on the veranda and have cups of tea. It's 2 a.m., and Nadi is asleep. So is my mother. I shall see her at dawn.

I spend most evenings of my week-long stay in Maigania, where I was born, a village on the banks of the Nadi River. Across the river is a Fijian village, Molowai. The river used to be our meeting place: we swam in its waters, built sandcastles on its banks, and played *pakki* in what was known as Kalpu's *kund* (waterhole). On the riverbank we played soccer, ate pawpaws, drank coconuts, boiled and roasted corn on the cob. There was always an abundance of food, even after a flood. Occasionally we fished, bathed cows and horses, and looked at the village women,

Indians and Fijians, washing clothes together in the ever-flowing water. The men worked on the farms, harvested tonnes of cane, ate copiously and copulated with wanton abandon. My collection of poems, *Voices in the River*, was about this life by the banks of the river.

My first published short story after the coup, "Bro's Funeral," appeared in the *Canberra Times* in 1988. Distance had sharpened my awareness of my lost childhood, and given me a feeling for that stolen world. Bro is my brother's neighbour and friend, more than twelve years older than my brother. We call him *kaka*, father's younger brother. When Bro hears I am visiting my brother, he comes to see me: washed, brushed, with his hair well-oiled and combed, and dressed in a new pair of trousers and an immaculate white shirt; suited-booted, as my mother would say.

Bro is a farmer on a ten-acre farm given to his mother by the CSR Company after her *girmit*. He arranged the marriages of his eleven children, and himself remarried after the death of his first wife. He speaks proudly of his achievements: his cane-cutting ability, his sexual prowess under increasingly difficult circumstances, the marriages of his children, and, above all, his gumption in talking in English to anyone of importance.

"Kaka, where did you learn English?" we ask.

"I'm learning at my working, boyo." Bro had worked at the airport as a waiter, and then as a night watchman — the first job that brought him in direct contact with a European boss. It seems he was given the task of guarding a crane that dredged sand from the river for the building of the tarmac. One night it rained. Bro hadn't kept watch, and by the next morning the crane was down a few chains from its original position, under the swirling water, with only the top visible.

"Boy, mountain flooding, waterfalling. Me guarding the bloody *zhaam* crane. Morning I no see *zhaam* I go mad. What I telling the boss when he coming. I see in Kalpu's *kund*, the top of *zhaam* showing. All things under water. I no guarding, night sleeping. I swim flooding river to *zhaam*. Climbing the top and sticky there like glue. On top, right on top, boyo. I hanging like a bat, upside down. The supervisor come in army jeep. The sahib he look me over. He taking his helmet off. His red mouth wide open like a monkey *chutter*, bum. He say: "Ram, down man; coming down!" I say "No, boss. It's me dootie." Sahib shout: "You die there, Ram. All night you sitting there?" I say humbly: "Yes, bosso." The sahib crying. I weeping too."

The overseer was so impressed by Bro's dedication to duty that he promised him a week's holiday on full pay. Now Bro said, "But, sahib, me no swimming." Then the supervisor sent some Fijian boys in a motor boat to winch Bro off the submerged crane. As Bro scrabbled onto the dry bank, his Fijian friend, Lesu, hissed under his breath, "*Kaisi, kaiindia! Sa lasu! Lia lia*" (Stupid Indian, telling lies!). "*Barchod, chutia, Kaiuiti*" (Bloody Fijian idiot!), hissed Bro with a grin.

Most of Bro's stories deal with his uncanny ability to outwit the Europeans or the Chinese. He tells us of his first visit to Suva, when he knocked on the wrong door by mistake: "All houses looking the same to me in Suva."

The highlight of Bro's life was a cane-growers' meeting at the Regent Hotel, Fiji's only five-star hotel, on the edge of Nadi. Bro went as a delegate from his cane-harvesting gang: he drove his tractor close to the hotel complex, and parked it behind a bush. Bro marched into the hotel and bought a couple of quick whiskies, only to realize that in another room the drinks were being served free by Fijian waiters, paid for by the cane farmers. In an hour he was high, and ventured into a larger room, where all kinds of delicious cakes and desserts were arranged. He began devouring them. Then he saw some people going into the adjacent room, with Ratu Napolioni Dawai in the lead. Bro hid his tray under a chair and followed the party. Inside this room was laid a feast fit for kings. Bro had begun his lunch with desserts, and now he let himself go. " Boys, I'm eating like a *suwar* pig. Like Taniela." When Chief Napolioni Dawai saw him, he said kindly, "Hey, Ram, Bula. Have more, *turanga*. You pay for this, you know." Now Ratu Napolioni is dead, and the Regent belongs to the Japanese. "But boyo, me never eating like that day. Phew. Farting all the way home!"

The Nadi Tennis Club used to be exclusively for whites. Then a few Indians and Fijians who were sponsored by the members were allowed in, depending on their income. I go to play tennis there on Saturday afternoon, two nights after my arrival. The place is full of Indian members, their wives and children splashing in the pool. The players are mainly young Indian businessmen and a few teachers. Playing tennis on one of the courts is Harish Sharma, Fiji Deputy Prime Minister in the Bavadra coalition government. Harish and I talk intermittently between games, and I am sorry to hear that he is no longer in Parliament, having lost his seat by three votes in the last election. He invites me home for a drink, but I have to refuse, as I am leaving for Suva in the morning.

On my way to Suva I go through the one-street Nadi Town. Where Sukhdeo's wooden shop and Angie's café used to be there is now a three-storey concrete building, the Bank of Baroda. On the second floor Jasbir, my lawyer friend from Suva, is running his lucrative law practice. Jasbir and his partner John Cameron risked a lot to get us out of the colonel's clutches during the coups. Soon after, he went to Wellington, but then returned to practise in Nadi. He took over this office and its business from the daughter of A. D. Patel, who was Fiji's most prominent Indian politician during the pre-independence days. Patel died just before Independence, while presenting the farmers' case against CSR. Lord Denning gave the farmers a fairer deal, the Australian company withdrew after a century in Fiji, and the Fiji Indians never recovered from the death of their leader.

John Cameron has emigrated, and is somewhere in Perth. Recently he was refused permission to enter Fiji to attend a friend's funeral. None of the lawyers and politicians seems to care. "We're only minting money," one says proudly, and the gadgets in Jasbir's office patently show it. Fijian politicians are happy with the banal corruption and cupidity they have spawned, and not a few acquisitive Indians are revelling in merchant politics. We talk briefly of establishing a Human Rights and Civil Liberties group. We've never had anything like that in Fiji, and the nightmare of the coups may yet be repeated. The guardians of the law have simply become witnesses to the persecution. After admiring the gadgets and having a cup of coffee, I am on my way to Suva, the capital of Fiji.

As I drive out of town I am suddenly confronted by a massive new structure on the left, just a little beyond the tramlines. Subramanyam temple, Fiji's largest, is under construction. The design is based on the traditional architecture of the great South Indian temples, and many of the artisans carving images and idols have come from South India. Once built, it will be a major tourist attraction, as well as a place of worship for thousands of Hindus.

Among rich Hindus the religious fervour before the coups was for material prosperity. For all its spirituality, Hinduism is essentially of this world; a life of things adds substance and permanence to an otherwise uncertain existence. One had to thank god or gods for every blessing. For my father's generation Saraswati, the goddess of learning and wisdom, was paramount; now it is Lakshmi, the goddess of wealth. Everything is economic, that is where real power resides. We walked the streets of Suva feeling we had created it all, until ten masked gunmen and a third-ranking colonel shattered the illusion. And now, once again, our fatalism finds expression in our religion. There is little else to inspire hope or faith: but as I drive past that temple, I wonder why we have failed to produce a newspaper or a university, so integral to any community that has so much image-building to do and possesses so little land. Some Hindus are multi-millionaires, but would they donate money to build a university or start an education foundation, even when a whole generation of Indian children goes without training? To be without higher education in Fiji today is to become an urchin of the second colonialism.

With these thoughts I arrive at Cuvu secondary school, built two decades ago by the local farmers. Now it is a large school, catering for Indian and Fijian children. I go to a senior English class where two of my short stories are being taught. A real writer, no matter how small, creates a buzz in a school. I talk to the students — Fijians and Indians, boys and girls — about stories, about how to read and write them. Fiji, I tell them, is an unwritten world, but their lives and the lives of their parents, grandparents, neighbours are worthy of being written about. Their questions come with shyness and a quiet sharpness. How lucky they are to be studying together, and to have qualified teachers guiding them! This is the most creative act of subversion against the regime, a regime that wants separation along racial lines, not realizing that there is an inseparable humanity of those in bondage.

A few kilometres from Cuvu secondary school is Sigatoka town — a dilapidated little place known primarily as the birthplace of two Indian multi-millionaires, Hari Punja and Kanti Tappoo. In Sigatoka town is also Sir Vijay Singh, a lawyer and Fiji's first Indian knight, who has had a chequered political career. When I was dismissed from the university after my first election victory in 1982, he successfully fought in the Supreme Court to have me reinstated. During the immediate aftermath of the first coup, Sir Vijay's Suva office was virtually our political headquarters. But now his friends say that greed and the new virulence in politics have alienated him from his political colleagues. He went to Australia, but returned after almost four years to resume his uprooted life among those who had so swiftly supplanted him. I'd once given him Naipaul's *The Mimic Men*, thinking he'd see himself in its pages. I don't think he ever read it.

Sir Vijay's office is on the second floor of a grey, shabby concrete building. There I find him seated on a varnished wooden chair, behind a rough-hewn table. A fan is whirring at his feet, and he is wiping sweat from his forehead. A fly buzzes against an unopened window. We have a brief chat. He is embittered by the reception his friends gave him when he returned. The new politics his taken its toll: it is rough, mean and moneyed, something I thought Sir Vijay would understand. We leave him scrutinizing a brown file. My companion comments that for once Sir Vijay is earning his bread by the sweat of his brow. I wonder how long it will be before he bounces back; he always had the knack of entering the revolving door of politics behind you and coming out in front.

Soil has been piled on the flood-damaged Sigatoka bridge to allow cars to pass. The river still whirls with thick muddy water. On the other side the sugar-cane fields give way to lush bush. The devastating impact of cyclone Kina is scarcely visible here, though the houses look battered, the palm trees sway with broken fronds, and landslides have gashed the face of many a hill. The floods and winds from the cyclone here were worse than the *bara toofaan* — the big hurricane of which my grandparents had talked in our childhood. After Rabuka's coups Fiji didn't experience any major natural disasters, and fundamentalist Fijians said the Lord was happy with the colonel's treachery. Now some Indians are saying *"Bhagwan ke insaaf mein der hai, andher nahin"*: in God's justice there may be delay, but not injustice.

As I whiz past on the sea road, I feel the deep vulnerability of island life. Indian farms, Fijian villages — where all are poor, what can be gained? We drive past like tourists in our Japanese car, winding up our windows as the hawkers wave and shout.

I drive through my old constituency, from Navua to Suva. I was their MP for thirty-three days. It starts drizzling. I've always liked a soft rain falling; it curtains you from the rest of the world. We turn left at Suva Cemetery, where the signs say "Welcome to Suva City" and "The Wages of Sin is Death." On Prince's Road a huge Australian High Commission complex is being built. Further down on the right stands India House, the Indian High Commissioner's residence, vengefully closed by the military regime. The High Commission gave much to the people of Fiji. Even Rabuka studied in India; so did I, when opportunities for Fijian children were few and far between. But no Indo-Fijian politician will protest against the closure now, because a week ago Rabuka floated the idea of forming a national government. Both Indian parties covet the few powerless Cabinet positions. The colonel understands the greed of coolie children, and has cast his old net like a spell. But the political clout lies with the chiefs, and their power relies on keeping the Indians out of reach of power. If Rabuka's republic began to destroy their *mana*, the chiefs would end up as undertakers of their own anachronistic tradition.

I've never been quite at home in Suva; home for me is Nadi, even though I lived in Suva for almost twenty years. A little up the Prince's Road, I built a house of my own in 1984. I jokingly called it "A House for Mr Biswas," for I'd bought the land from a friend at a cocktail party, and another friend had found me a contractor soon after I was sacked from the university. We lived in it for barely thirteen months. I feel quite detached looking at this house from outside. It has been rented for the past few years, but it evokes no emotion in me, although it is the only piece of property my wife and I have owned in Fiji. The roof needs a new coat of paint. I don't go inside; instead, I decide to sell it to the tenants. Within three days it is sold, and I am once again homeless in paradise.

I meet up with a few former political colleagues; the unelected Deputy Speaker invites me for lunch at the new Parliament House, which is in session. I decline, saying that I won't go to that House until a non-Fijian, especially an Indo-Fijian, can dream of holding the highest elected office in the land, guaranteed by the constitution. The old Parliament Chamber lies forgotten, a grey pile of imperial stones. I have no desire to see the new Parliament House, which is built on a foundation of guns called, literally, Battery Hill. The Parliament in session is a babel of racial politics. It must be hell to listen daily to racist vilification in a place that should be a haven of conscience in the land.

Meeting so many people – lawyers, academics, politicians, farmers, businessmen – I get the sinking feeling that a relentless culture of corruption is in the making. To get a birth certificate you have to pay $10 to a clerk, for a business licence a little more. Is it really that bad? "Yes," comes the chorus. "Right at the top, the rot has set in." Such a perception of political and business life can easily lead to cynicism and self-contempt. It is the unenviable, inevitable consequence of a coup in any part of the Third World. "Look around," they whisper. "Who's building? Who's expanding the shops? Checked the directors' list?" The hospitals remain neglected. The new rich, the coup men and a few politicians are doing well through intrigue and corruption. People who have been through uncertainty and insecurity, both at personal and communal levels, don't want to be caught without money again. Power belongs to those who can buy it, and can manipulate those who think they have power.

Next day I go to visit a few colleagues at the university. It is still an oasis for both students and staff. New buildings cast long dull shadows. Tupeni Baba, my colleague at the university and as Education Minister in the Bavadra Cabinet, is now installed in my old room. His interest in politics has waned since Bavadra's death and the dissolution of the Coalition. He is now co-owner of some exclusive apartments where politicians stay during parliamentary sessions. "You must see it, Satend," he says with pride.

A floor below Tupeni's office is Sudesh Mishra, furiously preparing his next volume of poetry, writing a paper on postmodernist theory, revising his thesis for publication and desperately waiting for a postdoctoral award from Australia. I ask after Raymond Pillay and Subramani, two short-story writers: Pillay has gone to Wellington, and Subramani is in Sydney "secretly writing" his Fijian novel on torture. The playwright Jo Nacola, the most creative Fijian academic I know and the Minister for Natural Resources in Bavadra's cabinet, has made a political comeback, and is now Minister for Ethnic and Multicultural Affairs.

I am surprised that there is no nostalgia in me as I walk out of the campus I once knew like my village. Those who denied me a job unwittingly gave me liberty, which I now prize above all else. And my young friend, P. R. Sharma, the longest-serving member of the university's general staff, is dead; he committed suicide after his lean-to home was burnt by his neighbour. The kava basin in his room remains empty and dry.

In the afternoon I visit the place where I hid for four days during the second coup. Even my wife didn't know where I had gone. That became a joke among my friends, who were caught napping and taken to Naboro, a notorious prison for Fiji's most hardened criminals. One of my brothers built his house a street away from here. He is no longer there: he sold it cheaply and went to Auckland, because his contract as the University's deputy librarian was in jeopardy. Supporters of the coup and sycophants ruled the roost: self-respect demanded that I leave.

In the evening I drive back to Nadi. With my mother and brother I visit my second village, Lega Lega, where I spent my youth. The village is there, but my two brothers, a sister and many of my childhood friends have emigrated. We sit and count: almost a hundred. My mother remembers every name, which pleases me; her memory is as sharp as a cane-knife file. Now she lives in Nadi town, but the faces of the village grieve in her. Our orchard has disappeared: the jungle has been cut and made into a field that now lies fallow. If the Indians left Fiji, it would be as terrible as a landscape without trees.

I have to catch the early-bird flight next morning. Saying goodbye to an almost 80-year-old mother is not easy, and mothers never say goodbye to their children gladly. My brother drives me to the airport. As we pass the houses, with their occupants still asleep, I see the damage the cyclone has wreaked, but already leaves are sprouting on the trees again. If only coups too were like cyclones, there would be some hope of regeneration. But the casual brutality of a coup and the cunning betrayals of men take longer to heal than nature's *dharma*. I drive past the village, faintly visible in pre-dawn darkness, so deceptively quiet, full of so many damaged lives.

The airport is well lit, and our flight is on time. Our aircraft soars into the dawn over blue hills and green cane-fields. The tawdry little village-town is awash in half-light. I think of "Josephine" — is she, too, returning home? Then our plane is above the clouds, like an island lost in the undivided, indifferent ocean-sky.

As my son drives me home from the airport, I see the first leaves turning to gold. It is the beginning of a new season in Canberra. It is autumn, something I never experienced in Fiji, an epiphany of age and youth, father and son. We drive on a road that is strewn and stippled with dry, fallen leaves. The tree will soon stand starkly bare, like grief itself. To flower in spring it has to survive a leafless winter.

# R.K. Narayan

## Mother and Son

Ramu's mother waited till he was halfway through dinner and then introduced the subject of marriage. Ramu merely replied, "So you are at it again!" He appeared more amused than angry, and so she brought out her favourite points one by one: her brother's daughter was getting on to fourteen, the girl was good-looking and her brother was prepared to give a handsome dowry; she (Ramu's mother) was getting old and wanted a holiday from housekeeping: she might die any moment and then who would cook Ramu's food and look after him? And the most indisputable argument: a man's luck changed with marriage. "The harvest depends not on the hand that holds the plough but on the hand which holds the pot." Earlier in the evening Ramu's mother had decided that if he refused again or exhibited the usual sullenness at the mention of marriage, she would leave him to his fate; she would leave him absolutely alone even if she saw him falling down before a coming train. She would never more interfere in his affairs. She realized what a resolute mind she possessed, and felt proud of the fact. That was the kind of person one ought to be. It was all very well having a mother's heart and so on, but even a mother could have a limit to her feelings. If Ramu thought he could do what he pleased just because she was only a mother, she would show him he was mistaken. If he was going to slight her judgement and feelings, she was going to show how indifferent she herself could be. . . .

With so much preparation she broached the subject of marriage and presented a formidable array of reasons. But Ramu just brushed them aside and spoke slightingly of the appearance of her brother's daughter. And then she announced, "This is the last time I am speaking about this. Hereafter I will leave you alone. Even if I see you drowning I will never ask why you are drowning. Do you understand?"

"Yes." Ramu brooded. He could not get through his Intermediate even at the fourth attempt; he could not get a job, even at twenty rupees a month. And here was Mother worrying him to marry. Of all girls, his uncle's! That protruding tooth alone would put off any man. It was incredible that he should be expected to marry that girl. He had always felt that when he married he would marry a girl like Rezia, whom he had seen in two or three Hindi films. Life was rusty and sterile, and Ramu lived in a stage of perpetual melancholia and depression; he loafed away his time, or slept, or read old newspapers in a free reading room. . . .

He now sat before his dining leaf and brooded. His mother watched him for a moment and said, "I hate your face. I hate anyone who sits before his leaf with that face. A woman only ten days old in widowhood would put on a more cheerful look."

"You are saying all sorts of things because I refuse to marry your brother's daughter," he replied.

"What do I care? She is a fortunate girl and will get a really decent husband." Ramu's mother hated him for his sullenness. It was this gloomy look that she hated in people. It was unbearable. She spoke for a few minutes, and he asked, "When are you going to shut up?"

"My life is nearly over," said the mother. "You will see me shutting up once and for all very soon. Don't be impatient. You ask me to shut up! Has it come to this?"

"Well, I only asked you to give me some time to eat."

"Oh, yes. You will have it soon, my boy. When I am gone you will have plenty of time, my boy."

Ramu did not reply. He ate his food in silence. "I only want you to look a little more human when you eat," she said.

"How is it possible with this food?" asked Ramu.

"What do you say?" screamed the mother. "If you are so fastidious, work and earn like all men. Throw down the money and demand what you want. Don't command when you are a pauper."

When the meal was over, Ramu was seen putting on his sandals. "Where are you going?" asked the mother.

"Going out," he curtly replied, and walked out, leaving the street door ajar.

Her duties for the day were over. She had scrubbed the floor of the kitchen, washed the vessels and put them in a shining row on the wooden shelf, returned the short scrubbing broom to its corner and closed the kitchen window.

Taking the lantern and closing the kitchen door, she came to the front room. The street door stood ajar. She became indignant at her son's carelessness. The boy was indifferent and irresponsible and didn't feel bound even to shut the street door. Here she was wearing out her palm scrubbing the floor night after night. Why should she slave if he was indifferent? He was old enough to realize his responsibilities in life.

She took out her small wooden box and put into her mouth a clove, a cardamom and a piece of areca nut. Chewing these, she felt more at peace with life. She shut the door without bolting it and lay down to sleep.

Where could Ramu have gone? She began to feel uneasy. She rolled her mat, went out, spread it on the *pyol* and lay down. She muttered to herself the holy name of Sri Rama in order to keep out disturbing thoughts. She went on whispering, "Sita Rama Rama . . ." But she ceased unconsciously. Her thoughts returned to Ramu. What did he say before going out? "I am just going out for a stroll, Mother. Don't worry. I shall be back soon." No, it was not that. Not he. Why was the boy so secretive about his movements? That was impudent and exasperating. But, she told herself, she deserved no better treatment with that terrible temper and cutting tongue of hers. There was no doubt that she had conducted herself abominably during the meal. All her life this had been her worst failing: this tendency, while in a temper, to talk without restraint. She even felt that her husband would have lived for a few more years if she had spoken to him less . . . Ramu had said something about the food. She would include more vegetables and cook better from tomorrow. Poor boy . . .

She fell asleep. Somewhere a gong sounded one, and she woke up. One o'clock? She called, "Ramu, Ramu."

She did not dare to contemplate what he might have done with himself. Gradually she came to believe that her words during the meal had driven him to suicide. She sat up and wept. She was working herself up to a hysterical pitch. When she closed her eyes to press out the gathering tears, the vision of her son's body floating in Kukanahalli Tank came before her. His striped shirt and mill dhoti were sodden and clung close to his body. His sandals were left on one of the tank steps. His face was bloated beyond all recognition.

She screamed aloud and jumped down from the *pyol*. She ran along the whole length of Old Agrahar Street. It was deserted. Electric lights twinkled here and there. Far away a *tonga* was rattling on, the *tonga*-driver's song faintly disturbing the silence; the blast of a night constable's whistle came to her ears, and she stopped running. She realized that after all it might be only her imagination. He might have gone away to the drama, which didn't usually close before three in the morning. She rapidly uttered the holy name of Sri Rama in order to prevent the picture of Kukanahalli Tank coming before her mind.

She had a restless night. Unknown to herself, she slept in snatches and woke up with a start every time the gong boomed. The gong struck six through the chill morning.

Tears streaming down her face, she started for Kukanahalli Tank. Mysore was just waking to fresh life. Milkmen with slow cows passed along. Municipal sweepers were busy with their long brooms. One or two cycles passed her.

She reached the tank, not daring even once to look at the water. She found him sleeping on one of the benches that lined the bund. For just a second she wondered if it might be his corpse. She shook him vigorously, crying "Ramu!" She heaved a tremendous sigh of relief when he stirred.

He sat up, rubbing his eyes. "Why are you here, Mother?"

"What a place to sleep in!"

"Oh, I just fell asleep," he said.

"Come home," she said. She walked on and he followed her. She saw him going down the tank steps. "Where are you going?"

"Just for a wash," Ramu explained.

She clung to his arm and said vehemently, "No, don't go near the water."

He obeyed her, though he was slightly baffled by her vehemence.

# Mudrooroo Narogin
(formerly Colin Johnson)

## *A Missionary Would I Have Been*

Into the mountains, into those heaped-up rocks, all rising, all curved and pointed like the breasts of women, I came strutting: a crusader with a tarnished cross, or rather one of Peter the Hermit's motley band of cranks — but without even his zeal to keep on striding towards the illusion of a new Jerusalem. Was it a wonder that the end soon came?

The clouds pressed against the mountain-tips: babies suckling, lovers in a breeze-blown fantasy. Too old to be a baby — and so the eyes stared: the soft curves half unveiled by the fabric. The eyes glanced covetously, wished to possess: below the hips the swathed cloth of sari hid all shape, and so the eyes slid to the face — clung, eyes to eyes, searching and seeking for a love returned. Always not to know: love was going to bed with the other, but that did not ease the pain that slipped to another: an endless round!

The clouds moved from tip to tip, sliding down into the deep valleys, misting and turning objects into uneasy lumps. The eyes never seemed, *I was never sure*, to really meet in that attitude called *touching*. My pair looked, gazed and finally wanted to rip into that other which seemed to be deliberately with-holding what I felt was a colossal lack. "*Ah, if she only knew.*" — I consoled myself with that thought.

The foaming waters penetrated deep into the mountain-slopes, pushing away at the red and uncovering the grey of rock. The wind creased the clouds: how naked the hills and mountains lay. How soft, how desirable was a woman's body! And so my round eyes gazed into her almond eyes seeking to find. How the sun sparkled — really sparkled in the vivid blue of the high-mountain sky, and this brightness caused an upsurge of joy: every desire was shining with all the promise of fulfilment. But the clouds humped on the horizon, surged up, the sun rushed to them — "*I am ashamed*" — my eyes flew away and the sun had gone. "*Lord Jesus*", I muttered, "*protect and cherish me; keep me away from all sin*" — and felt no answer. My eyes stared away and up.

Above the road the *gonpa* squatted: a few low, grey wooden shacks about a yellow concrete cube of temple topped by a smaller rectangle on which a short stubby spire of brass diminished rung by rung to the final cone. Above the road the monastery squatted: a noise of cymbals, bells and trumpets surrounded by the ceaseless flapping of prayer-cloth strips edging long tall poles. *"Oh Lord Jesus protect me from all alien creeds"* — and my eyes fell below to the safety of the thin black road twisting and looping along the side of the ridge and around and around and about the curving railway track that wound leading to Darjeeling.

Now along that narrow way I was walking to where, below the monastery and across the road hung a petrol station: swirling cars and labouring trucks curved in and out — and next to that garage lay the tea-shop-shack in which she lived.

There I drank tea and gazed and gazed into her face: a love-lorn *Krishna* aching for his *Radha*. There was too much useless suffering in the world: only the celibate knew how to suffer desire and the desire not to desire. She looked, she looked, her eyes held mine and I fell. Once she saw me and called me to her — and now I could not leave. "Gentleman," she sang — and I fell. She mocked me — never was I priest, father, *swamiji* — only a man! *"O Jesus, Mary and Joseph am I lost?"* My prayers unanswered, and the sun moved towards the earth. Long strips of clouds glowed, then reddened with passion. The earth lay quietly waiting — a bitch on heat! And lured, then hooked, then reeled in I was pulled again and again to the tea-shop where I sat and watched the holy strips of cloth tugging at the long poles black against the sky. *"St Francis keep me in thy bosom and protect me from pain, from sin and from the desire to sin!"*

And I came and came — to watch the tiny rail engines, loud with shrieks of whistles and sooty with great belchings of black smoke, struggling to pull lines of blue match-box carriages up and along the ridge towards Darjeeling. Her hair, so midnight black, falling about the pale oval of her face. Her beauty, a cliche from oriental mythology. Her glancing eyes, her lips shaping smiles, her tongue fully extended in the mountain gesture of appreciating a joke. And her English words increased as did my Nepali. *"Namestay,* how are you?" *"Tikay, beto hos." "Ek glass, chah timee."* So mixed up, all mixed up — stupid phrases like: "You are happy today"; "You look very beautiful"; "Don't laugh" — and my hand formed about my face her cliche beauty: the thick black glossy hair flowing about the heartshaped face in which the huge eyes, encircled by *kohl,* glowed, mocking my status and my God. Her lips were red and full, shaped like the cliche bow, and her small even teeth were milky white, while her cheeks were a vivid pink from

from too much rouge.

The sun flashed and was gone in an instant; the clouds heaved and struggled; rain tumbled down. Desire surged about, a bridge collapsed, and the rain fell and fell—pounding the ground and finally slashing the road in two. My face lost its smile. My idol believed all was God and paid homage to a holy-man with a halo of hair, who worked miracles. *"Thou sufferest that woman Jezabel to teach and mock thy servants and thy teaching."* And the bridge was repaired, the road made one, and again the trains rattled down towards the plains and heaved up to the mountain top. The clouds separated and roamed across the skies and across the valleys to smother the hillsides in ever-shifting mists. And I saw her stand in her doorway, her eyes drowsy and heavy-lidded, laden with the hot dreams of mystery cities like Bombay and Calcutta: the homes of her movie idols. And I watched her split her wood and wash her clothes, her face and even her feet. She was a peasant my mind screamed, and the *gonpa* vanished in an instant mist that veiled the hideous images grimacing down in mockery at my weakness. To have come so far for this!

The clouds heaved together, the heavy rain tumbled and tumbled: all was one heavy wet cloud—and my face had lost its smile. I felt like fleeing the beloved, I felt like tormenting the beloved with my torment. *"I will hurt her, I will never come here again—it's too wet anyway; besides she is a peasant while I am a teacher—almost a priest."* And through the rain I ran down to the shop to order *"Chah,"* and sipped watching the waters flow. Her laughing face, her eyes caused bliss—but I could not touch, only look. And if I did not see her the whole day collapsed about me in the gloom of the constantly dropping rain.

Impregnated the earth brought forth shrubs and grasses, which in their turn gave birth to buds that waited for the sun to flower. Rain and then a little warmth was all that was necessary—and next to the beloved, in her warmth I listened to the rain and wished to echo the rhythm of the rain. *"O gentle Jesus protect me from harm."* And she was vulgar, too many films she had dreamt herself into. The sidelong glance, the stance, a ludicrous wink, even the flung kiss from hand—all borrowed from films. How vulgar she was, with her forehead *tika* dot and lipstick a purple-pink and her sari a scarlet-red. The rains fell and fell. One goal could be gained, two opposing goals—never! To have desire was to lose one's pride. She looked at me, laughed "Gentleman"—and like a dog I pricked my ears. *"Kyahein, what?"*—to sip tea and talk to her in a mixture of English-Nepali in an effort to get her to Darjeeling, to get her alone, to have her: to be free of her.

"Darjeeling, *hami janoo bioscope*—one night, back." To gesture along the road and back. *"Ney, mata, pita"*—to finish in gestures of slapping and the pulling of hair.

To finish in the sound of gongs and bells from the monastery. How to end it? How to fulfil it? In homeopathic medicine a small quantity of poison was used to expel a larger dose of the same lethal venom. To be rid of the poison of the beloved I would use the venom of lust and disgust. Love would be expelled by love. An absurd plan born of the overheard whispers of boys telling of the evils of Darjeeling. Best to confess and do penance. Confession and penance was the answer. *"Bless me father for I have sinned. It is a week since my last confession and I am plagued by bad thoughts and dreams." "Say six Hail Marys every night before going to sleep. Go in peace and sin no more." "Thank you father."* The rain eased a little, then hesitated. *"Hail Mary full of grace the Lord is with thee—save me from temptation."* The sun streaked light across the mountain breasts—to vanish, and the rain rushed down upon me. But the road to Darjeeling remained open.

Darjeeling, that like a slut to her mop, clung to the mountain ridge with her dirty face flung towards the towers of the castle of Katchenjunga, gleaming pure-white in the season without clouds. But the town now rotted under the rain. And to that town I came, clinging like a leech to a cow, on a jeep—to be flung off into the bustle of the market place. Grey wooden stalls in grimy rows hanging with gaudy trinkets fondled by the light fingers of the dainty beautiful Nepali women, stacked with piles of bright cloth caressed by the dark fingers of the plainswomen. And I eased myself among them letting my eyes meet theirs and feeling the breath of their passing saris. I tossed a coin to a heap of grey rags and received a heathen *"Ram, Ram"* from thick bearded lips. A damp *sadhu*, clad only in an army greatcoat, strode along with swinging long matted locks. *"Bom Shankar!"* he grinned mockingly into my eyes. Too many heathen gods hung on their lips and walls: the blood of the Lamb had not cleansed this place—had only become one of the multitude to be grouped along with *Shiva, Ram, Krishna, Vishnu.* Perhaps one day he would be classified as: Jesus Christ, Indian god of Euro-Semitic origin. Only the pure sword could cleanse this land—and me! I thought of my plan and of the suffering that brought relief—to suffer, to descend into hell: to put the plan into action, to be dirty: by the grace of God to rise cleansed.

And so, anonymous, freed from the feeling of identity I was free to act. I slipped away from the bazaar area up steps leading towards the better part of the town. Then the rain again began to fall—like a white mist of sperm. The clouds bulged heavy with dripping lust. Passing girls talked, flat faces flashed smiles at one another, pointed faces threw discontent. Today I was not a priest-to-be teacher — no, today I was free to enter an eating house just edging into the class above the low and dirty. It was Tibetan, but with the eternal Indian calendar gods pushing against a shrine to the living god — the *Dalai Lama*. And I sat on a bench at the back feeling nervous, for I had done no such thing as this before.

I ordered a plate of meat from a grinning little-English speaking boy and picked at it while watching heavy-set Tibetan women muffled in thick full skirts, shape meat patties. A radio blared soprano-voiced, eastern-western music, and I watched a man gulping down a glass of the white spirit which I had heard called *Arak*. I thought to order, but afraid of its potency instead asked for the weaker Tibetan beer — *Chang*. The boy's grin broadened and he brought a bottle of the liquid together with a dirty glass. I sipped and watched the day drifting into the night. Today I had not seen her or drunk her tea.

The rain increased to a torrent; figures scurried past, and befuddled by the beer my plan hung in my head. To continue or let all be: how to get the bitter fruit and effect the cure? The light had fallen into the rushing darkness when a Nepali man, wearing the small *Gurkha* black-pot cap with a silver badge of crossed knives, staggered to my table, sneered at my beer and called for *"Arak."* We drank. Words — "Where from?"; "Where stay!"; "What doing?" — attempted to cross the void. Outside the water hissed down to the earth; inside the light escaped from a bare sealed glass bulb. The *Arak* rushed to my stomach, spread up and provided the courage to enquire about women. The man looked intently at me, smiled quite beautifully, then said: "I know, you friend, I tell you. Not far from here — I go with you." His eyes glazed, brightened: "You know Karventer's shop and motor stand behind. There railing, go through it, down steps and you find — number 99!" The rain stopped for a moment, the darkness hung, the radio stuttered, and another Nepali came to the table to firmly and gently lead the drunken man away. His feeble protests moved out of the door, but he had left his information behind.

The smell and taste of the *Arak* sickly clinging to my mouth. Darkness of the night spaced by a few weak lights. Shadows of things and one or two wayfarers. The rhythm of my footsteps and another's. Her: her face, her body flowed from my crushed mind to glide in front of me. I saw her there: to forget, to remember; to push physically with my hands at that image which had turned and faced me. To kill it, to push forward; to conquer and to win — to lose, to give away: shame! *"Jesus,*

*Mary and Joseph save me from myself. St Francis even now it's not too late to stop this thing!"* Unanswered: the railing, twin bars of cold iron dripping with the moisture of my fear. *"Even now it's not too late to stop this thing"* — no answer: through and bending forward, the rush of water beating at the umbrella fabric and scattering on the slippery stone steps.

Splashing feet and the dark shadows filled with the imaginary forms of beckoning women. *"Must I do this thing?"* A man, a sorrowful black dog, plodded past. Tunnel of alley oozing slime; failing steps slippery with my desire — worn with my countless thoughts. The way to destruction: a mis-shapen shadow of a sentinel tree. *"Then I saw that there was a way to hell, even from the gates of heaven, as well as from the city of destruction"* — thus, the roaming words of a song seemed to chant. *"Kab kahanthe"* — when, where? No one — how could I do this thing? Silence, blankness — emptiness: no whores, only the wind and the rain, my dripping umbrella, and the light which suddenly materialised a man: "You want girl?" "Yes." "Come."

Lightning suddenly seared across the great voidness called sky to show the emptiness of alleys down which two rats scurried. Again lightning seared to show the remounting of the slippery rocks called stairs. The dark rain rained water — like piss flooding a urinal. Lightning seared: the white rain spurting like sperm into the womb of the earth. "How far? Where going?" I asked my companion, a Nepali with a thick moustache and a supernatural smile. "Number 99 — come!" Followed to the sacrifice, to the release — the purging, the purification: the water was swallowing the earth!

Lightning flashed into existence an arched opening leading into the bowels of the earth. Such thick darkness within, a curtain seeming to be violently agitated by the moaning wind. A hand groped to my hand, touched and held — to pull me inside! A woman's hand — impossible to see her face or body. Nothing, except the felt solid existence of that hand pulling me into the tunnel; pulling me, stumbling along a passageway running with water running out of the subterranean depths. Nothing! — then a curtain pulled aside: a single candle flickering light onto dirty walls pasted with torn-out magazine pictures of cinema actresses staring fixedly out in simulated lust. Another flickering flame, a faint gleam level with my forehead: her god, four-armed and passively white, stared out of a boyish face, and below him danced a black devil in a foam of fire. Travesty of religion: to have religion in such a place. Barbaric idolism that Christ meant to banish from the world — with the sword: the cleansing by blood! *"Our Father, holy Mary, all the blessed Saints—I am lost!"* — in this dim dirty cave that reeked with vileness, that held the vileness of a filthy couch covered with a *grimy* sheet. *"Sweet Jesus, what must I do? Stay, be purified—or what?"* An answer not received I sat on the bed and waited for the cleansing fire. Before my eyes her demon-god flung a skull at my head. My face seemed to drip blood and my ears ached with the chanting of infernal vespers. And worst of all—Oh God!—she was monstrous and old. A witch: the devil had caught me.

*"Das rupee?"*

*"Achah."*

"All night—*bis rupee.*"

*"Achah—Arak?"*

"*Ek rupee, bis paisa* one bottle."

*"Achah."*

To get drunk, not to think or be. Once there had seemed to be love. How vile everything was. Especially that horribly leering face which struggled to hold the expression of a young girl. An old woman playing the part of a seductive film actress: how awful to watch a young girl struggling out of an old woman. But strangely desire begun; strangely in that hell lust quivered and arose—for her! She danced out and returned with the bottle, a blanket and a clean sheet—then began playing coy. Imprisoned in a nightmare I was forced to play her game bereft of the power to flee into the light. I sought a refuge in drunkenness. With drunkenness lust turned urgent—I reached for her and she recoiled. Then began a game of hide-and-seek with her body: offering, with-holding, coming together, pulling apart—an old virgin whore. *"Jesus, Mary, Joseph"*—she left the cave.

Tibetan gods leered down: sought to possess, to hold, to conquer. Heathen demons: ugly, corrupt—beyond corruption. Dancing on corpses—on death; rattling human bones, draining skulls of their brains; uniting in foul copulation—too soon to come true! I was lost! Hideous scene—beautiful scene of my damnation. No—of my purging! *Arak*, more *Arak* what matter—desire! The demons entered my heart and danced in my body. The witch returned, changed into a short shift: impossible travesty of a goddess. The soft curves beneath the fabric. Too ugly to be ugly—far beyond. *"Oh sweet Jesus, gentle Mary save me from strange compelling deities."* And I surrendered to the moment—to this thing! Her body so beautiful, the fluttering candle; the soft breasts flowing, flowing beneath my hands, the water pelting hard above—rattling, rushing down. The drops falling, gleaning in the light: jewels dripping one by one. And all the restless night fell into the rush of the rain, into the smell of urine, of vomit—the painted face: too real to be real. The body above, beneath; the foaming waters—the fall into the abyss. How soft, how desirable was a woman's body. The warmth, the time flowing towards the spent morning.

Dawn rising to flow in and over the night-time going away with the rain that overflowed in puddles lying cold and inert. Stillness of the early hours, neither morning nor night; stillness of the soul after its panic flight. I looked up into the dark-grey of the sky where a few piercing stars hung. I looked up into the pearl-grey of the sky and at the mountain-ridge behind which the full-flush of day lay. Then rays of light, God's fingers splayed up to reveal the hidden sun. The bazaar area lay empty and soaking with the fragile frames of the stalls leaning sleepily together in the growing light. A thin bearded beggar, wrapped in numberless rags, squatted in a doorway and yawned, rubbing his eyes into wakefulness. The motor-stand stood silent. Without noise or motion the vehicles were sleeping like old coolies worn and emaciated by life-times of profitless drudgery.

A man clanged into existence—a doctor performing an emergency operation; and another man emerged from behind the vehicle—the nurse. I approached them.

"Jeep?"

"*Gharry ney*—road broken, *bahut pani.*"

"Later?—"

A shrug, and I decided to walk the few miles to the school. The sun's golden hair showed above the ridge, and strands fell upon the trees and sparkled off the leaves. Its forehead appeared, and then its face. Above, the dark hue of sky gleamed with the new morning. A few tiny puffy clouds drifted far away. It was a beautiful clear bright day that had been purged by the lashings of the dark rain. And I seemed to feel the liquid eyes of God following my every moment—*but should it be the eyes of the Goddess?* Blasphemy: there was only one God and he was male. God was not, could not be female—she who was the lacerated earth terrorised by the male passion of God. I seemed to hear a snigger. The old prostitute's eyes glared in mockery: bloodshot and wise, accepting and giving: more goddess than demon-ness. No!—a witch's face: once such people were burnt.

Above the clear sky sparkled the earth below. A heavy trunk rested across the road; its roots poked up still shedding earth, while its leaves hung over the road-edge still into the sky. The streaming earth steamed, while the misty hills lay like a woman—and the road ran, black and glistening, littered with fallen boulders and debris, between her thighs, to end in a rush of converging red. I walked on and reached the place where the earth had miscarried, had laboured to bring forth shapeless mud. I stopped and looked for a way around, and saw that the hill-slopes had been raped, that the flesh of the earth had been rent and the skin slashed as if by the claws of a monstrous animal. I picked my way over the mud to come to a group of houses that once stood whole beside the roadway. Now they gaped open like the slashed bellies of pregnant women. The land had been raped, the road lay broken and the railway line spanned a chasm. I stepped onto the swaying tracks. Miraculously they held and I was across—to a man who stood: emotionless, expressionless. He sung out: "Sahib, Sahib, road dangerous—broken. Very bad, many people dead." "Yes."—unable to feel the many deaths. The day was so beautiful, the sun so warm, the faint breeze so pleasant on my skin: all felt so fresh and purified.

I walked on, closer and closer to her. What would I feel when I saw her? Now she seemed of the dead past. A bend, beyond was the petrol station. I saw its yellow *Shell* sign. Across a bridge, below the heavy rush of water rushed sparkling. Near to the garage, and beside it—emptiness! Mud had flowed like water down over the fragile boulders of the shacks. And I saw at the bottom of the slope tiny men poking in the mud and pulling a tinier thing from the slush. Two men carried it up and up towards where I stood and waited and watched. The night had purged the day. She was coming to me: purification sacrifice: a dead child born from a dead mother—what matter? I stared down until they reached me and laid her down at my feet. Dead matter: the body, the face broken: a red of flesh under the red of earth: the matted hair stiff and brown like a clump of dead grass. I looked at the dead thing and thought that perhaps I should arrange a burial and say the service. But I was not a priest—never to be a Priest! What matter?—dead matter!

"Five persons", a man gestured downwards where more things were being pulled forth. "Three *kuties,*" he gestured at the slope where the shacks once clung. "Many," he gestured about.

No more "Gentleman, gentleman"—oh God!

Numbed I stumbled off along the road. Above the road the *gonpa* squatted; the prayer-strips rose a little in the breeze, and the sun caused the spire to glisten golden. A patch of mud and I detoured along a path edging the road a few feet above. Then I jumped down, and onto a black coiled length of body. Struck!—I gazed down to watch the snake writhe away in terror. It was a miniature of the road, but whole not broken. I gazed at my leg, shrugged, then walked on.

# Njabulo S. Ndebele

## *Guilt and Atonement: Unmasking History For The Future*

A few years ago I began to write a novel which I called "The Mask of the Fatherland." It was meant to be about a young Afrikaner boy in the South African Defence Force who during the war in Angola discovers the many masks that he and his tribe have had to wear over the centuries as they tried to justify their mission on earth. After much planning and research, I found I could not write the novel. At the root of the problem was that I simply did not know my main character. I did not know the simplest things about him. What was his mother fond of saying to him? Did he dream of his childhood sweetheart? Did he have problems revealing his feelings? Who were his neighbourhood friends, and what kind of mischief as boys did they get into? Does he have any strong thoughts about TV, about the Space Shuttle? What kind of home conditions his thinking? All I had was a treasure house of stereotypes for which I had no use.

I look at the times in which we live right now and I ask the question: am I in a position to write this novel? I know that I still cannot write it. At bottom is the fact that I do not know the people that my hero belongs to as a real, living community. At this time when Berlin walls of various kinds are falling, I am aware of a wall that is as formidable as ever. It is the wall of ignorance. At this time when the spirit of reconciliation is supposed to bring South Africans together, South Africans don't know one another as a people. Can we as a nation write the novel of the future under these conditions? If so, what are the preconditions for such novels to be written? What does it take for us to know one another? What *will* it take?

The African struggle for liberation was coming along. Somewhere it appeared to flounder and then it stopped to take another form. What characterises the nature of the transformation is that those who opened the prison doors were not victorious crowds pursuing a defeated enemy in flight. They were opened by an enemy who had declared that he was now a friend. To date, he still holds the keys. When it suits him, he haggles over conditions, trying to prescribe the manner in which the new friendship is to be carried out, prompting the following questions. Are those who did not forcibly bring down the doors victorious? Have those who still hold the keys been defeated? There is a stand-off that offers no certitude. We are aware of those who are driven by hope, the supposed victors, and those who are driven by fear, the supposed losers. The danger is that a situation such as this can breed the most debilitating ambiguity in which we oscillate between hope and despair with a frequency that induces undefined bitterness and cynicism.

This situation of ambiguity may very well suggest that what we see is a chaotic play of masks: the masks of conciliation or reconciliation whose colourfulness may suggest a fragile essence, the absence of an underlying form. One such mask is the expression "the new South Africa." It is a sonorous expression fraught with much meaning and meaninglessness all at once. It spawns various masks that suggest many possible forms that this "new South Africa" may take. Who, anyway, invented the phrase? Was it the anxious "defeated" or the hopeful "victors"? Whatever the case might be, at the end of the day we still ask: what exactly is behind each mask? What is the reality so steadfastly hidden by the rhetoric of hope and anxiety?

It is part of the writer's task to strive to unmask. We are confronted by so many surfaces in our day-to-day lives. So many masks. Writing enables us to crack the surface and break through to the often deliberately hidden essence. What we find may either bring joy or sadness, hope or despair, but almost always yields insight. It is this masking and unmasking that often constitutes the terrain of conflict between the writer and official culture. Writers strive to remove the blanket which officialdom insists on spreading and laying over things. When officialdom is under attack and lacks confidence, it is the new one that constructs masks.

Let us step back and reconstruct the situation briefly. It is interesting to note that we have just come from a situation in which the South African government *(this very present government)* did not even attempt to mask anything. On the contrary, it seems to have even enjoyed what most of us saw as obscene exhibitionism. It was characterised by brazen acts of public cruelty and terrible laws. It was a public dance of indecency choreographed from parliament. Some masking, of course, took place at the level of ideology. Attempts were made to justify the manifest and most observable horror through the propounding of apartheid philosophy.

Of course the oppressed had no option but to live with and to subsist in the terrible reality created. From that perspective, denied a say in matters pertaining to their health, housing, education, employment, recreation, they focused their attention on the justificatory arguments, since we cannot but respond to speech. They grappled with the logic of apartheid.

February 2, 1990 represented the strategic withdrawal of the argument. "Strategic" because, indeed, it was known all along that the argument was a lie, that it had been constructed for a purpose: to systematically entrench white power through a range of instruments of domination. Now all is in place, the red herring can be done away with and it will all seem like defeat. In fact, this is victory at the very moment that defeat is being proclaimed.

Of course, it will take generations in a normal time sequence for blacks to produce enough academics, engineers, industrialists, doctors, corporate managers, archivists, pilots, etc. to make a real competitive difference in the actual play of power in the governance of the country. Their land of milk and honey, according to the current flow of events, still seems a remote possibility.

In fact, just as they had no option but to accept the conditions of life imposed on them, if they want to experience some semblance of freedom, in the short term, they may have no option but to fit into the available business and civil service culture and rise through the ranks. Suddenly, where the various structures of such a culture represented exclusion and repulsive, exploitative white power, now they may represent opportunity. The glitter of apartheid: buildings, banks, etc., previously an index of the oppressed's powerlessness, now represent, disturbingly, the possibility of fulfilment.

But such fulfilment comes at a price. Everything has been thought out for us: our inventive capacity is harnessed according to the demands of a structured business and industrial culture. The brazen oppression of the past can now become the seductive oppression of having to build and consolidate and enjoy what was achieved at our expense. There will be the attractive tendency to accept all this as the spoils of struggle. But who are likely to take advantage of this situation?

This situation is likely to split the black community into those who, worn out by the struggle, seek immediate relief, and those who, seeing the dangers of a short-term accommodation, wish to press ahead. Indeed, the ambiguities and contradictions of the times throw up painful choices to grapple with intellectually.

Terrible choices! We can choose between absorption and

accommodation on the one hand, and, on the other hand, the quest for a self-created reality. The former promises short-term relief for the few who can make it, and discontent for the vast masses who see no relief in sight. The latter choice may even prompt the question: was the armed struggle perhaps abandoned too soon? Could a year or two not have driven home more dramatically to the whites of our country the real nature of the demand of the oppressed for liberation? Did all the painful struggles of the past terminate so abruptly so that an all-white cricket team can go to India triumphantly without the baggage of guilt? Who did it represent? Certainly not me. Do people who still ask for old national emblems really know what is going on? Where is the future we have wanted to build with our hands and our imaginations from the ashes of the past?

Terrible choices! We can choose between freedom through the agony of destructive strife and struggle, on the one hand, and on the other, the anxiety born of the need for security, the choice to hang on to a known reality, no matter how problematic (after all there can be legitimate burn-out after long years of struggle and hope for deliverance); between reconstruction and accommodative consolidation; between war and negotiation.

One of the prices we can pay for choosing the illusion of freedom is to forget about the past and enjoy the present as much as we can. After all, apartheid laws are gone, what do we want now?

In fact, there is a concerted attempt by those responsible for apartheid to forget about the past and to convince everyone else to do so. Not too long ago, Roelof ("Pik") Botha, addressing the Australian press club, declared that he has also fought against apartheid. So the ANC, PAC and other liberation groups really have no special claim to the attention of the world. Of course, Pik Botha has his heroic, invisible scars to show for it: he has been banned, tortured, detained without trial, forced into exile, maimed in SADF raids in Lesotho and Botswana and then recalled to be rewarded with a cabinet post by the government of his nightmares. This tactic represents not only a brazen distortion of historical fact, but can also be regarded as an obscene attempt to appropriate the struggles of those who have been victims of his government in order to belittle the significance of the liberation struggle. What gives him the right to do this? I registered in myself the flickers of rage as I listened to our Minister of Foreign Affairs perform.

Certainly it now seems to me that the negotiation atmosphere has created a false moral equation between the Nationalist Party (the authors of our horror novel) and its government on the one hand, and the liberation movement on the other. It is an equation that has given our white compatriots a right they previously and still do not have: the right to judge our struggle. It is an equation in which the liberation movement perhaps saw the possibility of some strategic gains for the struggle. But clearly, the government saw the possibility of consolidating white power without the baggage of the past. In effect, there is no equation but conflicting interests in a balance in which one thing that is certain is the uncertainty of the future.

One should not be seen to be harping on the evils of the past. But we have to cry out when the past is being deliberately forgotten in order to ensure that what was gained by it can now be enjoyed without compunction. It is crucial at this point that the past be seen as a legitimate point of departure for talking about the challenges of the present and the future. The past, no matter how horrible it has been, can redeem us. It can be the moral foundation on which to build the pillars of the future. If so, what are the implications of keeping the past alive?

Should the oppressor now feel guilty about it? Guilt, in this situation, may be healthy. It may represent a healthy recognition of the moral flaws of the past and the extent of one's responsibility for them.

But guilt is like pain: not many of us would like or wish to inflict it on others. We cannot call forth the guilt of others. Guilty people are not pleasant people to live with. They are tense, unpredictable, and unhappy. Guilt on a massive social scale is not healthy.

And the oppressed? Should they feel shame? Yes, to the extent that they should recognise their humiliation and vow never to go through it again. Beyond that, a prolonged feeling of shame on a massive social scale may perpetuate inferiority.

Yes. It is at this point that we move away from shame and guilt to call for the atonement of justice. It is justice we must demand, not guilt. We must demand justice.

But the balance of forces at this juncture is such that we may not even be able to get justice. Is justice possible in a situation in which the following questions are still being asked? Given the current balance of forces and the need for democracy and equality in the short term:

How do we dispossess those who took the land by unfair means?
How do we remove from power those who won it by conquest?
How do we take away privileges and resources from those who
  accumulated them by unfair means?

Because of the balance of forces, I am unable to answer these questions. This inability I find debilitating. It spawns frustration and may even lead to something I have steadfastly fought in the past: bitterness. For indeed, to borrow from Jay Reddy's quotation in her address, "the end of apartheid seems to represent for the white minority a defeat in which they have lost nothing." It leads me to the uncomfortable perception that at a time when justice has to prevail (because the advent of freedom represents historical redress), there seems no objective basis on which to promote it. There is no manifest objective base to support the moral law. Entrenched privilege, entrenched and pervasive institutional and social power, entrenched poverty, ill health, joblessness, lack of opportunity, lack of housing: all these persist *with a vengeance*! All these still constitute the universal reality of our times.

Guilt? it is not something we need to spend too much time on. Guilt is irrelevant. But why is it likely to crop up in discussions of the need for redress? Essentially because the struggle is unresolved. Its end has not been decisive. Paradoxically, it may benefit the whites to keep us demanding their guilt. For guilt is a red herring that gives us the illusion that in dealing with it we are engaged in combat. It enables us to deal with the illusion while leaving the reality intact. It may even represent the reinvention of protest. The demand for justice, on the other hand, is more immediately and concretely threatening: *it keeps our attention firmly on the search for the actual process of redress.*

Those who have lost should properly experience loss, not guilt. Those who feel guilty may feel this way precisely because they have not lost, and yet see the legitimacy of the demands on them, and the possibility and even the need to lose something. The bold and the arrogant among them may even say: why should I feel guilty anyway? I deserve everything I have. Of course, yes. They deserve every bit of it, because at the individual level, people may very well have worked hard for what they possess. Of course, no. The entire social context in which those personal struggles took place was seriously flawed. Ultimately, individuals who have benefited from that flawed environment cannot deny responsibility. To deny responsibility is to affirm indirectly the perception that there has indeed been no change.

There is one area of negotiation that produces many heated words: Affirmative Action. It is designed not to make people lose jobs, but to ensure that those who have been left out previously through parliamentary injustice can find jobs. And there lie the problems.

Whenever I hear this expression, affirmative action, I boil inside. Affirmative action represents concessions that the powerful make for the oppressed. In the land of its origins, the United States of America, affirmative action is a strategy to manage the demand for redress for those who can never hope ever to seize the instruments of government as a group. The context of their struggle has been civil rights, not national liberation. In South Africa, to adopt this strategy is to distort our perceptions of the objective goal; it enables us to assume the mentality of being a dominated minority, rather than experience ourselves as a struggling, free majority, free even to make mistakes. Free, to quote Babel, to write our bad novels.

Affirmative action is a programme for the oppressed. Free people talk about the need for education and skills in a reconstructive national environment. Free people appreciate the need to learn from experience. They are not chained to keeping going something they had no part in establishing; they are not chained to the need to maintain efficiency that does not contain the content of their lives. They learn through the sweat and frustrations of reconstruction. They know that the future will not be easy; that there are new things to be learned; that during the struggle they accumulated so much experience that as a result there is so much that they are good at, and that it is that experience that must form the new society.

The maintenance of corporate efficiency will not be sufficient justification to keep people oppressed, to deny people freedom. Reference is always being made to the "chaos" in the north. One will not deny many of the allegations. But in reality, the "chaos" up north is the chaos of historically free people making their own and understandable mistakes, which they learn from. It is a much better lesson for it calls for the kind of creative involvement in the search for solutions which makes people experience themselves as true participants in history.

Paulo Freire has said that only the oppressed can free both themselves and their oppressors from the shackles of the past. But for the oppressed to feel that the moral high ground belongs to them, they have to experience themselves as having the power to be magnanimous, generous, and forgiving. Do the oppressed feel that power in our country at this point in our history?

No. I cannot and can never demand other people's guilt; but I do want justice. I cannot ask people to confess their sins, or to indulge in any kind of self-flagellation (unless they do so voluntarily—even though I would never enjoy the sight of them doing so). Guilt is too personal a feeling. To demand it of someone is to invade a personal domain that can result in humiliation. It results in no solace for both sides. Justice, on the other hand, yields not humiliation but knowledge and responsibility.

And the search for justice is the path by which the struggle for redress is dramatised, and the means by which the struggle between fairness and unfairness is made visible through a legitimate institutional instrument. It leads to decisive corrective action.

The past is knocking constantly on the doors of our perceptions, refusing to be forgotten, because it is deeply embedded in the present. To neglect it at this most crucial of moments in our history is to postpone the future.

# Ngitji Ngitji

(formerly Mona Tur)

## The Possum Woman

*This legend is dedicated to my late beloved mother, who passed away 9 December 1978. For many years, Mother told my sister and I this legend. Our mother was an Antagaringa Elder. — N.N.*

Long ago in the Dream Time, a man and his wife lived in a far-away country. These two would sleep by day. Each night, the woman would go hunting possums. She would take up her killing stick. Her husband would hear her singing in the distance:

"I'm going to kill the possums by pulling them out of the hollow of the trees."

The possum woman was very tall with beautiful long hair which hung to the ground. When she caught the possums she would tie them up on top of her head with her hair and a string made of animal hair. When she returned home in the morning she would undo her hair. All of the possums fell out. Her husband then cleaned the possums, cooked meat and later on, when ready, put the meat in a bark shelter to eat.

One night the husband felt uneasy when his wife was ready to go hunting. His nose made a cracking noise, which means bad luck. Even today Aboriginals believe this. He told her to take care. That night she set off singing until she was near the hills.

Suddenly her husband heard an echo of her song, then silence. He waited all night for her return. At daybreak he followed her footprints to the rocks near a hill. There were drops of blood but no strange footprints.

He climbed the rocks. As he looked over the rocks, to his amazement he saw a great giant asleep near the fire. The bones of his wife lay nearby, pieces of her beautiful hair everywhere, her blood spilled on the ground.

The angry husband speared the giant through the heart. He was a very clever man. He said, "I'll bring her back to life."

So he gathered up all the scattered bones, hair, blood, then brought her back to life as she was before. He told her, "I told you long ago not to sing while hunting. A devil or something worse can hurt you."

Later they went to live in another place. The possum woman never sang again as she hunted.

# Ngũgĩ wa Thiong'o

## Goodbye Africa

She was in the kitchen making coffee. She loved making coffee even in the daytime when the servants were around. The smell of real coffee soothed her. Besides, the kitchen was a world to her. Her husband never went in there.

He was now in the sitting room, and to him the noise from the disturbed crockery seemed to issue from another land. He picked a book from the glass-fronted shelf. He sat down on the sofa, opened the book at random, but did not read it. He just let it drop beside him.

She came in, holding a wooden tray with both hands. She enjoyed the feel of things made from wood. She put the tray on a table at the corner of the room. Then she arranged side tables, one for him and the other for herself. She sat down to her coffee, facing him. She saw his look was fixed past her. He did not seem to have noticed his cup of coffee. She stood up as if to go to him. But instead she picked up a tiny piece of paper on the floor and sat down again. She liked her house to be specklessly clean.

"The thought of leaving didn't bother me until tonight," she said, and knew it was not true. She felt the triteness of her comment and kept quiet.

He avoided her look and now played with the cup. He thought about everything and nothing. Suddenly, he felt bitter: why did she judge him all the time? Why couldn't she at least speak out her silent accusations?

And she thought he must also be sad at leaving. Fifteen years is not a small period of one's life and God, I don't make it easy for him. She was filled with sudden compassion. She made sweet, pious resolutions. I'll try to understand him. For a start, I'll open my heart to him, tonight. Now she walked up to his side, placed her left hand on his shoulder: "Come to bed, you must be tired, all that noise at the party."

He put down his cup and patted the hand on his shoulder, before removing it gently. "Go. I'll soon join you." She felt a suggestion of impatience in his voice. And he was angry because his hand was not steady.

My hands are losing their firmness, he was thinking. Or did I drink too much? No, my hand suddenly became weak, so weak. She was laughing at me. Was it my fault, what, what fault? I didn't mean to do it. I couldn't have meant it, he insisted harder now addressing himself to his absent wife. He drove me into it, he whispered uncertainly, going to the low cupboard by the wall, and taking out the only remaining bottle of whisky. Scotch, Johnny Walker born 1840 and still walking strong. He laughed a little. He poured himself a glass, and gulped it down, poured another, drank and then went back to the seat keeping the bottle beside him. Why then should a thing that never happened — well — perhaps it did happen, but he never meant it — how could it come to trouble him?

He had forgotten about the incident until these, his last months in Africa. Then he had started re-enacting the scene in his dreams, the vision becoming more and more vivid as days and months whistled by. At first the face had only appeared to him by night. His bed held terror for him. Then suddenly, these last few days, the face started appearing before him in broad daylight. Why didn't he get visitations from all the other Mau Mau terrorists he had tortured and killed? Except the man, that!

Yet he knew the man was not like the others. This man had worked for him as a shamba boy. A nice, God-fearing, submissive boy. A model of his type. He loved the boy and often gave him presents. Old shoes, old clothes. Things like that. He remembered the gratitude in the boy's face and his gestures of appreciation, a little comic perhaps, and it had made giving them worthwhile. It was this feeling of doing something for the people here that made the things you had to put up with bearable. Here in Africa you felt you were doing something tangible, something that was immediately appreciated. Not like in Europe where nobody seemed to care what you did, where even the poor in the East of London refused to seize opportunities offered them. The Welfare State. G-r-r-r! Such thoughts had made him feel that the boy was more than a servant. He felt somehow fatherly towards him . . . responsible, and the boy was his. Then one Christmas, the boy suddenly threw back at him the gift of a long coat and ten shillings. The boy had laughed and walked out of his service. For a long time, he could never forget the laughter. This he could have forgiven. But the grief and the misery in his wife's face at the news of the boy's disappearance was something else. For this he could never forgive the boy. Later when the Mau Mau War broke out, he, as a screening officer, was to meet the boy.

He drank steadily as if in vengeance for years of abstinence and outward respectability. The ceiling, the floor, the chairs swam in the air. I'll be all right if I go for a drive, for a small drive, he suggested to himself, and staggered out daring the man to appear before him with that sneering laughter.

He got into the car. The headlights swept away the darkness. He did not know where he was going, he just abandoned himself to the road. Sometimes he would recognize a familiar tree or a signpost then he would go into a blackout and drive blindly. In this way, dozing, waking, telling himself to hold on to the steering wheel, he swerved round sharp corners and bends, down the valley, avoiding, miraculously, one or two vehicles from the opposite direction. What am I doing? I am mad, he muttered and unexpectedly swerved to the right, leaving the road, and just managing to avoid crashing into a passing train at the crossing. He drove through the grass into the forest; he hit into bumps, brushed against tree stumps, again miraculously avoided hitting the tree trunks. I must stop this, he thought, and to prove that he had not yet lost his head, he braked the car to a sudden standstill.

He had heard of rituals in the dark. He had even read somewhere that some of the early European settlers used to go to African sorcerers, to have curses lifted. He had considered these things opposed to reason: but what had happened to him, the visions, surely worked against the normal laws of reason. No, he would exorcise the hallucinations from his system, here, in the dark. The idea was attractive and, in his condition, irresistible. Africa does this to you, he thought as he stripped himself naked. He now staggered out of the car and walked a little distance into the forest. Darkness and the forest buzzing crept around him. He was afraid, but he stood his ground. What next? He did not know anything about African magic. At home he had heard vague things like faerie folk, rowan trees, stolen babies and kelpies. He had heard, or read, that you could make waxen images of somebody you wanted to harm and at the dead of the night stick pins into the eyes. Maybe he ought to do this; he would make an image of that man, his former shamba boy, and prick his eyes. Then he remembered that he had not brought any wax and danced with fury, alone in the forest.

No, that'll never do, he thought, now ashamed of things of the dark. I want to know what went wrong that even my wife laughs at me. He went back to the car, hoping to find out why things in Kenya, everywhere, were falling, falling apart. He had never thought a day would come when a government would retire him and replace him with a black. The shame of it. And his wife looking at him with those eyes. Another idea more irresistible than the first now possessed him. I'll write to her. I'll write to the world. He fished out a notebook and started writing furiously. Inspiration already made him feel light and buoyant within. The light in the car dimly lit the pages, but he did not mind, because words, ideas, were all in his head, he butchered his life and tried to examine it, at the same time defending himself before her, before the world.

. . . I know you have seen me shake before that face. You have refused to comment, perhaps not to hurt me. But you laughed at me all the time, didn't you? Don't deny it. I've seen it in your eyes and looks. I know you think me a failure. I never rose beyond the rank of Senior D.O. Africa has ruined me, but I never got a chance, really. Oh, don't look at me with those blue eyes as if you thought I lied. Maybe you are saying there's a tide in the affairs of men. O.K. I neglected it. We neglected it. But what tide? Oh, I am tired.

He stopped and read over what he had written. He turned over another page. Inspiration came in waves. His hand was too slow for what begged to come out.

. . . What went wrong, I keep on asking myself? Was it wrong for us, with our capital, with our knowledge, with our years of Christian civilization to open and lift a dark country onto the stage of history? I played my part. Does it matter if promotion was slow? Does it matter if there were ups and downs? And there were many moments of despair. I remember the huts we burnt. Even then I did ask myself: had I fallen so low? My life reduced to burning down huts and yet more huts? Had my life come to a cul-de-sac? And yet we could not let atavistic violence destroy all that had taken so many years and so many lives to build. When I had reached the nadir of my despair, I met that man—our shamba boy. Do you remember him? The one who spurned my gift and disappeared, maybe to the forest? He stood in the office with that sneer in his face—like—like the devil. The servile submissive face when he worked for you had gone. He had that strange effect on me—when I remembered the grief he caused you—well—made me boil inside—I felt a violent rage within such as I had never felt before—I could not bear that grin. I stood and spat into his face. And that arrogant stare never left his face even as he cleared off the spit with the back of his left hand. Isn't it strange that

I forget his name now, that I never really knew his name? Did you? I only remember that he was tall and there in the office I saw the violence in his eyes. I was afraid of him. Can you believe it? I, afraid of a black man? Afraid of my former shamba boy? What happened later, I cannot remember, I cannot explain, I was not myself, I only saw the face of the man. At night, in the morning, I saw the grin, the sneer, the arrogant indifference. And he would not confess to anything. I gave command. He was taken to the forest. I never saw him again . . .

He wrote in fury; images flowed, merged, clashed: it was as if he had a few days to live and he wanted to purge his soul of something. A confession to a priest before the gallows fell. He was now shivering. But he was still possessed . . . I'm writing this to you, I am alone in the forest, and in the world. I want to begin a new life with you in England, after saying goodbye to Africa. . . . And now he discovered he had no clothes and that he was shivering. He felt ashamed of his nakedness and quickly put on his clothes. But he could not continue with his confession and he feared to read it over in case he changed his mind. He was now almost sober, but very excited at the prospect of giving his life to her, tonight.

She was not yet asleep. She too was determined to wait for him to come back so that they could share their last night in Africa. In bed, she allowed her mind to glance backwards over her life, over her relationship with him. At first, in their early days in Kenya, she had tried to be enthusiastic about his civilizing zeal and his ambitions. She too was determined to play her part, to give life a purpose. She attended a few meetings of African women in the ridges and even learnt a smattering of Swahili. Then she wanted to understand Africa, to touch the centre, and feel the huge continent throb on her fingers. In those days she and he were close, their hearts seemed to beat together. But with the passage of years, he had gone farther and farther away. She lost her original enthusiasm: the ideas that had earlier appeared so bright faded and became rusty in her eyes. Who were they to civilize anyone? What was civilization anyway? And why did he fret because he could not climb up the ladder as quickly as he wanted? She became slightly impatient with this rusty thing that took him away from her, but she would not disturb him, ruin his career. So she went to the parties, did her share of small talk, and wanted to cry. Ought she to have spoken, then, she wondered now, wriggling in bed, puzzled by his late night drive. She gave up meetings in the villages. She wanted to be alone. She did not want to understand Africa. Why should she? She had not tried to understand Europe, or Australia where she was born. No. You could never hope to embrace the meaning of a continent in your small palms, you could only love. She wanted to live her own life, and not as a prop to another's climb to a top that promised no fuller life.

So she went for walks alone in the countryside: she saw children playing and wondered what it would feel like to have a child. When would her first arrive in this strange world? She was awed by the thick crowds of banana plants, the thick bush and forests. That was just before the Emergency when you could walk down alone anywhere without fear.

It was during one of her walks that the boy had first made love to her among the banana plantations. Freedom. And afterward their fevered love-making had finally severed her from the world of her husband and other District Officers.

Arriving home, he found she was not yet asleep. He went towards her, riding on low exciting waves. He did not put on the light but sat on the bed without speaking.

"Where have you been?"

"I went for a drive — seeing the old place for the last time."

"Come into bed then, God, how cold you are! And here I was waiting for you to give me warmth."

"You know it's always chilly at night."

"Come on then."

She felt she had to tell him now in the dark, about her lover. She did not want to look into his face in case she changed her mind. She put out her hand and stroked his head, feeling for a way to start. Now. Her heart was beating. Was she scared?

"I want to tell you something," she removed her hand from his head, and paused, the next words refusing to come out. "Will you forgive me?"

"Of course I will, everything." He was impatient. What could she tell him greater than what he had written, red-hot, filling the notebook. He wanted to tell her how he had exorcised the ghost of the shamba boy from his life. He waited hoping she would finish quickly. He meant to give her the notebook and withdraw to the bathroom to give her time to see his bare soul.

"Of course I can forgive you anything," he said by way of encouragement. "Go on," he whispered gently into the dark room.

She told him about the shamba boy—her lover.

He listened and felt energy and blood leave his body.

Would he forgive her? She only wanted them to start a new life. She finished, her voice fading into dark silence. She listened to her heart-beat waiting for him to speak.

But he did not speak. A kind of dullness had crept into his limbs, into his mouth, into the heart. The man. His shamba boy. For an answer he stood up and started toward the door.

"Darling, please!" She called out, for the first time feeling dark terror at his lack of words. "Don't go. It was long way back, before the Emergency."

But he continued walking, out through the door, into the sitting room. He sat on the sofa exactly where he had earlier. Automatically, he started fingering the unfinished cup of coffee.

For all his visions of moral ideals in the service of British capitalism, he was a vain man: he never really saw himself in any light but that of an adequate husband. He had no cause, within himself, to doubt her fidelity to him as a man, or a husband. How then could this woman, his wife, bring herself to sleep with that man, that creature? How make herself so cheap, drag his thousand-year-old name to mud, and such mud?

He had followed a dream for too long. He would not let the dream go despite the reality around him. In his colonizing mission and his zeal to reach the top he had neglected his house and another had occupied it. In this, perhaps, he was not alone. But how could he know this as he sat in the middle of the room, the bare walls staring at him? The cup fell out of his hands and broke into pieces. He stood up and walked around the room, slowly, looking at nothing, seeing neither yesterday nor tomorrow. Then he took out his notebook and opened it at random:

> The white man in Africa must accept a more stringent moral code in the family and in the society at large. For we must set the ideals to which our African subjects must aspire.

He closed the notebook and walked into the kitchen where he never went before. He took a match, struck it, and watched the notebook burn. He watched the flame, saw his flesh burn, but he felt no pain, nothing. The man's ghost would forever pursue him. Africa.

# Oodgeroo Noonuccal

(formerly Kath Walker)


## Gooboora, the Silent Pool

*for Grannie Sunflower, last of the Noonuccals*


Gooboora, Gooboora, the Water of Fear
That awed the Noonuccals once numerous here,
The Bunyip is gone from your bone-strewn bed,
And the clans departed to drift with the dead.

Once in the far time before the whites came
How light were their hearts in the dance and the game!
Gooboora, Gooboora, to think that today
A whole happy tribe are all vanished away!

What mystery lurks by the Water of Fear,
And what is the secret still lingering here?
For birds hasten by as in days of old,
No wild thing will drink of your waters cold.

Gooboora, Gooboora, still here you remain,
But where are my people I look for in vain?
They are gone from the hill, they are gone from the shore,
And the place of the Silent Pool knows them no more.

But I think they still gather when daylight is done
And stand round the pool at the setting of sun,
A shadowy band that is now without care,
Fearing no longer the Thing in its lair.

Old Death has passed by you but took the dark throng;
Now lost is the Noonuccal language and song.
Gooboora, Gooboora, it makes the heart sore
That you should be here but my people no more!

# The Past

Let no one say the past is dead.
The past is all about us and within.
Haunted by tribal memories, I know
This little now, this accidental present
Is not the all of me, whose long making
Is so much of the past.

Tonight here in suburbia as I sit
In easy chair before electric heater,
Warmed by the red glow, I fall into dream:
I am away
at the camp fire in the bush, among
My own people, sitting on the ground,
No walls about me,
The stars over me,
The tall surrounding trees that stir in the wind
Making their own music,
Soft cries of the night coming to us, there
Where we are one with all old Nature's lives
Known and unknown,
In scenes where we belong but have now forsaken.
Deep chair and electric radiator
Are but since yesterday,
But a thousand thousand camp fires in the forest
Are in my blood.
Let none tell me the past is wholly gone.
Now is so small a part of time, so small a part
Of all the race years that have moulded me.

# Gabriel Okara

## *The Snowflakes Sail Gently Down*

The snowflakes sail gently
down from the misty eye of the sky
and fall lightly on the
winter-weary elms. And the branches
winter-stripped and nude, slowly
with the weight of the weightless snow
bow like grief-stricken mourners
as white funeral cloth is slowly
unrolled over deathless earth.
And dead sleep stealthily from the
heater rose and closed my eyes with
the touch of silk cotton on water falling.

Then I dreamed a dream
in my dead sleep. But I dreamed
not of earth dying and elms a vigil
keeping. I dreamed of birds, black
birds flying in my inside, nesting
and hatching on oil palms bearing suns
for fruits and with roots denting the
uprooters' spades. And I dreamed the
uprooters tired and limp, leaning on my roots —
their abandoned roots
and the oil palms gave them each a sun.

But on their palms
they balanced the blinding orbs
and frowned with schisms on their
brows — for the suns reached not
the brightness of gold!
Then I awoke. I awoke
to the silently falling snow

and bent-backed elms bowing and
swaying to the winter wind like
white-robed Moslems salaaming at evening
prayer, and the earth lying inscrutable
like the face of a god in a shrine.

# Michael Ondaatje

## Light

*for Doris Gratiaen*

Midnight storm. Trees walking off across the fields in fury
naked in the spark of lightning.
I sit on the white porch on the brown hanging cane chair
coffee in my hand midnight storm midsummer night.
The past, friends and family, drift into the rain shower.
Those relatives in my favourite slides
re-shot from old minute photographs so they now stand
complex ambiguous grainy on my wall.

This is my Uncle who turned up to his marriage
on an elephant. He was a chaplain.
This shy looking man in the light jacket and tie was infamous,
when he went drinking he took the long blonde beautiful hair
of his wife and put one end in the cupboard and locked it
leaving her tethered in an armchair.
He was terrified of her possible adultery
and this way died peaceful happy to the end.
My Grandmother, who went to a dance in a muslin dress
with fireflies captured and embedded in the cloth, shining
and witty. This calm beautiful face
organised wild acts in the tropics.
She hid the mailman in her house
after he had committed murder and at the trial
was thrown out of the court for making jokes at the judge.
Her son became a Q.C.
This is my brother at 6. With his cousin and his sister
and Pam de Voss who fell on a pen-knife and lost her eye.
My Aunt Christie. She knew Harold MacMillan was a spy
communicating with her through pictures in the newspapers.
Every picture she believed asked her to forgive him,

his hound eyes pleading.
Her husband Uncle Fitzroy a doctor in Ceylon had a memory
sharp as scalpels into his 80's
though I never bothered to ask him about anything
— interested then more in the latest recordings of Bobby Darin.

And this is my Mother with her brother Noel in fancy dress.
They are 7 and 8 years old, a hand-coloured photograph,
it is the earliest picture I have. The one I love most.
A picture of my kids at Halloween
has the same contact and laughter.
My Uncle dying at 68, and my Mother a year later dying at 68.
She told me about his death and the day he died
his eyes clearing out of illness as if seeing
right through the room the hospital and she said
he saw something so clear and good his whole body
for a moment became youthful and she remembered
when she sewed badges on his trackshirts.
Her voice joyous in telling me this, her face light and clear.
(My firefly Grandmother also dying at 68.)

These are the fragments I have of them, tonight
in this storm, the dogs restless on the porch.
They were all laughing, crazy, and vivid in their prime.
At a party my drunk Father
tried to explain a complex operation on chickens
and managed to kill them all in the process, the guests
having dinner an hour later while my Father slept
and the kids watched the servants clean up the litter
of beaks and feathers on the lawn.

These are their fragments, all I remember,
wanting more knowledge of them. In the mirror and in my kids
I see them in my flesh. Wherever we are
they parade in my brain and the expanding stories
connect to the grey grainy pictures on the wall,
as they hold their drinks or 20 years later
hold grandchildren, pose with favourite dogs,
coming through the light, the electricity, which the storm
destroyed an hour ago, a tree going down by the highway
so that now inside the kids play dominoes by candlelight

and out here the thick rain static the spark of my match
                                    to a cigarette
and the trees across the fields leaving me, distinct
lonely in their own knife scars and cow-chewed bark
frozen in the jagged light as if snapped in their run
the branch arms waving to what was a second ago the dark sky
when in truth like me they haven't moved.
Haven't moved an inch from me.

# Sasenarine Persaud

## *Tiger Swami*

Even as you leap
I leap with you
Across oceans, across continents
Across the kala pani.
On the clean coast of
South America, on the flat-
Lands of Guyana
Tracking the prey we plunge
Into Atlantic surf
And come up with the wet
Touchable moon only in our wistful eyes

You stalk the Guiana Coast
Searching, seeing
Manicured rice-fields more
orderly than heaven
Pin-prick multitudes of cattle
Sweeter than paradise
And where is the kill?

It is better to starve
So we starve until sunset
Calls of prayer from the mosque at the
Edge of the Corentyne river
Still our souls —

Just for a while we stop
And surrender
And begin our prowl again.

You springing into the South American
Rainforest and I your keeper

Clinging to your collar chain—
Milky white sands record our quest
For erasure by afternoon showers,
At night we see the many eyes of god
Twinkling overhead and aren't we
Too tired
or too satisfied/starved to spoil it
By a single breath?
Crickets, leaves, wind, deer, snakes crawling to
The creek hums
Hypnotic love-songs
From mountain top to river.

Quicksilver filled and empty
Samadhi-stilled, vacant-filled
We motor to the springboard coast

Across ocean, above Atlantis
We leap through time.
Through the asphalt jungles
Of North America
We sprint from overpass
To underpass, from overhead
To underground, from oven
To refrigerator. We pounce
On legalities and think, aha,
Maybe here . . .
Even as you leap in the subways
of my mind and I rise to prevent
The kill

I know, O tiger, tiger
—multi-coloured eyes
Shining in my darkened mind—
I must light Nirvana-touch
To tame you!

# M. Nourbese Philip

## *She Tries Her Tongue; Her Silence Softly Breaks*

*All Things are alter'd, nothing is destroyed*
Ovid, *The Metamorphoses* (tr. Dryden).

the me and mine of parents
the we and us of brother and sister
the tribe of belongings small and separate,
when gone . . .
on these exact places of exacted grief
i placed mint-fresh grief coins
sealed the eyes with certain and final;
in such an equation of loss tears became
a quantity of minus.
with the fate of a slingshot stone
loosed from the catapult pronged double with history
and time on a trajectory of hurl and fling
to a state active with without and unknown
i came upon a future biblical with anticipation

## *Transfiguration*

In the ceremony of White
The cyclamen girl would answer
To her name

*Aphrodite!*

Gives rote answers
About promises

Of the godfathers

*Ave Maria*!

Remembering
First the drums
Then the women
Called out her name

*Atabey!*

Her other name

*Oshun!*

As she whirls
Into the circle of grief
For her fleeting childhood
Passed like the blood
Of her first menses
Quick and painful
Name her

*Rhythm!*
*Song!*
*Drum!*

Mahogany-tipped breast catches
The glare of the fires
Women of the moon feast and fast
And feast again

Name her

*Aphrodite! Mary! Atebey!*
*Orehu! Yemoja!*
*Oshun!*

For her newly arrived wound
Name her!

# Jean Rhys

## I Used to Live Here Once

She was standing by the river looking at the stepping stones and remembering each one. There was the round unsteady stone, the pointed one, the flat one in the middle — the safe stone where you could stand and look round. The next wasn't so safe for when the river was full the water flowed over it and even when it showed dry it was slippery. But after that it was easy and soon she was standing on the other side.

The road was much wider than it used to be but the work had been done carelessly. The felled trees had not been cleared away and the bushes looked trampled. Yet it was the same road and she walked along feeling extraordinarily happy.

It was a fine day, a blue day. The only thing was that the sky had a glassy look that she didn't remember. That was the only word she could think of. Glassy. She turned the corner, saw that what had been the old pavé had been taken up, and there too the road was much wider, but it had the same unfinished look.

She came to the worn stone steps that led up to the house and her heart began to beat. The screw pine was gone, so was the mock summer house called the ajoupa, but the clove tree was still there and at the top of the steps the rough lawn stretched away, just as she remembered it. She stopped and looked towards the house that had been added to and painted white. It was strange to see a car standing in front of it.

There were two children under the big mango tree, a boy and a little girl, and she waved to them and called "Hello" but they didn't answer her or turn their heads. Very fair children, as Europeans born in the West Indies so often are: as if the white blood is asserting itself against all odds.

The grass was yellow in the hot sunlight as she walked towards them. When she was quite close she called again, shyly: "Hello." Then, "I used to live here once," she said.

Still they didn't answer. When she said for the third time "Hello" she was quite near them. Her arms went out instinctively with the longing to touch them.

It was the boy who turned. His grey eyes looked straight into hers. His expression didn't change. He said: "Hasn't it gone cold all of a sudden. D'you notice? Let's go in." "Yes let's," said the girl.

Her arms fell to her sides as she watched them running across the grass to the house. That was the first time she knew.

# Salman Rushdie

## *"Commonwealth Literature" Does Not Exist*

When I was invited to speak at the 1983 English Studies Seminar in Cambridge, the lady from the British Council offered me a few words of reassurance. "It's all right," I was told, "for the purposes of our seminar, English studies are taken to include Commonwealth literature." At all other times, one was forced to conclude, these two would be kept strictly apart, like squabbling children, or sexually incompatible pandas, or, perhaps, like unstable, fissile materials whose union might cause explosions.

A few weeks later I was talking to a literature don—a specialist, I ought to say, in *English* literature—a friendly and perceptive man. "As a Commonwealth writer," he suggested, "you probably find, don't you, that there's a kind of liberty, certain advantages, in occupying, as you do, a position on the periphery?"

And then a British magazine published, in the same issue, interviews with Shiva Naipaul, Buchi Emecheta and myself. In my interview, I admitted that I had begun to find this strange term, "Commonwealth literature," unhelpful and even a little distasteful; and I was interested to read that in *their* interviews, both Shiva Naipaul and Buchi Emecheta, in their own ways, said much the same thing. The three interviews appeared, therefore, under the headline: "Commonwealth writers . . . but don't call them that!"

By this point, the Commonwealth was becoming unpopular with me.

Isn't this the very oddest of beasts, I thought—a school of literature whose supposed members deny vehemently that they belong to it. Worse, these denials are simply disregarded! It seems the creature has taken on a life of its own. So when I was invited to a conference about the animal in—of all places—Sweden, I thought I'd better go along to take a closer look at it.

The conference was beautifully organized, packed with erudite and sophisticated persons capable of discoursing at length about the new spirit of experiment in English-language writing in the Philippines. Also, I was able to meet writers from all over the world—or, rather, the

Commonwealth. It was such a seductive environment that it almost persuaded me that the subject under discussion actually existed, and was not simply a fiction, and a fiction of a unique type, at that, in that it has been created solely by critics and academics, who have then proceeded to believe in it wholeheartedly . . . but the doubts did, in spite of all temptations to succumb, persist.

Many of the delegates, I found, were willing freely to admit that the term "Commonwealth literature" was a bad one. South Africa and Pakistan, for instance, are not members of the Commonwealth, but their authors apparently belong to its literature. On the other hand, England, which, as far as I'm aware, has not been expelled from the Commonwealth quite yet, has been excluded from its literary manifestation. For obvious reasons. It would never do to include English literature, the great sacred thing itself, with this bunch of upstarts, huddling together under this new and badly made umbrella.

At the Commonwealth literature conference I talked with and listened to the Australian poet Randolph Stow; the West Indian, Wilson Harris; Ngugi wa Thiong'o from Kenya; Anita Desai from India and the Canadian novelist Aritha van Herk. I became quite sure that our differences were so much more significant than our similarities, that it was impossible to say what "Commonwealth literature" — the idea which had, after all, made possible our assembly — might conceivably mean. Van Herk spoke eloquently about the problem of drawing imaginative maps of the great emptinesses of Canada; Wilson Harris soared into great flights of metaphysical lyricism and high abstraction; Anita Desai spoke in whispers, her novel the novel of sensibility, and I wondered what on earth she could be held to have in common with the committed Marxist Ngugi, an overtly political writer, who expressed his rejection of the English language by reading his own work in Swahili, with a Swedish version read by his translator, leaving the rest of us completely bemused. Now obviously this great diversity would be entirely natural in a general literature conference — but this was a particular school of literature, and I was trying to work out what that school was supposed to be.

The nearest I could get to a definition sounded distinctly patronizing: "Commonwealth literature," it appears, is that body of writing created, I think, in the English language, by persons who are not themselves white Britons, or Irish, or citizens of the United States of America. I don't know whether black Americans are citizens of this bizarre Commonwealth or not. Probably not. It is also uncertain whether citizens of Commonwealth countries writing in languages other than English—Hindi, for example—or who switch out of English, like Ngugi, are permitted into the club or asked to keep out.

By now "Commonwealth literature" was sounding very unlikeable indeed. Not only was it a ghetto, but it was actually an exclusive ghetto. And the effect of creating such a ghetto was, is, to change the meaning of the far broader term "English literature"—which I'd always taken to mean simply the literature of the English language—into something far narrower, something topographical, nationalistic, possibly even racially segregationist.

It occurred to me, as I surveyed this muddle, that the category is a chimera, and in very precise terms. The word has of course come to mean an unreal, monstrous creature of the imagination; but you will recall that the classical chimera was a monster of a rather special type. It had the head of a lion, the body of a goat and a serpent's tail. This is to say, it could exist only in dreams, being composed of elements which could not possibly be joined together in the real world.

The dangers of unleashing such a phantom into the groves of literature are, it seems to me, manifold. As I mentioned, there is the effect of creating a ghetto, and that, in turn, does lead to a ghetto mentality amongst some of it occupants. Also, the creation of a false category can and does lead to excessively narrow, and sometimes misleading, readings of some of the artists it is held to include; and again, the existence—or putative existence—of the beast distracts attention from what is actually worth looking at, what is actually going on. I thought it might be worth spending a few minutes reflecting further on these dangers.

I'll begin from an obvious starting place. English is by now the world language. It achieved this status partly as a result of the physical colonization of a quarter of the globe by the British, and it remains ambiguous but central to the affairs of just about all the countries to whom it was given, along with mission schools, trunk roads and the rules of cricket, as a gift of the British colonizers.

But its present-day pre-eminence is not solely—perhaps not even primarily—the result of the British legacy. It is also the effect of the primacy of the United States of America in the affairs of the world. This second impetus towards English could be termed a kind of linguistic neo-colonialism, or just plain pragmatism on the part of many of the world's governments and educationists, according to your point of view.

As for myself, I don't think it is always necessary to take up the anti-colonial—or is it post-colonial?—cudgels against English. What seems to me to be happening is that those peoples who were once colonized by the language are now rapidly remaking it, domesticating it, becoming more and more relaxed about the way they use it — assisted by the English language's enormous flexibility and size, they are carving out large territories for themselves within its frontiers.

To take the case of India, only because it's the one with which I'm most familiar. The debate about the appropriateness of English in post-British India has been raging ever since 1947; but today, I find, it is a debate which has meaning only for the older generation. The children of independent India seem not to think of English as being irredeemably tainted by its colonial provenance. They use it as an Indian language, as one of the tools they have to hand.

(I am simplifying, of course, but the point is broadly true.)

There is also an interesting North-South divide in Indian attitudes to English. In the North, in the so-called "Hindi belt," where the capital, Delhi, is located, it is possible to think of Hindi as a future national language; but in South India, which is at present suffering from the attempts of central government to *impose* this national language on it, the resentment of Hindi is far greater than of English. After spending quite some time in South India, I've become convinced that English is an essential language in India, not only because of its technical vocabularies and the international communication which it makes possible, but also simply to permit two Indians to talk to each other in a tongue which neither party hates.

Incidentally, in West Bengal, where there is a State-led move against English, the following graffito, a sharp dig at the State's Marxist chief minister, Jyoti Basu, appeared on a wall, in English: it said, "My son won't learn English; your son won't learn English; but Jyoti Basu will send his son abroad to learn English."

One of the points I want to make is that what I've said indicates, I hope, that Indian society and Indian literature have a complex and developing relationship with the English language. This kind of post-colonial dialectic is propounded as one of the unifying factors in "Commonwealth literature"; but it clearly does not exist, or at least is far more peripheral to the problems of literatures in Canada, Australia, even South Africa. Every time you examine the general theories of "Commonwealth literature" they come apart in your hands.

English literature has its Indian branch. By this I mean the literature of the English language. This literature is also Indian literature. There is no incompatibility here. If history creates complexities, let us not try to simplify them.

So: English is an Indian literary language, and by now, thanks to writers like Tagore, Desani, Chaudhuri, Mulk Raj Anand, Raja Rao, Anita Desai and others, it has quite a pedigree. Now it is certainly true that the English-language literatures of England, Ireland and the USA are older than, for example, the Indian; so it's possible that "Commonwealth literature" is no more than an ungainly name for the world's younger English literatures. If that were true or, rather, if that were all, it would be a relatively unimportant misnomer. But it isn't all. Because the term is not used simply to describe, or even misdescribe, but also to *divide*. It permits academic institutions, publishers, critics and even readers to dump a large segment of English literature into a box and then more or less ignore it. At best, what is called "Commonwealth literature" is positioned *below* English literature "proper" – or, to come back to my friend the don, it places Eng. Lit. at the centre and the rest of the world at the periphery. How depressing that such a view should persist in the study of literature long after it has been discarded in the study of everything else English.

What is life like inside the ghetto of "Commonwealth literature"? Well, every ghetto has its own rules, and this one is no exception.

One of the rules, one of the ideas on which the edifice rests, is that literature is an expression of nationality. What Commonwealth literature finds interesting in Patrick White is his Australianness; in Doris Lessing, her Africanness; in V. S. Naipaul, his West Indianness, although I doubt that anyone would have the nerve to say so to his face. Books are almost always praised for using motifs and symbols out of the author's own national tradition, or when their form echoes some traditional form, obviously pre-English, and when the influences at work upon the writer can be seen to be wholly internal to the culture from which he "springs." Books which mix traditions, or which seek consciously to break with tradition, are often treated as highly suspect. To give one example. A few years ago the Indian poet, Arun Kolatkar, who works with equal facility in English and Marathi, wrote, in English, an award-winning series of poems called *Jejuri*, the account of his visit to a Hindu temple town. (Ironically, I should say, it won the Commonwealth Poetry Prize.) The poems are marvellous, contemporary, witty, and in spite of their subject they are the work of a non-religious man. They aroused the wrath of one of the doyens of Commonwealth literary studies in India, Professor C. D. Narasimhaiah, who, while admitting the brilliance of the poems, accused Kolatkar of making his work irrelevant by seeking to defy tradition.

What we are facing here is the bogy of Authenticity. This is something which the Indian art critic Geeta Kapur has explored in connection with modern Indian painting, but it applies equally well to literature. "Authenticity" is the respectable child of old-fashioned exoticism. It demands that sources, forms, style, language and symbol all derive from a supposedly homogeneous and unbroken tradition. Or else. What is revealing is that the term, so much in use inside the little world of "Commonwealth literature," and always as term of praise, would seem ridiculous outside this world. Imagine a novel being eulogized for being "authentically English," or "authentically German." It would seem absurd. Yet such absurdities persist in the ghetto.

In my own case, I have constantly been asked whether I am British, or Indian. The formulation "Indian-born British writer" has been invented to explain me. But, as I said last night, my new book deals with Pakistan. So what now? "British-resident Indo-Pakistani writer"? You see the folly of trying to contain writers inside passports.

One of the most absurd aspects of this quest for national authenticity is that — as far as India is concerned, anyway — it is completely fallacious to suppose that there is such a thing as a pure, unalloyed tradition from which to draw. The only people who seriously believe this are religious extremists. The rest of us understand that the very essence of Indian culture is that we possess a mixed tradition, a *mélange* of elements as disparate as ancient Mughal and contemporary Coca-Cola American. To say nothing of Muslim, Buddhist, Jain, Christian, Jewish, British, French, Portuguese, Marxist, Maoist, Trotskyist, Vietnamese, capitalist, and of course Hindu elements. Eclecticism, the ability to take from the world what seems fitting and to leave the rest, has always been a hallmark of the Indian tradition, and today it is at the centre of the best work being done both in the visual arts and in literature. Yet eclecticism is not really a nice word in the lexicon of "Commonwealth literature." So the reality of the mixed tradition is replaced by the fantasy of purity.

You will perhaps have noticed that the purpose of this literary ghetto — like that of all ghettos, perhaps — is to confine, to restrain. Its rules are basically conservative. Tradition is all; radical breaches with the past are frowned upon. No wonder so many of the writers claimed by "Commonwealth literature" deny that they have anything to do with it.

I said that the concept of "Commonwealth literature" did disservice to some writers, leading to false readings of their work; in India, I think this is true of the work of Ruth Jhabvala and, to a lesser extent, Anita Desai. You see, looked at from the point of view that literature must be nationally connected and even committed, it becomes simply impossible to understand the cast of mind and vision of a rootless intellect like Jhabvala's. In Europe, of course, there are enough instances of uprooted, wandering writers and even peoples to make Ruth Jhabvala's work readily comprehensible; but by the rules of the Commonwealth ghetto, she is beyond the pale. As a result, her reputation in India is much lower than it is in the West. Anita Desai, too, gets into trouble when she states with complete honesty that her work has no Indian models. The novel is a Western form, she says, so the influences on her are Western. Yet her delicate but tough fictions are magnificent studies of Indian life. This confuses the cohorts of the Commonwealth. But then, where "Commonwealth literature" is concerned, confusion is the norm.

I also said that the creation of this phantom category served to obscure what was really going on, and worth talking about. To expand on this, let me say that if we were to forget about "Commonwealth literature," we might see that there is a kind of commonality about much literature, in many languages, emerging from those parts of the world which one could loosely term the less powerful, or the powerless. The magical realism of the Latin Americans influences Indian language writers in India today. The rich, folk-tale quality of a novel like *Sandro of Chegem*, by the Muslim Russian Fazil Iskander, finds its parallels in the work—for instance—of the Nigerian, Amos Tutuola, or even Cervantes. It is possible, I think, to begin to theorize common factors between writers from these societies—poor countries, or deprived minorities in powerful countries—and to say that much of what is new in world literature comes from this group. This seems to me to be a "real" theory, bounded by frontiers which are neither political nor linguistic but imaginative. And it is developments of this kind which the chimera of "Commonwealth literature" obscures.

This transnational, cross-lingual process of pollination is not new. The works of Rabindranath Tagore, for example, have long been widely available in Spanish-speaking America, thanks to his close friendship with the Argentinian intellectual Victoria Ocampo. Thus an entire generation, or even two, of South American writers have read *Gitanjali, The Home and the World* and other works, and some, like Mario Vargas Llosa, say that they found them very exciting and stimulating.

If this "Third World literature" is one development obscured by the ghost of "Commonwealth literature," then "Commonwealth literature's" emphasis on writing in English distracts attention from much else that is worth our attention. I tried to show how in India the whole issue of language was a subject of deep contention. It is also worth saying that major work is being done in India in many languages other than English; yet outside India there is just about no interest in any of this work. The Indo-Anglians seize all the limelight. Very little is translated; very few of the best writers—Premchand, Anantha Moorthy—or the best novels are known, even by name.

To go on in this vein: it strikes me that, at the moment, the greatest area of friction in Indian literature has nothing to do with English literature, but with the effects of the hegemony of Hindi on the literatures of other Indian languages, particularly other North Indian languages. I recently met the distinguished Gujarati novelist, Suresh Joshi. He told me that he could write in Hindi but felt obliged to write in Gujarati because it was a language under threat. Not from English, or the West: from Hindi. In two or three generations, he said, Gujarati could easily die. And he compared it, interestingly, to the state of the Czech language under the yoke of Russian, as described by Milan Kundera.

This is clearly a matter of central importance for Indian literature. "Commonwealth literature" is not interested in such matters.

It strikes me that my title may not really be accurate. There is clearly such a thing as "Commonwealth literature," because even ghosts can be made to exist if you set up enough faculties, if you write enough books and appoint enough research students. It does not exist in the sense that writers do not write it, but that is of minor importance. So perhaps I should rephrase myself: "Commonwealth literature" should not exist. If it did not, we could appreciate writers for what they are, whether in English or not; we could discuss literature in terms of its real groupings, which may well be national, which may well be linguistic, but which may also be international, and based on imaginative affinities; and as far as Eng. Lit. itself is concerned, I think that if all English literatures could be studied together, a shape would emerge which would truly reflect the new shape of the language in the world, and we could see that Eng. Lit. has never been in better shape, because the world language now also possesses a world literature, which is proliferating in every conceivable direction.

The English language ceased to be the sole possession of the English some time ago. Perhaps "Commonwealth literature" was invented to delay the day when we rough beasts actually slouch into Bethlehem. In which case, it's time to admit that the centre cannot hold.

# Samuel Selvon

## *Brackley and the Bed*

One evening Brackley was cruising round by the Embankment looking for a soft bench to rest his weary bones, and to cogitate on the ways of life. The reason for that, and the reason why the boys begin to call him Rockabye, you will find out as the ballad goes on.

Brackley hail from Tobago, which part they have it to say Robinson Crusoe used to hang out with Man Friday. Things was brown in that island and he make for England and manage to get a work and was just settling down when bam! he get a letter from his aunt saying that Teena want to come England too.

Teena was Brackley distant cousin and they was good friends in Tobago. In fact, the other reason why Brackley hustle from the island is because it did look like he and Teena was heading for a little married thing, and Brackley run.

Well, right away he write aunty and say no, no, because he have a feeling this girl would make botheration if she come England. The aunt write back to say she didn't mean to say that Teena want to come England, but that Teena left Tobago for England already.

Brackley hold his head and bawl. And the evening the boat train come in at Waterloo, he went there and start 'busing she right away not waiting to ask how the folks at home was or anything.

"What you doing in London?" Brackley ask as soon as Teena step off the train. "What you come here for, eh? Even though I write home to say things real hard?"

"What happen, you buy the country already?" Teena sheself giving tit for tat right away. "You ruling England now? The Queen abdicate?"

"You know where you going?" Brackley say. "You know where you is? You know what you going to do?"

"I am going straight to the Colonial Office," Teena say.

"What you think the Colonial Office is, eh? You think they will do anything for you? You have a god-father working there?"

Well, they argue until in the end Brackley find himself holding on to Teena suitcase and they on the way to the little batchy he have in

Golders Green at the time.

When they get there Teena take one look at the room and sniff. "But look at the state you have this room in! You ain't ashamed of yourself?"

"Listen," Brackley say, "you better don't let me and you have contention. I know this would of happen when you come."

Teena start squaring up the room brisk-brisk.

"It making cold," she say, putting chair this way and table that way and turning everything upside down for poor Brackley. "How you does keep warm? Where the gas fire I hear so much about?"

Brackley grudgingly put a shilling in the meter and light the gas.

"What you have to eat?" But even as she asking she gone in the cupboard and begin pulling out rations that Brackley had stow away to see him through the winter. Brackley as if he mesmerize, stand up there watching her as she start up a peas and rice on the gas ring.

"You better go easy with them rations," he say. "I not working now and money don't grow on tree here as in Tobago."

When they was eating Teena say: "Well, you have to get a job right away. You was always a lazy fellar."

"Keep quiet," Brackley say, enjoying the meal that Teena cook in real West Indian fashion — the first good meal he ever had in London. "You don't know nothing."

"First thing tomorrow morning," Teena say. "What time you get up?"

"About nine — ten," Brackley say vaguely.

"Well is six o'clock tomorrow morning, bright and early as the cock crow."

"You don't hear cock crowing in London," Brackley say. Then he drop the spoon he was eating with. "Six o'clock! You must be mad! Six o'clock like midnight in the winter, and people still sound asleep."

"Six o'clock," Teena say.

Brackley finish eating and begin to smoke, whistling a calypso softly, as if he in another world and not aware of Teena at all.

"Ah well," he say, stretching by the fire, "that wasn't a bad meal. Look, I will give you some old blankets and you could wrap up that coat and use as a pillow — you could sleep on the ground in that corner . . ."

"*Me?* On the floor? You not ashamed?"

"Well, is only one bed here as you see . . ."

"I using the bed."

"Girl, is winter, and if you think I going to sleep in the corner with two old blanket and wake up stiff . . ."

But, in the end, was Brackley who crouch up in the corner, and

Teena sound asleep in the bed.

It look to Brackley like he hardly shut his eyes before Teena was shaking him.

"Get up," Teena say, "six o'clock."

Brackley start to curse.

"None of that," Teena say. "No bad language when I around."

Teena move around fast and give Brackley breakfast and make him dress and get out on the cold streets mumbling, "Get a job, get a job," before he knew what was happening.

It was only about ten o'clock, when he was washing dishes in a café where he get a work, that Brackley realize what was happening to him.

When he get home in the evening, Teena have screen put up around the bed and everything spick and span, and Brackley don't know where to look even for chair to sit down.

"I see you make yourself at home," he say maliciously.

"And what you think?" Teena flares.

"The boys come here sometimes for a little rummy."

"None of that now."

"And sometimes a girl-friend visit me."

"None of that now."

"So you taking over completely."

"Aunty say to look after you."

"Why the hell you come England, eh?"

Well, a pattern begin to form as the weeks go by, but the main thing that have Brackley worried is the bed. Every night he curl up in the corner shivering, and by the time he doze off: "Six o'clock, get up, you have to go to work."

Brackley ain't sleep on bed for weeks. The thing like an obsession with him. He window-shopping on the way home and looking at them bed and soft mattress on show and closing his eyes and sighing. Single divan, double divan, put-you-up, put-you-down — all makes and sizes he looking at.

One night when frost was forming on the window pane Brackley wake up and find he couldn't move.

"Teena."

"What?"

"You sleeping?"

"Yes."

"Teena, you want to get married?"

"Married? To who?"

"To me."

"What for?"

"So-I-could-sleep-in-the-bed—I mean, well, we uses to know one another good in Tobago, and now that you are here in London, what do you think?"

"Well, all right, but you have to change your ways."

"Yes, Teena."

"And no foolishness when we married. You come home straight from work. And I don't want you looking at no white girls."

"Yes, Teena."

No sooner said than done. Brackley hustle Teena off to the registry office as soon as things was fixed, thinking only how nice the bed would be after the hard floor and the cold, with Teena to help keep him warm.

"What about honeymoon?" Teena say after the ceremony.

"In the summer," Brackley say. "Let we go home. I am tired and I feel I could sleep for weeks."

"Bracks," Teena say as they was coming away. "I have a nice surprise for you. Guess who coming to London this evening?"

"Father Christmas," Brackley says yawning.

"No. Aunty. I write telling her to come up, as the room not so small and we could manage until we get another place. And then she and me could get a work too, and that will help."

"You putting hell 'pon jackass back," Brackley moan. But it was only when they reach home that a great fear come to Brackley. He had was to sit down in a chair before he could talk.

"But Teena," he say quietly, "we ain't have no place for Aunty to sleep?"

"Don't worry," Teena say. "She can sleep with me until we find another place."

# Turning Christian

Foreday morning, in the hint of pearly light preceding dawn, Changoo opened his eyes but did not stir from the floor in the corner of the barrack room he lived in with Kayshee and their son Raman. He could feel the warmth of her knee against his side. The boy was near the doorway, where he usually slept.

Changoo always woke easily, as if sleep was part of an active function except that the mind rested and the body was horizontal. It was because of what he had to do today that he lay for a minute, thinking, before he sat up and pulled on a pair of ragged khaki trousers stained with mud and the labour of the canefields, holding them up with a frayed piece of thin rope as a belt. Standing, he moved quietly to the doorway and stepped over the sleeping boy. Tomorrow morning he ain't going to be here, he thought. Kayshee got to get up earlier to catch water by the standpipe, and tie-out the goat, and do all them things what the boy had to do. But most of all she got to stop grieving for him when he gone.

Outside, Changoo walked a few steps to the road—a wide gravelly track, really, with two worn parallel grooves from the traffic of mule and buffalo-drawn carts plying from the canefields to the sugarmills. He urinated into a clump of hibiscus, splattering loudly on the leaves before directing his stream to the ground. He was convinced his urine helped to thrive the growth and keep him supplied with toothbrushes. He took one now, breaking off a twig and stripping off the bark, chewing one end to a frazzle, with which he began to scrub his mouth as he stepped onto the trail.

This was the time of day he possessed—the stillness, the pale pearly light of foreday morning where everything loomed as imaginary shapes before the rising sun brought it all into focus. Then it would be waking sugarcane workers and their families, the clatter of buckets at the standpipe, the stir of movement and activity that was there even if he didn't see it all, because he preferred to witness the quick blur of bluejeans or listen to the raucous keskidees as they darted about the estate of Cross Crossing.

Changoo's feet were tough and did not feel the pebbly stones as he walked towards the canefields end of the barracks where his friend Gopaul lived. He was also an early riser, and had asked Changoo to do him a favour when he took Raman to San Fernando. When Changoo remonstrated that he had never been to town and would not know his way about, Gopaul said it was only something he wanted from the drugstore for his cough, everybody would know where the drugstore was, and he would give him the money. That was three mornings ago, and Gopaul knew that today was the day, and that this morning was his last chance to bring the money.

Changoo would not have bothered about it except that Gopaul was his best friend and knew all his business, how he and Kayshee came to Trinidad from Calcutta because of his younger brother Jaggernauth who had himself come some years before and had settled in the town as a jeweller with a small shop. Jaggernauth's encouragement had resulted in him and Kayshee landing up in the sugar estate in Cross Crossing, along with all the other indentured labourers taking the place of the black slaves in the canefields . . . and everytime he visited them, it was the same story, to join-up with the white Canadian missionary religion, as that was the only way they could get out of Cross Crossing, and come and live in town.

"You got to turn Christian," Jaggernauth said, "only those Indians who turn Christian making any headway. Is not enough to talk the language . . ."

Unable to make any headway with Changoo and Kayshee, Jaggernauth had turned his attention to the boy. Raman helped his parents, like all the children in the settlement, in the fields, but he had been spending all his spare time attending the classes that a Canadian missionary from San Fernando held in a small wooden house near the main road. He even ran away sometimes to go to the school. And he was eager to show off his English and what he was learning to his uncle.

"Jesus Christ is our Saviour."

"Good, good,"Jaggernauth encouraged. "What again? What about the Lord Prayer, you know the Lord Prayer?"

"Our father which art in heaven, hollow be thine name . . ."

"Look at that!" Jaggernauth turned to Changoo as if he was the father showing off his son's accomplishments.

"I know hymns too," Raman said, "Onwards Christian Soldiers . . ."

"Let him come and live with me in town," Jaggernauth urged. "The Canadian missionaries build a new school there, and all the smart Indians sending their children to learn and turn Christian. Give the boy a chance, Changoo."

"You will keep him and support him?" Changoo asked.

"Yes. I will give him clothes and shoes to wear, and send him to school and church. Bring him to town next week." Jaggernauth wanted a feather in his cap, though he did not know what it meant; it must be something good, for the Canadian minister in the church told the congregation it would be a feather in their cap if they could persuade any heathens to be converted to the Lord and Saviour Jesus Christ.

Changoo had discussed the matter with Gopaul, who was a strict Hindu and warned the Indians that in the years to come they would regret giving up their religion and beliefs. He kept a firm hold on his own family, but there were many who were lured by the promise of an easier life and the hope of wearing shoes, and it was true that those who turn Christian seemed to prosper and do better for themselves. Changoo and Kayshee had made up their minds to let Raman go. The decision threatened, then weakened, his friendship with Gopaul.

Now, as he saw Gopaul slowly approaching—also brushing his teeth—he had a feeling that if his friend didn't need the medicine for his cough he would not have turned up.

"So." Gopaul did not waste any time in preliminary talk. "Today is the day you taking your son to town to give him away to the white people religion?" He spat a bit of hibiscus as if to emphasise his words, and spat again some phlegm which had risen in this chest.

"I just going to give him a chance," Changoo said, compromising the doubts he still held. He really wanted to ask Gopaul what it was like in town, but his friend emanated all the coldness that had come between them. Indeed, Gopaul reinforced that thought now by shoving the money at him, and saying, "Look, the money for the medicine," and Changoo put it in his pocket, and then, as Gopaul turned to go back, Gopaul said, "You sure you doing the right thing?"

And Changoo said, "Yes," though he wasn't sure, and Gopaul left him standing there . . .

The police uniform doubled Norbert's concepts about himself: he felt like a giant. He did not walk, but swagger—look at me, I is the LAW, and every man-jack and his brother better get out the way, or else I lock them up and throw away the key!

Norbert grew from boyhood to manhood as a slave. When emancipation came, like many of his black countrymen, he celebrated in the intoxication of freedom by deserting the canefields for a carefree, idle life in the town of San Fernando, where they loafed about or turned their hands and wits to other means of survival. As the indentured labourers from India came in to replace the slaves, the blacks were as happy as the estate proprietors to have them. Let the coolies sweat with hoe and cutlass in the hot-sun for Massa, we done with that.

When Norbert joined the police force one of the laws he had to help enforce was to keep the Indians away from the town, unless they had a written pass from the foreman or overseer. Some of them couldn't stand the grind and absconded; others drifted away and ventured into town, or looked for another estate where conditions were not so hard. The sugar owners were concerned about this loss of labour and asked the police to watch out for them.

Norbert didn't need to be told. He was zealous in his duty; the locals cried "Call Norbert!" if they spotted an Indian looking out-of-place, or if they had an altercation with any of the few who lived legitimately in the town. Scarred with the atrocities and cruelties of slavery, Norbert had a dread that if the new labourers became rebellious, he and his friends might be called upon to return to the fields. He had nightmares about that when he couldn't sleep because the scars from the driver's whip still itched sometimes. What if the Indians gave trouble, and the white bosses and them squashed this "emancipation" business and ensnared the scattered slaves for the yoke again?

This morning, as he patrolled the one road out of the town to the nearest estate of Cross Crossing, he was looking forward to one of Tanty Matilda's sweetbreads. He could see her sitting by the wayside among a small group of women who were hawking sweetmeats and fruit and vegetables. Tanty was waving a rag over her tray of cakes to keep away the flies. In the doorway of a small shop nearby, a gang of men were gambling in a circle with a soiled pack of cards. Norbert knew the game – he played regularly before he became a policeman. The dealer turned up two cards, and after bets were placed turned up the rest of the pack until one showed up to match one of the original two. It was called *wapee*, and was illegal, but Norbert knew most of the players and turned a blind eye: one or two of the players even looked up as they saw him coming and waved out to him.

"I have your sweetbread here for you, Norb," Tanty said. She always kept a nice one for him: sweeten up the police and they go be sweet to you. Besides, she had slaved alongside Norbert's father, who had literally bled to death from a flogging a week before the emancipation thing came into force. "How things going, Tanty?" Norbert took a big bite, and winked at one of the younger women close by. She put her hand to her mouth to stifle a titter: Norbert thought he would remember her when he was off-duty.

"No thiefs and vagabonds about for you to catch, but I think I see a coolie man down the road coming? My eyesight bad in the hot sun."

"Eh-heh?" Norbert put his hand to his forehead to shade the sunlight, and looked. Like it was a coolie for true, and like he have a child with him. "You right, Tanty! On the other side of the road!"

Norbert liked public participation when he was called upon to do his duty; he pretended to be swayed by the public's reaction or opinion. So he raised his voice and shouted as Changoo and Raman drew near, "Aye, you, coolie man! Come over here!"

By the time the Indian and his son crossed the road, the gambling stopped, and the women vendors gathered around with the gamblers and idlers. There was drama in the air. They liked to watch Norbert in action, and he liked to perform for them. Furthermore, they considered themselves more as participators than spectators in what was to unfold.

"What you doing in town, coolie? You run away from the estate?"

Changoo was disconcerted by the crowd, and the black man in the police uniform. Though he had his pass safely knotted in his *dhoti*, it was the first time he had ever seen so many black people together.

"No, no," he said quickly.

"Where you from?"

"Cross Crossing."

"Where your free paper? You got a free paper?"

"Yes, yes." Changoo fumbled to undo the knot in his *dhoti* as the crowd laughed and jeered.

"He got it tie-up in he trousers!"

"You call that trousers? It look more like a sheet he got tie round he waist!" Those in the background pressed forward to see what was happening.

Norbert took the pass Changoo handed him and held it at arm's length, drawing it closer and closer to his eyes. The crowd jostled and elbowed, eager for blood.

"Take him down, Norb, take him down!"

"Lock him up and throw away the key!"

"H'mm," Norbert said, and "h'mm," and he frowned and rubbed his chin. "Cross Crossing, eh?"

Changoo was scared. The boy was gripping his arm tightly. He knew Raman was frightened, and that if he showed his own fear the boy's fright would turn to terror. Nothing was wrong with his pass, but this policeman was acting as if he had run away.

Norbert now, slowly, took a notebook out of the breast pocket of his tunic. The crowd acted silence when the notebook appeared. "I have to make a note of this." He licked the tip of the pencil. "What your name is, Ram or Singh?"

"No. Changoo."

"H'mm, that's a new one, how you spell it?"

Raman said, "C-h-a-n-g-o-o."

Norbert looked at the boy as if seeing him for the first time. "Oh, and what you call, boy?"

"I call Raman. R-a-m-a-n."

"Oho! Well, Mr R-a-m-a-n, this pass is only for Mr C-h-a-n-g-o-o. What you have to say about d-a-t?"

The witticism drew the laughter Norbert expected from his extras, and the inevitable comments:

"Is a spelling competition, Norb!"

"Ask him to spell policeman!"

"No, ask him to spell bound-coolie!"

It seemed to Changoo that the mood was changing from antagonism to derision, and suddenly his mood changed too, and he was angry.

"This boy is my son. I taking him to live by his uncle Jaggernauth who have a jewellery shop here in town."

"Aha!" Norbert cried, "this uncle sheltering runaways from the estates, eh!" For the first time, he began to write rapidly in the notebook.

"No no. He is a Christian, and the boy turning Christian too!" In a flash, Changoo thought that mention of this Christian business would end the interrogation, because Jaggernauth had told him so many times that it would take care of all his troubles.

And lo, there was a voice above the murmuring crowd. Tanty Matilda cried loudly, "Let him go, Norb, don't interfere with religious business, them coolies have their own *bassa-bassa* what work for them!"

Norbert's extras began to argue among themselves at this turn. He had never arrested a coolie who offered religion as an excuse, and was himself thinking that he would have to tote this man and boy all the way back up the road in the hot sun, to the police station. And too besides, nothing was wrong with the pass from the estate supervisor, though it ought to of had the name of the boy, too. The high-brown girl he had winked at was in front of the crowd, watching him to see what he would do. Somehow, he felt that if he let the coolie man go this time, she might favour him for future possibilities . . . but he felt he had to say something to save face. "Is all well and good for you to say so, Tanty, but is my job to investigate these things. If these coolies keep running away from the estates, all of we would be back to slavery!"

The word emoted a frenzied response from the crowd, shouts of: "Kill him!" and "Don't let the coolie go!"

The ultimate decision had always been to jail the coolies, and this yes-today, yes-tomorrow attitude on Norbert's part wasn't in keeping with his previous arrests. The crowd was still out for blood in spite of his unusual hesitation. The high-brown girl winked at Norbert, and shouted, "Let we see who is man today! Mr Norbert the policeman, or the coolie from the sugar estate!"

"Don't let that woman provoke you, Norb," Tanty Matilda cried. "Let him go!"

What the girl wanted, Norbert suspected, was to see if he was man enough to challenge the mood of the crowd and not allow himself to be swayed by their emotions. I would show she who is man, he thought, and then she could show me who is woman . . .

"All right, all right!" He raised his arms. "Keep quiet, the whole set of you!" He waited for the hubbub to die down. "Who all-you think all-you is, eh? Who is the police here, me or you? The jail big enough to hold all of you for disturbing the peace!" He paused. The high-brown girl was watching him with wide eyes, the top of her tongue moving slowly over her slightly-parted lips. "I letting this man go about his business, and that decide the case." He turned to Changoo. "You hear what I say and you still here?" Changoo crossed the road quickly with Raman. He did not look back as he tugged the boy along, fleeing from the scene.

As the crowd slowly dispersed, arguing and discussing the incident, Norbert looked for the girl. He saw her running up the road after the man and boy . . .

# Olive Senior

## *The Boy Who Loved Ice Cream*

They walked down the path in single file, first the father carrying the baby Beatrice on his shoulder, then the mother, then Elsa. He brought up the rear. Wearing unaccustomed sandals, Benjy found it hard to keep his footing on the slippery path. Once or twice he almost fell and throwing out his hands to break his fall, had touched the ground. Unconsciously he wiped his hands on his seat, so that his new Sunday-go-to-church pants that his mother had made from cutting down one of his father's old jackets was already dirty with bits of mud and green bush clinging to him. But there was nobody behind him to see.

They were already late for the Harvest Festival Sale, or so his father claimed. Papa also said that it was his fault. But then his father blamed him for a lot of things, even when he was not to be blamed. The boy wasn't sure why his father was sometimes so irritable towards him, and lived in a constant state of suspense over what his father's response to him was likely to be. Now, he had been the first ready. First his sister had taken him around to the side of the house for his bath. She held him and firmly scrubbed him down with a "strainer" covered in soap. Then she had stuck the long-handled dipper into the drum of rain water and poured it over him from head to foot. He made noises as the cold water hit him and would have run, but Elsa always had a firm grip on one of his limbs.

"Stan still yu jumbo-head bwoy or a konk yu till yu fenny," she hissed at him. Although he knew that her threats were infrequently accompanied by action beyond a slap or two, still he tried to get away from her grip for he hated this weekly ritual of bathing. But Elsa by now had learned to control him and she carried the bath through without mishap for she had whispered, "Awright. Doan have yu bath and see what happen. See if yu get no ice cream."

Ice Cream! The very words conveyed to him the sound of everything in his life that he had always wanted, always longed for, but could not give a name to. He had never tasted ice cream.

It was Elsa who had told him about it. Two years ago at the Harvest

Festival Sale, Mr Doran had brought an ice cream bucket and had spent the evening the most popular man at the sale, his very customers fighting to get an opportunity to turn the bucket. According to Elsa's description, this marvellous bucket somehow produced something that, she said, was not a drink and was not food. It was hot and it was cold. Both at the same time. You didn't chew it, but if you held it on your tongue long enough it vanished, leaving an after-trace that lingered and lingered like a beautiful dream. Elsa the excitable, the imaginative, the self-assured, told him, think of your best dream, when he didn't understand. Think of it in colours, she said, pink and mauve and green. And imagine it with edges. Then imagine licking it slowly round and round the edges. That's how ice cream was.

But this description only bewildered him more. He sighed, and tried hard to imagine it. But he couldn't because he didn't have a best dream or even a good dream, only nightmares, and his mother would hold him and his father would say, "what is wrong with this pickney eh? a mampala man yu a raise." Then the baby had come and he didn't have his mother's lap any more. Now imagining ice cream, he thought of sitting cuddled in his mother's arms again and saw this mysterious new creation as something as warm and beautiful. From Elsa's description, ice cream was the most marvellous thing he had ever heard of. And the strangest. For apart from anything else, he didn't know what ice was. His thoughts kept returning to the notion of ice cream throughout the year, and soon it became the one bright constant in a world full of changeable adults.

Then last year when he would have discovered for himself exactly what this ice cream was like, he had come down with measles. Elsa of course went to the sale for she had already had it, but he had to stay feverish and miserable with only toothless old Tata Maud to keep him company. And Elsa had come back and given him a description of ice cream that was even more marvellous than the first. This time Mr Doran had brought two buckets, and she alone had had two cones. Not even the drops, the wangla, and the slice of light cake they brought him could compensate for missing the ice cream.

This year he was well and nothing would keep him away.

Now with the thought of ice cream the cold water his sister kept splashing on him felt refreshing and he and she turned the bath into a game, both shrieking so loudly that their mother had to put her head out the window and promise to switch them both if they didn't stop.

His mother rubbed him down with an old cloth and put on his new clothes of which he was extremely proud, not noticing that the black serge was stitched very badly with white thread which was all his mother had, and the three buttons she sewed down the front were all of different sizes and colours. His shirt too, with the body of one colour, the sleeves of a print which was once part of mama's dress and the collar of yet another print, was just, Mama said, like Joseph's coat of many colours.

Then Mama had dressed the baby and she herself had got ready. By this time Papa had come up from the spring where he had had his bath and put on his Sunday suit and hat. Benjy, dressed and bored, had wandered off down to the cotton tree root to have another look at the marvellous colours and shapes of the junjo which had sprung up after the rains just a few days ago. He was so busy that it took him a long time to hear them calling. They were standing all ready to go to the Harvest Festival Sale and Papa was cross for he said that Benjy was making them late.

Papa dressed in his Sunday suit and hat was a sight to see, for he only dressed up for special occasions — funerals, weddings and the Harvest Festival Sale. Papa never went to church though Mama did every Sunday. Papa complained every Sunday that there was no hot food and dinner was always late for Mama never got back from church till late afternoon. Plus Papa never liked Mama to be away from him for any length of time.

Foolishness, foolishness, Papa said of the church going.

Mama didn't say anything but she prayed for Papa every Sunday. She wasn't that religious, but she loved every opportunity to go out. She loved to dress up and she loved to talk to people and hear all the news that was happening out there in the wide world, though she didn't believe half of it. Although Mama hadn't even been to Kingston in her life, if someone came along and said, "Let us go to the moon," quick as anything Mama would pick herself up and go. Or if Papa said to her "Let us give up all this hard life and move to town where we will have electric light and water out of a pipe and food out of a tin," Mama would not hesitate. Papa of course would never dream of saying anything of the sort. He was firmly wedded to the soil. She was always for Progress, though, as she sadly complained to the children, none of that ever came their way.

Now the Harvest Festival Sale was virtually the only time that Papa went into Springville these days. He hated to go into Springville even though it was where he was born for increasingly over the last four or five years, he had developed the feeling that Springville people knew something he didn't know but should, and they were laughing at him behind his back. It was something to do with his woman. It was one of those entirely intuitive feelings that suddenly occurred full-blown, then immediately took firm root in the mind. Even before the child was born he had had the instinctive feeling that it was not his. Then as the boy had grown, he had searched his face, his features, to discern himself there, and had failed utterly to find anything conclusive. He could never be sure. The old women used to say you could tell paternity sure thing by comparing the child's foot with that of the supposed father: "if the foot not the spitting image of the man then is jacket". He had spent countless surreptitious hours studying the turn of his son's foot but had come away with nothing. For one thing, the child was so thin and rickety that his limbs bore no resemblance to the man's heavily muscled body.

Now he had never known of the woman being unfaithful to him. But the minute she had come back from spending three weeks in Springville that time her mother was dying, from then on he had had the feeling that something had happened. Maybe it was only because she seemed to him so beautiful, so womanly that he had the first twinges of jealousy. Now every Sunday as she dressed in her neat white dress and shoes and the chaste hat which to him sat so provocatively on her head, his heart quickened as he saw her anew, not as the young girl he had taken from her mother's house so many years before, not as the gentle and good-natured mother of his children, but as a woman whom he suddenly perceived as a being attractive to other men.

But now everyone was in a good mood again as they set off down the road to the Harvest Festival Sale. First they walked a mile and a half down their mountain path where they saw no one, until they met up with the main path to the village. Always in the distance ahead of them now they could see people similarly dressed going to the sale. Others would call out to them from their houses as they passed by:

"Howdy Mis Dinah," said Papa.

"Mis Dinah," Mama said.

"Mis Dinah," the children murmured.

"Howdy Mister Seeter. Miss Mae. Children. Yu gone on early."

"Ai. Yu coming?"

"No mus'. Jus a wait for Icy finish iron mi frock Miss Mae. A ketch yu up soon."

"Awright Mis D."

Then they would walk another quarter mile or so till they got to another house perched on the hillside.

"Owdy Mister Seeter. Miss Mae. Little ones. A coming right behin."

And another family group would come out of the house and join them. Soon, a long line of people was walking in single file down the path. The family groups got mixed. The adults would walk behind other adults so that they could talk. The children bringing up the rear instinctively ranked themselves, putting the smallest ones in front. Occasionally one of the adults would look back and frown because the tail of the line had fallen too far behind.

"Stop! Jacky! Ceddie! Mavis! Merteen! What yu all doing back there a lagga lagga so? Jus' hurry up ya pickney."

Then all the offspring chastised, the adults would soon become lost in a discussion of the tough-headedness of children.

The children paid hardly any attention and even forgot to fight or get into any mischief, for they were far too excited about the coming afternoon.

Soon, the path broadened out and joined the lane which led to the Commons where the sale was being held. Benjy loved to come out from the cool and shadows of the path, through an archway of wild brazilwood with branches that drooped so much the adults had to lift them up in order to get through. From the semi-darkness they came suddenly into the broad lane covered in marl and dazzling white which to him was the broadest street in the whole world. Today the lane was full of people as far as the eye could see, all the men in their dark suits and hats and the women, abandoning their chaste Sunday white, wearing their brightest dresses. Now a new set of greetings had to take place between the mountain people who came from a place called One Eye and were regarded as "dark" and mysterious by the people who lived in the one-time prosperous market town of Springville. Springville itself wasn't much—a crossroads with a few wooden "upstairs" houses with fretwork balconies, built at the turn of the century with quick money made in Panama or Cuba. Now even though these houses were so old they leaned in the wind together, and had never seen a coat of paint, to the mountain people they looked as huge and magical as anything they hoped to see. Two of these upstairs houses had shops and bars beneath, with their proud owners residing above, and on one corner there was a large one-storey concrete building with huge wooden shutters which housed the Chinese grocery and the Chinese. A tiny painted house served as the post office and the equally tiny house beside it housed Brother Brammie the tailor. The most imposing buildings in the village were the school and the Anglican Church which were both on the main lane. The Baptists and the Seventh Day Adventists had their churches on the side road.

At Harvest Festival time, all the people in the village forgot their differences and came together to support each other's Harvest Festival Sales. But none could compare in magnificence to the Anglicans'. The sale took place on the Monday after the Harvest Service in the church. On Monday morning at dawn, the church members travelled from far with the bamboo poles and coconut boughs to erect on the Commons the booths for the sale. Because the sale was a secular event and liable to attract all kinds of sinners, it was not held in the church yard but on the Commons which belonged to the church but was separated by a barbed wire fence. Since the most prosperous people in the area were Anglicans, this was the largest and most popular of the sales. After a while it became less of a traditional Harvest Festival Sale and more of a regular fair, for people began to come from the city with goods to sell, and took over a little corner of the Commons for themselves. The church people frowned on this at first, then gave up on keeping these people out even when they began to bring games such as "Crown and Anchor," for they helped to attract larger and larger crowds which also spent money in the church members' booths. The church members also enjoyed themselves buying the wares of the town vendors, parson drawing the line only at the sale and consumption of liquor on the premises. A few zealots of the village strongly objected to this sale, forbidding their daughters to go to this den of wickedness and vice, but nobody paid these people the slightest attention. The Mothers Union ladies who had decorated the church for the Harvest Service the day before now tied up sprays of bougainvillea and asparagus fern over the entrance into each booth and radiated good cheer to everyone in their self-appointed role as hostesses.

The sale actually started at noon, but the only people who got there early were those who were involved in the arrangements. Most people turned up only after the men had put in at least a half-day in the fields and then gone home to bathe and dress and eat. They would stay at the sale until night had fallen, using bottle torches to light their way home.

When they got to the Commons, Benjy was the only person who was worried, for he wasn't sure that they wouldn't get there too late for the ice cream. Maybe Mr Doran would make the ice cream as soon as the sale started and then it would all be finished by the time they got there. Then another thought came: suppose this year Mr Doran was sick, or simply couldn't be bothered with ice cream any more. He would have to wait a whole year again to taste it. Perhaps never.

"Suppose, jus' suppose," he had said to his sister many times during the past week, "suppose him doan mek enough."

"Cho! As soon as him finish wan bucket him mek anadda. Ice cream nevva done," Elsa told him impatiently, wishing that she had never brought up the subject.

But this did not console him. Suppose his father refused to buy him ice cream? It was unthinkable! And yet his father's behaviour towards him was irrational: Benjy never knew just what to expect.

As soon as they turned into the Commons they could hear the sound of Mass Vass' accordion rising shrilly above the noise of the crowd, as much a part of the Harvest Festival sale as was Brother Shearer's fife and drum band that played at all fairs, weddings and other notable events for miles around.

There were so many people already in the Commons that Benjy was afraid to enter: the crowd was a living, moving thing that would swallow him up as soon as he crossed through the gate. And yet he was excited too, and his excitement won out over his fear so that he boldly stepped up to the gate where the ticket taker waited and Papa paid the entrance fee for them all.

"Now you children dont bother get lost," Mama warned them but not too sternly, knowing that sooner or later they would all become separated in this joyous crowd.

Benjy was in an agony just to see the ice cream. But Elsa would have none of it.

"Wait nuh," she said, grabbing his hand and steering him firmly in the direction of the fancy goods stall where Mama had headed. There were cake stalls and pickles and preserves stalls, fancy goods stalls, glass cases full of baked goods and all the finest in fruits, vegetables, yams and all the other products of the soil that the people had brought to the church as their offerings to the Harvest Service. Off to one side was a small wooden merry-go-round and all over the field were children playing and shrieking.

"Elsa, ice cream," Benjy kept saying, and finally to reduce this annoyance Elsa took him over to a corner of the field where a crowd had gathered. There, she said. But the crowd was so thick that he could see nothing, and he felt a pain in his heart that so many other, bigger people also wanted ice cream. How ever would he get any?

"Nuh mine, Benjy," Elsa consoled him. "Papa wi gi wi ice cream. When de time come."

"Suppose him forget, Elsa."

"Not gwine forget."

"Yu remin' him."

"Yes."

"Promise?"

"But wa do yu ee bwoy," Elsa cried. She angrily flung his hand away and took off into the crowd.

He did not mind being alone, for this rich crowd so flowed that sooner or later the same people passed each other.

Benjy wished he had some money. Then he would go and wiggle his way into the very centre of the crowd that surrounded the ice cream bucket. And he would be standing there just as Mr Doran took out the ice cream. But he didn't know anything about money and had no idea what something as wonderful as ice cream would cost.

So he flowed with the crowd, stopping here and there but not really looking at anything and soon he came across his mother with Beatrice. Mama firmly took hold of his hand.

"Come. Sister Nelson bring a piece of pone fe yu."

She took him to Sister Nelson who gave him the pone which he stuffed into his mouth.

"Say tank yu chile. Yu doan have manners?" his mother asked.

He murmured thank you through the pone. Sister Nelson smiled at him. "Growing a good boy," she said and patted his head.

"But baad!" Mama said, laughing.

Mama was always saying that and it frightened him a little, for he never knew for sure just how he was "baad."

"Mama," he said, "Ice cream."

"Chile! Yu mout full an yu talking bout ice cream aready!"

Tears started to trickle down his cheeks.

"Now see here. A bawl yu wan' bawl? Doan mek a give yu something fe bawl bout, yu hear bwoy. Hm. Anyway a doan know if there is money for foolishness like cream. Have to see yu father about dat."

His heart sank, for the day before he had heard his father complain that there was not enough money to buy all the things they needed at the Harvest Festival Sale and did she think money grew on trees. But everyone knew that Papa saved all year for that day, for the town vendors came and spread out their wares under the big cotton tree—cloth, pots and pans, fancy lamps, wicks and shades, readymade clothes, shoes, shoelaces, matches, knives, cheap perfume, plastic oilcloths for the table, glasses with birds and flowers, water jugs, needles, enamelware, and plaster wall hangings with robins and favourite bible texts. Even Miss Sybil who had the dry goods store would turn up and buy from them, and months later the goods would turn up in her dark and dusty shop at twice the price as the vendors'.

Mama had announced months in advance that she wanted an oilskin cloth, a new lampshade and shoes for the children. She hadn't mentioned anything for herself, but on these occasions Mama usually came home with a pair of new shoes, or a scarf, or a hat — anything that would put her in touch with what seemed another, glamorous life.

Papa, like his son, was distracted, torn between two desires. One was to enjoy the sale and to see if he could pick up anything for the farm or just talk to the farmers whom nowadays he never saw at any other time. Then the Extension Officer was there and he wanted to catch him to ask about some new thing he had heard that the government was lending money to plant crops though he didn't believe a word of it. Then he wanted to go and buy a good white shirt from the town vendors. Mama had insisted that he should. And he wanted to see the new games they had brought. In many ways one part of his mind was like a child's, for he wanted to see and do everything. But another part of his mind was spoiling the day for him: he didn't want to let Mama out of his sight. More and more the conviction had been growing on him that if there had been another man in her life, it wasn't anyone from around here. So it had to be a townman. And where else did one get the opportunity to meet strangers but at the sale. Walking down the mountain path he had started out enjoying the feeling of going on an outing, the only one he permitted himself for the year. But as they got nearer and nearer to Springville and were joined by other people, he became more and more uneasy. The way his woman easily greeted and chatted with people at first used to fill him with pride and admiration that she could so naturally be at ease where he was dull and awkward and clumsy. But by the time they entered the lane this pride had turned to irritation, for now he had begun to exaggerate in his mind precisely those qualities for which he had previously praised her: now she laughed too loudly, chattered too much, she was not modest enough, she attracted attention to herself — and to him, for having a woman so common and so visible. By the time they got to the Commons it was clear to her that he was in one of his "moods" though she did not know why and she hoped that the crowd would bring back his good humour again, for she was accustomed to his ups and downs. But she didn't dwell on the man's moods, for nothing would make her not enjoy herself at the sale.

Now the man surreptitiously tried to keep her under his eye but it was virtually impossible because of the crowd. He saw her sometimes only as a flash in the distance and he strained to see what she was up to, but he caught her only in the most innocent of poses—with church sisters and married couples and little children. She eagerly tried on hats and shoes. She looked at pictures. She examined tablecloths. She ate grater cake and snowballs. Looking at her from afar, her gestures seemed to him so pure, so innocent that he told himself that he was surely mad to think badly of her. Then he looked at the town folk gathered around the games, hawking yards of cloth, and stockings and ties and cheap jewellery. He looked at them and their slim hard bodies and their stylish clothes and their arrogant manners and their tough faces which hid a knowledge of the world he could never have. And he felt anxious and angry again. Now he turned all his attention to these townmen to see if he could single out one of them: the one. So engaged did he become on this lonely and futile pursuit that he hardly heard at all what anybody said to him. Even the children begging for ice cream he roughly brushed aside. He was immediately full of remorse, for he had planned to treat them to ice cream, but by the time he came to his senses and called after them, they had disappeared into the crowd. He vowed that once he met up with them again he would make up for his gruffness. He would treat them not only to ice cream but to sliced cake, to soft drinks, to paradise plums and jujubs. But the moment of softness, of sentiment, quickly passed for his attention became focussed on one man in black pants and a purple shirt and wearing a grey felt hat. The man was tall, brown-skinned and good looking with dark, curly hair. He couldn't tell why this man caught his attention except that he was by far the best looking of the townmen, seemed in fact a cut above them, even though like some of the others his arms were covered from wrist to elbow in lengths of cheap chains, and his fingers in the tacky rings that he was selling. He watched the man steadily while he flirted and chatted with the girls and finally faded out of sight—but not in the direction his woman was last seen.

Now Benjy was crying and even Elsa felt let down. Papa had refused to buy them ice cream! Although she cajoled and threatened, she couldn't get Benjy to stop crying. He was crying as much for the ice cream as for being lost from even his mother so happy and animated among all the people she knew, amid crowds and noise and confusion. Now she had little time for them and impatiently waved them on to "enjoy themselves." Elsa did just that for she found everything entertaining and school friends to chatter with. But not Benjy. She could not understand how a little boy could be so lacking in joy for such long periods of time, periods of time, and how his mind could become focussed on just one thing. If Benjy could not have ice cream, he wanted nothing.

Night was coming on and they were lighting the lamps. They hung up the storm lantern at the gate but all the coconut booths were lit with kitchen bitches, Only the cake stall run by Parson's wife and the most prosperous ladies of the church had a tilly lamp, though there wasn't much cake left to sell.

Benjy still stumbled along blindly, dragged by Elsa who was determined to get a last fill of everything. Benjy was no longer crying but his eyes were swollen and he was tired and his feet were dragging. He knew that soon they would have to go home. The lighting of the lamps was the signal for gathering up families together, and though they might linger for a while after that talking, making last minute purchases and plans, children were at this point not allowed to wander or stray from the group for the word of adults had once again become law, and when all the adults decided to move, woe onto the child who could not be found.

So everyone was rounding up everyone else, and in this confusion, Benjy started to howl again for he and Elsa were passing by Mr Doran and his bucket, only the crowd was so thick around it you couldn't see anything.

But just then they ran into Papa again and, miraculously, he was the one that suggested ice cream. Although Benjy's spirits immediately lifted, he still felt anxious that Papa would never be able to get through that crowd in time. Papa left him and Elsa on the fringes, and he impatiently watched as Papa, a big man, bore his way through. What is taking Papa so long? I bet Mr Doran has come to the end of the bucket. There is no more ice cream. Here comes Mr Manuel and Mars Edgy asking if they aren't ready. And indeed, everyone from the mountain was more or less assembled and they and Papa now seemed the only people missing from the group. They told Mars Edgy that Papa had gone to get them ice cream, and Mars Edgy was vexed because, he said, Papa should have done that long before. Now Mars Edgy made his way through the crowd around the ice earn vendor and Benjy's hopes fell again. He felt sure that Mars Edgy would pull Papa away before he got the ice cream. Torn between hope and despair, Benjy looked up at the sky which was pink and mauve from the setting sun. Just like ice cream! But here comes Papa and Mars Edgy now and Papa is carrying in his hands three cones and Papa is coming and Benjy is so excited that he starts to run towards him and he stumbles and falls and Elsa is laughing as she picks him up and he is laughing and Mars Edgy is moving off quickly to where the mountain people are standing and Papa bends down and hands him a cone and Papa has a cone and Elsa has a cone and Benjy has a cone and the three of them stand there as if frozen in time and he is totally joyous for he is about to have his first taste of ice cream but even though this is so long-awaited so precious he first has to hold the cone at arm's length to examine it and witness the ice cream perched just so on top and he is afraid to put it into his mouth for Elsa said it was colder than spring water early in the morning and suppose just suppose it burns his tongue suppose he doesn't like it and Elsa who is well into eating hers and Papa who is eating his are laughing at him . . . then he doesn't know what is happening for suddenly Papa sees something his face quickly changes and he flings away his cone and makes a grab for Benjy and starts walking almost running in the direction where Mama is standing she is apart from all the people talking to a strange man in a purple shirt and Papa is moving so fast Benjy's feet are almost off the ground and Benjy is crying Papa Papa and everything is happening so quickly he doesn't know the point at which he loses the ice cream and half the cone and all that is left in his hand is the little tip of the cone which he clutches tightly and he cannot understand why Papa has let go of his hand and is shouting and why Mama isn't laughing with the man anymore and why everyone is rushing about and why he has only this little tip of cone in his hand and there is no ice cream and he cannot understand why the sky which a minute ago was pink and mauve just like the ice cream is now swimming in his vision like one swollen blanket of rain.

# Vikram Seth

from *The Golden Gate*

12.1

John's nights are free, Jan's days. Their meetings,
On weekend afternoons, are rare.
And yet, the pattern of their greetings,
The counted hours that they share,
Drive him from his embittered brooding
Against the cosmos — all, excluding
His erstwhile friends. There, in his eyes,
There is no balm of compromise,
No herb of reconciliation.
To talk of them, to speak their names
Is to immerse him in the flames
Of hatred, the intoxication
Of a now long-fermented brew
That burns his spirit through and through.

12.2

A waste, a puerile waste and pity,
Jan thinks, that these three former friends
Will not meet somewhere in the city
— Some neutral café — make amends
Or peace or mutual restitution,
Perform some ritual ablution
Of their ill will, and recognize
That life is short and that time flies,
Etcetera — and that, all things taken
Into account, John, Liz, and Phil
Have less of ill than of goodwill;
But when she mentions this, so shaken
Is she by John's extreme response,
She drops the matter — for the nonce.

12.3

When one considers how pain mangles
John, who believes he's duped by love,
When one considers that triangles
Such as the one described above
Lent five-star tragedy material
To Shakespeare and the Greeks, ethereal
Dream bubbles such as Janet blows
Of universal love expose
An aspiration somewhat artless
In one whose art's far from naive.
It's true that Jan does not believe
John's stance is reasonless or heartless;
She sees it, though, as rigid. Well,
Perhaps that's so; it's hard to tell.


12.4

Some claim the coast of California
Is seasonless, that there's no snow
To flavor winter. Others, born here
Or fleeing here — glad to forgo
The option of frostbitten fingers
And housebound months as hoarfrost lingers
Upon the firs, less picturesque
Than deadening, while from their desk
They'd stare past dark eaves fringed with icicles
Well into March, and scarcely dare
To breathe the east or midwest air —
Now yield, with tank tops, frisbees, bicycles,
Dogs, cats, and kids and tans and smiles
To spring's precocious warmth and wiles.


12.5

It's spring! Meticulous and fragrant
Pear blossoms bloom and blanch the trees,
While pink and ravishing and flagrant
Quince bursts in shameless colonies
On woody bushes, and the slender
Yellow oxalis, brief and tender,
Brilliant as mustard, sheets the ground,
And blue jays croak, and all around

Iris and daffodil are sprouting
With such assurance that the shy
Grape hyacinth escapes the eye,
And spathes of Easter lilies, flouting
Nomenclature, now effloresce
In white and lenten loveliness.

12.6
John views his disregarded garden
Where flowers and weeds hold equal sway.
He feels his resolution harden:
"It's springtime, and it's Saturday.
Jan is an excellent adviser.
I ought to call her and apprise her
That I need help in my attempt
To keep my backyard couth and kempt."
But when Jan comes, instead of dealing
With mulch, mimosas, and manure
They take a ride along the shore
And, with a vernal verve of feeling,
Talk of the past, of the old days
Before they went their separate ways.

12.7
No wistfulness but, rather, laughter
Tinges their speech. Do they refer
To different beings? Even after
She says to him and he to her
That first love's best by definition
They seem to state a proposition
So distant from their lives that they
Are quite untouched by it today.
John lives each week, and takes things easy.
Love's a mere word. Though it's a blast
To screen old reels, the past's the past.
If it intrudes, it makes him queasy.
Singed once, he will not yield again
Words that might cause him future pain.

12.8
But week by week, as springtime urges

Him into the caressing sun,
And the rain lessens, and March merges
With April, and the benison
Of days, their tread and their profusion,
Distract his heart from its contusion,
His visits to the bars decrease.
If now and then he finds release
From his aloneness with a stranger,
His new companionship with Jan,
Confined to daylight, helps him span
The darkness safer from the danger
Of the crude misery that drove
Him into unknown arms for love. . .

# Philip Sherlock

## *The Warau People Discover the Earth*

The Caribs were the first people on earth. After them came the Warau from a land beyond the sky, rich in birds of rare beauty but without animals of any kind. No deer grazed on its grassy plains, no jaguar roamed through its scattered woods, no fish swam in its clear, shallow streams. Instead there were large flocks of birds of rare beauty. Some of these the Warau killed for food; and each man made for himself from the feathers of the birds a richly coloured headdress for wearing at great festivals.

One day while a young Warau hunter, Okonorote, was wandering through the fields he saw a bird more beautiful than any he had ever seen. In flight it was an exquisite jewel, the scarlet of its feathers more brilliant than those of the scarlet ibis, its green more vivid than the emerald feathers of the humming-bird. Enchanted by its rainbow loveliness, Okonorote swore not to return home until he had taken the bird. "How splendid a head-dress these feathers will make," he said to himself; "lovelier than any fashioned in ancient times. These feathers will give joy to many. I must have them."

For five days Okonorote followed the bird, using all his skill to come within bowshot while it settled to a meal of berries on some lofty branch. He crept towards the bird through the long grass, keeping out of sight, crawling, inching his way forward, holding his breath lest even that faint sound of breathing should startle it. Almost within range, he lifted the bow, put the arrow in place, then moved forward so gently that neither stirring of grass nor rustle of leaves told of his presence. Suddenly, even while he was pointing the arrow, the bird flew away and the pursuit began anew.

On the afternoon of the fifth day the bird settled on the low branch of a tree. Okonorote moved forward very slowly, making no sound. He kept his eyes fixed on the bird. His heart beat fast, for now he was nearer to it than he had ever been. He marvelled at the proud curve of the neck, the splendid crest of red and blue feathers, the rich hues of the rainbow plumage. He loosed his arrow. At that moment the bird flew up into the air. But it was too late. The arrow pierced the body. The bird fell back lifeless into the high grass.

Okonorote raced towards the place where the bird had fallen, shouting for joy. For five days he had watched, moving with care, making no sound, thinking only of the bird. Now he could throw caution to the winds. He raced at full speed towards the bird he had sought for so long. But it was not there. He thrust aside the dagger-points of the thorn-bush, the keen blades of the sword-grass and tore away the thick undergrowth covering the black swollen roots of the trees, but he could not find the bird. He had seen the arrow pierce its splendid body. He had seen it fall headlong into the thorn-bushes; but it was not there. Widening his circle of search, Okonorote came not to a gleaming bird but to a deep hole. Throwing himself face downward he looked over the edge of the hole, hoping to see the bird's body. To his astonishment he saw far below him a world of sunlit savannahs, green forests, and of animals grazing quietly—cattle, the fat, slow-moving tapir, and the swift deer.

With the skill of a hunter, Okonorote noted that the hole lay at the feet of a gentle hill, under the shelter of two cedar-trees that joined hands above it. Then he hurried back to tell of what he had seen, leaving signs to show the way: an arrow scratched on the bark of a mora-tree, a little heap of stones, a broken branch.

Many of the Warau people laughed at Okonorote's tale. Some said that he had fallen asleep and mistaken a dream for reality. The elders pointed out that for many years they had wandered far and wide through their land, and had never found this deep hole. Also, surely their fathers before them would have found it. After all, Okonorote was but a young man! Perhaps he had fallen into a hole hidden in the long grass and this had so shaken him that he was confused. Besides, no bird such as he described had been seen in their land. And even if Okonorote had seen such a bird, and he had put an arrow through it, how could it have vanished, leaving neither bones nor feathers?

A few of the young men, Okonorote's friends, believed him. They set off to find the hole, threw themselves face downwards beside it, and exclaimed in wonder at the beauty of the world below them, its sparkling streams, its forests, and, most wonderful of all, at the animals grazing on the savannahs.

"But how shall we get to that world?" asked the young men.

The wise men of the Waraus came together and talked, until at last one thought of a plan.

"Let us," he said, "make a long rope-ladder down which we can climb to this other world."

"That will take many months," said one.

"And who will be the first to climb down?" asked another.

"I will climb first," replied Okonorote; "for it may be that my bird lies on those savannahs that we can see. If I fail to return, only one man is lost. If I come back you will know that the way is safe."

For many weeks the Warau girls and women picked cotton in the forest and wove it into a rope-ladder of great strength. This the men lowered through the deep hole, trying out the length of the rope. At the first trial it was too short. The women picked more cotton and lengthened the rope-ladder, but still it was too short. At the third trial it touched the trees in the forest far below.

As soon as the ladder had been made fast, Okonorote climbed down, descending first through the dark hole whose sides were smooth and damp, and then beyond towards the savannahs, the ladder swaying but holding fast; so, after half a day, he came to the trees, and finally, to the floor of the forest. Having tied the end of the rope-ladder firmly to a tree, he moved out on to the savannahs where the animals were grazing. He shot a young deer, kindled a fire, roasted the flesh and found it good. Packing up the rest of the meat, he climbed with it to his own land.

When the Waraus tasted the flesh of the deer they longed for more. When Okonorote told them of the savannahs, forests, gleaming rivers, and high mountains, and above all of the deer and cattle, the tapir and the armadillo, they cried out, "Let us go to this world below and see its wonders."

So it came about that all the Warau people descended to the earth, climbing down the rope-ladder, passing first through the deep hole and coming at last to the forest. With Okonorote they searched for the bird, but there was no trace of it. Instead, they found guavas, pineapples, sapodillas, and bananas; and animals of many kinds.

Among the Warau people there was one only, a woman named Rainstorm, who did not like the earth. In the land above the sky she had been sad and lonely, keeping to herself, often full of tears. Because she often wept, her friends called her Rainstorm. On earth the forests and the savannahs gave her no pleasure, and the animals terrified her. After some months she decided to make her way back to the land above. But Rainstorm had grown fat on earth, and while she was climbing through the hole she stuck fast. Wedged tight, she could not move. There she remains to this day, wedged tightly in the hole, so that those who live on earth cannot see through the sky. And when clouds cover the sky and the rains begin to fall, the Warau people say, "Rainstorm is weeping today."

# Leslie Marmon Silko

*Yellow Woman*

## I

My thigh clung to his with dampness, and I watched the sun rising up through the tamaracks and willows. The small brown water birds came to the river and hopped across the mud, leaving brown scratches in the alkali-white crust. They bathed in the river silently. I could hear the water, almost at our feet where the narrow fast channel bubbled and washed green ragged moss and fern leaves. I looked at him beside me, rolled in the red blanket on the white river sand. I cleaned the sand out of the cracks between my toes, squinting because the sun was above the willow trees. I looked at him for the last time, sleeping on the white river sand.

I felt hungry and followed the river south the way we had come the afternoon before, following our footprints that were already blurred by lizard tracks and bug trails. The horses were still lying down, and the black one whinnied when he saw me but he did not get up — maybe it was because the corral was made out of thick cedar branches and the horses had not yet felt the sun like I had. I tried to look beyond the pale red mesas to the pueblo. I knew it was there, even if I could not see it, on the sandrock hill above the river, the same river that moved past me now and had reflected the moon last night.

The horse felt warm underneath me. He shook his head and pawed the sand. The bay whinnied and leaned against the gate trying to follow, and I remembered him asleep in the red blanket beside the river. I slid off the horse and tied him close to the other horse. I walked north with the river again, and the white sand broke loose in footprints over footprints.

"Wake up."

He moved in the blanket and turned his face to me with his eyes still closed. I knelt down to touch him.

"I'm leaving."

He smiled now, eyes still closed. "You are coming with me,

remember?" He sat up now with his bare dark chest and belly in the sun.

"Where?"

"To my place."

"And will I come back?"

He pulled his pants on. I walked away from him, feeling him behind me and smelling the willows.

"Yellow Woman," he said.

I turned to face him. "Who are you?" I asked.

He laughed and knelt on the low, sandy bank, washing his face in the river. "Last night you guessed my name, and you knew why I had come."

I stared past him at the shallow moving water and tried to remember the night, but I could only see the moon in the water and remember his warmth around me.

"But I only said that you were him and that I was Yellow Woman — I'm not really her — I have my own name and I come from the pueblo on the other side of the mesa. Your name is Silva and you are a stranger I met by the river yesterday afternoon."

He laughed softly. "What happened yesterday has nothing to do with what you will do today, Yellow Woman."

"I know — that's what I'm saying — the old stories about the ka'tsina spirit and Yellow Woman can't mean us."

My old grandpa liked to tell those stories best. There is one about Badger and Coyote who went hunting and were gone all day, and when the sun was going down they found a house. There was a girl living there alone, and she had light hair and eyes and she told them that they could sleep with her. Coyote wanted to be with her all night so he sent Badger into a prairie-dog hole, telling him he thought he saw something in it. As soon as Badger crawled in, Coyote blocked up the entrance with rocks and hurried back to Yellow Woman.

"Come here," he said gently.

He touched my neck and I moved close to him to feel his breathing and to hear his heart. I was wondering if Yellow Woman had known who she was — if she knew that she would become part of the stories. Maybe she'd had another name that her husband and relatives called her so that only the ka'tsina from the north and the storytellers would know her as Yellow Woman. But I didn't go on; I felt him all around me, pushing me down into the white river sand.

Yellow Woman went away with the spirit from the north and lived with him and his relatives. She was gone for a long time, but then one day she came back and she brought twin boys.

"Do you know the story?"

"What story?" He smiled and pulled me close to him as he said this. I was afraid lying there on the red blanket. All I could know was the way he felt, warm, damp, his body beside me. This is the way it happens in the stories. I was thinking, with no thought beyond the moment she meets the ka'tsina spirit and they go.

"I don't have to go. What they tell in stories was real only then, back in time immemorial, like they say."

He stood up and pointed at my clothes tangled in the blanket. "Let's go," he said.

I walked beside him, breathing hard because he walked fast, his hand around my wrist. I had stopped trying to pull away from him, because his hand felt cool and the sun was high, drying the river bed into alkali. I will see someone, eventually I will see someone, and then I will be certain that he is only a man — some man from nearby — and I will be sure that I am not Yellow Woman. Because she is from out of time past and I live now and I've been to school and there are highways and pickup trucks that Yellow Woman never saw.

It was an easy ride north on horseback. I watched the change from the cottonwood trees along the river to the junipers that brushed past us in the foothills, and finally there were only piñons, and when I looked up at the rim of the mountain plateau I could see pine trees growing on the edge. Once I stopped to look down, but the pale sandstone had disappeared and the river was gone and the dark lava hills were all around. He touched my hand, not speaking, but always singing softly a mountain song and looking into my eyes.

I felt hungry and wondered what they were doing at home now — my mother, my grandmother, my husband, and the baby. Cooking breakfast, saying, "Where did she go? — maybe kidnaped," and Al going to the tribal police with the details: "She went walking along the river."

The house was made with black lava rock and red mud. It was high above the spreading miles of arroyos and long mesas. I smelled a mountain smell of pitch and buck brush. I stood there beside the black horse, looking down on the small, dim country we had passed, and I shivered.

"Yellow Woman, come inside where it's warm."

## II

He lit a fire in the stove. It was an old stove with a round belly and an enamel coffeepot on top. There was only the stove, some faded Navajo blankets, and a bedroll and cardboard box. The floor was made of smooth adobe plaster, and there was one small window, facing east. He pointed at the box.

"There's some potatoes and the frying pan." He sat on the floor with his arms around his knees pulling them close to his chest and he watched me fry the potatoes. I didn't mind him watching me because he was always watching me — he had been watching me since I came upon him sitting on the river bank trimming leaves from a willow twig with his knife. We ate from the pan and he wiped the grease from his fingers on his Levis.

"Have you brought women here before?" He smiled and kept chewing, so I said, "Do you always use the same tricks?"

"What tricks?" He looked at me like he didn't understand.

"The story about being a ka'tsina from the mountains. The story about Yellow Woman."

Silva was silent, his face was calm.

"I don't believe it. Those stories couldn't happen now," I said.

He shook his head and said softly, "But someday they will talk about us, and they will say, 'Those two lived long ago when things like that happened.' "

He stood up and went out. I ate the rest of the potatoes and thought about things — about the noise the stove was making and the sound of the mountain wind outside. I remembered yesterday and the day before, and then I went outside.

I walked past the corral to the edge where the narrow trail cut through the black rim rock. I was standing in the sky with nothing around me but the wind that came down from the mountain peak behind me. I could see faint mountain images in the distance miles across the vast spread of mesa and valleys and plains. I wondered who was over there to feel the mountain wind on those sheer blue edges — who walks on the pine needles in those blue mountains.

"Can you see the pueblo?" Silva was standing behind me.

I shook my head, "We're too far away."

"From here I can see the world." He stepped out on the edge. "The Navajo reservation begins over there." He pointed to the east. "The Pueblo boundaries are over here." He looked below us to the south, where the narrow trail seemed to come from. "The Texans have their ranches over there, starting with that valley, the Concho Valley. The Mexicans run some cattle over there too."

"Do you ever work for them?"

"I steal from them," Silva answered. The sun was dropping behind us and shadows were filling the land below. I turned away from the edge that dropped forever into the valleys below.

"I'm cold," I said; "I'm going inside." I started wondering about this man who could speak the Pueblo language so well but who lived on a mountain and rustled cattle. I decided that this man Silva must be Navajo, because Pueblo men didn't do things like that.

"You must be a Navajo."

Silva shook his head gently. "Little Yellow Woman," he said, "you never give up, do you? I have told you who I am. The Navajo people know me, too." He knelt down and unrolled the bedroll and spread the extra blankets out on a piece of canvas. The sun was down, and the only light in the house came from outside – the dim orange light from sundown.

I stood there and waited for him to crawl under the blankets.

"What are you waiting for?" he said, and I lay down beside him. He undressed me slowly like the night before beside the river – kissing my face gently and running his hands up and down my belly and legs. He took off my pants and then he laughed.

"Why are you laughing?"

"You are breathing so hard."

I pulled away from him and turned my back to him.

He pulled me around and pinned me down with his arms and chest. "You don't understand, do you, little Yellow Woman? You will do what I want."

And again he was all around me with his skin slippery against mine, and I was afraid because I understood that his strength could hurt me. I lay beneath him and I knew that he could destroy me. But later, while he slept beside me, I touched his face and I had a feeling – the kind of feeling for him that overcame me that morning along the river. I kissed him on the forehead and he reached out for me.

When I woke up in the morning he was gone. It gave me a strange feeling because for a long time I sat there on the blankets and looked around the little house for some object of his – some proof that he had been there or maybe that he was coming back. Only the blanket and the cardboard box remained. The .30-30 that had been leaning in the corner was gone, and so was the knife I had used the night before. He was gone, and I had my chance to go now. But first I had to eat, because I knew it would be a long walk home.

I found some dried apricots in the cardboard box, and I sat down on a rock at the edge of the plateau rim. There was no wind and the sun warmed me. I was surrounded by silence. I drowsed with apricots in my mouth, and I didn't believe that there were highways or railroads or cattle to steal.

When I woke up, I stared down at my feet in the black mountain dirt. Little black ants were swarming over the pine needles around my foot. They must have smelled the apricots. I thought about my family far below me. They would be wondering about me, because this had never happened to me before. The tribal police would file a report. But if old Grandpa weren't dead he would tell them what happened—he would laugh and say, "Stolen by a ka'tsina, a mountain spirit. She'll come home—they usually do." There are enough of them to handle things. My mother and grandmother will raise the baby like they raised me. Al will find someone else, and they will go on like before, except that there will be a story about the day I disappeared while I was walking along the river. Silva had come for me; he said he had. I did not decide to go. I just went. Moonflowers blossom in the sand hills before dawn just as I followed him. That's what I was thinking as I wandered along the trail through the pine trees.

It was noon when I got back. When I saw the stone house I remembered that I had meant to go home. But that didn't seem important any more, maybe because there were little blue flowers growing in the meadow behind the stone house and the gray squirrels were playing in the pines next to the house. The horses were standing in the corral, and there was a beef carcass hanging on the shady side of a big pine in front of the house. Flies buzzed around the clotted blood that hung from the carcass. Silva was washing his hands in a bucket full of water. He must have heard me coming because he spoke to me without turning to face me.

"I've been waiting for you."

"I went walking in the big pine trees."

I looked into the bucket full of bloody water with brown-and-white animal hairs floating in it. Silva stood there letting his hand drip, examining me intently.

"Are you coming with me?"

"Where?" I asked him.

"To sell the meat in Marquez."

"If you're sure it's O.K."

"I wouldn't ask you if it wasn't," he answered.

He sloshed the water around in the bucket before he dumped it out and set the bucket upside down near the door. I followed him to the corral and watched him saddle the horses. Even beside the horses he looked tall, and I asked him again if he wasn't Navajo. He didn't say anything; he just shook his head and kept cinching up the saddle.

"But Navajos are tall."

"Get on the horse," he said, "and let's go."

The last thing he did before we started down the steep trail was to grab the .30-30 from the corner. He slid the rifle into the scabbard that hung from his saddle.

"Do they ever try to catch you?" I asked.

"They don't know who I am."

"Then why did you bring the rifle?"

"Because we are going to Marquez where the Mexicans live."

### III

The trail levelled out on a narrow ridge that was steep on both sides like an animal spine. On one side I could see where the trail went around the rocky gray hills and disappeared into the southeast where the pale sandrock mesas stood in the distance near my home. On the other side was a trail that went west, and as I looked far into the distance I thought I saw the little town. But Silva said no, that I was looking in the wrong place, that I just thought I saw houses. After that I quit looking off into the distance; it was hot and the wildflowers were closing up their deep-yellow petals. Only the waxy cactus flowers bloomed in the bright sun, and I saw every colour that a cactus blossom can be: the white ones and the red ones were still buds, but the purple and the yellow were blossoms, open full and the most beautiful of all.

Silva saw him before I did. The white man was riding a big gray horse, coming up the trail toward us. He was travelling fast and the gray horse's feet sent rocks rolling off the trail into the dry tumbleweeds. Silva motioned for me to stop and we watched the white man. He didn't see us right away, but finally his horse whinnied at our horses and he stopped. He looked at us briefly before he loped the gray horse across the three hundred yards that separated us. He stopped his horse in front of Silva, and his young fat face was shadowed by the brim of his hat. He didn't look mad, but his small, pale eyes moved from the blood-soaked gunny sacks hanging from my saddle to Silva's face and then back to my face.

"Where did you get the fresh meat?" the white man asked.

"I've been hunting," Silva said, and when he shifted his weight in the saddle the leather creaked.

"The hell you have, Indian. You've been rustling cattle. We've been looking for the thief for a long time."

The rancher was fat, and sweat began to soak through his white cowboy shirt and the wet cloth stuck to the thick rolls of belly fat. He almost seemed to be panting from the exertion of talking, and he smelled rancid, maybe because Silva scared him.

Silva turned to me and smiled. "Go back up the mountain, Yellow Woman."

The white man got angry when he heard Silva speak in a language he couldn't understand. "Don't try anything, Indian. Just keep riding to Marquez. We'll call the state police from there."

The rancher must have been unarmed because he was very frightened and if he had a gun he would have pulled it out then. I turned my horse around and the rancher yelled, "Stop!" I looked at Silva for an instant and there was something ancient and dark—something I could feel in my stomach—in his eyes, and when I glanced at his hand I saw his finger on the trigger of the .30-30 that was still in the saddle scabbard. I slapped my horse across the flank and the sacks of raw meat swung against my knees as the horse leaped up the trail. It was hard to keep my balance, and once I thought I felt the saddle slipping backward; it was because of this that I could not look back.

I didn't stop until I reached the ridge where the trail forked. The horse was breathing deep gasps and there was a dark film of sweat on its neck. I looked down into the direction I had come from, but I couldn't see the place. I waited. The wind came up and pushed warm air past me. I looked up at the sky, pale blue and full of thin clouds and fading vapor trails left by jets.

I think four shots were fired—I remember hearing four hollow explosions that reminded me of deer hunting. There could have been more shots after that, but I couldn't have heard them because my horse was running again and the loose rocks were making too much noise as they scattered around his feet.

Horses have a hard time running downhill, but I went that way instead of uphill to the mountain because I thought it was safer. I felt better with the horse running southeast past the round gray hills that were covered with cedar trees and black lava rock. When I got to the plain in the distance I could see the dark green patches of tamaracks that grew along the river; and beyond the river I could see the beginning of the pale sandrock mesas. I stopped the horse and looked back to see if anyone was coming; then I got off the horse and turned the horse around, wondering if it would go back to its corral under the pines on the mountain. It looked back at me for a moment and then plucked a mouthful of green tumbleweeds before it trotted back up the trail with its ears pointed forward, carrying its head daintily to one side to avoid stepping on the dragging reins. When the horse disappeared over the last hill, the gunny sacks full of meat were still swinging and bouncing.

## IV

I walked toward the river on a wood-hauler's road that I knew would eventually lead to the paved road. I was thinking about waiting beside the road for someone to drive by, but by the time I got to the pavement I had decided it wasn't very far to walk if I followed the river back the way Silva and I had come.

The river water tasted good, and I sat in the shade under a cluster of silvery willows. I thought about Silva, and I felt sad at leaving him; still, there was something strange about him, and I tried to figure it out all the way back home.

I came back to the place on the river bank where he had been sitting the first time I saw him. The green willow leaves that he had trimmed from the branch were still lying there, wilted in the sand. I saw the leaves and I wanted to go back to him — to kiss him and to touch him — but the mountains were too far away now. And I told myself, because I believe it, he will come back sometime and be waiting again by the river.

\* \* \*

I followed the path up from the river into the village. The sun was getting low, and I could smell supper cooking when I got to the screen door of my house. I could hear their voices inside — my mother was telling my grandmother how to fix the Jell-o and my husband, Al, was playing with the baby. I decided to tell them that some Navajo had kidnapped me, but I was sorry that old Grandpa wasn't alive to hear my story because it was the Yellow Woman stories he liked to tell best.

# Wole Soyinka

## The Trials of Brother Jero

### Characters

JEROBOAM *a Beach Divine*
OLD PROPHET *his mentor*
CHUME *assistant to Jeroboam*
AMOPE *his wife*
A TRADER
MEMBER OF PARLIAMENT

PENITENTS
NEIGHBOURS
WORSHIPPERS
A TOUGH MAMMA
A YOUNG GIRL

## SCENE I

*The stage is completely dark. A spotlight reveals the Prophet, a heavily but neatly bearded man; his hair is thick and high, but well-combed, unlike that of most prophets. Suave is the word for him. He carries a canvas pouch and a divine rod. He speaks directly and with his accustomed loftiness to the audience.*

JEROBOAM: I am a Prophet. A prophet by birth and by inclination. You have probably seen many of us on the streets, many with their own churches, many inland, many on the coast, many leading processions, many looking for processions to lead, many curing the deaf, many raising the dead. In fact, there are eggs and there are eggs. Same thing with prophets. I was born a Prophet. I think my parents found that I was born with rather thick and long hair. It was said to come right down to my eyes and down to my neck. For them, this was a certain sign that I was born a natural prophet.

And I grew to love the trade. It used to be a very respectable one in those days and competition was dignified. But in the last few years, the beach has become fashionable, and the struggle for land has turned the profession into a thing of ridicule. Some prophets I could name gained their present beaches by getting women penitents to shake their bosoms in spiritual ecstasy. This prejudiced the councillors who came to divide the beach among us.

Yes, it did come to the point where it became necessary for the Town Council to come to the beach and settle the Prophets' territorial warfare once and for all. My Master, the same one who brought me up in prophetic ways staked his claim and won a grant of land. . . . I helped him, with a campaign led by six dancing girls from the French territory, all dressed as Jehovah's Witnesses. What my old Master did not realize was that I was really helping myself.

Mind you, the beach is hardly worth having these days. The worshippers have dwindled to a mere trickle and we really have to fight for every new convert. They all prefer High Life to the rhythm of celestial hymns. And television too is keeping our wealthier patrons at home. They used to come in the evening when they would not easily be recognized. Now they stay at home and watch television. However, my whole purpose in coming here is to show you one rather eventful day in my life, a day when I thought for a moment that the curse of my old Master was about to be fulfilled. It shook me quite a bit, but . . . the Lord protects his own . . .

*[Enter Old Prophet shaking his fist.]*

OLD PROPHET: Ungrateful wretch! Is this how you repay the long years of training I have given you? To drive me, your old Tutor, off my piece of land . . . telling me I have lived beyond my time. Ha! May you be rewarded in the same manner. May the Wheel come right round and find you just as helpless as you make me now. . . .

*[He continues to mouth curses, but inaudibly.]*

JEROBOAM *[ignoring him.]*: He didn't move me one bit. The old dodderer had been foolish enough to imagine that when I organized the campaign to acquire his land in competition with *[ticking them off on his fingers]* — The Brotherhood of Jehu, the Cherubims and Seraphims, the Sisters of Judgement Day, the Heavenly Cowboys, not to mention the Jehovah's Witnesses whom the French girls impersonated — well, he must have been pretty conceited to think that I did it all for him.

OLD PROPHET: Ingrate! Monster! I curse you with the curse of the Daughters of Discord. May they be your downfall. May the Daughters of Eve bring ruin down on your head!

*[Old Prophet goes off, shaking his fist.]*

JEROBOAM: Actually that was a very cheap curse. He knew very well that I had one weakness — women. Not my fault, mind you. You must admit that I am rather good-looking . . . no, don't be misled, I am not at all vain. Nevertheless, I decided to be on my guard. The call of Prophecy is in my blood and I would not risk my calling with the fickleness of women. So I kept away from them. I am still single and since that day when I came into my own, no scandal has ever touched my name. And it was a sad day indeed when I woke up one morning and the first thing to meet my eyes was a Daughter of Eve. You may compare the feeling with waking up and finding a vulture crouched on your bedpost.

BLACKOUT

# SCENE II

*Early morning.*

*A few poles with nets and other litter denote a fishing village. Downstage right is the corner of a hut, window on one side, door on the other.*

*A cycle bell is heard ringing. Seconds after, a cycle is ridden on stage towards the hut. The rider is a shortish man; his feet barely touch the pedals. On the cross-bar is a woman, the cross-bar itself is wound round with a mat, and on the carrier is a large travelling sack, with a woman's household stool hanging from a corner of it.*

AMOPE: Stop here. Stop here. That's his house.

*[The man applies the brakes too suddenly. The weight leans towards the woman's side, with the result that she props up the bicycle with her feet, rather jerkily. It is in fact no worse than any ordinary landing, but it is enough to bring out her sense of aggrievement.]*

AMOPE *[Her tone of martyrdom is easy, accustomed to use.]*: I suppose we all do our best, but after all these years one would think you could set me down a little more gently.

CHUME: You didn't give me much notice. I had to brake suddenly.

AMOPE: The way you complain—anybody who didn't see what happened would think you were the one who broke an ankle. *[She has already begun to limp.]*

CHUME: Don't tell me that was enough to break your ankle.

AMOPE: Break? You didn't hear me complain. You did your best, but if my toes are to be broken one by one just because I have to monkey on your bicycle, you must admit it's a tough life for a woman.

CHUME: I did my . . .

AMOPE: Yes, you did your best. I know. Didn't I admit it? Please . . . give me that stool. . . . You know yourself that I'm not one to make much of a little thing like that, but I haven't been too well. If anyone knows that, it's you. Thank you *[Taking the stool.]* . . . I haven't been well, that's all, otherwise I wouldn't have said a thing.

*[She sits down near the door of the hut, sighing heavily, and begins to nurse her feet.]*

CHUME: Do you want me to bandage it for you?

AMOPE: No, no. What for?

*[Chume hesitates, then begins to unload the bundle.]*

CHUME: You're sure you don't want me to take you back? If it swells after I've gone . . .

AMOPE: I can look after myself. I've always done, and looked after you too. Just help me unload the things and place them against the wall . . . you know I wouldn't ask if it wasn't for the ankle.

*[Chume had placed the bag next to her, thinking that was all. He returns now to untie the bundle. Brings out a small brazier covered with paper which is tied down, two small saucepans . . .]*

AMOPE: You haven't let the soup pour out, have you?

CHUME *[with some show of exasperation.]*: Do you see oil on the wrapper? *[Throws down the wrapper.]*

AMOPE: Abuse me. All right, go on, begin to abuse me. You know that all I asked was if the soup had poured away, and it isn't as if that was something no one ever asked before. I would do it all myself if it wasn't for my ankle — anyone would think it was my fault . . . careful . . . careful now . . . the cork nearly came off that bottle. You know how difficult it is to get any clean water in this place . . .

*[Chume unloads two bottles filled with water, two little parcels wrapped in paper, another tied in a knot, a box of matches, a piece of yam, two tins, one probably an Ovaltine tin but containing something else of course, a cheap breakable spoon, a knife, while Amope keeps up her patient monologue, spoken almost with indifference.]*

AMOPE: Do, I beg you, take better care of that jar. . . . I know you didn't want to bring me, but it wasn't the fault of the jar, was it?

CHUME: Who said I didn't want to bring you?

AMOPE: You said it was too far away for you to bring me on your bicycle. . . . I suppose you really wanted me to walk. . . .

CHUME: I . . .

AMOPE: And after you'd broken my foot, the first thing you asked was if you should take me home. You were only too glad it happened . . . in fact if I wasn't the kind of person who would never think evil of anyone — even you — I would have said that you did it on purpose.

*[The unloading is over. Chume shakes out the bag.]*

AMOPE: Just leave the bag here. I can use it for a pillow.

CHUME: Is there anything else before I go?

AMOPE: You've forgotten the mat. I know it's not much, but I would like something to sleep on. There are women who sleep in beds of course, but I'm not complaining. They are just lucky with their husbands, and we can't all be lucky I suppose.

CHUME: You've got a bed at home.

*[He unties the mat which is wound round the cross-bar.]*

AMOPE: And so I'm to leave my work undone. My trade is to suffer because I have a bed at home? Thank God I am not the kind of woman who . . .

CHUME: I am nearly late for work.

AMOPE: I know you can't wait to get away. You only use your work as an excuse. A Chief Messenger in the Local Government Office—do you call that work? Your old school friends are now Ministers, riding in long cars . . .

*[Chume gets on his bike and flees. Amope shouts after him, craning her neck in his direction.]*

AMOPE: Don't forget to bring some more water when you're returning from work. *[She relapses and sighs heavily.]* He doesn't realize it is all for his own good. He's no worse than other men, but he won't make the effort to become something in life. A Chief Messenger. Am I to go to my grave as the wife of a Chief Messenger?

*[She is seated so that the Prophet does not immediately see her when he opens the window to breath some fresh air. He stares straight out for a few moments, then shuts his eyes tightly, clasps his hands together above his chest, chin uplifted for a few moments' mediation. He relaxes and is about to go in when he sees Amope's back. He leans out to try to take in the rest of her but this proves impossible. Puzzled, he leaves the window and goes round to the door which is then seen to open about a foot and shut rapidly. Amope is calmly chewing cola. As the door shuts she takes out a notebook and a pencil and checks some figures.*

*Brother Jeroboam, known to his congregation as Brother Jero, is seen again at the window, this time with his canvas pouch and divine stick. He lowers the bag to the ground, eases one leg over the window.]*

AMOPE *[without looking back.]*: Where do you think you're going?
*[Brother Jero practically flings himself back into the house.]*

AMOPE: One pound, eight shillings, and ninepence for three months. And he calls himself a man of God.

*[She puts the notebook away, unwraps the brazier, and proceeds to light it preparatory to getting breakfast.*

*The door opens another foot.]*

JERO *[Coughs]*: Sister . . . my dear sister in Christ . . .

AMOPE: I hope you slept well, Brother Jero. . . .

JERO: Yes, thanks be to god. *[Hems and coughs.]* I—er—I hope you have not come to stand in the way of Christ and his work.

AMOPE: If Christ doesn't stand in the way of me and my work.

JERO: Beware of pride, sister. That was a sinful way to talk.

AMOPE: Listen, you bearded debtor. You owe me one pound, eight and nine. You promised you would pay me three months ago but of course you have been too busy doing the work of God. Well, let me tell you that you are not going anywhere until you do a bit of my own work.

JERO: But the money is not in the house. I must get it from the post office before I can pay you.

AMOPE *[fanning the brazier.]*: You'll have to think of something else before you call me a fool.

*[Brother Jeroboam shuts the door.*

*A woman trader goes past with a deep calabash bowl on her head.]*

AMOPE: Ei, what are you selling?

*[The trader hesitates, decides to continue on her way.]*

AMOPE: Isn't it you I'm calling? What have you got there?

TRADER *[stops, without turning round.]*: Are you buying for trade or just for yourself?

AMOPE: It might help if you first told me what you have.

TRADER: Smoked fish.

AMOPE: Well, let's see it.

TRADER *[hesitates]*: All right, help me to set it down. But I don't usually stop on the way.

AMOPE: Isn't it money you are going to the market for, and isn't it money I'm going to pay you?

TRADER *[as Amope gets up and unloads her.]*: Well, just remember it is early in the morning. Don't start me off wrong by haggling.

AMOPE: All right, all right. *[Looks at the fish.]* How much a dozen?

TRADER: One and three, and I'm not taking a penny less.

AMOPE: It is last week's, isn't it?

TRADER: I've told you, you're my first customer, so don't ruin my trade with the ill-luck of the morning.

AMOPE *[holding one up to her nose.]*: Well, it does smell a bit, doesn't it?

TRADER *[putting back the wrappings.]*: Maybe it is you who haven't had a bath for a week.

AMOPE: Yeh! All right, go on. Abuse me. Go on and abuse me when all I wanted was a few of your miserable fish. I deserve it for trying to be neighbourly with a cross-eyed wretch, pauper that you are . . .

TRADER: It is early in the morning. I am not going to let you infect my luck with your foul tongue by answering you back. And just you keep your cursed fingers from my goods because that is where you'll meet with the father of all devils if you don't.

*[She lifts the load to her head all by herself.]*

AMOPE: Yes, go on. Carry the burden of your crimes and take your beggar's rags out of my sight. . . .

TRADER: I leave you in the hands of your flatulent belly, you barren sinner. May you never do good in all your life.

AMOPE: You're cursing me now, are you?

*[She leaps up just in time to see Brother Jero escape through the window.]*

Help! Thief! Thief! You bearded rogue. Call yourself a prophet? But you'll find it easier to get out than to get in. You'll find that out or my name isn't Amope. . . .

*[She turns on the trader who has already disappeared.]*

Do you see what you have done, you spindle-leg toad? Receiver of stolen goods, just wait until the police catch up with you . . .

*[Towards the end of this speech the sound of "gangan" drums is heard, coming from the side opposite the hut. A boy enters carrying a drum on each shoulder. He walks towards her, drumming. She turns almost at once.]*

AMOPE: Take yourself off, you dirty beggar. Do you think my money is for the likes of you?

*[The boy flees, turns suddenly, and beats a parting abuse on the drums.]*

AMOPE: I don't know what the world is coming to. A thief of a Prophet, a swindler of a fish-seller and now that thing with lice on his head comes begging for money. He and the Prophet ought to get together with the fish-seller their mother.

## LIGHTS FADE

## SCENE III

*A short while later. The beach. A few stakes and palm leaves denote the territory of Brother Jeroboam's church. To one side is a palm tree, and in the centre is a heap of sand with assorted empty bottles, a small mirror, and hanging from one of the bottles is a rosary and cross. Brother Jero is standing as he was last seen when he made his escape—white flowing gown and a very fine velvet cape, white also. Stands upright, divine rod in hand, while the other caresses the velvet cape.*

JERO: I don't know how she found out my house. When I bought the goods off her, she did not even ask any questions. My calling was enough to guarantee payment. It is not as if this was a well-paid job. And it is not what I would call a luxury, this velvet cape which I bought from her. It would not have been necessary if one were not forced to distinguish himself more and more from these scum who degrade the calling of the Prophet. It becomes important to stand out, to be distinctive. I have set my heart after a particular name. They will look at my velvet cape and they will think of my goodness. Inevitably they must begin to call me . . . the Velvet-hearted Jeroboam. *[Straightens himself.]* Immaculate Jero, Articulate hero of Christ's Crusade . . .

Well, it is out. I have not breathed it to a single soul, but that has been my ambition. You've got to have a name that appeals to the imagination — because the imagination is a thing of the spirit — it must catch the imagination of the crowd. Yes, one must move with modern times. Lack of colour gets one nowhere even in the Prophet's business. *[Looks all around him.]* Charlatans! If only I had this beach to myself. *[With sudden violence.]* But how does one maintain his dignity when the daughter of Eve forces him to leave his own house through a window? God curse that woman! I never thought she would dare affront the presence of a man of God. One pound eight for this little cape. It is sheer robbery.

*[He surveys the scene again. A young girl passes, sleepily, clothed only in her wrapper.]*

JERO: She passes here every morning, on her way to take a swim. Dirty-looking thing.

*[He yawns.]*

I am glad I got here before any customers — I mean worshippers — well, customers if you like. I always get that feeling every morning that I am a shopkeeper waiting for customers. The regular ones come at definite times.

Strange, dissatisfied people. I know they are dissatisfied because I keep them dissatisfied. Once they are full, they won't come again. Like my good apprentice, Brother Chume. He wants to beat his wife, but I won't let him. If I do, he will become contented, and then that's another of my flock gone for ever. As long as he doesn't beat her, he comes here feeling helpless, and so there is no chance of his rebelling against me. Everything, in fact, is planned.

*[The young girl crosses the stage again. She has just had her swim and the difference is remarkable. Clean, wet, shiny face and hair. She continues to wipe herself with her wrapper as she walks.]*

JERO *[follows her all the way with his eyes.]*: Every morning, every day I witness this divine transformation, O Lord.

*[He shakes his head suddenly and bellows.]*

Pray Brother Jeroboam, pray! Pray for strength against temptation.

*[He falls on his knees, face squeezed in agony and hands clasped. Chume enters, wheeling his bike. He leans it against the palm tree.]*

JERO *[not opening his eyes.]*: Pray with me brother. Pray with me. Pray for me against this one weakness . . . against this one weakness, O Lord . . .

CHUME *[falling down at once.]*: Help him, Lord. Help him, Lord.

JERO: Against this one weakness, this weakness, O Abraham . . .

CHUME: Help him, Lord. Help him, Lord.

JERO: Against this one weakness David, David, Samuel, Samuel.

CHUME: Help, him. Help him. Help am. Help am.

JERO: Job Job, Elijah Elijah.

CHUME *[getting more worked up.]* Help am God. Help am God. I say make you help am. Help am quick quick.

JERO: Tear the image from my heart. Tear this love for the daughters of Eve . . .

CHUME: Adam, help am. Na your son, help am. Help this your son.

JERO: Burn out this lust for the daughters of Eve.

CHUME: Je-e-esu, J-e-esu, Je-e-esu. Help am one time Je-e-e-e-su.

JERO: Abraka, Abraka, Abraka.

> *[Chume joins in.]*

> Abraka, Abraka, Hebra, Hebra, Hebra, Hebra, Hebra, Hebra, Hebra, Hebra . . .

JERO *[rising.]*: God bless you, brother. *[Turns around.]* Chume!

CHUME: Good morning, Brother Jeroboam.

JERO: Chume, you are not at work. You've never come before in the morning.

CHUME: No. I went to work but I had to report sick.

JERO: Why, are you unwell, brother?

CHUME: No, Brother Jero . . . I . . .

JERO: A-ah, you have troubles and you could not wait to get them to God. We shall pray together.

CHUME: Brother Jero . . . I . . . I *[He stops altogether.]*

JERO: Is it difficult? Then let us commune silently for a while.

> *[Chume folds his arms, raises his eyes to heaven.]*

JERO: I wonder what is the matter with him. Actually I knew it was he the moment he opened his mouth. Only Brother Chume reverts to that animal jabber when he gets his spiritual excitement. And that is much too often for my liking. He is too crude, but then that is to my advantage. It means he would never think of setting himself up as my equal.

> *[He joins Chume in his meditative attitude, but almost immediately*

*discards it, as if he has just remembered something.]*

Christ my Protector! It is a good job I got away from that wretched woman as soon as I did. My disciple believes that I sleep on the beach, that is, if he thinks I sleep at all. Most of them believe the same but, for myself, I prefer my bed. Much more comfortable. And it gets rather cold on the beach at nights. Still, it does them good to believe that I am something of an ascetic. . . .

*[He resumes his meditative pose for a couple of moments.]*

*[Gently.]* Open your mind to God, brother. This is the tabernacle of Christ. Open your mind to God.

*[Chume is silent for a while, then bursts out suddenly.]*

CHUME: Brother Jero, you must let me beat her!

JERO: What!

CHUME *[desperately.]*: Just once, Prophet. Just once.

JERO: Brother Chume!

CHUME: Just once. Just one sound beating, and I swear not to ask again.

JERO: Apostate. Have I not told you the will of God in this matter?

CHUME: But I've got to beat her, Prophet. You must save me from madness.

JERO: I will. But only if you obey me.

CHUME: In anything else, Prophet. But for this one, make you let me just beat am once.

JERO: Apostate!

CHUME: I n' go beat am too hard. Jus' once small small.

JERO: Traitor!

CHUME: Jus' this one time. I no' go ask again. Jus' do me this one favour, make a beat am today.

JERO: Brother Chume, what were you before you came to me?

CHUME: Prophet . . .

JERO *[sternly.]*: What were you before the grace of God?

CHUME: A labourer, Prophet. A common labourer.

JERO: And did I not prophesy you would become an office boy?

CHUME: You do am, brother. Na so.

JERO: And then a messenger?

CHUME: Na you do am, brother. Na you.

JERO: And then quick promotion? Did I not prophesy it?

CHUME: Na true, prophet. Na true.

JERO: And what are you now? What are you?

CHUME: Chief Messenger.

JERO: By the grace of God! And by the grace of God, have I not seen you at the table of the Chief Clerk? And you behind the desk, giving orders?

CHUME: Yes, Prophet . . . but . . .

JERO: With a telephone and a table bell for calling the Messenger?

CHUME: Very true, Prophet, but . . .

JERO: But? But? Kneel! *[pointing to the ground.]* Kneel!

CHUME *[wringing his hands.]*: Prophet!

JERO: Kneel, sinner, kneel. Hardener of heart, harbourer of Ashtoreth, Protector of Baal, kneel, kneel.

*[Chume falls on his knees.]*

CHUME: My life is a hell . . .

JERO: Forgive him Father, forgive him.

CHUME: This woman will kill me . . .

JERO: Forgive him, Father, forgive him.

CHUME: Only this morning I . . .

JERO: Forgive him, Father, forgive him.

CHUME: All the way on my bicycle . . .

JERO: Forgive . . .

CHUME: And not a word of thanks . . .

JERO: Out Ashtoreth. Out Baal . . .

CHUME: All she gave me was abuse, abuse, abuse . . .

JERO: Hardener of the heart . . .

CHUME: Nothing but abuse . . .

JERO: Petrifier of the soul . . .

CHUME: If I could only beat her once, only once . . .

JERO *[shouting him down]*: Forgive this sinner, Father. Forgive him by day, forgive him by night, forgive him in the morning, forgive him at noon . . .

*[A man enters. Kneels at once and begins to chorus "Amen," or "Forgive him, Lord," or "In the name of Jesus (pronounced Je-e-e-sus)." Those who follow later do the same.]*

. . . This is the son whom you appointed to follow in my footsteps. Soften his heart. Brother Chume, this woman whom you so desire to beat is your cross — bear it well. She is your heaven-sent trial — lay not your hands on her. I command you to speak no harsh word to her. Pray, Brother Chume, for strength in this hour of your trial. Pray for strength and fortitude.

*[Jeroboam leaves them to continue their chorus, Chume chanting "Mercy, Mercy" while he makes his next remarks.]*

They begin to arrive. As usual in the same order. This one who always comes earliest, I have prophesied that he will be made a chief in his home town. That is a very safe prophecy. As safe as our most popular prophecy, that a man will live to be eighty. If it

doesn't come true,
*[Enter an old couple, joining chorus as before.]*
that man doesn't find out until he's on the other side. So everybody is quite happy. One of my most faithful adherents — unfortunately, he can only be present at week-ends — firmly believes that he is going to be the first Prime Minister of the new Mid-North-East-State — when it is created. That was a risky prophecy of mine, but I badly needed more worshippers around that time.

*[He looks at his watch.]*

The next one to arrive is my most faithful penitent. She wants children, so she is quite a sad case. Or you would think so. But even in the midst of her most self-abasing convulsions, she manages to notice everything that goes on around her. In fact, I had better get back to the service. She is always the one to tell me that my mind is not on the service. . . .

*[Altering his manner—]*

Rise, Brother Chume. Rise and let the Lord enter into you. Apprentice of the Lord, are you not he upon whose shoulders my mantle must descend?

*[A woman (the penitent) enters and kneels at once in an attitude of prayer.]*

CHUME: It is so, Brother Jero.

JERO: Then why do you harden your heart? The Lord says that you may not beat the good woman whom he has chosen to be your wife, to be your cross in your period of trial, and will you disobey him?

CHUME: No, Brother Jero.

JERO: Will you?

CHUME: Praise be to God.

CONGREGATION: Praise be to God.

JERO: Allelu . . .

CONGREGATION: Alleluia.

*[To the clapping of hands, they sing "I will follow Jesus," swaying and then dancing as they get warmer.*

*Brother Jero, as the singing starts, hands two empty bottles to Chume, who goes to fill them with water from the sea.*

*Chume has hardly gone out when the drummer boy enters from upstage, running. He is rather weighed down by two "gangan" drums, and darts fearful glances back in mortal terror of whatever it is that is chasing him. This turns out, some ten or so yards later, to be a woman, sash tightened around her waist, wrapper pulled so high up that half the length of her thigh is exposed. Her sleeves are rolled above the shoulder and she is striding after the drummer in no unmistakable manner. Jeroboam, who has followed the woman's exposed limbs with quite distressed concentration, comes suddenly to himself and kneels sharply, muttering.*

*Again the drummer appears, going across the stage in a different direction, running still. The woman follows, distance undiminished, the same set pace, Jeroboam calls to him.]*

JERO: What did you do to her?

DRUMMER *[without stopping.]*: Nothing. I was only drumming and then she said I was using it to abuse her father.

JERO *[as the woman comes into sight]*: Woman!

*[She continues out. Chume enters with filled bottles.]*

JERO *[shaking his head.]*: I know her very well. She's my neighbour. But she ignored me . . .

*[Jeroboam prepares to bless the water when once again the procession appears, drummer first and the woman after.]*

JERO: Come here. She wouldn't dare touch you.

DRUMMER *[increasing his pace.]*: You don't know her . . .

*[The woman comes in sight.]*

JERO: Neighbour, neighbour. My dear sister in Moses . . .

*[She continues her pursuit offstage. Jero hesitates, then hands over his rod to Chume and goes after them.]*

CHUME *[suddenly remembering.]*: You haven't blessed the water, Brother Jeroboam.

*[Jero is already out of hearing. Chume is obviously bewildered by the new responsibility. He fiddles around with the rod and eventually uses it to conduct the singing, which has gone on all this time, flagging when the two contestants came in view, and reviving again after they had passed.*

*Chume has hardly begun to conduct his band when a woman detaches herself from the crowd in the expected penitent's paroxysm.]*

PENITENT: Echa, echa, echa, echa, echa . . . eei, eei, eei, eei.

CHUME *[taken aback.]*: Ngh? What's the matter?

PENITENT: Efie, efie, efie, efie, enh, enh, enh, enh . . .

CHUME: *[dashing off.]*: Brother Jeroboam, Brother Jeroboam.

*[Chume shouts in all directions, returning confusedly each time in an attempt to minister to the penitent. As Jeroboam is not forthcoming, he begins, very uncertainly, to sprinkle some of the water on the penitent, crossing her on the forehead. This has to be achieved very rapidly in the brief moment when the penitent's head is lifted from beating on the ground.]*

CHUME *[stammering.]*: Father . . . forgive her.

CONGREGATION *[strongly.]*: Amen.

*[The unexpectedness of the response nearly throws Chume, but then it also serves to bolster him up, receiving such support.]*

CHUME: Father, forgive her.

CONGREGATION: Amen.

*[The penitent continues to moan.]*

CHUME: Father forgive her.

CONGREGATION: Amen.

CHUME: Father forgive am.

CONGREGATION: Amen.

CHUME *[warming up to the task.]*: Make you forgive am, Father.

CONGREGATION: Amen.

*[They rapidly gain pace, Chume getting quite carried away.]*

CHUME: I say make you forgive am.

CONGREGATION: Amen.

CHUME: Forgive am one time.

CONGREGATION: Amen.

CHUME: Forgive am quick quick.

CONGREGATION: Amen.

CHUME: Forgive am, Father.

CONGREGATION: Amen.

CHUME: Forgive us all.

CONGREGATION: Amen.

CHUME: Forgive us all.

*[And then, punctuated regularly with Amens . . . ]*

Yes, Father, make you forgive us all. Make you save us from palaver. Save us from trouble at home. Tell our wives not to give us trouble . . .

*[The penitent has become placid. She is stretched out flat on the ground.]*

. . . Tell our wives not to give us trouble. And give us money to have a happy home. Give us money to satisfy our daily necessities. Make you no forget those of us who dey struggle daily. Those who be clerk today, make them Chief Clerk tomorrow. Those who are Messenger today, make them Senior Service tomorrow. Yes Father, those who are Messenger today, make them Senior Service tomorrow.

*[The Amens grow more and more ecstatic.]*

Those who are petty trader today, make them big contractor tomorrow. Those who dey sweep street today, give them their own big office tomorrow. If we dey walka today, give us our own bicycle tomorrow. I say those who dey walka today, give them their own bicycle tomorrow. Those who have bicycle today, they will ride their own car tomorrow.

*[The enthusiasm of the response, becomes, at this point, quite overpowering.]*

I say those who dey push bicycle, give them big car tomorrow. Give them big car tomorrow. Give them big car tomorrow, give them big car tomorrow.

*[The angry woman comes again in view, striding with the same gait as before, but now in possession of the drums. A few yards behind, the drummer jog-trots wretchedly, pleading.]*

DRUMMER: I beg you, give me my drums. I take God's name beg you, I was not abusing your father. . . . For God's sake I beg you...I was not abusing your father. I was only drumming . . . I swear to God I was only drumming. . . .

*[They pass through.]*

PENITENT *[who has become much alive from the latter part of the prayers, pointing . . .]*: Brother Jeroboam!

*[Brother Jero has just come in view. They all rush to help him back into the circle. He is a much altered man, his clothes torn and his face bleeding.]*

JERO *[slowly and painfully]*: Thank you, brother, sisters. Brother Chume, kindly tell these friends to leave me. I must pray for the soul of that sinful woman. I must say a personal prayer for her.

*[Chume ushers them off. They go reluctantly, chattering excitedly.]*

JERO: Prayers this evening, as usual. Late afternoon.

CHUME *[shouting after.]*: Prayers late afternoon as always. Brother Jeroboam says God keep you till then. Are you all right, Brother Jero?

JERO: Who would have thought that she would dare lift her hand against a prophet of God!

CHUME: Women are a plague, brother.

JERO: I had a premonition this morning that women would be my downfall today. But I thought of it only in the spiritual sense.

CHUME: Now you see how it is, Brother Jero.

JERO: From the moment I looked out of my window this morning, I have been tormented one way or another by the Daughters of Discord.

CHUME *[eagerly.]*: This is how it is with me, Brother. Every day. Every morning and night. Only this morning she made me take her to the house of some poor man, whom she says owes her money. She loaded enough on my bicycle to lay a siege for a week, and all the thanks I got was abuse.

JERO: Indeed, it must be a trial, Brother Chume . . . and it requires great . . .

*[He becomes suddenly suspicious.]*

Brother Chume, did you say that your wife went to make camp only this morning at the house of a . . . of someone who owes her money?

CHUME: Yes, I took her there myself.

JERO: Er . . . indeed, indeed. *[Coughs.]* Is . . . your wife a trader?

CHUME: Yes, petty trading, you know. Wool, silk, cloth, and all that stuff.

JERO: Indeed. Quite an enterprising woman. *[Hems.]* Er . . . where was the house of this man . . . I mean, this man who owes her money?

CHUME: Not very far from here. Ajete settlement, a mile or so from here. I did not even know the place existed until today.

JERO *[to himself.]*: So that is your wife . . .

CHUME: Did you speak, prophet?

JERO: No, no. I was only thinking how little women have changed since Eve, since Delilah, since Jezebel. But we must be strong of heart. I have my own cross too, Brother Chume. This morning alone I have been thrice in conflict with the Daughters of Discord. First there was . . . no, never mind that. There is another who crosses my path every day. Goes to swim just over there and then waits for me to be in the midst of my meditation before she swings her hips across here, flaunting her near nakedness before my eyes . . . .

CHUME *[to himself, with deep feeling.]*: I'd willingly change crosses with you.

JERO: What, Brother Chume?

CHUME: I was only praying.

JERO: Ah. That is the only way. But er . . . I wonder really what the will of God would be in this matter. After all, Christ himself was not averse to using the whip when occasion demanded it.

CHUME *[eagerly.]*: No, he did not hesitate.

JERO: In that case, since, Brother Chume, your wife seems such a wicked, wilful sinner, I think . . .

CHUME: Yes, Holy One . . .?

JERO: You must take her home tonight . . .

CHUME: Yes . . .

JERO: And beat her.

CHUME *[kneeling, claps Jero's hand in his.]*: Prophet!

JERO: Remember, it must be done in your own house. Never show the discord within your family to the world. Take her home and beat her.

*[Chume leaps up and gets his bike.]*

JERO: And Brother Chume . . .

CHUME: Yes, Prophet . . .

JERO: The Son of God appeared to me again this morning, robed just as he was when he named you my successor. And he placed his burning sword on my shoulder and called me his knight. He gave me a new title . . . but you must tell it to no one – yet.

CHUME: I swear, Brother Jero.

JERO *[staring into space.]*: He named me the Immaculate Jero, Articulate Hero of Christ's Crusade.

*[Pauses, then, with a regal dismissal—]* You may go, Brother Chume.

CHUME: God keep you, Brother Jero – the Immaculate.

JERO: God keep you, brother. *[He sadly fingers the velvet cape.]*

## LIGHTS FADE


## SCENE IV

*As Scene II, i.e. in front of the Prophet's home. Later that day. Chume is just wiping off the last crumbs of yams on his plate. Amope watches him.*

AMOPE: You can't say I don't try. Hounded out of house by debtors, I still manage to make you a meal.

CHUME *[sucking his fingers, sets down his plate.]*: It was a good meal too.

AMOPE: I do my share as I've always done. I cooked you your meal. But when I ask you to bring me some clean water, you forget.

CHUME: I did not forget.

AMOPE: You keep saying that. Where is it then? Or perhaps the bottles fell off your bicycle on the way and got broken.

CHUME: That's a child's lie, Amope. You are talking to a man.

AMOPE: A fine man you are then, when you can't remember a simple thing like a bottle of clean water.

CHUME: I remembered. I just did not bring it. So that is that. And now pack up your things because we're going home.

*[Amope stares at him unbelieving.]*

CHUME: Pack up your things; you heard what I said.

AMOPE *[scrutinizing.]*: I thought you were a bit early to get back. You haven't been to work at all. You've been drinking all day.

CHUME: You may think what suits you. You know I never touch any liquor.

AMOPE: You needn't say it as if it was a virtue. You don't drink only because you cannot afford to. That is all the reason there is.

CHUME: Hurry. I have certain work to do when I get home and I don't want you delaying me.

AMOPE: Go then. I am not budging from here till I get my money.

*[Chume leaps up, begins to throw her things into the bag. Brother Jero enters, hides, and observes them.]*

AMOPE *[quietly.]*: I hope you have ropes to tie me on the bicycle, because I don't intend to leave this place unless I am carried out. One pound eight shillings is no child's play. And it is my money nor yours.

*[Chume has finished packing the bag and is now tying it on to the carrier.]*

AMOPE: A messenger's pay isn't that much you know—just in case you've forgotten you're not drawing a minister's pay. So you better think again if you think I am letting my hard-earned money stay in the hands of that good for nothing. Just think, only this morning while I sat here, a Sanitary Inspector came along. He looked me all over and he made some notes in his book. Then he said, I suppose, woman, you realize that this place is marked down for slum clearance. This to me, as if I lived here. But you sit down and let your wife be exposed to such insults. And the Sanitary Inspector had a motor-cycle too, which is one better than a bicycle.

CHUME: You'd better be ready soon.

AMOPE: A Sanitary Inspector is a better job anyway. You can make something of yourself one way or another. They all do. A little here and a little there, call it bribery if you like, but see where *you've* got even though you don't drink or smoke or take bribes. He's got a motor-bike . . . anyway, who would want to offer cola to a Chief Messenger?

CHUME: Shut your big mouth!

AMOPE *[aghast.]*: What did you say?

CHUME: I said shut your big mouth.

AMOPE: To me?

CHUME: Shut your big mouth before I shut it for you. *[Ties the mat round the cross-bar.]* And you'd better start to watch your step from now on. My period of abstinence is over. My cross has been lifted off my shoulders by the Prophet.

AMOPE *[genuinely distressed.]*: He's mad.

CHUME *[viciously tying up the mat.]*: My period of trial is over. *[Practically strangling the mat.]* If you so much as open your mouth now . . . *[Gives a further twist to the string.]*

AMOPE: God help me. He's gone mad.

CHUME *[imperiously.]*: Get on the bike.

AMOPE [backing away.]: I'm not coming with you.

CHUME: I said get on the bike!

AMOPE: Not with you. I'll find my own way home.

[Chume advances on her. Amope screams for help. Brother Jero crosses himself. Chume catches her by the arm but she escapes, runs to the side of the house and beats on the door.]

AMOPE: Help! Open the door for God's sake. Let me in. Let me in . . .

[Brother Jero grimaces.]

Is anyone in? Let me in for God's sake! Let me in or God will punish you!

JERO [sticking his fingers in his ears.]: Blasphemy!

AMOPE: Prophet! Where's the Prophet?

[Chume lifts her bodily.]

AMOPE: Let me down! Police! Police!

CHUME [setting her down.]: If you shout just once more I'll . . . [He raises a huge fist.]

[Brother Jero gasps in mock-horror, tut-tuts, cover his eyes with both hands, and departs.]

AMOPE: Ho! You're mad, You're mad.

CHUME: Get on the bike.

AMOPE: Kill me! Kill me!

CHUME: Don't tempt me, woman!

AMOPE: I won't get on that thing unless you kill me first.

CHUME: Woman!

[Two or three neighbours arrive, but keep a respectful distance.]

AMOPE: Kill me. You'll have to kill me. Everybody come and bear witness. He's going to kill me so come and bear witness. I forgive everyone who has ever done me evil. I forgive all my debtors especially the Prophet who has got me into all this trouble. Prophet Jeroboam, I hope you will pray for my soul in heaven . . . .

CHUME: You have no soul, wicked woman.

AMOPE: Brother Jeroboam, curse this man for me. You may keep the velvet cape if you curse this foolish man. I forgive you your debt. Go on, foolish man, kill me. If you don't kill me you won't do well in life.

CHUME [suddenly.]: Shut up!

AMOPE [warming up as more people arrive.]: Bear witness all of you. Tell the Prophet I forgive him his debt but he must curse this foolish man to hell. Go on, kill me!

CHUME [who has turned away, forehead knotted in confusion.]: Can't you shut up, woman!

AMOPE: No, you must kill me . . .

*[The crowd hub-bubs all the time, scared as always at the prospect of interfering in man-wife palaver, but throwing in half-hearted tokens of concern—]*

"What's the matter, eh?" "You two keep quiet."

"Who are they?" "Where is Brother Jero?" "Do you think we ought to send for the Prophet.?" "These women are so troublesome! Somebody go and call Brother Jero."

CHUME *[lifting up Amope's head. She has, in the tradition of the "Kill me" woman, shut her eyes tightly and continued to beat her fists on the Prophet's doorstep.]*: Shut up and listen. Did I hear you say Prophet Jeroboam?

AMOPE: See him now. Let you bear witness. He's going to kill me . . .

CHUME: I'm not touching you but I will if you don't answer my question.

AMOPE: Kill me . . . Kill me . . .

CHUME: Woman, did you say it was the Prophet who owed you money?

AMOPE: Kill me . . .

CHUME: Is this his house? *[Gives her head a shake.]* Does he live here . . . ?

AMOPE: Kill me . . . Kill me . . .

CHUME *[pushing her away in disgust and turning to the crowd. They retreat instinctively.]*: Is Brother Jeroboam . . . ?

NEAREST ONE *[hastily.]*: No, no. I'm not Brother Jero. It's not me.

CHUME: Who said you were? Does the Prophet live here?

SAME MAN: Yes. Over there. That house.

CHUME *[Turns round and stands stock still. Stares at the house for quite some time.]*: So . . . so . . . so . . . so . . .

*[The crowd is puzzled over his change of mood. Even Amope looks up wonderingly. Chume walks towards his bicycle, muttering to himself.]*

So . . . so . . . Suddenly he decides I may beat my wife, eh? For his own convenience. At his own convenience.

*[He releases the bundle from the carrier, pushing it down carelessly. He unties the mat also.]*

BYSTANDER: What next is he doing now?

CHUME *[mounting his bicycle.]*: You stay here and don't move. If I don't find you here when I get back . . .

*[He rides off. They all stare at him in bewilderment.]*

AMOPE: He is quite mad. I have never seen him behave like that.

BYSTANDER: You are sure?

AMOPE: Am I sure? I'm his wife, so I ought to know, shouldn't I?

A WOMAN BYSTANDER: Then you ought to let the Prophet see to him. I had a brother once who had the fits and foamed at the mouth every other week. But the Prophet cured him. Drove the devils out of him, he did.

AMOPE: This one can't do anything. He's a debtor and that's all he knows. How to dodge his creditors.

*[She prepares to unpack her bundle.]*

LIGHTS FADE

SCENE V

*The beach. Nightfall.*

*A man in an elaborate "agbada" outfit, with long train and a cap, is standing right, downstage, with a sheaf of notes in his hand. He is obviously delivering a speech, but we don't hear it. It is undoubtedly a fire-breathing speech.*

*The Prophet Jeroboam stands bolt upright as always, surveying him with lofty compassion.*

JERO: I could teach him a trick or two about speech-making. He's a member of the Federal House, a back-bencher but with one eye on a ministerial post. Comes here every day to rehearse his speeches. But he never makes them. Too scared.

*[Pause. The Prophet continues to study the Member.]*

Poor fish. *[Chuckles and looks away.]* Oho, I had almost forgotten Brother Chume. By now he ought to have beaten his wife senseless. Pity! That means I've lost him. He is fulfilled and no longer needs me. True, he still has to become a Chief Clerk. But I have lost him as the one who was most dependent on me. . . . Never mind, it was a good price to pay for getting rid of my creditor. . . .

*[Goes back to the Member.]*

Now he . . . he is already a member of my flock. He does not know it of course, but he is a follower. All I need do is claim him. Call him and say to him, My dear Member of the House, your place awaits you . . . Or do you doubt it? Watch me go to work on him. *[Raises his voice.]* My dear brother in Jesus!

*[The Member stops, looks round, resumes his speech.]*

Dear brother, do I not know you?

*[Member stops, looks round again.]*

Yes, you. In God's name, do I not know you?

*[Member approaches slowly.]*

Yes indeed. It is you. And you come as it was predicted. Do you not perhaps remember me?

*[Member looks at him scornfully.]*

Then you cannot be of the Lord. In another world, in another body, we met, and my message was for you . . .

*[The Member turns his back impatiently.]*

MEMBER *[with great pomposity.]*: Go and practice your fraudulences on another person of greater gullibility.

JERO *[very kindly, smiling.]*: Indeed the matter is quite plain. You are not of the Lord. And yet such is the mystery of God's ways that his favour has lighted upon you . . . Minister . . . Minister by the grace of God . . .

*[The Member stops dead.]*

Yes, brother, we have met. I saw this country plunged into strife. I saw the mustering of men, gathered in the name of peace through strength. And at a desk, in a large gilt room, great men of the land awaited your decision. Emissaries of foreign nations hung on your word, and on the door leading into your office, I read the words, Minister for War. . . .

*[The Member turns round slowly.]*

. . . It is a position of power. But are you of the Lord? Are you in fact worthy? Must I, when I have looked into your soul, as the Lord has commanded me to do, must I pray to the Lord to remove this mantle from your shoulders and place it on a more God-fearing man?

*[The Member moves forward unconsciously. The Prophet gestures him to stay where he is. Slowly—]*

Yes . . . I think I see Satan in your eyes. I see him entrenched in your eyes . . .

*[The Member grows fearful, raises his arms in half-supplication.]*

The Minister for War would be the most powerful position in the Land. The Lord knows best, but he has empowered his lieutenants on earth to intercede where necessary. We can reach him by fasting and by prayer . . . we can make recommendations. . . . Brother, are you of God or are you ranged among his enemies . . .?

*[Jeroboam's voice fades away and the light also dims on him as another voice—Chume's—is heard long before he is seen. Chume enters from left, downstage, agitated, and talking to himself.]*

CHUME: . . . What for . . . why, why, why, why 'e do am? For two years 'e no let me beat that woman. Why? No because God no like am. That one no fool me any more. 'E no be man of God. 'E say 'in sleep for beach whether 'e rain or cold but that one too na big lie. The man get house and 'e sleep there every night. But 'in get peace for 'in house, why 'en no let me get peace for mine? Wetin I do for am? Anyway, how they come meet? Where? When? What time 'e know say na my wife? Why 'e dey protect am for me? Perhaps na my woman dey give am chop and in return he promise to see say 'in husband no beat am. A-a-a-ah, give am clothes, give am food and all comforts and necessities, and for exchange, 'in go see that 'in husband no beat am . . . Mmmmmm.

*[He shakes his head.]*

No, is not possible. I now believe that. If na so, how they come quarrel then. Why she go sit for front of 'in house demand all 'in money. I no beat am yet . . .

*[He stops suddenly. His eyes slowly distend.]*

Almighty! Chume, fool! O God, my life done spoil. My life done spoil finish. O God a no' get eyes for my head. Na lie. Na big lie. Na pretence 'e de pretend that wicked woman! She no' go collect nutin! She no' mean to sleep for outside house. The Prophet na 'in lover. As soon as 'e dark, she go in go meet 'in man. O God, wetin a do for you wey you go spoil my life so? Wetin make you vex for me so? I offend you? Chume, foolish man, your life done spoil. Your life done spoil. Yeah, ye . . . ah ah, ye-e-ah, they done ruin Chume for life . . . ye-e-ah, ye-e-ah. . . .

*[He goes off, his cries dying offstage.*

*Light up slowly on Jero. The Member is seen kneeling now at Brother Jero's feet, hands clasped, and shut eyes raised to heaven . . .]*

JERO *[his voice gaining volume.]*: Protect him therefore. Protect him when he must lead this country as his great ancestors have done. He comes from the great warriors of the land. In his innocence he was not aware of his heritage. But you know everything and you plan it all. There is no end, no beginning . . .

*(Chume rushes in, brandishing a cutlass.]*

CHUME: Adulterer! Woman-thief! Na today a go finish you!

*[Jero looks round.]*

JERO: God save us! *[Flees.]*

MEMBER *[unaware of what is happening.]*: Amen.

*[Chume follows out Jero, murder-bent.]*

MEMBER: Amen, Amen. *[Open his eyes.]* Thank you Proph . . .

*[He looks right, left, back, front, but he finds the Prophet has really disappeared.]*

Prophet! Prophet! *[Turns sharply and rapidly in every direction, shouting.]* Prophet, where are you? Where have you gone? Prophet! Don't leave me, Prophet, don't leave me!

*[He looks up slowly, with awe.]*

Vanished. Transported. Utterly transmuted. I knew it. I knew I stood in the presence of God. . . .

*[He bows his head, standing. Jeroboam enters quite collected, and points to the convert.]*

JEROBOAM: You heard him. With your own ears you heard him. By tomorrow, the whole town will have heard about the miraculous disappearance of Brother Jeroboam. Testified to and witnessed by no less a person than one of the elected Rulers of the country. . . .

MEMBER *[goes to sit on the mound.]*: I must await his return. If I show faith, he will show himself again to me . . . *[Leaps up as he is about to sit.]* This is holy ground. *[Takes off his shoes and sits. Gets up again.]* I must hear further from him. Perhaps he has gone to learn more about this ministerial post . . . *[Sits.]*

JEROBOAM: I have already sent for the police. It is a pity about Chume. But he has given me a fright, and no prophet likes to be frightened. With the influence of that nincompoop I should succeed in getting him certified with ease. A year in the lunatic asylum would do him good anyway.

*[The Member is already nodding.]*

Good . . . He is falling asleep. When I appear again to him he'll think I have just fallen from the sky. Then I'll tell him that Satan just sent one of his emissaries into the world under the name of Chume, and that he had better put him in a strait-jacket at once . . . And so the day is saved. The police will call on me here as soon as they catch Chume. And it looks as if it is not quite time for the fulfilment of that spiteful man's prophecy.

*[He picks up a pebble and throws it at the Member. At the same time a ring of red or some equalling startling colour plays on his head, forming a sort of halo. The Member wakes with a start, stares open-mouthed, and falls flat on his face, whispering in rapt awe—]* "Master!"

## BLACKOUT

## THE END

# Subramani

## *Sautu*

That evening Dhanpat returned early from the mill barracks. Most of the night, lying on his string bed, he struggled with Kanga's remarks. He felt immensely uneasy and distressed.

His friend had brought out the tobacco and, wrapped up in their blankets, they filled their clay pipes and smoked. They talked of indenture but the period was no longer clearly defined; it seemed like a labyrinth full of shadows and memories.

Then Kanga told him a story he had read in a Hindi paper. It was about an old Hindu who was afraid of dying. Is it true, he asked Dhanpat, that a man's memory sharpens before death?

It didn't take long for Dhanpat to notice that his friend wasn't his usual self. He was less jocular and more introspective. Consequently there were long stretches of silence in their conversation when Kanga seemed tense and irascible one moment (the prattling of women and children next door seemed like an irritation which grated upon his nerves) and next moment he sank into a state of acute depression.

When Dhanpat saw him to bed, his friend held his arm and tried to talk. But Kanga's mouth merely opened and shut like that of a stranded fish.

Dhanpat couldn't sleep though he felt weary and his limbs ached. He coughed badly. After rubbing on some pain balm he slept. But not for long. Soon he was awakened by the barking of dogs and harsh whispers outside his hut. He went out with his lantern to see what was amiss: they were carrying Bansi's wife to the hospital.

And then he had those nightmares again: Ratni's madness, the pool of blood in dry sugar cane leaves, the frightening pursuit by apparitions on horse-back and Ratni's dismembered limbs in the *machaan*.

Dhanpat got up early. The minah birds were squawking angrily again on the bare branches of the tamarind tree. It made the cattle and goats restless. He donned his *dhoti*, picked his white cotton shirt, now coarsely patched and mildewed, from a nail and staggered to the window to shoo the birds away.

Dulari was up early too; she was already milking the cows. After her mother Ratni's death, Dulari looked after the animals for her father. In return, she took some milk for her baby.

A cloud had descended on Dhanpat's life after the simultaneous departure of Ratni and the children. Immediately after Ratni's death, Dulari was married. Then Dhaniram found work with a tailor and he shifted to town with his wife. And Somu disappeared from Sautu. With these exits a great deal of love was banished from Dhanpat's life.

When he had Ratni and the children, he saw the need for the body to be fine and the mind strong. Now his body was without motives or consequences. Detachment and acceptance of life came easily and quickly to him. He had read in the Gita "Desire nothing so that you'll have everything." Once this was a line he quoted in *mandali* debates; now it was held with conviction.

The village was stirring again. It stirred only in mornings and evenings with departure and arrival of men from the fields and the sugar mill. The women hurried in and out of their huts minding their *orhini*, while the bare-backed children squatted and rolled in the dirt-yard.

Dhanpat had observed the unchanging life of that village for nearly fifty years. Sautu wasn't an old village. After indenture a group of men and women scratched a little clearing from which the present squalid little huts sprang up.

The site was badly chosen. There were no rivers and the sea was thirty miles away. The village was hemmed in by an irregular stretch of unprosperous sugar cane fields in the south and in the north by partly barren soapstone hills bearing occasional guava bushes and stunted rain trees and reeds.

Sautu was regarded as insignificant, and it turned its back on the world beyond. More thatch and bamboo structures appeared as the families became larger. They continued to till the obstinate earth; there was nowhere else to go. Besides they were no longer moved by a momentum of their own. Habit and custom held them fettered to the place. Ultimately, Sautu, like its inhabitants, became an aberration, a contortion of history, on that landscape.

Near the coast, in the west, there were several small Fijian villages. Much of the land was owned by local chiefs. When Dhanpat came with Ratni, who was in late stages of pregnancy, he looked desperately for land to build a hut. The villages counselled him to see Ratu Epeli who gave Dhanpat a plot at the edge of Sautu, and sent Tomasi to help build his hut.

Dhanpat's reverie was broken: a waft of breeze brought the damp odour of old hay and cowdung from the pen. He turned from the window and sat heavily on his string bed.

Now in disarray, his hut spoke of a past order in the faded limewash on matted bamboo walls, in the arrangement of dull, discoloured photographs, and ripped up crêpe on soap-box shelves.

The reeds in the roof had thinned and the walls sagged. Cobwebs hung in shabby strands from rafters. The mud floor was uneven. Where it was damp the cowdung plaster had come off and the red earth showed.

It was always dismal and dark in the hut. The windows and doors rarely opened completely. The years had added nothing significant to his worldly possessions. A much-battered grey heavy tin suitcase under his string bed held his and Ratni's old clothes and odd cups and saucers, glass jugs, a large looking-glass and several combs and some jewellery — their wedding presents.

In a corner, where the wall and rafters were black with soot from cooking, lay copper and aluminum utensils and earthenware. His broken *dholak*, brought from India, stood on an empty wooden box in another corner.

He looked reflectively at his earthly belongings: a great emptiness seemed to unfold within him.

Then he did something he hadn't done for a long time — he pulled out his suitcase and picked up the large jagged mirror, a gift from Kanga, and examined himself.

The piercing brown eyes, narrow and heavily wrinkled, an aquiline nose and the thin line of his rather well-formed lips were the only visible parts; the rest of his face and head were concealed behind grey tangled hair.

Long years in the fields had bent his constitution. His long and bony arms and legs were cracked and creased like the earth outside. He was reminded of Kanga — his withered and shrunken husk — and the mask of death on his face.

He felt old, exhausted and bereft.

Ignoring the bowl of milk Dulari had left for him, he scrambled out, and went behind the hut to urinate.

Now slumped back against the wall of his hut, he watched the somnolent village minding its dull business.

He was relieved when Bhairo, the village barber, greeted him. He went inside the hut to get a mat. Bhairo pulled off his dusty canvas shoes, and squatted on the mat in the hot sun, resting his elbows on his scrawny legs.

"Acha, Dhanpat, I don't see you at *mandali* these days. Why?" he asked, fanning himself vigorously with his skull cap.

This was the correct way to begin. Bhairo knew it would lead, by way of discourse on comparative merits of illness and treatment, ancient and modern, to the scriptures. Bhairo trusted his own knowledge of Vedic literature. He often embellished his arguments, secretly elated, with learned quotations from the ancient books.

Bhairo, like most other villagers, respected Dhanpat less for his knowledge than his common sense and fairness. But he was too much of a free thinker, too much at times like the despicable *Samajis*. No wonder, thought Bhairo, he bred a renegade (according to the norms of Sautu, the highest form of delinquency) for a son.

Bhairo was disappointed when Tomasi appeared. He hurriedly opened his bundle and took out a wedding card for Dhanpat. It caught Tomasi's eyes.

"Aha, Bhairo. This modern thing catching fast. Where's the yellow rice?" asked Tomasi in broken Hindi.

Bhairo frowned. This wedding card was an odiously un-Hindu custom which he regretted but nevertheless propagated. But he understood well Tomasi's sinister fondness for asking awkward questions. He didn't answer.

Tomasi watched him and waited to be contradicted. Bhairo simply wilted under his stare, his face revealing the expression of self-denigration which unmistakably showed whenever he lost a verbal duel.

Bhairo resented the way Tomasi seemed to be appraising him. He resented most of all the way Tomasi's nostrils stared at him. Bhairo's effort to keep up an appearance of good companionship with Tomasi was inevitably resulting in suppressed hostility.

He observed this at a *Kali Puja*. Bhairo was the protagonist in the rituals. He was in a trance, singing and dancing in complete abandon round and round the grotesque brass idol. When he turned a corner his eyes arrested a familiar figure in the crowd—a ponderous head with thick fuzzy hair and a dark face. And those nostrils—they stared at him. When their eyes met, Tomasi grinned. The trance was broken.

Bhairo gathered his bundle, nodded and slipped away.

Dhanpat, however, derived certain pleasure from Tomasi's friendly antagonism. Tomasi, eager to test Dhanpat's response to his newly acquired ideas (from the visiting *misnari*) waited for an opportunity to begin. But today, scenting a certain dullness and abstract preoccupation in his friend, he asked instead after Somu.

Somu was planning to come back. "Only for a visit. At Christmas," Dhanpat told his friend with a nonchalance which wasn't real. He hadn't told anyone, however, that Somu wanted to take him to Canada. He waited to burst it on them when it became a recognized and established fact.

Tomasi didn't take this aspect of Dhanpat's conversation seriously. He couldn't conceive of Dhanpat and Somu in any other setting. He was convinced that Somu was hiding in another village.

Tomasi flapped his large hands against his sleeveless blue coat in disappointment. For a moment he gazed, with a kind of proprietorial concern, at the sagging hut and the bare garden patch. The kasava sticks he had given Dhanpat for planting still lay under the tamarind.

Dhanpat anticipated Tomasi's half-patronizing, half-admonitory glance.

Tomasi stood there without saying anything while Dhanpat's mangy dog licked the sores on Tomasi's ankles. He crossed the yard to the tamarind tree where the ground was thick with leaves and tamarind fruits in various stages of decomposition. He examined a handful of fruits, dropped a couple into his coat pocket, and left.

In the pelting heat of two o'clock sun, Dhanpat picked up his walking stick and turban and headed for the village school. With his head slightly in advance of his body, he walked like one balked with a nagging problem.

He trudged on a ribbon of well-beaten dusty soapstone path, past the straggle of huts where women went listlessly about their tasks or sat under a mango or a tamarind tree picking lice from their hair.

The huts looked desolate and the dirt-yards showed ugly cracks. There were no gardens to speak of, no decorative trees, except occasional marigold plants which bore small gawdy flowers. For the first time Dhanpat was overwhelmed by the dereliction.

He rested for a while at Rambaran's store where the latter sold groceries from the front door and very bad rum from the back. Some men were drinking *kava* and smoking *bidi* cigarettes on the veranda. Two or three others were snoring on empty sugar bags. Rambaran was inside, in his black shorts, chewing a match-stick with which he picked his teeth.

In a dilapidated *bure* outside the shop, Rambaran's attractive daughter-in-law was in her customary hammock singing mournfully a song from *Barsaat*. Bhairo's deaf-mute son was sitting in front devouring her with his gaze. Now and then Bimla would throw a mischievous glance at him, seductively, fluttering her eyelids. In response, his toothless grin would stretch from ear to ear, revealing the spittle at the corner of his mouth.

From somewhere inside the shop Rambaran's wife whispered reproachfully "Dulahin!" And Bimla straightened her *orhini*, slowly and deliberately, over her ample bosom, studiously avoiding her mother-in-law's eyes.

Dhanpat was distressed. He climbed down the veranda and took the path towards the swamp. At the swamp, Bansi was peeling pandanus leaves under a tree.

The swamp had swallowed several animals and children when it was wet and soggy. Mangal's eldest son had buried himself alive here twenty years ago. Now the swamp was dry. It carried only pandanus trees. And cattle and goats searched for anything edible all day.

Dhanpat waited for Bihari on a crooked wooden bench outside the school room. Bihari was inside prowling behind rows of exceptionally silent learners hoping to catch someone talking. There was a loud clamour when the bell rang. Bihari dismissed his class and came straight to Dhanpat.

He had a letter for Dhanpat. Dhanpat limped along with Bihari across a parched playground, strewn with lunch wrappings, as the schoolmaster translated the letter, his reading punctuated by a regular asthmatic wheeze. Bihari prided himself upon his knowledge of Hindi and English and his ability to translate from both languages. He glowed in his superior knowledge as he explained every nuance, every shade of meaning in Somu's letter.

The letter was sad. It was unlike those letters Somu wrote from New Zealand. Those early letters mainly described landscapes and expressed bewilderment at the complexity of social life. They were enthusiastic letters.

Dhanpat didn't hear from Somu for a long time after he stowed away to India. However, he received reports of his levity with women and money, and the frequent bouts of depression he suffered. Rambaran once spread the story that Somu was in a mental hospital in India.

Dhanpat was alarmed; he worried about his son. Now more than ever when he heard so regularly from him. This was strange. He never had much affection for Somu. He wasn't like Dhaniram who went through all stages of life like a true Hindu. Dhanpat could trust Dhaniram. But his younger son invited only suspicion. He was far too restless, discontented and given to secret thinking.

The villagers regarded Somu as special. He didn't go to Bihari's school; instead he was taken into a mission school in town. They shook their heads in amazement and disbelief when he talked about books and ideas. This attitude changed to perplexity when he abruptly left his father. Finally, they were comforted in their initial belief that Somu was always a renegade.

Dhanpat saw quite early that Somu refused to be absorbed in the life of the village. These letters from Somu told more than he ever expected to know about his son. They were not addressed to him; it was always Somu talking to himself. At times he had wished that his son would come back. Life would change; it would become whole and fine again for both.

Somu, of course, didn't return. But in a curious way Dhanpat's life was changing. There were words in the letters which echoed, and arguments which festered, in his mind. It seemed that some unknown force had confronted him with truths he had hidden from himself.

His world was becoming rapidly disorientated. Things didn't seem to regroup again. His days oscillated between a past order and new anguish. At times he felt his life hovering at the edge of new perceptions.

There was, however, a loneliness now which was intense and complete. Was it because he feared desolation that he wanted Somu back?

The pale amber of receding sunlight rested on the distant Makai Hills and on top of tired and empty trees. It sharpened the grim profiles of the lugubrious huts.

The village was stirring again: the men were back from the fields and the mill. Dhanpat was at his prayer house under the tamarind tree. The door was open and the mixed smell of camphor and sandalwood paste was sharp and, to Dhanpat, reassuring. But when he confronted the icons and the brass idols the momentary exhilaration, like a sudden inspiration, was followed by corresponding hopelessness. The gods looked old and ravaged.

He heard someone stir behind him. It was Bhairo.

"*Aré, Aré* Dhanpat, you carry on. Don't worry about me," he protested, gesticulating.

Dhanpat placed the *lota* he was carrying at the door, and turned towards Bhairo.

They sat on the ground in front of the prayer house, and talked in low whispers. When Bhairo had left, Dhanpat sat there for a long time feeling old and withered.

This drought had laid so many old people in their graves, among them some of his closest acquaintances from the indenture days. Now it was Kanga's turn. How was he, thought Dhanpat, to regard all these deaths as quirks of fate?

Dhanpat had always considered himself inviolate. That is why he moved through life with such splendid reassurance. Now sitting in front of the temple, he saw how the protective armour had gradually disintegrated. The tenuous bond that existed among disparate items of his life was breaking. More than ever he felt the pointlessness of daily rituals of toil and rest, prayer and persistence. Once they were, however, the only affirmations of his existence.

He felt oddly defeated and humiliated.

Dhanpat hurried into his hut like one excited over an unknown thing or one expecting an eruption. He fretfully closed the doors and windows and crept onto his string bed, and lay there in a delirium, his energies completely drained.

That night there was more looting and stone throwing in the neighbouring village. More sugar cane was burnt.

It was Bimla's husband who, creeping and crawling home after a rum party, noticed the fire in Dhanpat's hut. He dragged himself from hut to hut yelling for help.

The villagers came with their machetes and cane knives, and with whatever water they could spare. They broke the door with their machetes and pulled Dhanpat out of the blaze.

The dry and brittle thatch and bamboo crackled, wilted and then flared into flames. They were soon reduced to cinders. The rafters and poles also came down with an explosion, and burnt on the ground giving off a pale glow.

A moment ago there was total hush. Now the village broke into a tumult and then pandemonium.

Dhanpat sat silently amidst wailing and shrieking women and children. Someone had thrown an old blanket around him. A couple of urchins crept close to him and stared, their faces revealing a mixture of fear and mute incomprehension.

Bhairo searched hard for any indication of guilt or shame on Dhanpat's face.

There was no sign of stress: he was stoic and inscrutable like the gods in the prayer house.

Dulari consoled her father in a low and husky voice, blowing her nose, and wiping her tears with the corner of her *orhini*. She helped him to his feet and directed him towards her hut.

Dhanpat felt something cold and damp on his thighs and down his legs. He examined his *dhoti*: he was wet.

In the weeks that followed, Dhanpat's insanity was argued and disputed. Then those outrageous stories began circulating. Bimla complained that she found Dhanpat peeping into her bath-shed. Henceforth the women moved in pairs or groups, and avoided him at the village well.

Bansi's son reported to his mother that the old man tried to molest him at the marshes. As a result the children refused to walk through the marshes to school. And Bimla's husband said one night when he was slouching back after a rum party he met Dhanpat, apparently sleep-walking. He was stark naked.

Other stories were equally scandalous. Finally, the village elders met at the *mandali* and proclaimed Dhanpat imbecile. They agreed he was bent on inviting the wrath of the gods on the entire village.

Dulari wept with shame. Her husband was embarrassed. One morning, instead of going to the fields, he left for town. When he came back late in the evening, he was angry and disappointed.

The following day he took a village elder with him. Weeks later a government van halted in the village amidst great shouting and clamour.

Dhanpat was taken away for observation. And the chief took possession of his land.

# Mary TallMountain

## *There Is No Word for Goodbye*

Sokoya, I said, looking through
    the net of wrinkles into
    wise black pools
    of her eyes.

What do you say in Athabaskan
    when you leave each other?
    What is the word
    for goodbye?

A shade of feeling rippled
    the wind-tanned skin.
    Ah, nothing, she said,
    watching the river flash.

She looked at me close.
    We just say, Tlaa. That means,
    See you.
    We never leave each other.
    When does your mouth
    say goodbye to your heart?

She touched me light
    as a bluebell.
    You forget when you leave us,
    You're so small then.
    We don't use that word.

We always think you're coming back,
    but if you don't,
    we'll see you some place else.
    You understand.
        There is no word for goodbye.

# Edwin Thumboo

## *Ulysses by the Merlion*

for Maurice Baker

I have sailed many waters,
Skirted islands of fire,
Contended with Circe
Who loved the squeal of pigs;
Passed Scylla and Charybdis
To seven years with Calypso,
Heaved in battle against the gods.
Beneath it all
I kept faith with Ithaca, travelled,
Travelled and travelled,
Suffering much, enjoying a little;
Met strange people singing
New myths; made myths myself.

But this lion of the sea
Salt-maned, scaly, wondrous of tail,
Touched with power, insistent
On this brief promontory . . .
    Puzzles.

Nothing, nothing in my days
Foreshadowed this
Half-beast, half-fish,
This powerful creature of land and sea.

Peoples settled here,
Brought to this island
The bounty of these seas,
Built towers topless as Ilium's.
    They make, they serve,

They buy, they sell.

Despite unequal ways,
Together they mutate,
Explore the edges of harmony,
Search for a centre;
Have changed their gods,
Kept some memory of their race
In prayer, laughter, the way
Their women dress and greet.
They hold the bright, the beautiful,
Good ancestral dreams
Within new visions,
So shining, urgent,
Full of what is now.

Perhaps having dealt in things,
Surfeited on them,
Their spirits yearn again for images,
Adding to the dragon, phoenix,
Garuda, naga, those horses of the sun,
This lion of the sea,
This image of themselves.

# M. G. Vassanji

## *The London-returned*

We still went back for our holidays then and we formed a rambunctious group whose presence was hard to miss about town. We were the London-returned. For two or three joyously carefree months the city became a stage for us and we would strut up and down its dusty pavements parading overseas fashions, our newly acquired ways. Bare feet and Beatle-style haircuts were in then, drawing conservative wrath and doomsday prophecies. We sported flashy bell-bottoms, Oxford shirts and bright summer dresses. And fat pinkish-brown thighs below the colourful miniskirts of our female companions teased the famished adolescent eyes of our hometown. Come Saturday morning, we would gather at a prearranged rendezvous and conscious of every eye upon us, set off in one large and rowdy group towards Independence Avenue. There to stroll along its pavements a few times over, amidst fun and laughter, exchanging jokes and relating incidences in clipped, finished accents.

The acacia-lined avenue cut a thin margin at the edge of town. It looked out at the ocean a short block away, black and rust red steamers just visible plying in and out of the harbour. Behind it was crammed the old town, a maze of short dirty sidestreets feeding into the long and busy Uhuru Street, which then opened like a funnel back into the avenue. From here Uhuru Street went down, past downtown and the Mnazi Moja grounds into the interior: the hinterland of squat African settlements, the main-road Indian stores, the Arab corner stores — in which direction we contemptuously sniffed, suppressing a vague knowledge of our recent roots there.

On Saturday morning you came to Independence Avenue to watch and to be seen. You showed off your friends, your breeding, your money. It was here that imported goods were displayed in all their glory and European-looking mannequins threw temptation from store windows. And yes, hearts too were on sale on these pavements. Eyes could meet and the memory of a fleeting instant live to fuel one's wildest dreams . . .

We walked among tourists and expatriate shoppers, civil servants and messengers in khaki. And we passed other fugitive groups like ours, senior boys and girls (always separate) from the high schools, who somehow had managed to walk away this Saturday. Our former classmates, many of these. With some I had managed to keep up a brief correspondence. Now some exchanged short greetings, others pretended not to see, and a few turned up their noses with the moral superiority of the uncontaminated. Yet they stoked our merriment no end — these innocents — by their sidelong glances at our mini-skirted companions, or their self-conscious attempts at English accents and foreign manners while sipping iced capuccinos in the European surroundings of Benson's.

It was at Benson's where it began.

She was sitting with a group of friends sipping iced capuccino. They were all in uniform, of course. How can I forget, the green and white, the skirt and blouse? For a brief instant, between two intervening sandy-haired tourist heads, our eyes met. And lowered. And then again a fleeting, fugitive appointment. She had me then.

I think of her as she was then. A small figure, not too thin, with a heart-shaped face: a small pointed chin, high cheekbones, a large forehead. Her hair was tightly combed back and tied into a plain pony tail. She sat sipping through a straw, stirring the frothy contents in the tall frosted glass to turn them more liquid. I hadn't heard her voice and I didn't know her. Yet I sat there a few tables away, flustered, self-conscious, saying silly things, laughing uncertainly.

At her table an animated conversation was underway. They talked in Cutchi, not too loudly nor timidly. How self-contained they looked, how comfortable with each other! I felt a little envious, looking in from outside. My subject never looked up again although she must have known I was watching. Presently they waved at the uniformed waiter and went out through the frosted glass door.

We had a word for the kind of state I was in in the few days that followed. Pani-pani: liquid. It means, perhaps, melted. With stylish and refined company — at least as I saw it then — beside me, what made me turn pani-pani at the sight of so plain a figure? The mating instinct, I tell myself a little cynically many years later; how surely it singles out and binds! Kismet, our elders called it. You could walk to the end of the world and not find the right partner, they told you, until your kismet opened up for you. And when it did, as surely and beautifully as a flower, no amount of reason could dissuade you from your choice. In our case it sought to bridge our two worlds. And where else should it strike but on Independence Avenue where these two worlds met.

\* \* \*

She lived in what I called the hinterland: not in a squat mud and limestone dwelling but a modern two-storey affair that had replaced it. They were newly rich and moving up; they owned the building and ran the bustling store on the street floor. It had a perpetual sale on, announced by huge signs painted on the walls, pillars, and display windows. And periodically leaflets would be distributed in the area, announcing "Sale! Sale! Sale!" This much I knew as soon as I came home and gave her description to my sister; it was common knowledge. I learned that she was the daughter of Amina Store. Four times a day an elegant blue hydraulic-suspensioned Citroën sailed smoothly over the potholes and gravel of our backroads, carrying the daughter of the house and her neighbourhood friends to school and back.

\* \* \*

On Saturday nights, after a rest from our frolics of the day, we partied. We met on the rooftop of a modern residential building called Noor-e-Salaam in our new suburb of Upanga well away from the bustle of the downtown shops and streets. The latest from the London hit parade wafted down from here. We swung to the rhythms of the Mersey beat while our former friends still drooled over the lyrics of Elvis and Jim Reeves. And to friendly locals we dispensed some of the trendier scraps from our new lifestyles. We talked about nights out in London and trips to the Continent. We introduced new words and naughty drinks.

The Saturday night following my first sight of her I managed to get Amina invited, and also her gang just to keep talk from spreading that I had been stricken. Yet how long can one hide the truth where even the slightest conjecture or suspicion could become truth merely by the force of suggestion? The blue Citroën dutifully unloaded its passengers outside the garden of Noor-e-Salaam and sailed away. They had all come. But I paid attention only to her and what pleased me was that she let me. I had come prepared for the kill, to sweep her off her feet before anyone else realised that she was available. With these unspoilt maidens who haven't left home, I told myself, you can't go wrong with books. And so on the dance floor under a modestly bright series of coloured lightbulbs, while the Rolling Stones sang "Satisfaction," while we sipped Coke and looked down over the sidewall at the rustling trees and the few people walking on the dark street below, we talked in soft tones about nothing but books. Books!

But it was by her books that my sister swore, a few days later, when she came back from school. Two years younger, she knew I was stricken and had me on the rack, torturing me with bits of information about Amina.

"Look! I swear by holy knowledge!" Brown-papered exercise books held up solemnly as if they meant that much to her.

"Don't lie, or I'll . . ."

"Okay, then." A mock sullenness. The books are thrown on the sofa. She sits with a long face and draws her knees up close, looks from the corners of her eyes.

"So? What was she asking?"

"But you said I was lying! So I was lying."

"Come on now, *what*?"

"What will you give me if I tell you?"

"You'll get a slap if you don't!"

"She was asking about you. They are teasing her about you, you know. The news has got around!"

"They are stupid."

"Well, what do you expect? You danced with no one else. And to talk of studies all the time!" She chuckles.

"I don't know her, silly! What if she is the pious type?"

It didn't hurt, being laughed at like that in the Girls' School. To be studious was still a virtue in those days. No small matter. It was the way out. And it tickled my vanity no end to learn that I had been talked about in a conversation among girls. But perhaps she had found out about me only to reject me?

Because she never came to those parties again. That was the last time, for the entire group. It indicated a certain rejection on her part: of my lifestyle and my friends. She's chosen against me I thought. Perhaps she thinks I'm a loafer. Doesn't she know I go to school, I don't go around London cutting people's hair? I go to school. To have come this close to victory — and to lose out without explanation. Maybe she was teasing, testing me, to show how vulnerable even we could be, the sophisticates who seemed to have the world in the palms of our hands.

What agonising days I spent, keeping a lookout for her up and down Independence Avenue, entering Benson's on impulse and coming out pretending to have forgotten something, a ridiculous figure altogether. There was no way of contacting her; you needed an excuse for that. I could not think of any that would not have seemed a direct proposition.

But she could, and she did.

* * *

I stand on our balcony looking down on the street. It's five-thirty in the evening or thereabouts. There's not a moving car on the road but some pedestrians are about. Except around noon this sidestreet is shielded from the sun by buildings and it always feels like five-thirty in the evening. A gloomy street. The sun always shines on Uhuru Street a block away. There the heat roasts you and you seek the shelter of the shadier streets.

Below me two boys play marbles on the pavement. Some distance away a figure walks towards them. A circle with a diameter is drawn in charcoal, two marbles placed on the straight line. A game of "pyu" beginning. I look away to the figure that is closer now and I see it's a girl. Below me a marble gets projected by a forefinger pulled back, lands on the ground, rolls for a while, then takes a sudden turn and sweeps away towards the road—Oh God, it's her! as she walks around them—"Aaaaaaah!" Rage and disappointment, fists clenched. What did he expect, on such a surface? It's the other one's turn now. My heart leaps: she's entered the doorway of our building. I picture her walking through the courtyard past the boys playing cricket against the wall and taking the stairs. I keep looking down at the road, chest pounding away, face flushed to a fever. Who could she be visiting? —four possibilities . . . no, three . . .

A knock on the door.

"Yes," says my sister behind me in a voice obviously spilling over with glee, "he's right here!" I turn away from the balcony and greet her.

She is in a hurry. "Can I borrow Tranter's book from you? I need it for my revision."

I bring the book, careful to avoid the mischief in my sister's eyes.

"You can keep it as long as you want—I'll tell you when I want it back."

"Only for a few days. I have to rush now. Our driver's waiting. Thanks!"

So it was Tranter's *Pure Mathematics* to begin with. She kept it for two months. Meanwhile I borrowed Cooke's *Organic Chemisty* from her, and so it went on. Other books, other excuses, the books untouched. Anything for a chance to meet and talk under plausible cover. Education was not to be tampered with. I would on occasion miss my stroll on Independence Avenue and walk two miles down Uhuru Street with a book in my hand, past the barren grounds, the small dingy shops packed close together, to the flat above Amina Store where she lived. How delicious, luxurious, the anxieties of those days; how joyful the illusion of their pain! They consumed my existence. Her mother fed me hot bhajias when she was there, inviting me in with: "Come on in, babu, don't stand there in the door-way!" The servant would bring in the delights. At other times her young brother would sit at the dining table doing sums in an old exercise book while we sat on the sofa. I tried sending him downstairs to buy Coke or something, but he wouldn't budge. And the two of us would smile, embarrassed.

People noticed—and they talked, made up their minds. But for us nothing was decided—it could not be—the future was open. This was a chance to be together, to explore the bounds of possibility; and if it lasted long enough, it would lead to an eventuality that was acceptable. But of course, meanwhile, I had to leave. At the end of the holidays, when it was time for me to go back, I asked her: "Can I write to you?" "You may, if you want to," she said. And so we corresponded.

\* \* \*

All this is eighteen years ago, and dead: but surely, the dead deserve their due? Or, as our elders said, they come to haunt your dreams.

I sit here in the cosy embrace of a north Scarborough living room in winter, looking out through glass doors, mulling over the last years of our marriage. An intimacy that turned insipid, dried up. Not for us the dregs of relationships, the last days of alternating care and hatred. "I need a life of my own," she said. "I can change; we both can change. You can quit work and go back to college. Is that it?" "Alone," she said, "we've moved apart." "And she?—I'll want to keep her." "You may, if you want to."

The open field before me stretches northwards—a vast desert of snow. There are towns out there, I tell myself, cities full of people. Yet I see only endless stretches, a bleak landscape with a few brambles blown by a light wind. And way beyond, beyond which I cannot see a thing, there is a point marked by a pennant strangely still on a short pole. The North Pole as I've always imagined it. In that landscape I see a figure from the past, a former hero . . . Captain Scott from my Standard Six reader, cowering from biting winds . . . Why Captain Scott, out of the blue, as it were and at the wrong Pole? I cannot say for sure . . .

I tell myself I walked too far, too north, and left too much behind. We inhabited a thin and marginal world in Toronto, the two of us. Barely within a community whose approval we craved, by whose standards we judged ourselves the elite; the chic and educated. Our friends we counted on our fingers—and we proudly numbered Europeans, Asians, North Americans. Friends to talk about, not to bring together: points on our social achievement score. Not for us the dull weekend nights of nothing to do. We loved to entertain. And we clamoured for invitations; when we missed one we would pretend not to care and treat ourselves to an expensive dinner instead. We had things to do.

This marginal life she roundly rejected now—just as she did once many years ago. But then she sought me out in spite of it. She came to borrow Tranter's blue and red book though I don't believe she ever needed it . . . and now? She's back in the bosom of Uhuru Street. Or rather the companionship that's moved up Uhuru Street and into the suburban developments of Toronto. Her friends gradually came, one by one, and set themselves up with their families long after we ourselves had moved from London. And it bloomed once more, that old comradeship of Uhuru Street with Amina at the centre—first helping them to settle and then being with them just like old times. Slowly, Toronto, their Toronto became like Dar, and I was out of it.

She came to London exactly a year after the summer in which we had exchanged books and shy but satiated looks in her sitting room, while her little brother pretended to do sums in his warped exercise book on the dining table. This was a time of political change in our country: Asian students from all backgrounds were now desperately trying to go abroad. Her arrival was therefore a surprise; a cousin went to pick her up. A week later, on a Sunday morning, she telephoned me and with heart beating wildly I went to see her. It had been a long wait, a year in which we exchanged letters which delicately hinted at increasing affection. At least I did, and she did not object. I told her I missed her, she reminded me of a funny thing I'd said. I graduated from signing "Sincerely" to "Affectionately" and finally "With love." She stuck to "Affectionately."

She had put up in a hostel on Gloucester Road not far from High Street Kensington run by a Mr Toto, our townsman and reputedly a former valet to an oriental prince. It was a dismal place, this hostel, and I had been through it too. It was your first stop in London when you hardly knew a soul there. It picked you up and prepared you, sometimes for the worst.

Here you could see what might become of you in a week, a month, a year. Previously it had been more pleasant, a hangout for rich kids, when Mr Toto let you have parties on Saturdays. Now, in the sixties, the faces were more desperate, lonely and white from the cold since they all flew in in September and October. Boys who left early in the morning in home-made Teteron suits carrying attaché cases full of certificates, returning late, hopeless, to a night of exchanging notes on the old, sunken mattresses Mr Toto provided for his iron bedsteads, English pop songs mingled with tear-drenched Hindi film songs, the atmosphere was darkly nostalgic supported by a hollow boisterousness in the corridors. I knew the place so well, its mildew-smelling interior, the migrant Spanish maids in black, landings full of clutter to be picked up, bathrooms stained, taps leaking. I had come here many times, to meet relatives, pick up parcels from home, give advice. Over the years how many must have wept on those soiled, striped mattresses of Mr Toto, prayed on them or indulged themselves in the cold, lonely nights of London!

I entered through the black door with the brass knocker that opened directly onto the street and went straight up to the first floor and knocked on Number One as instructed. There was a shuffle of feet behind the door, which was then opened by a girl in a faded pink home-style nightie with a laced neckline. Behind her, sitting on a bed already made, was my Amina, writing letters. On Sunday you write home I said to myself.

It was still breakfast time and we went down three flights of creaky stairs into the basement. There a narrow pathway through junk and clutter led into a medium-sized brightly lit room laid with blue linoleum, long tables and some benches. There was a steady trickle of traffic in and out of this room and up and down the stairs. Here you could get onion omelettes, cornflakes, and black tea and milk ("English style") from waiters with strangely familiar faces who added advice and humour to the morning's fare.

Later we went out sightseeing. She made her pilgrimage to Trafalgar Square and with her Instamatic I took a picture of her feeding the pigeons to send back home. Then Buckingham Palace and finally Parliament with Big Ben, which for ages had chimed out the nine o'clock hour to us over the radio. "Eighteen hours, Greenwich Mean Time," she echoed with amusement in a mock BBC accent.

That night we had dinner at my flat. Rice and curry from a takeaway Indian store in Earls Court. After dinner we sat side by side on the sofa to watch television. From the floor below came the sounds of female laughter and hilarity. I knew them well, a group of Asian girls from back home who in their inimitable way mothered the boys they knew. I often stopped at their place and had dinner there. Later I was to introduce Amina to them, but meanwhile I hoped they wouldn't come up to fetch me this night. They didn't and we sat quietly holding hands. Then we went to bed. I slept on my box spring and she on my mattress on the floor. She would not have it otherwise. "I have to learn to be tough," she said. For a while we talked in the dark, holding hands. We caressed, touched, our hands trembling, groping for each other in the space between us. Finally the tension reached a breaking point and I looked down in the darkness at the figure below me. "Can I come down?" I asked, my voice straining. "Yes," she said.

How frail our defences, how easily cast aside when the time comes. Nothing could have been more natural. Yet nothing could have shocked more, caused greater pain, in a different setting. How easy it was to judge and condemn from there. Yet no sooner were you here than a layer of righteousness peeled down from your being.

* * *

Last night we took a drive down Yonge Street, my daughter Zahra and I. We drove among the Saturday night traffic, among the Camaros and Thunderbirds swooping down south for the evening, or just a zoom past downtown, as we'd done before. This time we parked the car and started walking with the crowd, caught by the summerlike festive mood. People waited outside restaurants and cinemas; vendors of popcorn and nuts called out; cars hooted; stores were open and display windows lighted. At Bloor Street we exchanged salaams with a Sikh vendor, then stopped and I bought the little lady some flowers from him. We walked along Bloor Street for some time, arm in arm, talking about our joint future. Fortunately loneliness is not a word in her vocabulary yet. We reached the end of a queue outside an ice cream shop and joined it. We were happy, the two of us. We kept walking on Bloor Street. Somewhere nearby was her mother's apartment; she knew where, but I didn't ask. We reached a repertory cinema where another crowd was queueing and I picked up a schedule. Then, at a whim, I turned on her and asked, "How would you like to see *Wuthering Heights*?"

Tugging my arm playfully she pulled me along. "How about seeing *Star Wars*? Finally?"

# Alafina Vuki

## *Four-Year Wisdom*

Yesterday
My kid sister
asked me
why the sun
was dying
into the sea?

Inside
I was bleeding
red
into
Pure misery.

The sun
I sobbed
has run
across the sky
not to die
but to sleep
deep
in the sea.

Lips of four-year
wisdom
ask
"Why do you cry?
If you say the
sun does not die?"

In my hand
a telegram
that ran

"ALL UNITS FAILED"
Efforts gone to sand.

Eyes of four-year
wisdom

piercing
waiting
searching
needing
an answer
While I fumbled
the paper
stuttered
stammered
could not stop
the crying
choking
"I wish I was the
sun
asleep forever in the sea."

Hand of four-year
wisdom
holding my hand
crying along with
me
as we watched the
fiery kingdom
slipping into the
sea.

# Fred Wah

from *Breathin' my name with a sigh*

my father hurt-
ing at the table
sitting hurting
at suppertime
deep inside very
far down inside
because I can't stand the ginger
in the beef and greens
he cooked for us tonight
and years later tonight
that look on his face
appears now on mine
my children
my food
their food
my father
their father
me mine
*the* father
very far
very very far
inside

# Derek Walcott

## *Ruins of a Great House*

> *though our longest sun sets at right*
> *declensions and makes but winter*
> *arches, it cannot be long before we*
> *lie down in darkness, and have our*
> *light in ashes . . .*
>     BROWNE: *Urn Burial*

Stones only, the *disjecta membra* of this Great House,
Whose moth-like girls are mixed with candledust,
Remain to file the lizard's dragonish claws;
The mouths of those gate cherubs streaked with stain.
Axle and coachwheel silted under the muck
Of cattle droppings.

               Three crows flap for the trees,
And settle, creaking the eucalyptus boughs.
A smell of dead limes quickens in the nose
The leprosy of Empire.

              "Farewell, green fields"
              "Farewell, ye happy groves!"

Marble as Greece, like Faulkner's south in stone,
Deciduous beauty prospered and is gone;
But where the lawn breaks in a rash of trees
A spade below dead leaves will ring the bone
Of some dead animal or human thing
Fallen from evil days, from evil times.

It seems that the original crops were limes
Grown in the silt that clogs the river's skirt;
The imperious rakes are gone, their bright girls gone,

The river flows, obliterating hurt.
I climbed a wall with the grill ironwork
Of exiled craftsmen, protecting that great house
From guilt, perhaps, but not from the worm's rent,
Nor from the padded cavalry of the mouse.
And when a wind shook in the limes I heard
What Kipling heard; the death of a great empire, the abuse
Of ignorance by Bible and by sword.

A green lawn, broken by low walls of stone
Dipped to the rivulet, and pacing, I thought next
Of men like Hawkins, Walter Raleigh, Drake,
Ancestral murderers and poets, more perplexed
In memory now by every ulcerous crime.
The world's green age then was a rotting lime
Whose stench became the charnel galleon's text.
The rot remains with us, the men are gone.
But, as dead ash is lifted in a wind,
That fans the blackening ember of the mind,
My eyes burned from the ashen prose of Donne.

Ablaze with rage, I thought
Some slave is rotting in this manorial lake,
And still the coal of my compassion fought:
That Albion too, was once
A colony like ours, "Part of the continent, piece of the main"
Nook-shotten, rook o'er blown, deranged
By foaming channels, and the vain expense
Of bitter faction.

           All in compassion ends
So differently from what the heart arranged:
"as well as if a manor of thy friend's . . ."

# A Letter From Brooklyn

An old lady writes me in a spidery style,
Each character trembling, and I see a veined hand
Pellucid as paper, travelling on a skein
Of such frail thoughts its thread is often broken;
Or else the filament from which a phrase is hung
Dims to my sense, but caught, it shines like steel,
As touch a line, and the whole web will feel.
She describes my father, yet I forget her face
More easily than my father's yearly dying;
Of her I remember small, buttoned boots and the place
She kept in our wooden church on those Sundays
Whenever her strength allowed;
Grey haired, thin voiced, perpetually bowed.

"I am Mable Rawlins," she writes, "and know both your parents;"
He is dead, Miss Rawlins, but God bless your tense:
"Your father was a dutiful, honest,
Faithful and useful person."
For such plain praise what fame is recompense?
"A horn-painter, he painted delicately on horn,
He used to sit around the table and paint pictures."
The peace of God needs nothing to adorn
It, nor glory nor ambition.
"He is twenty-eight years buried," she writes, "he was called home,
And is, I am sure, doing greater work."

The strength of one frail hand in a dim room
Somewhere in Brooklyn, patient and assured,
Restores my sacred duty to the Word.
"Home, home," she can write, with such short time to live,
Alone as she spins the blessings of her years;
Not withered of beauty if she can bring such tears,
Nor withdrawn from the world that breaks its lovers so;
Heaven is to her the place where painters go,
All who bring beauty on frail shell or horn,

There was all made, thence their lux-mundi drawn,
Drawn, drawn, till the thread is resilient steel,
Lost though it seems in darkening periods,
And there they return to do work that is God's.

So this old lady writes, and again I believe,
I believe it all, and for no man's death I grieve.


## Midsummer: LII

I heard them marching the leaf-wet roads of my head,
the sucked vowels of a syntax trampled to mud,
a division of dictions, one troop black, barefooted,
the other in redcoats bright as their sovereign's blood;
their feet scuffled like rain, the bare soles with the shod.
One fought for a queen, the other was chained in her service,
but both, in bitterness, travelled the same road.
Our occupation and the Army of Occupation
are born enemies, but what mortar can size
the broken stones of the barracks of Brimstone Hill
to the gaping brick of Belfast? Have we changed sides
to the mustached sergeants and the horsy gentry
because we serve English, like a two-headed sentry
guarding its borders? No language is neutral;
the green oak of English is a murmurous cathedral
where some took umbrage, some peace, but every shade, all,
helped widen its shadow. I used to haunt the arches
of the British barracks of Vigie. There were leaves there,
bright, rotting like revers or epaulettes, and the stenches
of history and piss. Leaves piled like the dropped aitches
of soldiers from rival shires, from the brimstone trenches
of Agincourt to the gas of the Somme. On Poppy Day
our schools bought red paper flowers. They were for Flanders.
I saw Hotspur cursing the smoke through which a popinjay
minced from the battle. Those raging commanders
from Thersites to Percy, their rant is our model.
I pinned the poppy to my blazer. It bled like a vowel.

# Albert Wendt

## *Crocodile*

Miss Susan Sharon Willersey, known to all her students as Crocodile Willersey, was our House Mistress for the five years I was at boarding school. I recall, from reading a brief history of our school, that she had been born in 1908 in a small Waikato farming town and, at the age of ten, had enrolled at our Preparatory School, had then survived (brilliantly) our high school, had attended university and graduated MA (Honours in Latin), and had returned to our school to teach and be a dormitory mistress, and, a few years later, was put in charge of Beyle House, our House.

So when I started in 1953, Crocodile was in her fit mid-forties, already a school institution more myth than bone, more goddess than human (and she tended to behave that way!).

Certain stories, concerning the derivation of her illustrious nickname, prevailed (and were added to) during my time at school.

One story, in line with the motto of our school (which is: Perseverance is the Way to Knowledge), had it that Miss Willersey's first student called her Crocodile because she was a model of perseverance and fortitude, which they believed were the moral virtues of a crocodile.

Another story claimed that because Miss Willersey was a devout Anglican, possessing spiritual purity beyond blemish (is that correct?), an Anglican missionary, who had visited our school after spending twenty invigorating years in the Dark Continent (his description), had described Miss Willersey in our school assembly as a saint with the courage and purity and powers of the African crocodile (which was sacred to many tribes). Proof of her steadfastness and purity, so this story went, was her kind refusal to marry the widowed missionary because, as she reasoned (and he was extremely understanding), she was already married to her church, to her school and students, and to her profession.

The most unkindly story attributed her nickname to her appearance: Miss Willersey looked and behaved like a crocodile – she was long,

long-teethed, long-eared, long-fingered, long-arsed, long-everythinged. Others also argued she had skin like crocodile hide, and that her behaviour was slippery, always spyful, decisively cruel and sadistic and unforgiving, like a crocodile's.

As a new third-former and a naive Samoan who had been reared to obey her elders without question, I refused to believe the unfavourable stories about Miss Willersey's nickname. Miss Willersey was always kind and helpful (though distant, as was her manner with all of us) to me in our House and during her Latin classes. (Because I was in the top third form I *had* to take Latin though I was really struggling with another foreign language, English, and New Zealand English at that!) We felt (and liked it) that she was also treating all her "Island girls" (there were six of us) in a specially protective way. "You must always be proud of your race!" she kept reminding us. (She made it a point to slow down her English when speaking to us so we could understand her.)

During her Latin classes, I didn't suffer her verbal and physical (the swift ruler) chastisements, though I was a dumb, bumbling student. Not for ten months anyway.

However, in November, during that magical third-form year, I *had* to accept the negative interpretations of Miss Willersey's nickname.

I can't remember what aspect of Latin we were revising orally in class that summer day. All I remember well were: Croc's mounting anger as student after student (even her brightest) kept making errors; my loudly beating heart as her questioning came closer and closer to me; the stale smell of cardigans and shoes; Croc's long physique stretching longer, more threateningly; and some of my classmates snivelling into their handkerchiefs as Croc lacerated them verbally for errors (sins) committed.

"Life!" she called coldly, gazing at her feet. Silence. I didn't realize she was calling me. (My name is Olamaiileoti Monroe. Everyone at school called me Ola and *translated* it as Life which became my nickname.) "Life!" she repeated, this time her blazing eyes were boring into me. (I was almost wetting my pants, and this was contrary to Miss Willersey's constant exhortation to us: ladies learn early how to control their bladders!)

I wanted desperately to say, "Yes, Miss Willersey?" but I found I couldn't, I was too scared.

"Life?" She was not advancing towards me, filling me with her frightening lengthening. "You *are* called Life, aren't you, Monroe? That *is* your nickname?"

Nodding my head, I muttered, "Yes—yes!" A squeaking. My heart was struggling like a trapped bird in my throat. "Yes, yes, Miss Willersey!"

"And your name is Life, isn't it?"

"Yes!" I was almost in tears. (Leaking everywhere I was!)

"What does Ola mean exactly?"

"Life, Miss Willersey."

"But Ola is not a noun, is it?" she asked.

Utterly confused, leaking every which way, and thoroughly shit-scared, I just shook my head furiously.

"Ola doesn't mean Life, it is a verb, it means "to live", "to grow", doesn't it?" I nodded furiously.

"Don't you know even your own language, young lady?" I bowed my head (in shame); my trembling hands were clutching the desk-top. "Speak up, young lady!"

"No, Miss Willersey!" I swallowed back my tears.

"Now, Miss Life, or, should I say, Miss To-Live, let's see if you know Latin a little better than you know your own language!" Measuredly, she marched back to the front of our class. Shit, shit, shit! I cursed myself (and my fear) silently. Her footsteps stopped. Silence. She was turning to face me. Save me, someone!

"Excuse me, Miss Willersey?" the saving voice intruded.

"Yes, what is it?"

"I think I heard someone knocking on the door, Miss Willersey." It was Gill, the ever-aware, always courageous Gill. The room sighed. Miss Willersey had lost the initiative. "Shall I go and see who it is, Miss Willersey?" Gill asked, standing up and gazing unwaveringly at Miss Willersey. We all focused our eyes on her too. A collective defiance and courage. For a faltering moment I though she wasn't going to give in.

Then she looked away from Gill and said, "Well, all right and be quick about it!"

"You all right, Miss To-Live?" Gill asked me after class when all my friends crowded round me in the corridor.

"Yes!" I thanked her.

"Croc's a bloody bitch!" someone said.

"Yeah!" the others echoed.

So for the remainder of my third-form year and most of my fourth year I *looked* on Miss Susan Sharon Willersey as the Crocodile to be wary of, to pretend good behaviour with, to watch all the time in case she struck out at me. Not that she ever again treated me unreasonably in class despite my getting dumber and dumber in Latin (and less and less afraid of her).

In those two years, Gill topped our class in Latin, with little effort and in courageously clever defiance of Crocodile. Gill also helped me to get the magical 50% I needed to pass and stay out of Crocodile's wrath.

Winter was almost over, the days were getting warmer, our swimming pool was filled and the more adventurous (foolhardy?) used it regularly. Gill and I (and the rest of Miss Rashly's cross-country team) began to rise before light and run the four miles through the school farm. Some mornings, on our sweaty way back, we would meet a silent Crocodile in grey woollen skirt and thick sweater and boots, striding briskly through the cold.

"Morning, girls!" she would greet us.

"Morning, Miss Willersey!" we would reply.

"Exercise, regular exercise, that's the way girls!"

In our fourth-form dormitory, my bed was nearest the main door that opened out to the lounge opposite which was the front door to Crocodile's apartment, forbidden domain unless we were summoned to it to be questioned (and punished) for a misdemeanour, or invited to it for hot cocoa and biscuits (prefects were the usual invitees!). Because it *was* forbidden territory we were curious about what went on in there: how Croc lived, what she looked like without her formidably thick make-up and stern outfits, and so on. As a Samoan I wasn't familiar with how papalagi (and especially Crocodile) lived out their private lives. I tried but I couldn't picture Miss Willersey in her apartment in her bed or in her bath in nothing else (not even her skin) but in her make-up, immaculately coiffured hair and severe suits. (I couldn't even imagine her using the toilet! Pardon the indiscretion which is unbecoming of one of Miss Willersey's girls!)

The self-styled realists and sophisticates among us — and they were mainly seniors who had to pretend to such status — whispered involved and terribly upsetting (exciting) tales about Crocodile's men (and lack of men), who visited (and didn't visit) her in the dead of night. We, the gullible juniors, inexperienced in the ways of men and sex, found these lurid tales erotically exciting (upsetting) but never admitted publicly we *were* excited. We all feigned disgust and disbelief. And quite frankly I couldn't imagine Miss Willersey (in her virgin skin) with a man (in his experienced skin) in her bed in the widely lustful embrace of *knowing each other* (our Methodist Bible-class teachers's description of the art of fucking!). No, I really tried, but couldn't put Crocodile into that forbidden but feverishly exciting position. At the time I *did* believe in Miss Willersey's strict moral standards concerning the relationship between the sexes. (I was a virgin, and that's what Miss Willersey and my other elders wanted me to retain and give to the man I married.)

One sophisticate, the precociously pretentious and overweight daughter of a Wellington surgeon and one of Crocodile's pet prefects, suggested that Croc's nightly visitors *weren't* men. That immediately put more disgustingly exciting possibilities into our wantonly frustrated (and virgin) imaginations.

"Who then?" an innocent junior asked.

"What then?" another junior asked.

"Impossible. Bloody filthy!" the wise Gill countered.

"It happens!" the fat sophisticate argued.

"How do you know?" someone asked.

"I just know, that's all!"

"Because your mother is a lesbian!" Gill, the honest, socked it to her. We had to break up the fight between Gill and the Wellington sophisticate.

"Bugger her!" Gill swore as we led her out of the locker room. "She sucks up to Miss Willersey and then says Croc's a les!"

"What's — what's a les...lesbian?" I forced myself to ask Gill at prep that evening. She looked surprised, concluded with a shrug that I didn't really know, printed something on a piece of paper and, after handing it to me, watched me read it.

A FEMALE WHO IS ATTRACTED TO OTHER FEMALES!!!

"What do you mean?" I whispered. (We weren't allowed to talk during prep.)

She wrote on the paper. *"You Islanders are supposed to know a lot more about sex than us poor pakehas. A les is a female who does it with other females. Savvy?"*

*"Up you too!"* I wrote back. We started giggling.

"Gill, stand up!" the prefect on duty called.

"Oh, shit!" Gill whispered under her breath.

"Were you talking?"

"Life just wanted me to spell a word for her!" Gill replied.

"What word?"

"Les —," Gill started say. My heart nearly stopped. "Life wanted to know how to spell 'lesson'?" Relief.

"Well, spell it out aloud for all of us!" And Gill did so, crisply, all the time behind her back giving the prefect the up-you sign.

After this incident, I noticed myself observing the Crocodile's domain more closely for unusual sounds, voices, visitors, and, though I refused to think of the possibility of her being a lesbian, I tried to discern a pattern in her female visitors (students included), but no pattern emerged. Also, there were no unusual sounds. (Croc didn't even sing in the bath!)

Some creature, almost human, was trapped in the centre of my head, sobbing pitifully, mourning an enormous loss. It was wrapping its pain around my dreaming and I struggled to break away from its tentacles. I couldn't. I woke to find myself awake (and relieved I wasn't strangling in the weeping) in the dark of our dormitory. Everyone else was fast asleep.

Then I knew it was Miss Willersey. I knew it and tried not to panic, not to give in to the feeling I wasn't going to be able to cope. I wrapped the blankets round my head. It was none of my business! But I couldn't escape.

I found myself standing with my ear to Miss Willersey's door. Shivering. Her light was on, I could tell from the slit of light under the door. The sobbing was more audible but it sounded muffled, as if she was crying into a pillow or cushion. Uncontrolled. Emerging from the depths of a fathomless grief. Drawing me into its depths.

My hand opened the door before I could stop it. Warily I peered into the blinding light. My eyes adjusted quickly to the glare. The neat and orderly arrangement of furniture, wall pictures, ornaments, and bookcases came into focus. Miss Willersey was enthroned in an armchair against the far wall, unaware of my presence, unaware of where she was and who she was, having relinquished in her grief all that was the Crocodile. She was dressed in a shabby dressing-gown, brown slippers, hair in wild disarray, tears melting away her thick make-up in streaks down her face, her long-fingered hands clasped to her mouth trying to block back the sound.

Shutting the door behind me quietly, I edged closer to her, hoping she would see me and order me out of her room and then I wouldn't have to cope with the new, fragile, vulnerable Miss Willersey. I didn't want to.

All around us (and in me) her grief was like the incessant buzzing of a swarm of bees, around and around, spiralling up out of the hollow hive of her being and weaving round and round on my head, driving me towards her and her sorrow which had gone beyond her courage to measure and bear.

And I moved into her measure and, lost for whatever else to do, wrapped my arms around her head, and immediately her arms were around me tightly and my body was the cushion for her grief.

At once she became my comfort, the mother I'd never had but had always yearned for, and I cried silently into her pain. Mother and daughter, daughter and mother. A revelation I hoped would hold true for as long as I was to know her.

Her weeping eased. Her arms relaxed around me. She turned her face away. "Please!" she murmured. I looked away. Got the box of tissues on the table and put it in her shaking hands. I looked away. Tearing out a handful of tissues, she wiped her eyes and face.

I started to leave. "It is Ola, isn't it?" she asked, face still turned away. In her voice was a gentleness I have never heard in it before.

"Yes."

"Thank you. I'm . . . I'm sorry you've had to see me like this." She was ripping out more tissues.

"Is there anything else I can do?" I asked.

"No, thank you." She started straightening her dressing-gown and hair. The Crocodile was returning. I walked to the door. "Ola!" she stopped me. I didn't look back at her. "This is our secret. Please don't tell the others?"

"I won't, Miss Willersey. Good-night!"

"Good-night, Ola!"

I shut the door behind me quietly, and on *our* secret.

Next morning there was a short article in the newspaper about her mother's death in Hamilton, in an old people's home. Miss Willersey left on the bus for Hamilton that afternoon.

"The Croc's mother's crocked!" some girls joked at our table at dinner that evening.

Yes, Crocodile Willersey remained married to her school and students until she died in 1982. By becoming a school tradition and a mythical being in the memories of all her students (generations of them) she has lived on, and we will bequeath her to our children.

Miss Susan Sharon Willersey, the Crocodile, I will always think of you with genuine alofa. (And forgive me — I've forgotten nearly all the Latin you taught me!) By the way, you were wrong about the meaning of Ola; it can also be a noun, Life.

# May Wong

## *The Shroud*

The little childish happiness
Is taken off, together
With the old school uniform.

Never will I be in that uniform again.
And who will remember
The little girl with her two pigtails
With her petticoats always too long
And her thousand naughty and silly ways?

The old school uniform
With the little childish delights and giggles
Is folded and locked up in the top drawer
Forever.

Shall I cry?
I am no longer a child
My eyes so dry
It's not easy to cry.

Yet I hear somebody weeping —
Crying louder and louder — howling
I feel her tears —
She is the girl locked up in the top drawer.

# Arthur Yap

## *2 Mothers In A HDB Playground*

ah beng is so smart,
already he can watch tv & know the whole story.
your kim cheong is also quite smart,
what boy is he in the exam?
this playground is not too bad, but i'm always
so worried, car here, car there.

    at exam time, it's worse.

because you know why?

    kim cheong eats so little.

give him some complan. my ah beng was like that,
now he's different. if you give him anything
he's sure to finish it all up.

    sure, sure. cheong's father buys him
    vitamins but he keeps it inside his mouth
    & later gives it to the cat.
    i scold like mad but what for?
    if i don't see it, how can i scold?

on saturday, tv showed a new type,
special for children. why don't you call
his father buy some? maybe they are better.

    money's no problem. it's not that
    we want to save. if we buy it
    & he doesn't eat it, throwing money
    into the jamban[1] is the same.
    ah beng's father spends so much,

takes out the mosaic floor & wants
to make terazzo or what.

we also got new furniture, bought from diethelm.
the sofa is so soft, i dare not sit. they all
sit like don't want to get up. so expensive.
nearly two thousand dollars, sure must be good.

that you can't say. my toa-soh
bought an expensive sewing machine,
after 6 months, it is already spoilt.
she took it back but . . . . beng,
come here, come, don't play the fool.
your tuition teacher is coming.
wah! kim cheong, now you're quite big.

come, cheong, quick go home & bathe.
ah pah wants to take you chya-hong² in new motor-car.

¹ toilet      ² literally, "to eat wind," a Hokkien idiom for "car-ride"

# Biographical Notes

ACHEBE, Chinua (b. 1930) Born in Ogidi, Nigeria, he studied in Ibadan and London. His novels include *Things Fall Apart* (1958), *A Man of the People* (1966), and *Anthills of the Savannah* (1986). He has published stories, poetry, and essays, and has held teaching positions in Nigeria and the United States. He has been awarded honorary degrees in Canada, the USA, and the UK.

AIDOO, (Christina) Ama Ata (b. 1942) Born in Ghana, she was educated there and at Stanford University and now lives in the USA. A poet, playwright, and novelist, she has written the novel *Our Sister Killjoy* (1977), the play *Anowa* (1970), and several short stories.

ALI, Agha Shahid (b. 1949) Originally from Kashmir, he was educated in India and the USA. He currently lives in the USA, where he has taught at several universities and colleges. His publications include *The Half-Inch Himalayas* (1987) and *A Nostalgist's Map of America* (1990).

ANAND, Mulk Raj (b. 1905) Born in Peshawar, India (now in Pakistan), he was educated in Punjab and in London. He earned his PhD in Philosophy in 1929. Actively involved in India's struggle for independence, he served later as cultural advisor to the government. *Untouchable* (1935) was the first of many novels, stories, essays, and children's books.

ARASANAYAGAM, Jean (b. 1940) Born in Sri Lanka into a Dutch Burgher family, she was educated there and in Scotland. She has published six volumes of poetry, including *Out of our Prisons We Emerge* (1987) and *Red Water Flows Clear* (1991), a collection of short stories, and a novel. She lectures at a teachers' college in Sri Lanka.

BEGAMUDRE, Ven (b. 1956) Born in South India, he moved to Canada when he was six years old. He studied in the USA, Paris, and Ottawa. His publications include a collection of short stories, *A Planet of Eccentrics* (1990), and a novel, *Van de Graff Days* (1993).

BENNETT, Louise (b. 1919) Born in Jamaica, she originally wrote poems in Standard English but abandoned that for Jamaican creole. She went to England on a drama scholarship and had a regular programme on the BBC. Now based in Jamaica, she has written several volumes of poetry including *Jamaica Labrish* (1966), and has retold Jamaican folk tales in several published collections.

BISSOONDATH, Neil (b. 1955) Born and educated in Trinidad, he came to Canada in 1973 to attend York University. His publications include *Digging Up the Mountains* (a collection of stories, 1986), *A Casual Brutality* (a novel, 1988), and *Selling Illusions: The Cult of Multiculturalism in Canada* (1994).

BOSTOCK, Gerry (b. 1942) Born in New South Wales, Australia, he became involved in street theatre and later in the political struggles for Aboriginal rights. He has written poetry, including *Black Man Coming* (1980), and several plays. He has done work for television. His documentary film *Lousy Little Sixpence* was produced in 1981.

BRAND, Dionne (b. 1953) Born in Trinidad, she immigrated to Canada in 1970. She is involved in the black community and in the educational system in Toronto. She has written *Sans Souci and Other Stories* (1988) and several volumes of poetry, including *Chronicles of the Hostile Sun* (1984) and *No Language is Neutral* (1990).

BRATHWAITE, Edward Kamau (b. 1930) Born in Barbados, he was educated at Harrison College, Barbados, and Cambridge University. His many volumes of poems include *The Arrivants: A New World Trilogy* (1973), *Masks* (1968), and *Sun Poem* (1982). He has written several studies on Caribbean social and cultural history and has lectured in History at the University of the West Indies.

BRUTUS, Dennis (b. 1924) Born in Zimbabwe, he was educated in South Africa, where he studied English and Law. Because of opposition to apartheid, he was banned from South Africa. He currently lives and writes in the USA. His poetry collection *Letters to Martha* (1968) tells of his experiences of violence and degradation in prison.

BUHKWUJJENENE (b. c.1815-1900) He was the Ojibway chief who, in 1878, told the story of Nanaboozhoo creating the world to a group to Englishmen.

CHEN, Willi (b. 1934) Born In Trinidad, he is a short-story writer, poet, dramatist, painter, and sculptor. Some of his stories are collected in *King of the Carnival and Other Stories* (1988).

CLARKE, Austin (b. 1934) Born and educated in Barbados, he came to Canada in 1955 to study economics. He has published several novels, including *Survivors of the Crossing* (1964), *The Meeting Point* (1967), and *Growing Up Stupid Under the Union Jack* (1980) and several collections of short stories, including *Nine Men Who Laughed* (1986) and *In This City* (1992).

COWASJEE, Saros (b. 1931) Born in India, he studied at Agra University and the University of Leeds and now teaches English at the University of Regina. He has written two novels, including *Goodbye to Elsa* (1974), two collections of stories, and several essays and commentaries, and has edited several volumes of Indian stories.

CRUSZ, Rienzi (b. 1925) Born in Sri Lanka of Portuguese ancestry, he was educated at St. Joseph's College in Colombo and later taught there. In 1951, he studied library science in London. He immigrated to Canada in 1965 and has worked as a librarian. His volumes of poetry include *Flesh and Thorn* (1974) and *A Time for Loving* (1986).

D'AGUIAR, Fred (b. 1960) Born in London, he grew up in Guyana, but returned to England, where he now resides. A poet and dramatist, his volumes of poems include *Mama Dot* (1985) and *Airy Hall* (1989).

DABYDEEN, Cyril (b. 1945) Born in Guyana, he came to Canada in 1970 and attended Queen's University. He has published several volumes of poetry, including *Distances* (1977) and *Coastland* (1989), two volumes of short stories, and two novellas.

DABYDEEN, David (b. 1955) Born in Berbice, Guyana, he immigrated to England when he was thirteen years old. He attended the universities of Cambridge and London. His publications include a scholarly work, *Hogarth's Blacks* ((1987), several volumes of poetry, including *Slave Song* (1984), and a novel, *The Intended* (1991).

DAS, Kamala (b. 1934) Born and educated in India, she has written several volumes of poetry, including *The Descendants* (1967), short stories, and an autobiography, *My Story* (1975).

DAS, Manoj (b. 1934) Born in Orissa, India, he has written several volumes of short stories, fables, and fantasies, including *The Vengeance and Other Stories* (1980).

DAVIS, Jack (b. 1917) Born in Australia, he has been active as a poet, dramatist, and critic since the 1960s. He was the editor of the Aboriginal magazine *Identity*. His poetry collections include *The First-Born and Other Poems* (1970).

DESAI, Anita (b. 1937) Born in India to a German mother and Bengali father, she has written several novels, including *Fire on the Mountain* (1977) and *Baumgartner's Bombay* (1988), children's books, and a volume of short stories, *Games at Twilight* (1978). She currently teaches in the USA and Delhi.

DE SOUZA, Eunice (b. 1940) Born in Poona, India, she was educated in the

USA and in Bombay, where she is now Lecturer in English. She has written three volumes of poetry, including *Ways of Belonging* (1990), and children's books.

EZEKIEL, Nissim (b. 1924) Born in Bombay, India, of Jewish parents, he was educated in Bombay and London. He worked as a journalist, broadcaster, and teacher. He has written several volumes of poetry, including *The Unfinished Man* (1960), plays, reviews, and art criticism.

GOODISON, Lorna (b. 1947) Born in Jamaica, she attended the University of Iowa and Radcliffe College. An artist and poet, she has written several volumes of poetry, including *I Am Becoming My Mother* (1986) and *Heartease* (1988), and a collection of short stories, *Baby Mother and the King of Swords* (1990).

GORDIMER, Nadine (b. 1923) Born in Springs, near Johannesburg, she attended the University of Witwatersrand. She published her first collection of stories, *Face to Face,* in 1949. Since then she has published many other volumes of stories and such novels as *The Conservationist* (1974) and *My Son's Story* (1990). She was awarded the Nobel Prize for Literature in 1991.

HAGEDORN, Jessica (b. 1949) Born and raised in the Philippines, she now lives in the USA. She has performed in the theatre and has published numerous poems, reviews, essays, and fiction, including two volumes of poetry and a novel, *Dogeaters* (1990).

HARRIS, Claire (b. 1937) Born in Trinidad, she was educated in Trinidad, Ireland, Jamaica, and Lagos. She now lives in Calgary. She has written many volumes of poetry, including *Fables from the Women's Quarters* (1984) and *The Conception of Winter* (1988).

HARRIS, Wilson (b. 1921) Born and educated in Guyana, he immigrated in 1959 to England. Among his novels are *Palace of the Peacock* (1960), *Ascent to Omai* (1970), and *Carnival* (1985). He has written poetry and essays, including *The Womb of Space: The Cross-Cultural Imagination* (1983). He has lectured widely at universities around the world.

HEAD, Bessie (1937-86) Born in South Africa of a Scottish mother and black father, she became a teacher and later a journalist. She left South Africa in 1964 and spent the rest of her life in Botswana. She wrote four novels, including *Maru* (1971) and *A Question of Power* (1974), and two short-story collections.

HULME, Keri (b. 1947) Born in New Zealand, she lives in Okarito on the West Coast. She is of Maori (Kai Tahu) and Pakeha ancestry. She has written poetry and fiction. Her novel *the bone people* (1984) won the Pegasus Prize for Maori literature and the 1985 Booker Prize.

IHIMAERA, Witi (b. 1944) Born in New Zealand of Maori and Scottish ancestry, he has published several novels and stories, including *Tangi* (1973), *The Whale Rider* (1987), and *Dear Miss Mansfield* (1989). He has written an opera, *Waituhi: The Life of the Village* (1985), and a cultural history, *Maori* (1975).

ITO, Sally (b. 1965) Born in Alberta, Canada, of Japanese ancestry ("my mother having come from Japan and my father being a third generation Japanese Canadian"), she studied in Japan and at the University of British Columbia. Her poems have appeared in Canadian magazines.

ITWARU, Arnold (b. 1942) Born in Guyana, he immigrated to Canada in 1969. He has written three collections of poetry, including *Entombed Survivals* (1987), a novel, *Shanti* (1988), and three non-fiction works, the most recent being *The Invention of Canada: Literary Texts and the Immigrant Imagination* (1990).

JAIN, Sunita (b. 1941) Born in India, she has studied in the USA and India. She writes in both Hindi and English and has published two volumes of stories, including *Eunuch of Time and Other Stories* (1982).

JHABVALA, Ruth Prawer (b. 1927) Born in Germany to a Polish/Jewish family, she immigrated to Britain in 1939. Educated in England, she lived in India for 25 years after her marriage. Her novels include *The Householder* (1960) and *Heat and Dust* (1975). She has written several collections of short stories and screenplays. She has been living in the USA since 1976.

KINCAID, Jamaica (b. 1949) Born in Antigua, she now lives and writes in the USA. Her fiction includes *At the Bottom of the River* (short stories, 1984) and *Annie John* (novel, 1985). She has written many critical essays.

KING, Thomas (b. 1943) Born in Canada of a Cherokee father and a Greek-German mother, he was Chair of Native American studies at the University of Minnesota. He also teaches at the University of Guelph, Canada. His publications include *Green Grass, Running Water* (novel, 1993), a number of short stories, poems, and a children's book.

KOGAWA, Joy (b. 1935) Born in Vancouver, Canada, of Japanese ancestry, she grew up in Saskatchewan, Alberta, and British Columbia. She and her family were interned during the Second World War. Her volumes of poetry include *A Choice of Dreams* (1974). She has written a novel, *Obasan* (1981), based on her experiences during the war.

LAM, Dominic Man-Kit   Raised in Hong Kong, he attended the University of British Columbia, and now divides his time between Hong Kong and Texas; he is a scientist as well as an internationally recognised artist.

LIM, Shirley Geok-Lin (b. 1843) Born in Malaysia, she immigrated to the USA and is a poet, critic, and academic. Her poetry collections include *Crossing the Peninsula*, which won the 1980 Commonwealth Poetry Prize. She is co-editor of *The Forbidden Stitch: An Asian American Women's Anthology* (1989).

MAHAPATRA, Jayanta (b. 1928)  Born and educated in Calcutta, India, he taught Physics for many years in Orissa. He has written thirteen volumes of poetry, including *The False Start* (1980), short stories and essays and has won several awards for his poetry.

MARACLE, Lee (b. 1950)  Born in Canada, she is a Native poet, who is immersed in the social and cultural life of her people. She was part-time writer in residence at the International School for Native People in British Columbia. She now lives in Toronto. Among her books of fiction is *Sojourner's Truth and Other Stories* (1990) and *Ravensong* (1993).

MARECHERA, Dambudzo (1952-87)  Born in Zimbabwe, he was educated at the University of Zimbabwe and Oxford University. He travelled extensively in Europe and Africa. He was a controversial but acclaimed writer whose publications include *The House of Hunger* (novel, 1978) and *Cemetery of Mind* (poetry, 1992).

MELVILLE, Pauline  Born in Guyana, she immigrated to London, working there on stage and in film. Her poems have been published in various anthologies. *Shape-shifter* (1990) is her first collection of short stories.

MISHRA, Sudesh  Born in Suva, Fiji, he received his doctorate from the Flinders University of South Australia. He has published three volumes of poetry, including *Memoirs of a Reluctant Traveller* (1994), and has recently made his debut as a playwright and actor. He is working on a novel set in Fiji.

MISTRY, Rohinton (b. 1952)  Born in Bombay, India, he came to Canada in 1975. He studied at the University of Bombay and the University of Toronto. His publications include *Tales from Firozsha Baag* (stories, 1987) and *Such a Long Journey* (novel, 1991).

MO, Timothy (b. 1950)  Born in Hong Kong to English and Cantonese parents, he has spent much of his life in the UK. His works include the novels *Sour Sweet* (1982) and *An Insular Possession* (1986).

MORI, Toshio (b. 1910)  Born in California, of Japanese ancestry, he has written several volumes of fiction, including *Woman from Hiroshima* (novel, 1979) and *Yokohama, California* (stories, 1949).

MOLLEL, Tololwa Marti  Born in Tanzania, he immigrated to Canada and has been teaching at the University of Alberta. His stories, many written for children, have been broadcast on the BBC, and have been published in such periodicals as *Kunapipi* and the *Greenfield Review*.

MORRIS, Mervyn (b. 1937) Born in Jamaica, he was educated there and at Oxford University on a Rhodes Scholarship. He has published several collections of poetry, including *The Pond* (1973), has edited a number of anthologies, and is a journalist and theatre critic. He teaches at the University of the West Indies in Jamaica.

MPHAHLELE, Es'kia (b. 1919) Born in Pretoria, South Africa, he has taught at universities in the USA and in South Africa, where he currently lives. His publications include *The Wanderers* (novel, 1971), *Man Must Live* (stories, 1946), and *The African Image* (essays, 1962, rev. 1974).

MUKHERJEE, Bharati (b. 1940) Born and educated in Calcutta, India, she attended universities in India and the USA. She spent some years in Canada before returning to the USA in 1981. Her publications include *Wife* (novel, 1975), *Darkness* (stories, 1985), and *The Sorrow and the Terror: The Haunting Legacy of the Air India Tragedy* (1987), with Clark Blaise.

NAIPAUL, V. S. (b. 1932) Born in Trinidad and educated at Queen's Royal College, Trinidad, he left for Oxford University in 1950, and has lived in England since then. His novels include *The Mystic Masseur* (1957), *A House for Mr Biswas* (1961), *The Enigma of Arrival* (1987), and *A Way in the World* (1994). He has published several collections of essays and travel books, including *Among the Believers* (1981) and *India: A Million Mutinies Now* (1990).

NANDAN, Satendra (b. 1939) Born in Fiji, he was educated the in UK and Australia. He moved to Australia after the Fijian coups in 1987. He has published several volumes of poems, including *Voices in the River* (1985), and a novel *The Wounded Sea* (1991). His autobiography, *Relics of a Rainbow: A Fijian Story,* is due in 1995.

NARAYAN, R. K. (b. 1906) Born in Madras, India, he has spent most of his life in Mysore. He has published fourteen novels including *Swami and Friends* (1935) and *The World of Nagaraj* (1990), and numerous collections of stories, essays, and memoirs. He has travelled and lectured in the USA, and has received India's highest literary award, the Padma Bhushan award.

NAROGIN, Mudrooroo / Colin Johnson (b. 1938) Born in Narogin, Western Australia, he changed his name to reaffirm his tribal identity. He writes poetry, fiction, and literary criticism. His publications include *Wild Cat Falling* (novel, 1965) and *The Song Circle of Jacky and Selected Poems* (1986). He has taught Aboriginal Literature at Murdoch University and at the University of Queensland.

NDEBELE, Njabulo S. (b. 1948) Born in Johannesburg, South Africa, he was educated there, at Cambridge University, and the University of Denver. His publications include *Fools and Other Stories* (1983) and *South African Literature and Culture* (1994).

NGITJI, Ngitji / Mona Tur  Born in South Australia, she writes poetry and prose, and is a teacher and translator of Aboriginal languages. She has written several critical articles on Aboriginal literature in *Identity*.

NGUGI WA THIONG'O  (b. 1938)  Born in Kenya, he was educated at universities in Uganda and Britain. His novels include *A Grain of Wheat* (1967) and *Petals of Blood* (1977). He has written plays and cultural and political commentaries, including *Decolonising the Mind: The Politics of Language in African Literature* (1986).

NOONUCCAL, Oodgeroo / Kath Walker  (1920-93)  Born in Australia, she was a member of the Noonuccal tribe and was an activist for her people. She published several poetry volumes, including *We Are Going* (1964), children's stories, and such traditional tales as *Stradbroke Dreamtime* (1972).

OKARA, Gabriel  (b. 1921)  Born and educated in Nigeria, he worked as a schoolteacher, bookbinder, and businessman until 1953, when his poem "Call of the River Nun" won a poetry award. His publications include *The Fisherman's Invocation* (poetry, 1978) and *The Voice* (novel, 1964).

ONDAATJE, Michael  (b. 1943)  Born in Sri Lanka of mixed Tamil, Sinhalese, and Dutch ancestry, he immigrated to Canada in 1962. His many volumes of poetry and prose include *Coming Through Slaughter* (1976), *There's a Trick with a Knife I'm Learning to Do* (1979), *Running in the Family* (1982), and *The English Patient* (1992), for which he won the Booker Prize. He is also a filmmaker and has written a critical study on Leonard Cohen (1970).

PERSAUD, Sasenarine  Born in Guyana, he now lives in Canada. A poet, novelist, and critic, his publications include *The Ghost of Bellow's Man* (novel, 1992) and *Demerara Telepathy* (1988).

PHILIP, M. Nourbese  (b. 1947)  Born in Trinidad (Tobago), she moved to Canada in 1968. A lawyer and activist against racism, she has published several volumes of poetry, including *She Tries Her Tongue: Her Silence Softly Breaks* (1989) and *Looking for Livingstone: An Odyssey of Silence* (1991).

RHYS, Jean  (1890-1979)  Born in Dominica to a Welsh father and Creole mother, she spent the first seventeen years of her life there. She left for Britain and Paris where she spent the rest of her life. She wrote five novels, including *Voyage in the Dark* (1934) and *Wide Sargasso Sea* (1966), several short-story collections, and an autobiography.

RUSHDIE, Salman  (b. 1947)  Born in Bombay, India, Rushdie was educated at Rugby and Cambridge, England, graduating with a degree in History. His novels include *Grimus* (1975), *Midnight's Children* (1981), and the controversial *The Satanic Verses* (1988), which led to death threats against him. He has published also *Imaginary Homelands: Essays and Criticism* (1991).

SELVON, Sam (1923-94) Born in Trinidad, the son of an East Indian father and half-Scottish mother, he immigrated to England in 1954 and moved to Calgary in 1978. He wrote ten novels, including *An Island Is a World* (1955), *The Lonely Londoners* (1956), and *Moses Migrating* (1983), numerous short stories, essays, screenplays, and plays for radio and television.

SENIOR, Olive (b. 1941) Born in Jamaica, she was educated there, in Canada, and in Britain. An editor and journalist, her publications include *Talking of Trees* (poems, 1985), *Summer Lightning* (stories, 1986), and *The Arrival of the Snake Woman* (stories, 1989).

SETH, Vikram (b. 1952) Born in Calcutta, India, he left India at the age of eleven to study in England. A graduate of Oxford and of Stanford, his publications include *Mappings* (poetry, 1982), *From Heaven Lake: Travels Through Sinkiang and Tibet* (1983), *The Golden Gate* (a novel in verse, 1986), and *A Suitable Boy* (novel, 1993).

SHERLOCK, Philip (b. 1902) Born in Jamaica, he became Vice-Chancellor of the University of the West Indies. He is the author and editor of more than fifteen volumes of poetry, history, and folk tales, including *Anansi the Spider Man* (1954).

SILKO, Leslie Marmon (b. 1948) Born in New Mexico, she is of mixed ancestry, part Laguna, part Mexican, and part white. She is the author of the novel *Ceremony* (1977), and several collections of stories, including *Laguna Woman* (1974). *Storyteller* (1981) is a selection of her poems and stories.

SOYINKA, Wole (b. 1934) Born in Nigeria and educated at universities in Ibadan and Leeds, he has published several novels and volumes of essays, plays, and poetry, including *A Dance of the Forests* (play, 1963), *The Interpreters* (novel, 1965), *Poems from Prison* (1969), *The Man Died: Prison Notes of Wole Soyinka* (1972), and *Mandela's Earth and Other Poems* (1988). He was awarded the Nobel Prize for Literature in 1986.

SUBRAMANI (b. 1943) Born in Fiji, he has studied in Suva, New Zealand, and Canada. His publications include *The Fantasy Eaters* (1988) a collection of stories and a number of critical essays. He now teaches at the University of the South Pacific in Suva.

TALLMOUNTAIN, Mary / Mary Randle (1918-94) Born in Alaska, the daughter of a Koyukon-Athabascan Indian mother and Scottish-Irish father, she published several collections of poems and short stories, including *Nine Poems* (1979), *There Is No Word For Goodbye* (1981), and *Light on the Tent Wall* (1990).

THUMBOO, Edwin  (b. 1933)  Born in Singapore to a Tamil father and a Chinese mother, he now lectures at the University of Singapore. He has published six volumes of poetry, including *Gods Can Die* (1977) and *Ulysses by the Merlion* (1979).

VASSANJI, M. G.  (b. 1950)  Born in Kenya, he grew up in Tanzania but moved to London and later to the USA, where he obtained a doctorate in Physics. His publications include *The Gunny Sack* (novel, 1989) and *Uhuru Street* (stories, 1992). He currently lives in Toronto.

VUKI, Alafina  Born in Suva, Fiji, she is a graduate of the University of the South Pacific and has taught at Dudley High School.

WAH, Fred  (b. 1939)  Born in Saskatchewan, Canada, he has written several collections of poetry, including *Selected Poems* (1980), *Breathin' My Name with a Sigh* (1981), and *Waiting for Saskatchewan* (1986), which won the Governor General's Award for Poetry, and *Rooftops* (1988). He teaches at the University of Calgary.

WALCOTT, Derek  (b. 1930)  Born in St. Lucia, he has lived in Trinidad and the USA. He currently teaches at Boston University. His volumes of poems include *25 Poems* (1948), *In a Green Night: Poems 1948-1960* (1962), *Midsummer* (1984), and *Omeros* (1989). He has written several plays, including *Henri Christophe* (1950) and *Dream on Monkey Mountain* (1970). He received the Nobel Prize for Literature in 1992.

WENDT, Albert  (b. 1939)  Born in Western Samoa, he is of Samoan and German ancestry. He has taught at the University of the South Pacific in Fiji and at the University of Auckland. His novels include *Pouliuli* (1976) and *Leaves of the Banyan Tree* (1979). He has published several collections of stories and poems.

WONG, May  Born in Singapore, she has published three volumes of poetry: *A Bad Girl's Book of Animals* (1969), *Reports* (1972), and *Superstitions* (1978).

YAP, Arthur  (b. 1943)  Born in Singapore, he has written four collections of poetry, including *Commonplace* (1977) and *Man Snake Apple and Other Poems* (1986).

# Index of Titles

*Of related interest:*

## THE BROADVIEW ANTHOLOGY OF POETRY

*edited by*
*Herbert Rosengarten & Amanda Goldrick-Jones*

This new anthology presents a wide range of poetry from Chaucer to Margaret Atwood and Maya Angelou and representing authors from around the English speaking world. Many of the poems that have become accepted as central to our literature are included, but the book also reflects the reassessments of the traditional canon of literature that have been carried out in recent years. It includes careful annotation, biographical notes, an appendix on Reading Poetry, and a glossary of literary terms.

"In reconsidering the canon of English language poetry, the editors have been as creative as they are generous. This is a lively anthology—it shows views where previous anthologies hadn't planned for windows."

David Shevin, Tiffin University

"Excellent, wide-sweeping anthology!"
Warren Anderson, Judson College

"Commendable in every way, especially in its unusually healthy selection of *pre-modern* female poets!"
Jennifer Wise, Malaspina University College

6x9 996pp 1-55111-006-7